Playgoing in Shakespeare's London

This is a newly revised edition of Andrew Gurr's classic account of the people for whom Shakespeare wrote his plays. Gurr assembles evidence from the writings of the time to describe the physical structure of the playhouses, the services provided in the auditorium, the cost of a ticket and a cushion, the size of the crowds, the smells, the pickpockets, and the collective feelings generated by the plays.

As well as revising and adding new material which has emerged since the second edition, Gurr develops new sections. He considers the difference between Shakespearean and modern thinking about early staging, the complex historical process which established the permanent playhouses, and the development of a distinctly different acting style in the open-air playhouses from that of the indoor halls. Fifty new entries have been added to the list of playgoers and there are a dozen fresh quotations about the experience of playgoing.

Andrew Gurr is Emeritus Professor, University of Reading. His many books include *The Shakespearean Stage 1574–1642* (third edition 1993), *Writers in Exile, Playgoing in Shakespeare's London* (second edition 1996), *The Shakespearian Playing Companies* (1996), and (with Mariko Ichikawa) *Staging in Shakespeare's Theatres* (2000).

Playgoing in Shakespeare's London

Third edition

ANDREW GURR
Emeritus Professor
University of Reading

CAMBRIDGE
UNIVERSITY PRESS

PUBLISHED BY THE PRESS SYNDICATE OF THE UNIVERSITY OF CAMBRIDGE
The Pitt Building, Trumpington Street, Cambridge, United Kingdom

CAMBRIDGE UNIVERSITY PRESS
The Edinburgh Building, Cambridge, CB2 2RU, UK
40 West 20th Street, New York, NY 10011–4211, USA
477 Williamstown Road, Port Melbourne, VIC 3207, Australia
Ruiz de Alarcón 13, 28014 Madrid, Spain
Dock House, The Waterfront, Cape Town 8001, South Africa

http://www.cambridge.org

First published 1987
First paperback edition 1988
Reprinted 1989, 1991, 1994
Second edition 1996
Reprinted 1997, 2000, 2002
Third edition 2004

Printed in the United Kingdom at the University Press, Cambridge

Typeface Trump Mediaeval 9.75/12 pt.   *System* LaTeX 2_ε [TB]

A catalogue record for this book is available from the British Library

First edition ISBN 0 521 25336 5 hardback
ISBN 0 521 36824 3 paperback

Second edition ISBN 0 521 58014 5 hardback
ISBN 0 521 57449 8 paperback

ISBN 0 521 83560 7 hardback
ISBN 0 521 54322 3 paperback

TAG

'The action of the theatre, though modern states esteem it merely ludicrous unless it be satirical and biting, was carefully watched by the ancients, so that it might improve mankind in virtue; and indeed many wise men and great philosophers have thought it to the mind as the bow to the fiddle; and certain it is, though a great secret in nature, that the minds of men in company are more open to affections and impressions than when alone.'

Francis Bacon, *The Advancement of Learning*

Contents

Illustrations

Preface to third edition

Sydney's Darling Harbour contains a Chinese 'Garden of Friendship' created by its sister-city Guangzhou in 1988 as a symbol of friendship between China and Australia. At the highest point of its beautifully intricate hectare of trees, rocks, pools and traditional houses stands a three-storeyed, gold-tiled pavilion. It is known in English as the 'Clear View Pavilion', because of its position as the best place to see the surrounding countryside. Its Chinese name is the Gurr.

This third edition of *Playgoing* is in its own way the book's highest and certainly its final storey. It now offers, thanks to the many helpful criticisms it has received and the development its subject has undergone since the first edition in 1987, my own clearest view of the complex process and experience of early modern playgoing and its many differences from the modern experience as I understand it. It continues to offer no pretensions to authority. A crowd, the best word for the complex of individuals making up the early modern theatre audiences, could never be described or explained with any adequacy, either in its composition, its collective mental structure and actions, or the history and mind-set of its individual components. This book is therefore necessarily a subjective and impressionistic picturing of those gatherings of Londoners and visitors who saw the original performances of the plays written for them by Shakespeare and his peers and successors.

Essentially it is a history, because in the remarkable seventy-five years between 1567 and 1642 not only did the kind of play offered at the different playhouses undergo some extraordinary transformations thanks to the creations of Marlowe, Shakespeare, Jonson, Fletcher and others, but the conditions of playgoing changed radically too. In the first years it was afflicted by massive hostility from the succession of magnates who served as Lord Mayor of London. Preachers consistently condemned it, and it continued to be disliked by the more strait-laced members of society at all of its many levels. For all that, its development followed a remarkably steep upward curve. In 1594 two lords on the Privy Council, the monarch's chief governing body, intervened to foster its growth in quality and to secure it a fixed place to perform in the suburbs of London. When King James replaced Elizabeth in 1603 he wasted little time making himself and his family patrons of the four companies then licensed to perform in London, a mighty affirmation for the rising status of playing. In time the leading playhouse became the most vaunted showplace after the court for anyone with high social ambitions. Under King Charles the whole business of playmaking gradually grew so close to its patrons the royal family that it had to share in the king's downfall in 1642. What it felt like to attend a performance through those seven decades altered with this sequence of growth and elevation.

The term 'Shakespearean' is used here with deliberate looseness. It covers a period starting when Shakespeare was only three years old in far-away Stratford, and ends twenty-six years after he died. The generosity of giving it his name is justified by the scale of his achievement, not least in the long duration of the company he helped to found and which ran as the theatre's leading light for forty-eight years up to the general closure of 1642. Ultimately the peculiar distinction of Shakespeare's plays was the magnet attracting this accumulation of bits and pieces of evidence and inspiring the labour of trying to assemble them in a coherent shape.

Most of the bits and pieces, while they are invoked throughout the book, are also bagged up together in the two appendices. Appendix 1 names and describes the 250 real persons known to have attended plays on some occasion through the period, augmenting the 196 named in the second edition of 1996 by 25 per cent. Appendix 2 quotes as many as possible of the hundreds of contemporary references which have something significant to say about the early audiences, real or fictional, adding 14 to the 210 in the list of 1996. The references in Appendix 2 are set out in their chronological sequence, affirming the process of historical change in as precise an order as the evidence for their provenance permits. Wherever such comments are cited in the text, the reference is to their number in Appendix 2.

There are too many people than I can name here who deserve my thanks for help with the work and the time that lies beneath this book, but some mention of the main contributors is essential. In the twenty years since I began, too many have died (Charles Barber, Philip Brockbank, Theo Crosby, E. R. Gurr, John Orrell, Alan Wardman, Sam Wanamaker). More happily, others are still there giving help, notably Mary Blackstone, Al Braunmuller, Cedric Brown, Martin Butler, Bernard Capp, John R. Elliott Jr, Henk Gras, E. A. Gurr, Christopher Hardman, Richard Hosley, Mariko Ichikawa, Grace Ioppolo, Mac Jackson, Ron Knowles, Ian Laurenson, Cameron Louis,

Carolyn Lyle, Scott McMillin, Michael Neill, Barbara Palmer, Alan Pritchard and Michael Shapiro. Special thanks to John Astington for his assiduous checks on my accuracy and reliability, not least with the illustrations. For this third edition I should like to add my particular thanks to Charles Whitney, who not only gave me good advice about various features of the book but supplied names and descriptions for several of the items in the two appendices. And as always, the quietest arm-twister in the business, Sarah Stanton of Cambridge University Press.

ANDREW GURR
Reading, 2003

Acknowledgements

We should like to thank the following for permission to reproduce the illustrations: the Guildhall Library, City of London (nos. 1, 7, 10 and 11 – photographs by Geremy Butler); the Bibliotheek der Rijksuniversiteit, Utrecht (3 and 5); the Mellon Foundation (4); the National Portrait Gallery (6, 9, 17, 18 and 20); the Provost and Fellows of Worcester College, Oxford (8); the Royal Library, Windsor (12); the Society of Antiquaries of London (14); the British Library (13, 15 and 16); the Folger Shakespeare Library (19); Abbot Hall Art Gallery (21); and the President and Fellows of St John's College, Oxford (22).

1
Introduction

The strongest way of registering the essential difference between play-going in Shakespeare's time and now is to register the etymological difference of an audience from a spectator. 'Audience' is a collective term for a group of listeners. A 'spectator' is an individual, seeing for him or herself. Modern playgoers are set up, by their physical and mental conditioning, to be solitary spectators, sitting comfortably in the dark watching a moving picture, eavesdroppers privileged by the camera's hidden eye. In fundamental contrast the early modern playgoers were audiences, people gathered as crowds, forming what they called assemblies, gatherings, or companies. They sat or stood in a circle round the speakers who were enacting what they came to hear and see. An audience comes to hear, and therefore it clusters as closely as possible round the speaker. Spectators come to see, and so they position themselves where they can confront the spectacle. The Elizabethan stage, being the centre of a circle, had no front.

This difference between then and now, between the early audiences and modern spectators, is both a consequence and a cause of the fundamental changes the design of theatres underwent in the centuries since the Shakespeare period. Almost all modern theatres and cinemas are based on the assumption that viewing is two-dimensional. The viewer sits in front of the screen or the stage, acquiring information primarily with the eye. Shakespearean playgoers were members of a crowd surrounding the speakers, their priority listening, not viewing. Early playhouses were designed to position audiences in a complete circuit all around the stage. Like anything in the centre of a circle, the stage had therefore no two-dimensional front or back. While fewer members of the playgoing community were positioned at what we think of as 'behind' the stage, their smaller numbers were counterbalanced by their higher social eminence. The playgoers who sat at what we think of as the rear of the stage were the richest and the highest in social status. Proximity to the speakers was far more important than a 'frontal' viewing position.

One of the basic difficulties that modern reconstructions of early playhouses like the new Globe in London suffer from is that modern

1

spectators, trained for viewing, automatically position themselves at the 'front', and modern actors therefore automatically play to them in two dimensions instead of the original three. This may be unavoidable, since the social distinctions that gave weight and potency to the elements of the audience positioned at what we think of as the 'back' of the stage have also gone, even when they are media celebrities, with the result that no modern audience, whether spectator-minded or not, can reproduce the conditions that prevailed at the original Globe. This change in mental conditioning from early audiences to modern spectators is only the most obvious of the many differences that can help us to identify the telling features of that dynamic interaction between plays and playgoers that is the essence of theatre, and what Shakespeare and his peers were catering for.

Those regrettable differences give an enormous incentive to study of the complex interactive process that was early modern theatre, the subject of this book. Its interactivity makes it a far from simple matter, not least because the participants of the time had widely divergent views about the process they were involved in, whether on the stage or around it. Spectator-minded playgoers were a major component in the interactive process then too. Writers for the stage like Ben Jonson strongly preferred their audiences to listen to their words rather than view the actors, a position with implications that will be looked at in detail later. The inclination even of the earliest players and some of their playgoers was to favour spectacle. Since it was the players who controlled what playgoers paid for, in a sense Jonson and Shakespeare were on the losing side from the outset. Priorities varied hugely, not just between writers and players but between categories of playgoer such as the handicraft apprentices who applauded *The Shoemaker's Holiday* in 1599 on the one hand and the Earl of Pembroke who quarrelled with the king's uncle over priority for a box at the Blackfriars in 1636 on the other.

It was of course the playwrights who voiced the best-publicised views. In the argument about satire and raillery which occupies the Induction to Jonson's *Every Man Out of his Humour*, the principal railer Asper is prodded by his friends into expressing the poet's ambition for his play and its reception:

> To please, but whom? attentive auditors,
> Such as will joine their profit with their pleasure,
> And come to feed their understanding parts.

Auditors, not spectators. Asper is not Jonson, but here he voices the hope Jonson put into his prologues in the plays he wrote between 1599 and 1626. Ignorance, says Asper at the end of his speech, is the enemy to art. A good playhouse audience will listen to the poetry and be properly rewarded in the mind. A poet wants listeners, not spectators, merely viewing the scene without the thought that listening entails.

Every Man Out was performed at the Globe in 1599. Some time later in the same year Jonson left Shakespeare's company for the company of boys at the newly opened Blackfriars playhouse. His reasons may not have been entirely divorced from his sense of the Globe audience, and the wrong kind of 'understanding' which he felt a large proportion of them displayed. The prologue to his first play for the boys, *Cynthia's Revels*, openly appeals to the 'learned eares' at the new venue. There can be no doubt that he expected a better-educated and more attentive audience at the smaller and more expensive playhouse. It would be nice to know how far this new 'auditory' met his expectations. By 1626 he was looking to the court to give him the audience of 'Schollers' who might understand his play. We might also wonder how many of his fellow poets wrote for the scholars of the time.

Drama, especially Shakespearean drama, is a performance art. Francis Beaumont called the printed text of a play a 'second publication' after the first on the stage (see Appendix 2, no. 91; hereafter in the form 2.91). Shakespeare himself was evidently not concerned to immortalise his plays by any second publication, and rested content with the transient fame of his company's performances. As performance texts, the plays were composed for a tight grouping of people, a more immediate and readily recognisable social entity than the individuals who might buy a printed text. Performed texts of course also supply an immediate response from the recipients, so that playwrights engage in a form of communication more thoroughly intercommunicative than any other form of publication. The more intimately you know your audience, the less simply verbal will the communication be. We should never lose sight of the wide gulf between the fixative written text and the flexible basis out of which the play was actually performed.

For Shakespeare's contemporaries the intimacy that grew up between player and playgoer when commercial theatre became a daily event in London was an extraordinary and uniquely rewarding novelty. London playgoers in the 1580s and 1590s created the unprecedented phenomenon of an audience paying money to hear poetry. For the poets this novelty gave them the first direct and regular contact with a large and committed crowd of hearers that poets in England had ever enjoyed. For the poets who were also players it must have been a revelation: poetry as a performing art speaking directly to an expectant crowd who had paid money to enjoy the offering. Audience response could be directly manipulated, known audience tastes could be catered for, fresh devices could be tested in the confidence that they would be welcomed as novelties. What we see in the texts of plays composed between about 1590 and 1610 is very largely an exploration of the new possibilities seen in this direct relationship between poet and playgoer.

All we have now of these early novelties is their second publication. It is a commonplace that the written play-texts of Shakespeare's time need supplementing and amplifying through knowledge of the stage conventions and the iconography of performance, what has been called the 'art of orchestration' of the performance text.[1] This approach has brought substantial dividends both to our understanding of the texts in detail at the verbal level and to the larger performance dimensions. Mostly however it has worked by identifying conventional techniques of staging evident either implicitly in the play-texts themselves or explicitly in the stage structures they were written for. We now know quite intimately how a play like *Hamlet* might have been staged at the Globe in 1600. What we do not know is how the players and playgoers interacted with it to create the performance experience. Indeed, unless we take the contemporary audiences into account, the full complex of intercommunication through performance for which Shakespeare designed his plays must remain uncertain. We do know that *Hamlet* was first staged at the Globe in 1600, in the broad daylight of what was probably an autumn afternoon on Bankside. We do not know how the audience in the heat and daylight of that London afternoon received the news, delivered in the play's opening lines, that the time was supposed to be shortly after midnight and the weather bitterly cold. We know that they would recognise Hamlet's pun about the distracted Globe he finds himself in, and possibly connect it with the 'distracted multitude' which Claudius later says loves Prince Hamlet. We cannot be so sure how they would receive Hamlet's soliloquies, spoken ostensibly in solitude when in fact he was visibly surrounded by thousands of people, some of whose heads and ears were literally at his feet. A performance text is a transmission tuned to a highly specific wavelength, and a specific set of atmospheric conditions. The receivers are a part of the mechanism of transmission, and need to be incorporated in the business of trying to recompose the performance text for what it can add to our knowledge of Shakespearean dramaturgy.

Shakespearean receivers were far from passive objects. They are likely all too often nowadays to be invoked in a vicious circle of internal evidence, as arbiters of this or that otherwise inexplicable or undesired feature of the plays. Understandably, because they are the most inconstant, elusive, unfixed element of the Shakespearean performance text, their contribution is presented as an easy means of explaining away features of the dramaturgy which seem incongruous to modern audiences. Shakespearean theatre is such a complex phenomenon that historians have found it easy to spin the evidence until it reflects their own wishes for an ideal performance text by means of the shapes they manufacture from that plastic entity the audience.

Of the many complicating factors that make assessing the nature of Shakespearean audiences difficult the chief one is historical change. The seventy-five years between the building of the first amphitheatre playhouse in 1567 and the closing of the three hall playhouses and three amphitheatres operating in 1642 saw huge shifts, in audience taste as much as in the physical nature of the auditoria and the social composition of the playgoers. The reopening of the hall playhouses in 1599, which Jonson tried to exploit for the learned ears he expected them to provide, entailed a complete switch of priorities in the auditorium, for instance. Whereas at the Globe and the other amphitheatres the nearest people on three sides of the stage were the poorest, the groundlings who paid a minimal penny for the privilege of standing on their feet next to the stage platform, at the Blackfriars and the other hall playhouses the wealthier a patron was the closer he or she could come to the action. In those precursors of modern theatres the cheapest places were furthest from the stage.

That transfer reflects a social shift in playgoing priorities that splits the period in two. The gentlemen students of the Inns of Court and the city's artisan apprentices were equally prominent as playgoers throughout the period, but not always in the same proportions, the same positions, or the same playhouses. And just as the social composition of playgoing crowds varied, so did their mental composition and their expectations. The establishment of a popular repertory by the end of the 1580s gave the poets a chance to build an intimate framework of allusion to familiar traditions and conventions which by the very process of building became subject to constant change. A historical perspective, applied to the physical structure of playhouse auditoria and to the varying social and mental structure of the playgoers, will underline the importance not just of the play as performance text but of the original performance text. A properly detailed historical perspective is a necessary component in any analysis of the original audiences and their contribution to performance.

The evidence about audiences falls into four main categories, each determining the contents of one chapter. Each builds on its predecessor. We have to start with the first and most tangible category, the physical circumstances of performance. This includes the shape and design of the auditorium, the numbers in an audience, and the consequent behaviour patterns characteristic of Shakespearean playgoing, down to the material provision the playhouses made for the playgoer's physical comfort in such things as cushions and toilets. The second body of evidence is demographic. It entails identifying the main social groupings in Elizabethan and Jacobean society, which helps to clarify the elements and conditions most likely to have generated playgoers. A detailed analysis – audience sampling – can show the people in these social groupings known to have attended plays at the time, whether real people or types identified by contemporary comment. The most potentially valuable body of evidence that follows is the kind of contemporary comment that says or implies something about the type of playgoer who would be regarded as a normal (or exceptional: the distinction is important) member of the audience at a particular playhouse at a particular time in its history. This third body of evidence, most elusive but potentially by far the most rewarding, is used to identify the mental composition, the collective mind of people in company, the kind of playgoer the hopeful poet might expect to find in the crowd at the venue intended for his play. The hermeneutics of the theatre, the complex interactive communication between stage and audience, depends as much on the audience's state of mind as it does on the author's and the players' expectations of what, mentally, their audience will be prepared for. That mind-set is a consequence of the mental furniture the Shakespeare playgoer might have been equipped with much more than it is a consequence of his or her state of stomach or bladder. It comprises the education, the routine prejudices, the playhouse traditions, and everything the playgoer expected from the playgoing experience.

That kind of evidence then needs to be anchored firmly in the more solid matter of the preceding kinds, and given its place in a historical sequence of play fashions. It has also to be approached with the reservation that the detail is fragmentary, and that even when framed carefully in its historical place it can more easily lead to misinterpretation than any other sort of evidence. This study takes only the most tentative steps towards the final kind of evidence. Perhaps, though, the solidity established with the other three may provide an anchorage for further exploration of this fourth kind, and a reduction in the speculation which has stood in for it in the past.[2]

The majority of the available evidence is contemporary comment. It may be useful to cite one example as a measure of what can reasonably be extracted from any one comment when it is properly located in its context. It should also indicate the importance of that context. A not untypical anecdote appears in a small pamphlet by Henry Peacham the younger which he published in 1642. It must have been written before March of that year, when the playhouses were closed, because it gives no hint that playgoing was not currently available, but it was probably made not long before, since the pamphlet was clearly written for publication and there is no reason why the printing should have been delayed. It made a small supplement to Peacham's *Compleat Gentleman*, originally published in 1622 and reprinted in 1625, 1627 and 1634. Its title is *The Art of Living in London*, and basically it describes the dangers of London life for a gentleman newly arrived from the country. The principal dangers of course were the idle pastimes of gambling, drinking and playgoing, together with their attendant costs. Near the end of the pamphlet Peacham offers a little story.

A tradesman's wife of the Exchange, one day when her husband was following some business in the city, desired him he would give her leave to go see a play; which she had not done in seven years. He bade her take his apprentice along with her, and go; but especially to have a care of her purse; which she warranted him she would. Sitting in a box, among some gallants and gallant wenches, and returning when the play was done, returned to her husband and told him she had lost her purse. 'Wife, (quoth he,) did I not give you warning of it? How much money was there in it?' Quoth she, 'Truly, four pieces, six shillings and a silver tooth-picker.' Quoth her husband, 'Where did you put it?' 'Under my petticoat, between that and my smock.' 'What, (quoth he,) did you feel no body's hand there?' 'Yes, (quoth she,) I felt one's hand there, but I did not think he had come for that.'

There is more than a hint in this anecdote of Peacham's gentlemanly contempt for a money-conscious citizen and his wife who is little more than a foolish and vulnerable sex object. But there is a good deal more too, and when it is stitched into the pattern made by equivalent pieces of evidence it makes a surprisingly strong fabric.

The wife's seat in a box, for instance, means that she went to one of the indoor playhouses. In the 1630s the boxes flanking the stage at Blackfriars and the Cockpit were customarily filled by ladies and their escorts. Squeezed in amongst the gentry and their ladies ('gallants and gallant wenches') she might well have felt a little ill at ease, sufficiently so to give her one reason for not objecting in public to the intrusive hand. A seven-year absence from playgoing might well have intensified her discomfort, even though it is apparent from Massinger's *City Madam* of 1632 that the wives of the wealthier London citizens did try to imitate the behaviour of court ladies in boxes at playhouses. This city madam was certainly the wife of a magnate, since her husband was

Marchants wife of
London

W. Hollar fecit

Ciuis Londinenſis melioris qualitatis Vxor.

2

1. A merchant's wife, one of a series of engravings by Wenceslas Hollar made
in the early 1630s.

busy at the Royal Exchange, which meant that he was either a merchant trader or a goldsmith-banker, one of the affluent city families living on the borderline between citizenship and gentrification which was the subject of Massinger's play. No respectable lady went alone to a playhouse, so in the absence of her husband his apprentice was there to ape the pages that court ladies took with them to playhouses. He might possibly have had a pretension to being gentry himself. One-third of the apprentices in the Goldsmith's Company were younger sons of gentry. The wife was clearly an affluent city madam, since her purse had four 'pieces' of gold in it. The cheapest gold coins were marks or nobles, at three to a pound, or royals at two to a pound, so she seems to have taken at least £2 in cash to the playhouse, plus the half-crown or more which admission to the box would have cost the two of them. Finally it is evident that the box was crowded enough for the cutpurse to have got his hand inside the wife's dress without being noticed by anyone else, and that not all gallants were as gentlemanly, either in their thieving ways, or in the lecherous groping which the wife expected, as Peacham's own *Compleat Gentleman* would have us assume. The wife's reaction to the groping hand says something about how usual it was for lechery to thrive in playhouse crowds and perhaps how unusual it was for cutpurses to operate in those conditions.

If we were to milk this possibly fanciful anecdote for rather more than it can reasonably be expected to give, we might associate Peacham's city madam with the wife of the Citizen in Beaumont's *Knight of the Burning Pestle*. In the play's Induction the wife explains that she has been trying for twelve months to get her husband to bring her to a play, and she subsequently entertains the gentry amongst whom she sits by her thoroughgoing ignorance of dramaturgy and her innocently lecherous *double entendres*. Her taste is for romance and old-fashioned tales of knight errantry, and she enjoys the stage spectacle with comic literal mindedness. After seven years without seeing plays it would not be inconceivable that Peacham's city madam should also be romantic in her tastes and gullible in her enjoyment of the spectacle.

The anecdote is useful, then, for deducing some tangible details about the physical conditions the wife endured in her box, the somewhat less tangible details about her social circumstances, and a few markedly fragile conclusions about her mental outlook. These can be related to the repertory of the indoor playhouses in the early 1640s, though the fact that it is the wife's first visit to a play for seven years would hardly make her a typical or normative playgoer. In itself the anecdote offers only a tiny sampling from the range of audience types.

If several hundred such pieces of evidence are put together, though, the fabric becomes both long and finely detailed. The anecdote certainly tells us something about the normal expectations of playgoing for the wealthier citizens and citizens' wives in the 1630s and early 1640s. It also indicates that we should use constraint because of the increasingly speculative nature of any deductions we make as we move from the tangible details of the physical setting into attempts to calculate what might have been in the particular playgoer's head on that visit.

Despite all the constraints, these possibilities, weaving the evidence into a fabric and limiting speculation over the precise mental processes, have established the structure of this analysis of Shakespearean playgoing. Following the building process identified above, it begins with the physical circumstances of the playgoing exercise, as the playhouses developed and changed through the seventy-five years between 1567 and 1642 when there were specially built commercial playhouses in London, and varied provisions at the different playhouses. It continues with analysis of the social structure and an attempt to identify the social types who are known to have been playgoers throughout the period. It investigates the more tangible pieces of evidence for the composition of the minds of different playgoers, both the learned ears and the 'Nutcrackers, that only come for sight', as Jonson called them in the prologue written for the court in *The Staple of News*, and tentatively it identifies some of the doors to further investigation which the evidence leaves open. Finally it seeks to emphasise the strength of the pressure for continual change inherent in the exercise of playgoing, by sketching a history of the changing tastes and the different kinds of repertory offered by the different playhouses. That history is also, by implication and rather covertly, an attempt to flesh out some of the questions raised by the chapter on the mental composition of playgoers. A history of the evolution of playgoers' tastes in plays has some value in suggesting the preferences which made one kind of play more popular at a given time than another. It also provides an outline of the interaction between the poets and their audiences.

The closing date for the period covered by this study is obvious. Parliament may not have intended to do more in September 1642 than to batten down the hatches in a time of political storm by ordering the closure of all places of public assembly such as playhouses.[3] The order explicitly offered the judgement that the times were too seriously disturbed for such frivolities as plays to be tolerable. It was in its macabre way a repetition of the lengthy closures ordered because of the plague epidemics when Elizabeth and James I died. Charles was not to die for another seven years, but the interim was not unlike a long wake so far as the lighter distractions of town life were concerned. Nobody could have anticipated in 1642 that the storm would last for eighteen years. Nonetheless, it was the longest interval in theatre history, and whatever flickers of life lit up that long closure the lamp was of a different kind when Davenant set it going again at the Restoration. Both the amphitheatres and the version of their open stage-playing which the hall playhouses maintained went out of existence in 1642, and that cessation provides the terminus for this study.

The opening date is necessarily a more arbitrary point in the long evolution of playgoing. Most histories still fix on 1576 as the significant date, since James Burbage's Theatre and the first Blackfriars both opened in that year. But we know that Burbage's brother-in-law and partner John Brayne built the Red Lion playhouse on the pattern followed by the Theatre and the later playhouses as early as 1567.[4] If the significance of the Theatre is that it indicates the size of the potential market for popular plays, leading Brayne and Burbage to invest money in an auditorium like those of the animal-baiting arenas where the owners could take money at the door and accommodate thousands of paying Londoners, then the building of its predecessor the Red Lion must make 1567 the watershed. At first this watershed was probably more important for the impresarios than the plays. It gave them better control of their income than they had passing a hat around in a market place or hiring an inn-yard or baiting arena to put on their shows. But it must also have made a difference fairly rapidly to the playgoers. By enclosing the plays inside a special building the players made the customers who paid to see what was on offer more selective, and no doubt more demanding. Only those who paid got in. They got in for the exclusive purpose of seeing a play, and they handed their money over to the impresarios and players whose sole interest was in satisfying their demand for entertainment. Moreover a single fixed venue needed a much larger turnover of plays than was needed when the players were on their travels from one town to another. So the London playhouses became a massive stimulus to the production of new plays. It was the years between 1567 and 1576 that saw the professional playing companies stamp their first durable footprint on London.

The first commercial playhouses of 1567 and 1575–6 offered a system for playgoers which differed significantly from previous arrangements. Groups of travelling players who performed in market places had to take a hat around for their income, and were likely to be paid by results, haphazardly, rather than systematically in advance. Players who secured an inn-yard venue were dependent on the innkeeper's willingness and the variable physical facilities he could provide. Players who performed in halls, whether at the behest of the local mayor or the lord of the manor, were paid chiefly by their host to use the facilities and to entertain the guests he provided. Audiences at such venues did not have any direct financial link with the pleasures the players gave them. To that extent the first purpose-built playhouses signal not just an escalation of impresario investment in playgoing but a change of motive and circumstance for the playgoers. The first playhouses were a rationalisation of the growing fashion for seeing plays for money at the inns more than they were a radical innovation, but they made as precise a growth point in the evolution of London playgoing as any from that rather obscure region of theatre history. The vicinity of 1567 is therefore the best starting date.

A study of the evidence about Shakespearean playgoing cannot afford to be hopeful of reconstructing a Shakespearean performance with any amplitude. Performances are ephemeral, audiences are disparate, and the poet, especially if he was of the tribe of Ben, was far more likely to have aimed at the individual (ideal) intellect than the collective emotion. Identifying the relative proportions in a playhouse crowd of artisan 'understanders', city madams and gallants sitting on their benches in judgement does not throw much light on these darker issues of a performance text. But it does light up the context, and that kind of illumination is certainly worth having. Shakespeare reads differently once the evidence set out in this kind of study is taken fully into account. The question of wordplay, for instance, and the learned '*lusus*' or witty allusion, which seems of primary importance to the reader, has to be treated with heavy scepticism by those who take seriously the physical circumstances of high-speed performances in noisy open-air amphitheatres. Even in the relative quietness of a hall like the Blackfriars a Shakespeare play, with no serious cuts and with four short intervals for candle-trimming between the acts, a performance that took well under three hours to perform as it did in Shakespeare's time, could have given its audience little time to take either breath or thought. The emotional sweep of a tragedy gains in intensity and concentrated power when played in a short span of time, as the performance removes attention from the minutiae of the text or its enactment.

We have, however, our own limitations which a knowledge of the context for Shakespearean performance can help to minimise. It is not only the actors and their directors who take Shakespeare more slowly these days. Sitting in padded armchairs in an artificially darkened auditorium is not good training for anyone's experience of Elizabethan plays. If we were habituated to hearing sermons, if we were used to standing in a muddy yard or even sitting on wooden benches by candlelight, we might perhaps be more alert to many features that Elizabethans would have taken for granted. The metatheatrical and 'all the world's a stage' aspects are much easier to recognise when the auditorium is not darkened and the audience is as visible and palpable a presence as the players. The verbal tropes and quibbles are quicker of access when listening is a more natural habit than reading. The physical features, that awareness of where you are and what you are doing that modern cinemas do so much to conceal, was an invariable feature of every Shakespearean performance. Knowing the context helps us to be more attentive to such factors and to give them better weight.

In the epistle accompanying the printed text of a sermon he gave at Paul's Cross in October 1578, the Cambridge divine Laurence Chaderton apologised for the defectiveness of his second publication.

Let no man thinke, that the reading of this can be half so effectuall and profitable to him, as the hearyng was, or might be. For it wanteth the zeale of the speaker, the attention of the hearer, the promise of God to the ordinary preaching of his word, the mighty and inwarde working of his holy spirite.

(Epistle, 'To the Christian Reader', A3)

Whether or not we want to think of Shakespeare as a sacred spirit, the player's zeal and the playgoer's attentiveness were essential elements in the collective process that created a performance event in the Shakespearean playhouse.

2
Physical conditions

London developed two quite different types of commercial playhouse when it first went into the business of housing professional playing companies. One type opened in 1567, the other in 1575. The 'public' playhouses or open amphitheatres, the first of which appeared in Stepney in 1567, were versions of the animal-baiting houses and galleried inn-yards. The 'private' playhouses or halls were built in large rooms on the model of the banqueting halls in the royal palaces and great houses where plays were provided for banqueting guests. One was opened in 1575 in the precinct of St Paul's Cathedral, and another in the following year in the Blackfriars precinct. Both were in liberties free from the Lord Mayor's jurisdiction, as were the amphitheatres in London's surburbs. These ventures precipitated a brief flood. In all, five commercial playhouses, three of them amphitheatres and two halls, opened in the years between 1575 and 1577. The terms 'public' and 'private' were not used to differentiate the two types until about 1600, and they say more about their social antecedents than any difference of commercial function. The terms 'amphitheatre' and 'hall' are better indications of their character. The value of the terms 'public' and 'private' lies chiefly in the way they mark the social snobbery that separated the two kinds.

The 'public' amphitheatres were all built out in the suburbs. The first of them, so far as we know, was the Red Lion, built in Whitechapel in 1567, and replaced in 1576 by the Theatre in Shoreditch, on the main road north out of the city. The dimensions of the Red Lion's stage are known, but nothing about its history or what might have been performed there. In 1576 a smaller amphitheatre was also built nearly a mile south of London Bridge at Newington Butts. Much of what we know about James Burbage's Theatre and its near neighbour, the Curtain, built in the following year, has to be inferred from the evidence for the later playhouses, which are rather better documented. The Theatre was dismantled in 1598 so that its timbers could be used as the frame for the Globe. In its basic

14

layout and audience capacity the later playhouse must have closely resembled it.

Much more is known about the Rose, built in 1587 on Bankside in Surrey, from the evidence in Philip Henslowe's records and from its foundations, partly uncovered in 1989. We also know something of the Swan, built in 1595 on the south bank of the Thames some distance west of the Rose, close to Paris Garden, where the chief bear-baiting house stood. We know about the Swan largely thanks to the drawing which the Dutchman Johannes De Witt made of it on a visit in 1596, surviving in a copy made by his friend Arend van Buchell in Amsterdam.

Different kinds of evidence, including builder's instructions and lawsuits, give information about the last five major amphitheatres, the Globe (1599) built on Bankside barely fifty yards from the age-ing Rose, the Fortune (1600) to the north, the Boar's Head (1601) in Whitechapel to the east, the Red Bull (1604) in Clerkenwell to the north-west, and the Hope, built on the Bankside in 1614 to double as a baiting house and playhouse.[1] The main features of the auditorium seem to have been basically similar in all the amphitheatres, though some were polygonal and others were built in a square, so it is possible to identify something like a typical setting for hearing a play at any of the 'public' venues. John Brayne, who built the Red Lion playhouse in 1567, partnered James Burbage in building what was probably its replacement, the Theatre, in 1576. Burbage's sons built the Globe. Philip Henslowe built the Rose in 1587, the Fortune in 1600 and the Hope in 1614. Most likely all of these earliest amphitheatres had an auditorium similar in structure to the galleried animal-baiting rings which had stood on the south bank of the Thames for the previous forty or more years. The Rose, built close to the baiting houses in 1587, was at first constructed without a stage, as if Henslowe's intention was to run a multipurpose amphitheatre, as twenty-seven years later he tried to do with the Hope.

The amphitheatres probably also resembled the great coaching inns, which had square yards and surrounding galleries. In fact two later playhouses, the Boar's Head and the Red Bull, were converted from inns, and the square-built Fortune may have been similar to them. The 1576 edition of William Lambarde's *Perambulation of Kent* describes playgoing at the Bel Savage inn on Ludgate Hill, and the 1596 edition adds the Theatre to the account without otherwise altering what is described. The arrangements for playgoing at the two venues were evidently similar. Inns, however, had galleries at only one level, and two or three allowed a much larger number of paying customers. The

2. A map of London, showing the playhouses built between 1567 and 1629. The map is from Braun and Hogenberg's *Civitates Orbis Terrarum*, 1572. The playhouses and the inns used for playing are marked in their approximate locations, with the date of building where known. In the seventy years from 1572 London grew to cover most of the territory shown on the map.

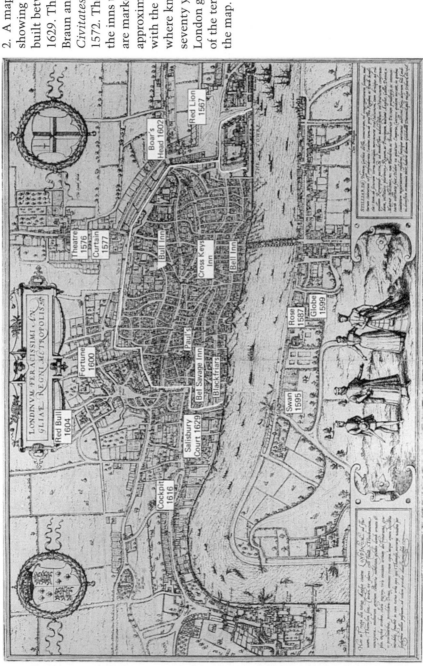

Boar's Head, converted from an inn to a playhouse in 1599 after the Privy Council banned the use of London's inns for playing, had only one level of galleries and did not last long. The inns and amphitheatres provided standing room in the 'yard' around three sides of the stage, an area obviously not available to audiences at the baitings, but apart from that extra space the auditorium layout probably did not differ in any fundamental way.[2] The playhouses certainly copied their three levels of galleries from the baiting houses.

Samuel Kiechel, a German merchant visiting London in 1584, reported that both of the playhouses in Shoreditch to the north had three levels of galleries.[3] These served as the chief accommodation for playgoers, offering seating on wooden 'degrees' or steps, and a roof to fend off the London weather. The stage itself, jutting from one side into the middle of the yard, was also protected by a cover or 'heavens', but the yard was open to the sky, and the playgoers who gathered there closest to the stage had nothing but their legs to uphold them and their hats to protect them from rain or snow. This minimal provision – no seating, and no protection from the rain – helps to explain one of the curious features of the earliest playhouses which seems to have altered when new ones began to appear in the 1590s. Admission to the first playhouses was a gradual progression from the minimal comfort of the yard to the better and more sheltered places in the galleries. As Lambarde put it in the 1596 edition of his *Perambulation* (p. 233):

such as goe to *Parisgardein*, the *Bell Savage*, or *Theatre*, to beholde Beare baiting, Enterludes or Fence play, can account of any pleasant spectacle, [if] they first pay one pennie at the gate, another at the entrie of the Scaffolde, and the thirde for a quiet standing.

Thomas Platter, a young Swiss visitor in 1599, described the same system with the added detail that the best seats were cushioned (2.37). You went in by the entrance doors directly to the yard, as you would enter a coaching inn-yard through its great double gates. Once in the yard you could choose to enter the galleries for a seat, and if you wanted more privacy and a cushion you could pay once again for a room in the galleries closest to the stage. This arrangement, a sequence of choices, may have owed something to the design of the inns, and it must have been acceptable to the players familiar with the traditions of booth stages in market squares, where the entire audience simply stood around the stage. It can hardly have been used in baiting houses, where the yard was the baiting arena, but in the playhouses it must have seemed entirely natural to those who assumed that a normal

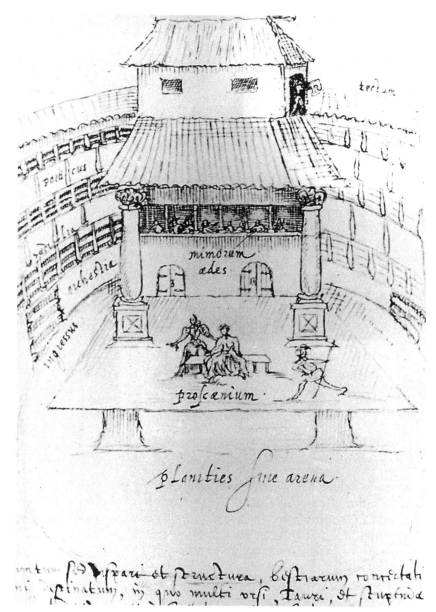

3. A drawing of the interior of the Swan, copied in Amsterdam by Arend van Buchell from one made in London in 1596 by Johannes De Witt. Its galleries were polygonal, with external stair turrets, and an 'ingressus' that provided access from the yard to the lowest level of gallery.

audience would principally be a crowd of men and women clustered on their feet around the stage platform. So you were admitted to the yard, and could go elsewhere only if you chose to separate yourself from the principal audience, the crowd standing around the stage platform. If it rained, you had the choice of getting wet or paying a second penny for shelter in the galleries.

The second generation of playhouses, including possibly the Rose (1587), and certainly the Swan (1595), the Globe (1599) and the Fortune (1600), seem to have been designed with a less clumsy system of admission, one that acknowledged from the start that the gallery sitters were different from the standers of the yard. De Witt's drawing of the Swan has caused some debate about this, because the openings marked 'ingressus' in the gallery walls surrounding the yard seem to mark the same cumbrous sequential system as Kiechel described, where the first penny gaining entrance to the yard required the gallery-goer to push his or her way through the crowd in the yard before surrendering another penny for a seat and a roof. But the Globe and the Fortune, built as exact rivals – James Burbage transported the timbers of his Theatre from the northern suburb to the Bankside near to Philip Henslowe's Rose, and Henslowe promptly built the Fortune as the Rose's replacement in the north, using as his builder the man who had just completed the Globe – had a more sophisticated admission system. Access to the galleries in these playhouses did not entail passing through the yard. Once in one of the two entrance-ways you chose either to enter the yard or to mount the stairs which rose in towers above the entrance-ways directly into the galleries.[4] The 'twopenny galleries' in fact could accommodate twice as many playgoers as the yard, so it is understandable that the financiers eventually came to feel that gallery patrons deserved better treatment than to be siphoned through the crowd who were paying least for their pleasure. By 1614 the Swan also had stair turrets.

The 'two small doors', which were all that the audience at the Globe had to escape by in 1613 when a performance of *Henry VIII* set the thatching over the galleries alight and destroyed the playhouse, were said to admit more than three thousand people. With such numbers when the house was full, the crowding was intense. At the Fortune, built in an 80-foot square, the yard measured 55 feet along each side, with the stage jutting into the centre from a tiring-house front occupying 43 of the 55 feet on the side opposite the entry gates. It thus gave the standers in its yard a total space of 1,842 square feet. The Boar's Head playhouse, converted from an inn-yard in 1599, had rather less than that, and only two levels of gallery. The Globe, built on a circular

4. The second Globe, as drawn by Wenceslas Hollar for his famous 'Long View' of London.

or polygonal frame almost 100 feet in outside diameter, and with a yard of about 70 feet across, offered nearly 2,500 square feet.[5]

There is no firm evidence about how many people this space could hold, and it would not have been really packed very often. But it could be enough of a squeeze to be an uncomfortable experience, if we are to judge by Marston's reference to being 'pasted to the barmy Jacket of a Beer-brewer', and Dekker's frequent mentions of garlic-breathing stinkards.[6] The only actual figures we have allocating a set number of standing spectators to a fixed space come from documents about the king's visit to Oxford in 1605 and the play performed before him at Christ Church.[7] There 400 square feet were allowed for 130 people standing. But that ratio – 3 square feet each – was actually more than the average gentleman or lady was allowed for sitting at the same play ($2\frac{1}{4}$ square feet), which cannot bear much relation to the level of crowding acceptable at the Globe or Fortune. Calculations of 600 or 800 in the yard at these playhouses probably rather underestimate the maximum capacity. At the nine performances of *A Game at Chesse* at the rebuilt Globe in 1624 the squeeze must have been fearsome,

5. A detail from De Witt's drawing of the Swan, showing the stage balcony and its audience in the 'lords' rooms'. Note the hats several of them are wearing.

and there could hardly have been fewer than a thousand people in the yard for each performance, since the Spanish ambassador claimed that there were 'more than 3000 persons there on the day that the audience was smallest'.[8]

The possible change in the admission system for the later playhouses may indicate a shift in priorities to favour the gallery audience over the 'understanders' in the yard. The yard's standers were always the lowest level of society, as Hamlet illustrated when he coined the term 'groundlings' for them. The only other use of this term contemporary with *Hamlet* was Philemon Holland's word in his translation of Pliny's *Natural History* (1601) for a small fish or ling, a species which fed by sucking the algae off the stones in a river bottom, so its mouth was a huge yawn. Prince Hamlet was calling the crowd of understanders surrounding the stage small fish with gaping mouths, just what he would have observed from his superior posture looking down on them. The amphitheatre auditoria reproduced quite precisely the Elizabethan social hierarchy, from the lowest in the yard below to the lords' rooms on the stage balcony above the actors, placed at the middle level between the stage as earth and the stage cover as the heavens.

The wealthiest patrons most likely had separate access to their places, since the 'lords' rooms'[9] on the balcony immediately over the stage were reached directly through the tiring house. The sixpence which a lord's room cost would have been paid at the tiring-house door at the back of the playhouse, and the privileged who went to their superior places could chat to the players in the tiring house on the way, as did the gallants who chose to sit on stools on the Blackfriars stage, where access for the stool-sitters was also through the tiring house, as Dekker's *Gull's Hornbook* testifies.

The entry system set up for the Swan, the Globe and Fortune with their stair turrets went some distance towards giving comparably separate access for the gallery patrons. John Harington wrote an epigram about a lady who was caught on the stairs by a pair of thieves, which dates from the 1590s and shows that access to the galleries at that time was no longer through the yard. We need not assume that the anecdote in the epigram really happened, since Harington was developing a bawdy pun on the stock term for stealing, 'cony-catching' (catching rabbits), but the material circumstances of the stairway must be genuine.

> A lady of great Birth, great reputation,
> Clothed in seemely, and most sumptuous fashion
> Wearing a border of rich Pearl and stone,
> Esteemed at a thousand crowns alone,
> To see a certaine interlude, repaires,
> To shun the press, by dark and privat staires.
> Her page did beare a Torch that burnt but dimly.
> Two cozening mates, seeing her deckt so trimly,
> Did place themselves upon the stayres to watch her,
> And thus they laid their plot to cunny-catch her:
> One should as 'twere by chance strike out the light;
> While th'other that should stand beneath her, might
> Attempt (which modestie to suffer lothes)
> Rudely to thrust his hands under her clothes.
> That while her hands repeld such grosse disorders,
> His mate might quickly slip away the borders.
> Now though this act to her was most unpleasant
> Yet being wise (as womens wits are present:)
> Straight on her borders both her hands she cast,
> And so with all her force she held them fast.
> Villaines, she cryde, you would my borders have:

6. A portrait of Sir John Harington, in the National Portrait Gallery.

But I'll save them, tother it selfe can save:
Thus, while the Page had got more store of light,
The coozening mates, for fear slipt out of sight.
Thus her good wit, their cunning over-macht,
Were not these cony-catchers conycatchd?[10]

If this anecdote relates to an amphitheatre, as its dating indicates it must, then it suggests a few additional points about gallery audiences. Wealthy noblewomen could expect to see plays there unescorted except by their pages. Cutpurses were regularly in attendance, and crowds did not come to the playhouse so thick and so fast that a gallery-goer might not find herself climbing the stairs alone. This last point fits in with the implications of Philip Henslowe's takings from the galleries of the Rose. His average income was less than half the maximum.[11] Overcrowding, except at new plays and exceptionally scandalous events like *A Game at Chesse*, was not usually a playgoer's main hazard.

Access to the upper gallery levels through a stair turret may have created a further social distinction between the groundlings and their superiors. The pair of major stairways with doors leading off to the two higher gallery levels need not have given access to the lowest gallery level, just behind and above the groundlings. It may be that De Witt's drawing of the Swan shows the form of access for the lowest gallery level. Those who wanted to occupy that space got there through the 'ingressus' from the yard that De Witt's drawing shows. We know that the Swan had stair turrets, since the contract for building the Hope specifies them as the model for its builder. If it also had a separate means of access to the lowest galleries, perhaps it was meant to provide a more distinct form of separation, one that kept the upper-level gallery-goers apart from those in the lowest galleries, who were associated rather with the standers in the yard. If so, the playhouse owners had profit from giving the standers easy access (on payment of an extra penny) to a gallery seat whenever it rained and they wanted to take cover.

By John Orrell's calculations, allowing an 18-inch spread and also 18 inches fore and aft for each person on the 'degrees', the Globe's galleries could hold almost 1,000 people on each of the two lower levels, and on the third level, where sight-lines would have required a steeper rake and less depth of degrees, about 750.[12] By the same criterion the Fortune galleries could hold 880 in the lower galleries and 660 in the upper tier. The allocation of space for the Christ Church performance in 1605 which Orrell used to obtain his figures in fact allocated 18 inches in width for everyone, but gave a relatively generous 30 inches fore and aft for lords and 24 inches fore and aft for court ladies and the king's servants. The gentlemen in the upper tier were confined to 18 inches each way. It seems plausible to assume that the public amphitheatres would only provide a minimum spacing for their customers, though of course Lambarde's third penny 'for a quiet standing' (i.e. a seat or standpoint) might have given access to a more spacious arrangement, like the Oxford allocation for court ladies, close to the stage. If so, the totals for the lower galleries would be less than a thousand each. The lords' rooms must have been spacious, supplied with benches or stools. On the Swan's balcony De Witt sketched not more than two people to a room. More amply, a reference from 1609 to a gallant who 'Plays at Primero over the stage'[13] shows that there was easily enough space for a card-game in the lords' rooms. Primero was a gambling game rather like poker involving three or more players.

This disposition, with space for 800 or more in the yard and over 2,000 in the various galleries, matches the estimates from the time for the total capacity of the amphitheatres, although we should note rather suspiciously that they all seem to specify exactly the same round figure of three thousand. Like earlier commentators, all identifying the same total capacity, the Spanish ambassador reckoned over three thousand people attending *A Game at Chesse* at the second Globe, which, being built on the same foundations as the first, must have had a similar capacity. De Witt gave three thousand for the Swan in 1596.[14] In the absence of allocated seating, and with everyone ready to shuffle more closely together as more people arrived, a rounded figure for the maximum of squeezed audience is as good as we can get.

Questions have been asked about the location of the lords' rooms above the stage at the Globe, and the consequent problem the highest payers must have had with sight-lines, viewing the 'spectacles' or 'discoveries' set out inside the central opening beneath Juliet's balcony. It has been claimed that the places 'o're the stage' (2.34) must have been favoured only by people who were keener to be seen than to see. That in the first place presupposes that they came as spectators rather than as an audience for proximity to the players. Early experiments at the new Globe, built in Southwark as a near-replica of the original design, indicate that Elizabethan playgoers seated in positions that we think of as being 'behind' the stage got better value for their money than the claim allows. Elizabethan designers did not find sight-lines a problem. If your access was poor, in the absence of any allocated seat you could move to wherever you could see or hear better. The rooms on the balcony and adjacent upper-gallery bays, which the early playgoers paid most for, were the best seats in the house for hearing because they were closest to the stage. What might be lost from a view of discovered set-pieces like Volpone's gold or Hermione's statue was offset by the bird's-eye perspective you got on the entire action of the play, and the dialogue which took care to explain what you might not see. The players and their theatre-owners knew what they were charging for.

Writers always expected their audience to have impeded views at times, whether from the large posts holding up the front of the galleries, the headgear of other audience members, the stage posts or (mostly with the groundlings) from the crowd of players standing on the stage. When Shakespeare gave his characters lines like 'Why sinks that cauldron?' in *Macbeth* (4.1.121) he was catering for the many in the crowd who might not have a clear view of the trapdoor, surrounded as the cauldron was by the circle of witches. Similar verbal descriptions of the spectacle were commonly provided for the more privileged playgoers who could see only part of what was 'discovered' when the central hangings beneath them were drawn back.

THE HALL PLAYHOUSES

The huge capacity of the amphitheatres with their open yards was the first of the many obvious differences of the 'public' playhouses from the more intimate 'private' halls. Francis Beaumont spoke of the Blackfriars in 1609 as a court where 'a thousand men in judgement sit' (2.91), but modern estimates put its capacity rather lower. Field in another verse in the same book (2.92) wrote of the monster clapping his thousand hands, which, taken literal-mindedly, meant an audience of 500. The set of drawings for a playhouse which Inigo Jones made in about 1616, almost certainly for the Cockpit, has been calculated as providing seating at 18 inches per bottom for fewer than 700 people.[15] There was no yard or standing area of any kind in the hall playhouses – the 'pit' was filled with bench seating – so it is possible to make a reasonable estimate of their capacity using the Christ Church figures. On that basis the indoor halls could take in no more than a quarter of the amphitheatre capacity.

The first 'private' playhouses came into use shortly before the Theatre opened, since Paul's choir school started using a small playhouse adjacent to the Chapter House in 1575.[16] It accommodated perhaps fewer than 200 people, and was used intermittently between 1575 and 1590 and again from 1600 to 1606. The master of the rival boy company to Paul's, the Chapel Children, built a playhouse in a hall in the Blackfriars precinct for his boys a year later. Little is known about it, and it was in use only for eight years, up to 1583–4, when for a brief season a combined company of Chapel and Paul's Children under John Lyly played there. All playing by boy companies was stopped in 1590, and from then till 1600 no boy companies and no indoor playhouses except rooms at a few of the city inns like the Cross

Keys in Gracechurch Street were available in London. The beginnings of durable hall playhouse use came towards the end of the century, through a peculiar combination of circumstances.

The most famous of all the hall venues, the second Blackfriars playhouse, was built in 1596 by James Burbage, builder of the original Theatre, for his adult player-tenants, Shakespeare's company. They were licensed to play at the Theatre in May 1594, and as their first winter approached they persuaded their new patron, Henry Carey the Lord Chamberlain, the first Baron Hunsdon, to ask the Lord Mayor if they could use the indoor Cross Keys inn for the winter. It was an intriguing request for a member of the Privy Council to make, because less than six months before the Council had agreed with the Lord Mayor that playing at all city inns was to be banned. The two newly licensed companies, the Lord Chamberlain's own and another set up by his son-in-law the Lord Admiral, also a Privy Councillor, were authorised by the Council to play exclusively in the suburbs, at the Theatre and the Rose. The Lord Mayor rejected the Chamberlain's request, but a desire to play at enclosed city inns like the Cross Keys in the winter stayed in the company's minds. Consequently the following winter James Burbage set about constructing a hall theatre that stood inside the city, like the lost inns, but in a precinct free from mayoral control. By 1596 the twenty-one-year lease of the ground he had built the Theatre on was nearly up, and he had reason to doubt whether he would be able to renew it. The ban on using city inns that the two Councillors had agreed when they set up their duopoly of companies in May 1594 did give the two companies a licensed playhouse, but the Theatre did not offer them a long future. That, plus their preference for playing indoors in winter, probably persuaded Burbage into the gamble of building a new hall playhouse inside the city walls in place of the lost city inns. The players using the Rose were evidently more willing than Shakespeare's company to continue running at their open-air venue through winter.

Burbage chose his site advisedly. He bought part of an imposing building built of stone in the liberty of Blackfriars, an area on the fashionable western side of the city close to the City of Westminster. It stood inside the London walls but was free of the City of London's jurisdiction because of its ancient status as a monastic precinct. There Burbage had no more need to worry about the city's hostility than he did with his Theatre in the suburbs of Middlesex, or the sponsors of the Paul's playhouse in the cathedral precinct. Moreover the new hall playhouse was close to the area where the wealthiest playgoers lived. Potentially it was an ingenious solution to the problem of

7. A section of Hollar's 'Long View' of London printed in 1644. The long
steep-pitched roof with two slender chimneys or lanterns jutting up
from the middle, below and to the left of St Bride's four-spired church tower,
is probably the Blackfriars Hall, containing the playhouse built in 1596.

replacing or supplementing the Theatre. It even raised the prospect of
the company using alternate summer and winter playing-places, and
certainly would have given them an emphatic shift up-market, from
the amphitheatre serving primarily the penny-paying standers in the
yard to the 'private' or 'select' kind of audience which could pay a lot
more and expected seats and a roof over their heads. It reflected the
company's desire to play in better conditions indoors through the winter months, a desire that as it happened they did not satisfy for another
fourteen years.[17]

Sadly for Burbage he miscalculated his popularity among the wealthy. After he had spent £600 on the acquisition of a great chamber once used for meetings of Parliament, and converted it into his playhouse, the wealthy and influential residents of Blackfriars petitioned the Privy Council to forbid the players using it, on the grounds that it

will grow to be a very great annoyance and trouble, not only to all the noblemen and gentlemen thereabout inhabiting but allso a generall inconvenience to all the inhabitants of the same precinct, both by reason of the great resort and gathering together of all manner of vagrant and lewde persons that, under cullor of resorting to the players, will come thither and worke all manner of mischeefe, and allso to the great pestring and filling up of the same precinct . . . and besides, that the same playhouse is so neere the Church that the noyse of the drummes and trumpetts will greatly disturbe and hinder both the ministers and parishioners in tyme of devine service and sermons.   (2.28)

This last point of objection reveals some of the grounds for the petition. It was not just the standard view that churchgoing and playgoing were antithetical – plays were officially forbidden on days of divine service anyway – but that the characteristic noises of adult players at the public amphitheatres were about to be imported into a neighbourhood which had previously tolerated only the Chapel Children in a hall playhouse. The martial noise of drums and trumpets was an affliction the amphitheatres visited on their neighbours, but not the boy companies at the small enclosed playhouses. 'Public' playing was trying to penetrate a superior residential area. Such effrontery roused the opposition even of Burbage's own new patron, Henry Carey's son, who happened to live close by the new playhouse. As the petition carefully noted,

one Burbage hath lately bought certaine roomes in the . . . precinct neere adjoining unto the dwelling houses of the right honorable the Lord Chamberlaine and the Lord of Hunsdon . . .

and in case anyone thought that this signified the second Lord Hunsdon's personal protection for his company's new venture, he himself signed the petition to the Privy Council, on which his neighbour the new Lord Chamberlain was the executive member for all matters that concerned playing. It was either a great betrayal by the company's new patron (his father, the Lord Chamberlain, died in July 1596 while the Blackfriars was still in building), or a disastrous failure of consultation. The new patron was obviously prejudiced by the fact that he lived close to the new playhouse. Burbage miscalculated disastrously the willingness of the nobility and especially of his company's own patron to tolerate adult players in that vicinity.

Had the times not been so prosperous for the two adult companies which then shared the monopoly of London playing, this ban on the Blackfriars would probably have destroyed the Chamberlain's Men. Burbage, violently at odds with the owner of the land on which his Theatre stood, had purchased the Blackfriars property, a heavy financial commitment even before he added the cost of converting it into a playhouse. Now he was about to lose the Theatre while his money was trapped in the abortive Blackfriars venture. Moreover the other lucrative central city locations, the inns, had been firmly barred to the players. As the Blackfriars petition protested,

now all players being banished by the Lord Mayor from playing within the Cittie by reason of the great inconveniences and ill rule that followeth them, they now thincke to plant themselves in liberties.   (2.28)

Once the inhabitants of the Blackfriars put a stop to that idea, the players had to retreat to their suburban amphitheatre, and then evacuate it when the lease expired, moving to its neighbour the Curtain. Out of that retreat, and out of Burbage's financial straits, came that rather desperate, second-best expedient, the Globe.

The Globe was an afterthought in the wake of the Blackfriars disaster, and a blessing that must have seemed well disguised at the time. Burbage himself died early in 1597 and his two sons and heirs, Cuthbert and Richard, had to invent a new arrangement to finance the rebuilding of the old Theatre as the Globe. They contributed the Theatre's timbers, but there was no Burbage money to pay the builder. To cover that cost they offered five one-eighth shares in the building to the leading players in the company, including Shakespeare.[18] Six of the eight leading sharers, the five who paid up plus Richard Burbage, thus became the first and only co-owners of the playhouse in which they performed. This arrangement, arising as it did fortuitously out of the Burbage misfortunes, became the guarantee for the stability and security of tenure which Shakespeare's company enjoyed from then on, all the way to the closure of the playhouses in 1642. Not for them the mere three-year tenancies allowed to the companies renting from Henslowe, Alleyn, Beeston and the other playhouse-owning impresarios. They were both impresarios and their own tenants. The disaster of 1596 did more for Shakespeare's art, and his income, than he knew. The unique reputation that the King's Men built for themselves in the years following Shakespeare's retirement from the company was largely based on the esteem the Blackfriars acquired as the most prestigious place for playgoing in the country.

The success of Shakespeare's company in the ten years they now spent at the Globe must not be allowed to obscure the fact, with its implications about audience preferences, that it came second to the Blackfriars in James Burbage's planning in 1596. Since the Blackfriars swallowed up his available funds he may not have expected then to provide both an indoor city playhouse and a new suburban amphitheatre for his players, as happened after 1608. He left his sons two playhouses, both unusable, and no spare cash. When Thomas Platter visited the new Globe to see *Julius Caesar* in September 1599 he noted it as 'the house with the thatched roof'. That economy, for which the owners paid a high price in 1613 when its gallery thatching caught fire, was one consequence of James Burbage's disastrous plan. He considered that the future of the adult playing companies lay in the city's hall playhouse. Building the Globe in Southwark was his sons' retreat in the face of the unexpected opposition by the company's patron and the nobility in the precinct.

The 1596 Blackfriars playhouse was the future for playing. It differed from the Red Lion and the Theatre in three major ways.[19] Each of the three differences indicates a drastic shift that took place between 1567 and 1596 in the kind of playgoer at whom Burbage's company aimed its plays. The first difference was in the sharply reduced size of the auditorium, and the switch of allegiance from the 'public' tradition to the 'private' tradition of playing in halls. The second was the far higher admission prices. Where the basic price at the Theatre was one penny, and sixpence could buy a lord's room, at the Blackfriars once it came into use as a playhouse the minimum admission price was set at between three and six pennies. A box alongside the stage cost five times the top price at the Globe, half a crown or two shillings and sixpence, thirty pennies.[20] For apprentices, who earned no wages and were dependent on their master's generosity even for the penny-worth of admission to an amphitheatre or baiting house, the prices at the hall playhouses were quite out of reach. Contemporary comments acknowledge the occasional 'shops Foreman . . . That may judge for his *six-pence'* (2.90), but the main clientele must have been the privileged, principally the gallants, law students, wealthier citizens and the nobility. They were a 'select' audience, as Marston called them,[21] selected by their affluence, relishing the fiction that they attended a 'private' playhouse, away from the common throng.

The third difference of the Blackfriars from the Globe reflected the shift in priorities even more precisely. In the amphitheatres the poorest patrons were closest to the stage, standing round its rim while the wealthier sat behind them in the galleries. In the hall playhouses not only were the boxes given a better position than the lords' rooms in the amphitheatres, flanking the stage instead of behind it, but the more you paid the closer you were to the stage. One shilling and six-pence gave you a bench in the pit immediately facing the 3-foot-high stage. All that the minimal sixpence provided was room in the topmost gallery, farthest from the stage. The Blackfriars auditorium established for the first time in England the disposition of seat prices that rules in every modern indoor theatre. The highest prices are for the stalls and boxes, the lowest for the balcony or the 'gods' at the top and rear of the house. If proximity to the stage is any reflection of priorities, Burbage's reversed themselves between his building the Theatre for the common penny-payer in 1576 and setting up the Blackfriars for the wealthy in 1596.

The upper frater at the Blackfriars where Burbage constructed his playhouse was a long hall 46 feet wide by 100 feet in length. He built his auditorium not in the round but longitudinally, setting the stage across the shorter dimension to make a playhouse measuring alto-gether 66 feet by 46 feet. A great circular stone stairway gave admission at the end farthest from the stage. The central pit was approximately 28 feet square, probably the same width as the stage itself. The *frons scenae* at the Blackfriars must have been similar to Inigo Jones's 1616 design (see Fig. 8), with degrees or benches for audience on the stage balcony at each side of the music room. On each flank of the stage stood boxes, probably at two levels as in Jones's design, and along the two long sides and over the stone stairway, in a semicircle round the pit, ran curved galleries, either two or three levels – the hall had a very high roof – which would have been about 8 feet 6 inches in depth.[22] The pit and the boxes flanking the stage could not have seated more than about 200 people. Three galleries of 8 feet 6 inches depth with four degrees each and some walkway space at the back could take another 200 at each level. The total capacity of a two-gallery house would thus have been barely 600, and of a three-gallery house (allowing for fewer degrees at the top level because of the steeper sight-lines) perhaps 700.

The boxes, judging by Peacham's story, appear to have accommo-dated a higher number than the lords' rooms shown in the Swan drawing, although the wealthiest patrons might well have reserved exclusive use of a box for themselves by paying more. In 1632 the Lord Chamberlain, the Earl of Pembroke, got into a quarrel with the king's cousin, the Duke of Lennox, over possession of a key to a box at Blackfriars. Their argument was not over who had precedence but who had the exclusive right to occupy the box. The Lord Chamberlain, whose function was in part the control of plays and playing, might have

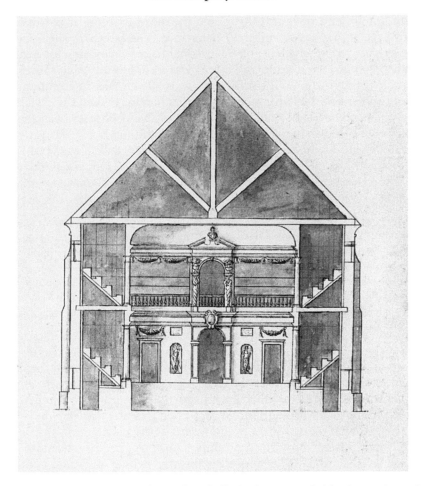

8. Part of the Inigo Jones design for a hall playhouse, probably the Cockpit of 1616, showing the stage and its flanking boxes. Its most costly audience accommodation, besides the four boxes on each side of the stage, was the two sets of benches at each side of the music room on the stage balcony. The original is in Worcester College, Oxford.

thought he had a special claim on the playhouse owners, and consequently a right to a key to the best box in the house. The royal family evidently had its own ideas about such a right. An affray that reveals rather more about the physical shape of the auditorium was recorded at the same playhouse in 1632. It tells us that the Countess of Essex occupied a box there, squired only by her stepson Captain Essex. The affray was between a stander on the stage and the captain in a box behind him. It tells a number of things about the more aristocratic patrons at this type of playhouse and their behaviour. The lady was the Earl of Essex's new wife, who had an already-established reputation for sexual indiscretions. Her stepson and escort was a soldier on leave from the Dutch army. In the civil conflict of the 1640s he was to command a foot regiment in the Parliamentary army under his cousin the earl. His opponent at the Blackfriars in 1632, the Irish Lord Thurles, was about twenty-one, newly arrived in London from Edinburgh. He became the Earl of Ormond only three weeks after the affray, and in the civil war served as the king's commander in the field and Lord Deputy of Ireland.

The Essex version lays the whole blame on the bad manners of the younger man. According to the record,

This Captaine attending and accompanying my Lady of Essex in a boxe at the playhouse at the blackfryers, the said lord coming upon the stage, stood before them and hindred their sight. Captain Essex told his lordship they had payd for their places as well as hee, and therefore intreated him not to deprive them of the benefitt of it. Whereupon the lord stood up yet higher and hindred more their sight. Then Capt. Essex with his hand putt him a little by. The lord then drewe his sword and ran full butt at him, though hee missed him.[23]

The affray's immediate outcome was a hearing in Star Chamber, the Privy Council wearing its judicial hats, which secured a verbal apology from Lord Thurles the newcomer, evidently anxious to establish his reputation as a gentleman ahead of his pride as a nobleman. What is most revealing about Blackfriars audiences in all this, though, is not just the social background of these two truculent rufflers but the stations they took up for their enjoyment of the play.

Captain Essex was with the countess in a box flanking the stage, at stage level. Lord Thurles chose the position which the most exhibitionistic of gallants tended to adopt in the indoor playhouses, on the stage itself. The practice of hiring a stool for an extra sixpence and emerging with it from the tiring house to sit and watch the play on the stage itself was a long-established custom at the Blackfriars. In this case whether out of ignorance, being new to London, or because other young sprigs had already commandeered the limited number of stools, Lord Thurles was on his feet, standing at the stage edge in front of the box occupied by the Essex party. Captain Essex's attempts to shift him so that the box-holders could see the play were what provoked the quarrel. The whole affair was an ironic endorsement of Dekker's advice to a gullible gallant in *The Gull's Hornbook*:

let our Gallant . . . presently advance himselfe up to the Throne of the Stage. I meane not into the Lords roome (which is now but the Stages suburbs):

9. The Duke of Ormond (Lord Thurles), from a portrait.

No, those boxes, by the iniquity of custome, conspiracy of waiting women and Gentlemen-Ushers, that there sweat together, and the covetousness of Sharers, are contemptibly thrust into the reare, and much new Satten is there dambd, by being smothred to death in darknesse. But on the very Rushes where the Comedy is to daunce, yea under the state of *Cambises* himselfe, must our fethered *Estridge*, like a piece of Ordnance, be planted valiantly (because impudently) beating downe the mewes and hisses of the opposed rascality.[24]

Dekker goes on to advise his gull to wait until the play is about to begin before appearing with stool and sixpence to occupy the most conspicuous position on the stage. Captain Essex was bound to occupy a box, since he had a lady with him, and ladies did not sit on the stage itself. Lord Thurles was positioning himself where any noble and wealthy young man-about-town visiting the play on his own would think of going, especially if he was newly arrived and keen to show himself to his peers in London. A not dissimilar squabble over a stool on stage happened to Sir Richard Cholmley, a celebrated Catholic from Yorkshire, at the Blackfriars in 1603, when he was aged about twenty-three. More modest than Lord Thurles, he claimed in his memoirs to have taken a stool only because there was so little room in the playhouse, and, 'as the custom was, between every scene stood up to refresh himself'. Another young gallant took the opportunity when he stood up to snatch away his stool, leaving him to stay on his feet for the rest of the performance or, as he chose, to challenge the thief to meet him with his sword outside the playhouse. When demand for stools exceeded the supply it does seem that latecomers stood around the flanks of the stage. In 1639 the king issued a ban on stool-sitting at the smallest of the hall playhouses, the Salisbury Court.

The practice of allowing important patrons to sit on the stage began with the first boy companies probably as early as the 1570s. Adult players never allowed it at the open amphitheatres. There the interference which stool-sitters would have created for everyone else's vision was worse, given the greater height of the stage and the numbers occupying the lower galleries and standing around the flanks of the stage. Moreover the public stages, lacking the rails which divided actors from audience in the hall playhouses, and raised 5 feet above the ground, would have seemed more precarious even without the mews and hisses of the penny-payers standing close up against the stage platform. Webster wrote an induction for a play that Shakespeare's company took from the Blackfriars boys in 1604, in which he burlesqued the behaviour of two gallants who try importing to the Globe the hall playhouse custom of viewing the play from stools on stage.[25] Contrariwise Beaumont's Induction for *The Knight of the Burning Pestle* for the Blackfriars boys in 1607 burlesqued the expectations of the Grocer and his wife and apprentice by bringing them up onto the stage and seating them on stools to comment on the play. Jonson wrote a chorus of 'gossips', 'four gentlewomen ladylike attired', who sit on the Blackfriars stage in *The Staple of News* in 1626. Sitting on stools on stage was clearly taken to be a very distinct mark of the difference between the audiences for the adult plays in the amphitheatres and those for boy plays in the hall playhouses through the decade 1600–1609 when they were competing for audiences. That immediate rivalry faded when Shakespeare's company took over the Blackfriars. Stool-sitting remained as a divide thereafter, but more as a mark to distinguish the types of playhouse and their clientele than the kinds of playing company using them.

Once James was on the throne, and had graced the leading companies with his family's patronage, the impresarios who built the playhouses concentrated almost exclusively on building the hall type. Henslowe replaced the old Bear Garden in 1614 with the Hope, intending it to function in a multipurpose way as both playhouse and baiting house. But the bears won against the players, as Hollar's label in his 'Long View' engraving indicates, and all the other new projects were indoor playhouses. After the tiny Paul's playhouse finally closed in 1606 and the Blackfriars controller surrendered his lease to Richard Burbage in 1608, a boy company from Blackfriars set themselves up for a while in another hall at Whitefriars. When the King's Men started the practice of adult companies offering daily performances at Blackfriars several attempts were made to emulate them. Edward Alleyn's plan for a new hall playhouse at Porter's Hall in 1615 failed, but a year later Christopher Beeston opened the Cockpit in Drury Lane with an adult company, and in 1629 Richard Gunnell, formerly of the Fortune, opened a third at Salisbury Court in Whitefriars. Near the closure Davenant was prevented from launching a grandiose scheme for an indoor playhouse in Fleet Street even closer to the Inns of Court, to show scenic and musical plays. It was blocked, and Davenant's plan to introduce operatic theatre was not realised until after the Restoration more than twenty years later.

The acting companies for all these projects were adults, and some companies seem to have changed from amphitheatre to hall – for instance from the Red Bull to the Cockpit – as readily as the King's Men made their annual switches between the Blackfriars and the Globe. Whatever the company, and whatever its repertory, the social trend moved emphatically towards the hall type of playhouse. The distinctive features of the hall playhouses, their all-seat auditorium, the roof, the higher prices keeping apprentices away, and the opportunities for self-display which stools on stage provided, were part of that trend. Hot-blooded young men jockeying for social prominence were always likely to regard the crowds in the amphitheatre yards and the lack of stools on their stages as tokens of an unfavourable environment. By the time the king was provoked into banning the use of stools at the smallest hall playhouse the division between the hall playhouses with their 'gentle' clientele and the plebeian amphitheatre was nearly complete.

PERFORMING CONDITIONS

The physical conditions of the two types of playhouse did not change widely between 1576 and 1642. There may have been some improvement in the design of the amphitheatres, particularly in the system of admitting people to the different sections of the auditorium, but there were no such changes in the private playhouses. When Burbage built the Blackfriars in 1596 he must have designed it along familiar lines, certainly at the stage and tiring-house end. Shakespeare's company found little trouble alternating between the Globe and Blackfriars with the same plays, even though the Blackfriars stage was less than half the size of the Globe's and lacked any stage posts. The Blackfriars auditorium was very different from the Globe's, having seating for everyone and putting the cheapest places furthest from the stage, but it was still spartan by modern standards, functional, however ornate were its carvings and its sconces for candles. Even Inigo Jones's design for an indoor playhouse, made probably in 1616 for Beeston's rival to the Blackfriars, the Cockpit or Phoenix,[26] seems colourful in its decoration but conservative in its other provision. It certainly made no allowance for such comfort stations as a bar or toilets. The whole early playgoing experience and its wide range of physical discomforts call for detailed comment.

The amphitheatres needed optimum daylight for their plays, so they established a pattern of performances starting at 2 or 3 p.m., depending on how close to midsummer it was. This habit prevailed even when the chief playhouses became the candle-lit halls. In October 1594 the Lord Chamberlain's letter to the Lord Mayor on behalf of Shakespeare's company assured him

that, where heretofore they began not their Plaies till towards fower a clock, they will now begin at two, & have don betwene fower and five.[27]

This was a shift in timing, and not just as an adjustment to the earlier darkness of the winter. Afternoon church services began at 2 p.m., and the clash between churchgoing and playgoing was a constant irritant to the more puritanical divines and city fathers. A 4 p.m. start for the performances, and shorter performance times, was one solution. The other was the Lord Chamberlain's, offering a time of performance more directly in competition with the churches, ostensibly in the interest of getting playgoers home before dark.

Perhaps it was in an oblique response to this that most playwrights insisted that the performances would not usually last for more than two hours. Whetstone wrote in 1578 that plays took 'three howers', probably at court or other private shows, and Dekker in 1609 mentioned players 'glad to play three houres for two pence', but most of them, even Shakespeare, refer to 'these two short hours', or the 'two hours' traffic of the stage'.[28] Even in 1639 Thomas Nabbes could call it 'two houres time of action' (2.207). In the absence of watches, of course, and the kind of precise timekeeping that only became necessary when railway timetables were invented, an hour was a fairly flexible measurement. The likely duration of most performances, which at the amphitheatres were followed by a jig and in the halls were preceded by music, was likely to have been close to three hours. Some such length, plus the time for arrival and dispersal of the crowd of playgoers before and after the show, is indicated by a second petition sponsored in 1619 by the puritan minister of the church adjacent to the Blackfriars playhouse. It spoke of unruly crowds gathering

almost everie daie in the winter tyme (not forbearinge the tyme of Lent) from one or twoe of the clock till sixe att night, which beinge the tyme alsoe most usuall for Christeninges and burialls and afternoones service, wee cannot have passage to the Church for performance of those necessary duties, the ordinary passage for a great part of the precinct aforesaid being close by the play house dore.[29]

Sir John Davies's courtier 'Fuscus' usually spent from 1 p.m. till 6 p.m. at a play in the 1590s (2.20), confirming the complaint of the Blackfriars petitioners. Allowing an hour for the crowds to arrive and another for them to disperse, that meant close to three hours for an actual performance starting at 2 p.m. It was probably a token of the prestige that Shakespeare's company was wrapped in by 1619, with its now routine alternation between the Blackfriars in winter and the Globe in summer, that it could sustain against this kind of local pressure its old amphitheatre tradition of afternoon performances even at Blackfriars.

The practice that Shakespeare's company introduced at the Blackfriars, once it reopened after a long plague closure in late 1609, of performing on every afternoon through the winter in contrast with the boy company's once-weekly performances throughout the year, must have been a major reason for its predominance as the most highly regarded of the London playhouses. The Blackfriars was much closer than the Bankside or the northern suburbs to the homes of the city's rich residents. Through the first decade of the century adults playing daily in the amphitheatres gradually outran the boys playing weekly

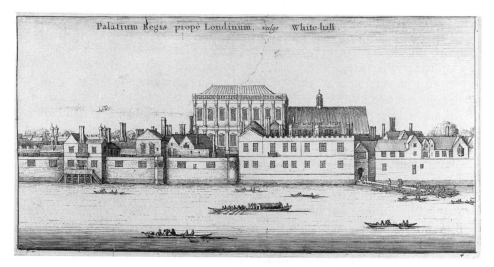

Palatium Regis propē Londinium, *vulgo* White-hall.

10. Wherries plying their trade in front of Whitehall Palace. An engraving by Wenceslas Hollar.

in the halls. Once the adults could play daily in the halls their success was beyond question. It certainly brought major discomfort to the local inhabitants. The regular daily flow of large numbers of playgoers was an unpleasant novelty in London, which had no means of policing it. So long as the amphitheatres were in the fields to the north of the city accessible on foot or on the southern bank of the river, there was no great difficulty. The Theatre and the Curtain were placed near the beginning of the Great North Road, a well-travelled thoroughfare. The land across London Bridge, having supported bull- and bear-baiting houses and whorehouses for most of the century, could also carry the flow of playgoers easily enough. The poorest crossed the bridge, while the wealthier patrons paid sixpence for a boat to get them to the Globe or the Rose, since the Thames wherries offered the nearest thing to a taxi service London had at the time. In 1604 a prodigal gallant had the choice, as Middleton described it, to

venture beyond sea, that is, in a choice paire of Noble mens Oares, to the Bankside, where he must sit out the breaking up of a Comedie, or the first cut of a Tragedie; or rather (if his humour so serve him) to call in at the Black-fryers, where he shall see a neast of Boyes able to ravish a man.[30]

Recalling the late legend about Shakespeare starting his writing career by holding horses at the playhouse, it is worth noting Sir John Davies's mockery of a gallant who went everywhere on horseback. In

Epigram 7, 'In Faustum', written in 1594 before the hall playhouses reopened, Davies wrote:

> Faustus not lord, nor knight, nor wise, nor olde,
> To every place about the towne doth ride,
> He rides into the fieldes, Playes to behold,
> He rides to take boate at the water side,
> He rides to Powles, he rides to th'ordinarie,
> He rides unto the house of bawderie too.
> Thither his horse so often will him carry,
> That shortlie he will quite forget to go. (2.24)

There was a playhouse of some kind within a mile of nearly every Londoner.

So long as the boy company occupied Blackfriars Middleton's option of ravishment only produced difficulties for the locals once a week. But from 1609 it became a daily event, and by that time the relatively novel habit of playgoing was drawing the privileged to travel through the city by the equally novel habit of going by coach, and had created a fresh problem, the traffic jam. The Blackfriars petition of 1619 described it in these terms:

there is daylie such resort of people, and such multitudes of Coaches (whereof many are Hackney Coaches, bringinge people of all sortes) that sometymes all our streetes cannott containe them. But that they Clogg up Ludgate alsoe, in such sort, that both they endanger the one the other breake downe stalles, throwe downe mens goodes from their shopps. And the inhabitantes there cannott come to their howses, nor bringe in their necessary provisions of beere, wood, coale or haye, nor the Tradesmen or shopkeepers utter their wares, nor the passenger goe to the common water staires without danger of their lives and lymmes.[31]

Coaches and their wealthy occupants soon became a major nuisance in the Blackfriars precinct. In January 1634 George Garrard wrote about the Privy Council failing to control parking:

Here hath been an Order of the Lords of the Council hung up in a Table near *Paul's* and the *Black-Fryars*, to command all that Resort to the Play-House there to send away their Coaches, and to disperse Abroad in *Paul's Church-Yard, Carter-Lane*, the Conduit in *Fleet-Street*, and other Places, and not to return to fetch their Company, but they must trot afoot to find their Coaches, 'twas kept very strictly for two or three Weeks, but now I think it is disorder'd again. (2.183)

The city authorities never had much reason to be grateful to the players.

Sala Regalis cum Curia Weſt monaſtery vulgo Weſtminſter haall.

11. Coaches standing in New Palace Yard, Westminster, an engraving by
Hollar made in the 1630s.

Once at the playhouse, whether summoned by flag, trumpet and
drum to the suburbs, ferried across the river or carried by coach into
the city, the two or three hours' traffic of the stage would be jammed
in with a variety of other distractions: the weather, food and drink,
smells, noise, cutpurses, and occasionally riots.

Of all these the weather seems strangely to have been the least irk-
some difficulty. Edmond Howes's extension of Stow's *Annales* mentions prolonged bad weather through eleven periods up to 1631, and
yet there is not a single reference in the entire seventy-five years of
playgoing to the deterrent effect of rain or snow. The galleries of course
could shelter more than two-thirds of the total capacity from rain, and
the stage itself was covered. Socially, of course, to stay in the yard when
it rained would prove that you had little spare money, so rain was not
a common cause for complaint.[32] Overcast wintry weather blighted
the first performance of *The White Devil* at the Red Bull in 1610, by
reducing the available daylight, but that was always a potential problem. The later open-air amphitheatres aligned their stages with their
backs to the midsummer solstice, so that the players would have a
uniformly shadowed stage to work on. It is possible that a low winter
sun, shining from just above the roof behind the stage, would have
bothered spectators in the upper galleries even more than rain. Sun-
shine does that at the new Globe even in midsummer for those foolish
enough to position themselves in the galleries where they sit 'in front'

of the stage on the modern spectator principle, instead of getting close to the stage like an Elizabethan audience.

On the whole it seems probable that playgoing at the open-air playhouses was troubled more by acoustic problems than by bad weather. A large open auditorium with a good proportion of the audience on its feet would certainly generate a level of background noise much greater than the smaller gatherings, all seated, in the hall playhouses. The players must have had remarkable volume control if they managed the transfer from amphitheatre to hall without damaging a few eardrums. Some late comments about players with extra-wide mouths may reflect the need to shift the decibel level between the different kinds of venue.

Once settled in place it was possible for playgoers at an amphitheatre to distract themselves with refreshments while the play was in progress. Until the hall playhouses, which had a practical need for pauses between the acts so that the lights could be trimmed, began to predominate over the amphitheatres, performances were continuous. Even the hall playhouses paused only for a minute or so between the acts. Consequently food and drink and the need for toilets became a distraction from the play while it was in performance. Thomas Platter reported in 1599 that 'during the performance food and drink are carried round the audience, so that for what one cares to pay one may also have refreshment' (2.37). The food seems principally to have been apples (there are several references to 'pippins' being used as ammunition) and nuts. Jasper Mayne spoke of the audience in the cheapest gallery of a hall playhouse who 'sixpence pay and sixpence crack'.[33] Fletcher has a character in *Wit Without Money* (1614) describe youths who 'break in at playes like prentices for three a groat, and crack Nuts with the Scholars in peny Rooms again, and fight for Apples' (2.111). John Tatham mentions pears used as ammunition in 1640 (2.212), and Overbury's Character 'A Puny-Clarke' (a puisne or junior law clerk) 'eates Ginger bread at a Play-house' (2.114). The drink offered was either water or bottle ale. In 1615 John Stephens, writing a set of 'Characters' in imitation of Overbury's recently published collection, included among the features of 'a base Mercenary Poet' that 'when he heares his play hissed, hee would rather thinke bottle-Ale is opening'. Webster, who probably composed many of the 'Characters' in Overbury's volume and who wrote a reply to Stephens's character of 'A Common Player', was the likely target of this jibe. Henry Fitzgeoffery describes him sitting in the gallery at Blackfriars in 1617, where bottled ale was presumably available, although the restricted circulation at the indoor playhouses where all the audience were seated must have

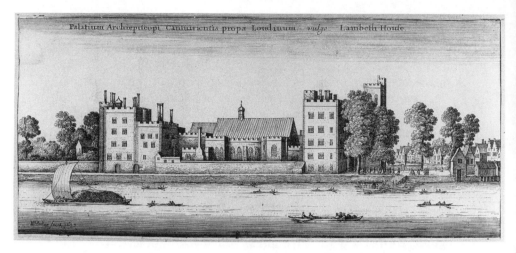

12. A view of Archbishop Laud embarking at Lambeth, as engraved by Hollar in the 1630s. The sheds hanging over the river on the right may be privies.

made life more difficult for the itinerant sellers than the amphitheatre yards. It was claimed that bottle ale was used when the Globe burned down to put out the fire in one man's breeches.

The form of distraction that results from refreshments, the need for toilets, is a feature of early playgoing for which there is regrettably little evidence. There is no provision for it anywhere in Inigo Jones's two sets of theatre plans. We have to look for such circumstantial evidence as we can find, and even this is patchy. Harington's celebrated *Metamorphosis of Ajax* gives a hint of the likely provision at playhouses, by its clear differentiation between the defecation of solids, the subject of his treatise, and urinating. The former required elaborate constructions. The latter was too trivial a business for Harington to bother with. Platter offers some help here by describing what was available for the latter purpose in the central pedestrian precinct in London, St Paul's. It was, to put it mildly, minimal.

Outside one of the doors is a hewn stone, and a standard nearby where water may be obtained, and often a vessel stands by it for passing urine, giving a pleasant odour to the passers-by![34]

The one piece of evidence I have found about the public supply of privies, Wenceslas Hollar's picture of the Thames at Lambeth Palace (Figure 12), is suggestive of riverbank supply, although archaeological studies of the Bankside have not yet revealed any such structure. I would suspect that the Globe offered no privy for the defecation of solids closer than the river, and that buckets in the corridors at the back of the galleries served for the passing of urine. Privacy there was none, and how women managed we can only guess. Evidence from Spain suggests that women carried glass or pewter containers under their skirts, for later discharge into any convenient bucket or ditch.

The smells that large crowds generated were the subject of comment in a number of ways. Perfume was popular as a disguise for other odours. Predictably when the hall playhouses were resurrected in 1599 and 1600 their supporters made the point that the more select audiences there were freed from the occupational smells that artisans carried with them. Marston wrote about the audience at Paul's in 1600 that 'A man shall not be choakte / With the stench of Garlicke, nor be pasted / To the barmy Jacket of a Beer-Brewer' (2.46). Dekker first published his dislike of garlic-breathed 'stinkards' in 1606 and used the term regularly thereafter. By implication all such stinkards were gathered in the yards of the amphitheatres. Apart from perfumes, the most distinctive smell at the indoor playhouses, and in the lords' rooms at the amphitheatres, was tobacco. Sir John Davies praised it ironically in an epigram written in or about 1593:

> . . . that vile medicine it doth far excell,
> Which by sir Thomas Moore hath bin propounded,
> For this is thought a gentleman-like smell.[35]

The equally ironic More had recommended eating onions to take away the smell of leeks and then garlic to take away the smell of onions. Guilpin recorded the gentleman-like feature at an amphitheatre playhouse in 1598:

> See you him yonder who sits o're the stage,
> With the Tobacco-pipe now at his mouth?   (2.34)

and in the same year Henry Buttes commented on the cheaper local form of tobacco which was being tried as an alternative to the novelty from Virginia:

> It chaunced me gazing at the Theater,
> To spie a Lock-Tobacco-Chevalier
> Clowding the loathing ayr with foggie fume
> Of Dock-Tobacco, friendly foe to rume.   (2.36)

Presumably it was rheum, not room, of which tobacco was the enemy. The meticulous Thomas Platter described the habit with his customary detail at about the time of his visit to the newly opened Globe in September 1599.

In the ale-houses tobacco or a species of wound-wort are also obtainable for one's money, and the powder is lit in a small pipe, the smoke sucked into the mouth, and the saliva is allowed to run freely, after which a good draught of Spanish wine follows. This they regard as curious medicine for defluctions, and as a pleasure, and the habit is so common with them that they always carry the instrument on them, and light up on all occasions, at the play, in the taverns or elsewhere, drinking as well as smoking together, as we sit over wine, and it makes them riotous and merry, and rather drowsy, just as if they were drunk.[36]

Dekker inevitably made his gullible young gallant follow the habit, and Fitzgeoffery included a complaint about smokers in his survey of the Blackfriars audience in 1617. In 1631 Richard Brathwait spoke of ruffians smoking and making themselves equally offensive in other ways while sitting in the twopenny gallery of an amphitheatre playhouse (2.166).

Sitting on stools to display their fine clothes and smoking to show their wealth were not the only marks that distinguished gallants at playhouses. By no means the least obtrusive feature of any Elizabethan gathering was the headgear. Hats were worn indoors as well as out, and there is no reason to suppose that a gallant minded like Lord Thurles would bother to lower his feather for the sake of the multitude behind him. Hats were worn in an ascending social order of obtrusiveness. Gallants wore crowned hats with feathers which might be as broad and opaque as an ostrich plume. Citizens, and most ladies, wore shorter hats with smaller or no feathers. Artisans wore woollen caps or bonnets. Caps were the wear for women, children, old men and lawyers, although some men wore bonnets or brimmed hats on top of them. Generally, the higher your status the higher your hat. Harrison's *Description of England* says of the artisan class, 'They also wore flat Caps, both then and many yeares after, as well Apprentizes as Journey-men and others, both at home and abroad, whom the Pages of the court in derision called "Flat Caps".' You were likely to suffer least from finding yourself behind obtrusive headgear if you stood in the yard. In the galleries hats could get in the way, but the steep rake of the degrees and the relative narrowness of the galleries would have made the problem fairly manageable. The worst position must have been in a box at Blackfriars in the dark behind half a dozen stool-sitting gallants in their ostrich plumes and tobacco clouds.

Human beings, even when long-haired, lose more than 30 per cent of their body heat from the head, and in the little ice age of Elizabethan times it must have seemed sensible to keep the head covered for most of the day and night. Hats, in the whole range from royal crowns to domestic night-caps, were a particularly prominent feature of Elizabethan costume. Philip Stubbes saw them as a sign of the evil times in 1583:

Sometymes thei use them sharpe on' the crowne, pearking up like the spere, or shaft of a steeple, standying a quarter of a yarde above the croune of their heades . . . Othersome be flat, and broad in the croune, like the battlementes of a house. An other sorte have round crounes, sometymes with one kinde of bande, sometymes with an other, now blacke, now white, now russet, now red, now grene, now yellowe: now this, now that, never content with one colour or fashion two daies to an ende . . . some are of silke, some of Velvet, some of Taffetie, some of Sarcenet, some of Wooll, whiche is more curious, some of a certain kind of fine haire . . . And so common a thing it is, that every Servyng man, countreiman, and other, even all indifferently, do weare of these hattes . . . And an other sort (as phantasticall as the rest) are content with no kind of Hat, without a great bunche of feathers of divers and sundrie colours.

Women were equally liable to suffer from the urge to show colourful variety:

Then, on top of these stately turrets (I meane their goodly heads wherein is more vanitie then true Philosophie now and then) stand their other capitall ornaments . . . according to the variable fantasies of their serpentine minds.

(*The Anatomy of Abuses*, D7v–8r, F4v)

It would have been an unusually modest, or considerate, or warm-blooded male playgoer in any of the playhouses, indoors or out, who kept his headgear off during the performance.

The 'plumed dandebrat' as Fitzgeoffery called him, with his feather and his sword, was a constant presence in the playhouses throughout the period. As early as 1563 Lawrence Humphrey noted the idler who 'licentiously roames in ryot, coasting the stretes with wavering plumes, hangd to a long side blade, & pounced in silkes . . . haunteth plaies, feastes, bathes and banketings' (2.1). Feathers were not popular with most observers. Samuel Rowlands wrote in 1600 of a gallant's feather as 'his heades lightness-proclaymer',[37] a jibe which Middleton elaborated a few years later:

13. Hats and fans were a conspicuous feature of early dress. They did help to prioritise hearing over viewing.

His head was drest up in white Feathers like a Shuttle Cock, which agreed so wel with his braine, being nothing but Corke, that two of the biggest of the Guard might very easily have tost him with Battledores, and made good sport with him in his Majesties great Hall.   (*Father Hubburds Tale*, C2r–2v)

Webster in his Induction to *The Malcontent* makes the point that the feather-merchants lived in the Blackfriars district. It was probably outside the Blackfriars playhouse in 1620 that the target of the anonymous *Haec-Vir: or the Womanish-Man* prepared himself for his grand entry:

(in the midst of his pride or riches) at a Play-house . . . (before he dare enter) with the *Jacobs*-staffe of his owne eyes and his Pages, hee takes a full survey of himselfe, from the highest sprig in his feather, to the lowest spangle that shines in his Shoo-string.   (2.140)

Since the highest sprig in a gallant's feather was likely to be a good foot or more above eye-level for the unfortunates sitting behind, there was good reason why this fashion was unpopular.

It was, nonetheless, normative wear in the hall playhouses. In *The Roaring Girl*, 2.1, Mistress Tiltyard at her stall selling feathers advertises them as vital for any playgoing gallant:

> These are the most worne and most in fashion,
> Among the Bever gallants the stone riders,
> The private stages audience, the twelve penny stool Gentlemen.   (D1r)

Feathers in the playhouses were not only on hats, and hats were not worn only by gallants, of course. Davenant's prologue for *The Unfortunate Lovers* (1638), a Blackfriars play, speaks of thc citizenry in the twopenny galleries at the amphitheatre playhouses of a previous generation.

> . . . they . . . to th' Theatre would come
> Ere they had din'd to take up the best room;
> Then sit on benches, not adorn'd with mats,
> And graciously did vail their high-crowned hats
> To every half-dress'd Player, as he still
> Through th'hangings peep'd to see how th'house did fill.
> Good easy judging souls, with what delight
> They would expect a jig, or target fight.   (2.197)

Citizenry in high-crowned hats are clearly visible in the picture of an audience for one of the celebrated open-air sermons at St Paul's Cross in 1620.

Citizens' hats did not usually include the frivolity of feathers, but women, even citizens' wives, not infrequently came to the playhouse with fans made of feathers, which no doubt could in a crowded hall prove as obtrusive as a plumed hat. They also wore starched ruffs around their necks. Their attire bulked them out to the point where a box would certainly have been more convenient for them than the 18-inch buttock space of the Christ Church Oxford entertainment, or the degrees in the galleries of Inigo Jones's 1616 plan. Rowlands described the trappings for a woman in 1600 as

> A Buske, a Mask, a Fanne, a monstrous Ruffe,
> A Boulster for their Buttockes and such stuffe.
> (*The Letting of Humours Blood*, F2r)

Jonson in 1609 wrote of the indoor playhouse '*Lady*, or *Pusill*, that weares maske or fan, / *Velvet*, or *Taffeta* cap' (2.90). The woodcuts attached to broadsheet ballads of the time show the fans and the bolster, and Hollar's engravings made in the 1630s show masked ladies. In the prologue to *Rule a Wife and Have a Wife* (1624) Fletcher indicated one use for the fans:

> Nor blame the Poet if he slip aside,
> Sometimes lasciviously if not too wide.
> But hold your Fannes close, and then smile at ease,
> A cruel Sceane did never Lady please.

Such ladies seem to have characteristically placed themselves in the boxes of the indoor playhouses, like the Countess of Essex in 1632

14. Detail from a painting of a public sermon at Paul's Cross, 1620. The audience are all in the clothing of citizens.

at Blackfriars, though by the 1620s the term 'boxes' may have been extended to include what were originally known as the 'lords' rooms' over the stage in the amphitheatres. Thomas May's *The Heir*, written for the Red Bull in 1620, has an elegiac passage about Richard Burbage, who had died the previous year, which says:

> . . . Ladies in the boxes
> Kept time with sighs, and teares to his sad accents
> As had he truely been the man he seem'd.   (*The Heir*, 1.1)

May was probably thinking of the Blackfriars boxes, but the same ladies frequented the Globe in summer, where the equivalent places were on the balcony over the stage. In the Praeludium written for Thomas Goffe's *The Careless Shepherdess* at Salisbury Court in 1638, a country gentleman summarises the place of ladies fairly precisely. After an exchange with a courtier and a gallant, they leave to take their places, and the gentleman forgets to worry about the expense and says:

> I'le follow them, though't be into a Box.
> Though they did sit thus open on the Stage
> To shew their Cloak and Sute, yet I did think
> At last they would take sanctuary 'mongst
> The Ladies, lest some Creditor should spy them.
> 'Tis better looking o're a Ladies head
> Or through a Lettice-window, then a grate.   (2.202)

The grate was the window in a debtors' prison.

AUDITORIUM BEHAVIOUR

The final matter for consideration among the physical conditions of Shakespearean playgoing is not strictly physical, though on occasions it could have an emphatically physical impact. Audience behaviour, in individuals and in crowds, is a complex but vital part of the physical environment for playgoing. Marking togetherness by explicit, usually vocal, signals such as laughter is a natural part of crowd behaviour. It is more easily noted in its extreme forms than its everyday features, but a large and visible crowd is always an active entity, and its responses interact powerfully with those speaking to it. The extremes of response, of course, give some hints by their very notability about where the lines for acceptable crowd behaviour were usually drawn. It is certainly possible to identify some of the normative as well as the extreme features of audience interaction, and even to see how the patterns of behaviour changed between different playhouses.

The most prominent feature of the amphitheatres was the physicality of audience responses to the play. The sitters in the galleries matched the reactions of the crowd on its feet in the yard. As Gosson said in 1596, 'in publike Theaters, when any notable shew passeth over the stage, the people arise in their seates, & stand upright with delight and eagernesse to view it well' (2.27). Whether because of the greater numbers, the quantity of people on their feet next to the stage or the broader social catchment, the crowds at the amphitheatres seem to have been markedly noisier than those in the hall playhouses. Nor, if John Lyly is to be believed, was the noise so much incidental shuffling or coughing as direct vocal response to the performance. Lyly's prologues written in the 1580s for boy plays at the first Blackfriars and Paul's more than once express the hope that the gentlemanly audience in the halls would react with 'soft smiling, not loude laughing', or at worst would be too courteous to hiss. These were evidently common reactions elsewhere.

Applause too was delivered with voice as well as hands. Drayton has a sonnet written in about 1600, which refers to his writing plays for Henslowe at the Rose amphitheatre and sitting in the 'thronged Theater' listening to the 'Showts and Claps at ev'ry little pawse, / When the proud Round on ev'ry side hath rung' (2.47). Shakespeare, Marston, Dekker and many other poets used epilogues to appeal for applause at the end of their plays, but applause clearly did not only come at the end. Moreover it was not just 'Brawny hands' which delivered the audience's opinion.[38] William Fennor, bringing to the reader's eye in 1616 the text of a performance recently given to a royal audience, offered a pained account of his play's original reception at the Fortune amphitheatre:

> Yet to the multitude it nothing shewed;
> They screwed their scurvy jawes and look't awry,
> Like hissing snakes adjudging it to die:
> When wits of gentry did applaud the same,
> With silver shouts of high lowd sounding fame:
> Whil'st understanding grounded men contemn'd it,
> And wanting wit (like fooles to judge) condemn'd it.
> Clapping, or hissing, is the onely meane
> That tries and searches out a well writ Sceane,
> So it is thought by *Ignoramus* crew,
> But that good wits acknowledge's untrue;

> The stinkards oft will hisse without a cause,
> And for a baudy jeast will give applause.
> Let one but aske the reason why they roare
> They'll answere, cause the rest did so before. (2.123)

Hearing this kind of doggerel it is perhaps hardly surprising that audiences would feel free to applaud or hiss at any point throughout the performance. In 1640 John Tatham characterised the behaviour of audiences at the Fortune as 'a noyse / Of *Rables*, *Applewives* and Chimneyboyes, / Whose shrill confused Ecchoes loud doe cry, / Enlarge your *Commons*, We hate *Privacie*' (2.212). Crowds affirm their collective spirit by vocal expression of their shared feelings. The audience, as an active participant in the collective experience of playgoing, had no reason to keep its reactions private. Tatham was a judge no less biased than Fennor. His lines were written for a company expelled from the Fortune and forced to play instead at the Red Bull, and therefore understandably hostile to the Fortune and its playgoers. Not that the Red Bull, the other citizen playhouse in 1640, was noticeably quieter. Tatham's verses confirm the suspicion that when an audience was addressed as 'Gentlemen' or 'Gentles' the poet was likely to ask for less disruptive behaviour than he was accustomed to expect.

> Here Gentlemen our Anchor's fixt; And wee
> (Disdaining Fortunes mutability)
> Expect your kinde acceptance; then wee'l sing
> (Protected by your smiles our ever-spring;)
> As pleasant as if wee had still possest
> Our lawfull Portion out of Fortunes brest:
> Onely wee would request you to forbeare
> Your wonted custome, banding *Tyle*, or Peare,
> Against our *curtaines*, to allure us forth. (2.212)

Tatham evidently called them gentlemen because their wonted custom was so markedly ungentle. Other commentators suggest that missiles might be used not only to hasten the beginning of a performance but to stop it altogether, and even to make the players offer a different play, though that was an extreme and probably rare example of customers insisting on getting what they wanted.[39] The usual form of audience behaviour is better indicated by the rare cases when authority laid down its laws for proper conduct. When the court visited Cambridge in March 1632, for instance, and a play was provided for Charles's entertainment, the university authorities issued an order prescribing exactly what the student audience might and might not do.

Item: That no tobacco be taken in the Hall nor anywhere else publicly, and that neither at their standing in the streets, nor before the comedy begin, nor all the time there, any rude or immodest exclamations be made, nor any humming, hawking, whistling, hissing, or laughing be used, or any stamping or knocking, nor any such other uncivil or unscholarlike or boyish demeanour, upon any occasion; nor that any clapping of hands be had until the *Plaudite* at the end of the Comedy, except his Majesty, the Queen, or others of the best quality here, do apparently begin the same.[40]

The performance for which this instruction was issued entailed a seven-hour play, *The Rival Friends*, by the ambitious young academic Peter Hausted. The performance was a disaster, and helped drive the university's Vice-Chancellor to suicide on 1 April following the royal visit. In that retrospect his directive over student behaviour reads rather naively. But it does indicate that even a student audience at Cambridge in the presence of the king was expected to react vocally in the course of a performance, and to maintain a distracting level of background noise and activity.

At the amphitheatres the vastly greater crowds, the packed mass of 'understanders' and the open-air acoustics could generate a higher intensity of audience reaction and hubbub than the halls with their padded benches and seated clientele. Small and darker as the candlelit halls were, though, they did not change the most basic feature of the amphitheatre auditorium. They had windows to let in some light, and whereas at the 'Torchy Fryers' (2.157) the auditorium could not enjoy the supreme candle power of the Globe's daylight, at neither playhouse was there any thought of using darkness to conceal the playgoers from the players and from themselves. Concealing the audience by darkening the auditorium did not come until the nineteenth century. Thus at every performance, while the play was on, Dekker's gull and his fellow gallants in the audience were free to distract themselves and others by their attention-seeking antics. Not surprisingly, there was a good deal of comment on their behaviour.

In the 1590s before the halls reopened, gallants occupied the lords' rooms, or the front places in the galleries. Jonson's *Every Man Out* (1599), written for Shakespeare's company, identifies a gallant

> Who (to be thought one of the judicious)
> Sits with his armes thus wreath'd, his hat pull'd here,
> Cryes meaw, and nods, then shakes his empty head . . .   (2.39)

in visible and self-advertising response to the action on the stage platform. This kind of overt criticising was taken by Marston a year or two
later at Paul's to be a matter for words as well as gestures. In the induction to *What You Will* (1601) Phylomusus, friend of the author and
speaker of the prologue, complains of 'some halfe a dozen rancorous
breasts' who come to the play in order to advertise their hostility to
the poet. The outcome would be that

> . . . some juicles husk
> Some boundless ignorance should on sudden shoote
> His grosse knob'd burbolt, with *thats not so good*,
> *Mew, blirt, ha, ha, light Chaffy stuff* . . .   (2.49)

Deliberate interjections of that kind were probably most fashionable
during the early years of the revived boy companies, when the so-called
War of the Theatres harnessed the fashion for poetic railing, and put the
attacks of one poet on another in front of titillated playgoers. Outside
that phase, which did not outlive the boy companies of 1599–1608, the
gallants in the hall playhouses would have made their peacock display
as Jonson has Fitzdottrell describe it in *The Devil is an Ass* (1616):

> Today I goe to the *Blackfryers Play-house*,
> Sit i' the view, salute all my acquaintance,
> Rise up betweene the *Acts*, let fall my cloake,
> Publish a handsome man, and a rich suite
> (As that's a speciall end, why we goe thither,
> All that pretend, to stand for't o' the *Stage*)
> The Ladies aske who's that?   (2.126)

Such behaviour by would-be gallants is exemplified in detail by the
ambitious Nim's account of his fictional visit to the Blackfriars in the
1620s (2.160).

It may serve as a rough measure of the changes in playhouse
behaviour which developed through the seventeenth century if we
set Jonson's parody of a gallant at Blackfriars in 1616 against what
Clitus-Alexandrinus (the Inns of Court poetaster Richard Brathwait)
wrote about an amphitheatre playhouse in the 1620s. His Theophras-
tan character 'A Ruffian' is a belligerent swaggerer who attends plays
on his own terms.

. . . To a play they will hazard to go, though with never a rag of money:
where after the *second Act*, when the *Doore* is weakly guarded, they will
make *forcible entrie*; a knock with a Cudgell is the worst; whereat though
they grumble, they rest pacified upon their admittance. Forthwith, by violent
assault and assent, they aspire to the two-pennie roome; where being furnished

with Tinder, Match, and a portion of decayed *Barmoodas*, they smoake it most terribly, applaud a prophane jeast unmeasurably, and in the end grow distastefully rude to all the Companie. At the conclusion of all, they single out their *dainty Doxes*, to cloze up a fruitlesse day with a sinnefull evening.   (2.166)

According to Brathwait such rufflers, probably paid-off soldiers, wore the swords and spurs of would-be gentlemen, though their behaviour was a crude burlesque of the gallants whom Jonson and Fitzgeoffery claimed to see at Blackfriars in 1616.

Playhouse crowds, for all their incidental violence and exhibitionism, seem to have used an effective if anarchic regime of self-regulation. Authority of any kind was signally absent. If a pickpocket was caught, for instance, he could expect to be dealt with by a form of mob rule. Will Kemp in 1600 wrote of cutpurses being tied to one of the stage pillars 'for all the people to wonder at, when at a play they are taken pilfring' (2.43). In such a prominent position they would be exposed to more than wonder. Cutpurses had to be expected at plays as readily as the whores whom Brathwait's ruffians looked for. Dekker described their favourite localities as 'the antient great grandfather Powles, & all other little churches his children, besides Parish Garden, or rather (places of more benefit) publick, & by your leave private play houses'.[41] All the attendant characteristics of large gatherings could be found there, from the secretive thief to the exhibitionist gentleman and whore. Such figures, though, were a fairly small proportion of the total throng, parasites as they were upon the many whose first purpose was to see the play.

Affrays at playhouses there were, no doubt many besides the most noted ones with swords at the Blackfriars in 1632 (2.175) and the quarrel over a key in 1636 (2.194). In the 1580s there were riots outside playhouses involving apprentices, and many others especially at the Rose in the 1590s which Guildhall claimed were started by apprentices laying plans there for their riots outside. In 1626 the Privy Council warned the Surrey magistrates about an intended riot by seamen meeting at the Globe. They had previously headed off an assembly of apprentices at the Fortune in 1618, when they planned to wreck the Red Bull and Cockpit.[42] But considering the alarm so regularly voiced by the civil authorities, particularly in the 1580s and 1590s, the number of affrays that actually engaged audiences inside the playhouse was almost nil. The throngs gathering outside a playhouse provided an obvious opportunity for gangs to foregather, and possibly the leaders laid their plans to rally their gangs while inside. But there are no records of any gangs fighting inside any playhouse. There is one record of another gang of seamen assembling outside the Fortune, but their intention was to attack the playhouse itself in reprisal for a fancied insult (see Appendix 1, Thomas Alderson). Chettle in *Kind-Harts Dreame* (1592) suggested that 'some lewd mates that long for innovation' might provoke fights between apprentices and serving-men, and that 'These are the common cause of discord in publike places', like the opening of *Romeo and Juliet*. But if such affrays did actually happen in the playhouse auditorium rather than on stage none of them came to the authorities' attention.

3

Social composition

Renaissance societies were much more sharply divided into distinct social roles and functions than modern societies. Money, dress, education: the entire pattern of living enforced a rigid social identity from which there was little chance of escape. The range in London was enormous, from the Earl of Salisbury, whose income as Lord Treasurer in the central years 1608–12 was almost £50,000 a year, down to the wife (and hence dependant) of a glover or shoemaker who might earn for his family no more than £3. 6s. 8d. a year.[1] There was nothing like the amorphous 'middle class' which provides the great bulk of modern theatre audiences. Within the broad social process which Louis B. Wright identified as a rising middle class in Elizabethan England[2] there were distinct individual growths: a large urban artisan class, chiefly in London; a citizen class of merchants and manufacturers in the major cities and ports; an increasingly literate class of schoolmasters, scriveners and clergy. Such growths imply a fairly high level of social mobility. But each class was distinct from the others in education, occupation, dress and income, and would have been shocked to find itself lumped in with any of the others. Almost all of these distinct classes in the middle stratum can be found amongst Shakespearean playgoers. Their composition broadly defines the composition of a majority in the London playhouse audiences, though the complete social range goes all the way from earls and even a queen to penniless rogues (Brathwait's rufflers), families of beggars, and the unemployed.

The Elizabethans who wrote about their society agreed in distinguishing four principal classes. Sir Thomas Smith, utilising his years of service representing England to the French court, wrote his account in the 1560s. William Harrison contributed his 'Description' of England to Holinshed's *Chronicles* of 1577.[3] The two accounts agree to such an extent that one must be largely a copy of the other, a fact which is probably better seen as a confirmation of the accuracy of the first account than a sign of laziness in the second writer. Thomas Wilson's account of 'The State of England, Anno Dom. 1600'[4] broadly agrees with the two earlier descriptions, though it supplies enough additional categories within the four principal classes to suggest that there had been changes between the 1560s and 1600, and that Wilson was hostile to the social mobility which the broadness of Harrison's and Smith's categories tended to conceal. Whatever shifts the process of social change imposed on contemporary commentators, it seems sensible to base a picture of Elizabethan society on the four main classes of Harrison and Smith. Modern analyses of social process suggest anyway that in the first half of the seventeenth century social divisions were if anything strengthening the separate identity of the main categories.[5] It is probably also fair to say that the polarisation of social allegiances that helped to promote the war between king and Parliament in 1640 was one reason why the cultural appeal of the repertories in the different types of playhouse came to vary so distinctly. There is not much direct evidence of links between social polarisation and the playhouse repertories favoured by different classes of playgoer, but the two phenomena are well worth setting alongside each other.

William Harrison's four classes were, in order of income and status, first the nobles and gentlemen, next citizens and burgesses, thirdly yeomen, the rural smallholders, and finally artisans and labourers. These categories reflect the extent to which land more than money was seen as the great divider, and they are therefore less precise than is really helpful in reflecting the class divisions of urban and suburban London, which provided almost all the Shakespearean playgoers and were the section of English society least dependent on landowning. In all the seventy-five years up to 1642, for instance, I have found only five references to a yeoman going to a playhouse. On the other hand there are quite a few to young heirs of landed estates selling their patrimonial land for the sake of a high life in London. The transfer of wealth from land to what Wemmick called portable property, the rapid growth of a cash nexus based in London, made a by no means insignificant contribution to the rise of playgoing.

The newly rich and the big spenders alike used playgoing to advertise their status, whether their social mobility was upward as prosperous citizens or downward as young and extravagant gallants.[6] That consideration – the distorting effect of London's magnetism on the wealthy – should be borne in mind when looking at Harrison's or Wilson's categories. London's population doubled from 100,000 to 200,000 between 1580 and 1600, and doubled again by 1650 to 400,000, at a time when the total population of England grew only about 20 per cent, from a little over 4 million in 1600.[7] London's economic dynamism attracted the wealthy and the unemployed alike.

The nobles and gentry comprised all social ranks below the monarch down to, as Harrison put it, 'they that are simplie called gentlemen'.[8] The nobles were all called 'lords' – 'the prince, dukes, marquesses, earls, viscounts, and barons' – along with the bishops. Amongst the lesser gentry of knights, esquires and simple gentlemen Harrison included lawyers, doctors and army captains, provided that a man with those qualifications 'can live without manuell labour, and thereto is able and will beare the port, charge, and countenance of a gentleman'. If he does so, 'he shall for monie have a cote and armes bestowed upon him by heralds . . . and thereunto being made so good cheape be called master, which is the title that men give to esquiers and gentlemen, and reputed for a gentleman ever after'. Shakespeare, knowing Harrison as he did from the volumes of Holinshed in which Harrison's *Description* appeared, was evidently not bothered by these sarcasms about being made so good cheap when he secured an esquire's coat of arms for his father in 1596.

John Shakespeare's elevation to the gentry was a piece of vanity illustrating the upward shift from citizen to gentleman which was one of the principal forms of mobility in this period. If a citizen bought himself a new status it was most likely a reflection of his financial well-being. Rather more often entry to the rank of gentleman came through that commonest of mobilising forces, education. Barnaby Rich, in *Roome for a Gentleman* (1609), defined the categories of people just above the boundary between gentry and citizenry in terms almost as sceptical as Harrison's:

there are comprised under the title of Gentry, all Ecclesiastical persons professing religion, all Martial men that have borne office, and have commaund in the field; all Students of Artes and Sciences, and by our English custome, all Innes of Court men, professors of the Law: it skilles not what their Fathers were, whether Farmers, Shoomakers, Taylers or Tinkers, if their names be inrolled in any Inne of Court, they are all Gentlemen.   (E1r)

Rich, himself a soldier, was partly reacting to the threefold increase at this time in students of the London Inns, which deposited eight hundred young gentlemen at a time on Fleet Street and its environs.[9] Members of the Inns who wrote plays, such as Marston and Beaumont, were gentlemen more automatically than the products of citizen households like Middleton and Webster, and even the son of a bishop like Fletcher. Shakespeare, despite the coat of arms bought for his father, did not become a gentleman until his glover father died in 1601, less honoured in fact than the shoemaker's son Marlowe, who was gentrified by his Cambridge degree. His fellow John Heminges became a gentleman too, but in his will he still defined himself as a member of the Grocers' Company of London, the freeman citizen status which authorised his extra role as tapster and provider of the Globe's foodstuffs.

Shakespeare, Jonson, Dekker, Heywood, Webster and others almost never secured the right to put 'Gent.' after their names on their books. Of the major playwrights whose plays were published with their names on the titlepages before 1642, Armin, Brome, Day, Dekker, Field, Glapthorne, Heywood, Jonson, Marston, Nabbes, Peele, the Rowleys, Shakespeare, Tourneur, Webster, Wilkins and Robert Wilson were never called 'Gent.'. Jonson was technically gentrified only by his honorary degree from Oxford in 1619. Beaumont and Fletcher were occasionally awarded the honour, as were Chapman in 1598, Daborne, Ford in 1638, Lodge, Marlowe, Massinger, Thomas May, Middleton (occasionally), Shirley (once) and Whetstone. A few, Daborne, Goffe, Greene, William Heminges, Lyly and Marmion, were implied as being gentlemen by the title 'M.A.'. Perhaps the most intriguing evidence of the care with which this line was drawn is Middleton's title 'Gent.' on the titlepage of *A Chaste Maid* and *A Fair Quarrel*, and its absence from Webster's titlepages. Middleton came from London gentry, and made a good deal of theatrical capital from social climbing in his city comedies, especially *A Trick to Catch the Old One* and *A Chaste Maid*. Webster's links with his family coach-building firm confirmed his rank as that of a citizen, derided by Fitzgeoffery as a *'Play-wright Cart-wright'*, in 1617.

It is difficult to be sure quite how deliberate these titlings were. Day, who was the son of a husbandman and never completed his degree at Cambridge because he was expelled for stealing a book, was never called 'Gent.'. On the other hand Marston, whose presence as an Inn of Court student was well publicised, never received the title either. The use could be quite specific, as with Tom May and Lodowick Carlell, who were called 'esq.', the rank Shakespeare had secured for his father, just above a mere gentleman. That was in the 1630s, by when even Shakespeare had finally secured the rank of 'Gent.'. Of the other well-known play-names, Henslowe, Alleyn, the Burbages and Beeston could never comfortably claim to be more than citizens. The distinction between a gentleman and a citizen was most unclear when the citizen was a wealthy merchant or from a family of merchants, and especially when he was educated. Players, unlike writers, were never thought to be educated.

Harrison acknowledged this blurred boundary in his account of the second class. Technically citizens were 'those that are free within the cities, and are of some likelie substance to beare office in the same'. In this sense 'free' meant being a member of a city guild who was an employer as distinct from an employee or artisan. James Burbage and Ben Jonson kept themselves 'free of the city' by paying their dues to the Carpenters' Guild and the Tilers and Bricklayers respectively. Jonson went on paying his dues to be a freeman of London up to 1612. Among citizens Harrison included merchants, with the proviso that merchants 'often change estate with gentlemen, as gentlemen doo with them, by a mutuall conversion of the one into the other'. The key determinant of a gentleman was freedom from the need to work, whether manually or with money. Barnaby Rich's point about law students indicates one method for conversion. The other method is indicated by the fact that of the 8,000 apprentices in the fifteen London livery companies through the period 1570–1646, 12.6 per cent were the sons of knights, esquires and gentlemen.[10] Younger sons usually had to find other means than a patrimony to keep themselves in London. In the wealthiest companies, such as the Goldsmiths', nearly a third of apprentices were the sons of gentlemen. Gold was the principal alchemy for converting citizenry into gentry. Lack of it, for younger sons, took them the opposite way.

The third class, yeomen, were the country equivalent of citizens in being also 'free' as landowners. Harrison's definition makes them 'free men borne English, and may dispend of their owne free land in yearelie revenue, to the summe of fortie shillings sterling, or six pounds as monie goeth in our times'. This financial freedom gave them 'more estimation than labourers & the common sort of artificers', but placed them below gentlemen, on whose behalf they might work as farmers. At their best,

with grasing, frequenting of markets, and keeping of servants (not idle servants, as the gentlemen doo, but such as get both their owne and part of their masters living) do come to great welth, in somuch that manie of them are able and doo buie the lands of unthriftie gentlemen, and often setting their sonnes to the schooles, to the universities, and to the Ins of the court; or otherwise leaving them sufficient lands whereupon they may live without labour, doo make them by those meanes to become gentlemen.

These examples of social mobility did not really blur the distinctions between classes. They were transfers from one distinct class to another.

The fourth and final class in Harrison's account was made up of 'daie labourers, poore husbandmen, and some retailers (which have no free land) copie holders, and all artificers, as tailers, shomakers, carpenters, brickmakers, masons, &c'. Apart from the 'poore husbandmen', who farmed land they did not own, most of these categories were employees, men who sold their labour or its products to the larger retailers and employers. The grades in the London livery companies reflect this distinction. Citizens were 'free' of their company, and employed skilled artisans as day labourers or journeymen while training apprentices to become day labourers. Apprentices were trained for seven years or more in return for their board and lodging before they could rise to the level of wage earners. The employer-citizens were in Harrison's second class, their employees in the fourth class.

Near the bottom of the fourth class was a group much in evidence at the playhouses. Artisans and apprentices who took an afternoon off to see a play were cutting their working time. The same was not so true of the last category Harrison distinguished in this class, house servants. Harrison took a low view of 'our great swarmes of idle serving men', devoting a lengthy paragraph to their evil ways. They were the unskilled workers, taking board and lodging as part of their wage. Below them lay only the depths of beggary and vagabondage, the unhoused and unemployed layer of people who ranked nowhere in Harrison's busy commonwealth and for whom he found no place at all.

Vagrants and vagabonds, according to the City of London authorities, had a great deal to do with the playhouses. The Lord Mayor's stream of complaints to the Privy Council about how playhouse audiences were largely made up of vagrants needs some explanation. Vagrants were basically the unemployed. Most of them were young men – thirty out of the thirty-seven vagrants registered at Bridewell in 1602 were aged between eleven and twenty. Three-quarters of them were unemployed servants or ex-apprentices.[11] Most of the London vagrants were immigrants from country areas. London's fourfold growth in the seventy years from 1580 produced an even larger growth in vagrancy, eightfold between 1560 and 1601 and twelvefold by 1625.[12] The unemployed lived mostly in the suburbs, where the playhouses were, since they were the poorest parts of London. That fact possibly swayed the minds of successive Lord Mayors, whose jurisdiction did not extend beyond the city itself, and who would naturally assume that most troubles were generated from the areas outside their control. But they must also have made the assumption that playgoing, being an occupation for the idle, was also largely a recreation for the unemployed. Nashe in 1592 pointedly ignored the fact that an 'afternoon's man' was a euphemism for a drunkard, and characterised London's idlers as chiefly 'men that are their owne masters (as Gentlemen of the Court, the Innes of the Courte, and the number of Captaines and Souldiers about *London*)'. These man 'do wholy bestow

themselves upon pleasure, and that pleasure they devide (howe vertuously it skils not) either into gameing, following of harlots, drinking, or
seeing a Playe' (2.15). This observation, together with the multitude of
evidence for 'mechanicals' or working men attending the playhouses,
suggests that the city definition of vagrancy was a little simple-minded.

Harrison does give a chapter to the poor, among whom, understandably, he includes all the known varieties of thief. In this chapter, and
in his ambitious section on the twenty-three types of known thief,
he makes his only acknowledgement of the female half of his commonwealth. Women had no property rights, and little in the way of
employment. Even women with respectable jobs, apple-wives and fishwives, or Ursula the pig-woman in *Bartholomew Fair*, were assumed
for Harrison's purposes to be attachments or extensions of their husbands' business affairs. The only women acknowledged to be self-
employed were whores. The absence of women from the active members of Harrison's commonwealth is the most conspicuous example
of a number of ways in which Harrison's picture of the four classes
in the nation differs from the evidence we have for the identity of a
Shakespearean playhouse audience. Those differences are important.

SOCIAL CLASSES IN LONDON

London itself was in many ways different from the nation at large, and
the distinctive character of the London population obviously makes
its social divisions much more like those of its playhouse audiences
than the nation as a whole. Literacy, for instance, was markedly higher
in London than elsewhere. Only 18 per cent of London apprentices and
31 per cent of servants in this period were unable to sign their names,
whereas in the rest of the country the same class appears to have been
little more literate than husbandmen and labourers, of whom 73–
100 per cent were unable to sign their names.[13] In the country as a
whole the gentry and clerics were the most literate, tradesmen and
yeomen next, labourers and women least. Amongst the citizenry of
London and Middlesex there was a distinct hierarchy:

At one end the civic elite of merchants, joined by the pen-wielding scriveners,
wholesale dealers and polite shopkeepers, had complete possession of literacy.
Specialist distributors and craftsmen came next, followed by a miscellany of
people in servicing and processing trades. Industrial workers and craftsmen
occupied the fourth metropolitan cluster, with less-skilled craftsmen and outdoor workers at the bottom. Most of these people were more literate than their
provincial and rural counterparts.[14]

London could provide the playhouses with an exceptionally high number of literate urban workers, as well as a huge population of the unemployed, and by far the greatest concentration of gentry and rich citizenry in the country. It is a reasonable presumption that London's playgoers had a similarly exceptional level of literacy, wealth and poverty.

Literacy, however, like the other general components of London's population, is by no means a straightforward guide to the make-up of playhouse audiences. Playgoing must have had a special appeal as a leisure activity to the illiterate, since the playgoer's involvement with the written word need have gone no further than the playbills posted to advertise performances. The high proportion of women at the playhouses testifies to the popularity of playgoing for the illiterate, since few women of any class, even in London, could write their names. Illiteracy among women in the country as a whole approached 90 per cent, and did not drop significantly until the last quarter of the seventeenth century.[15] On the other hand, a few women were very thoroughly educated. Queen Elizabeth herself established the model, having gained the benefit of a Tudor experiment allowing well-born women to follow the teaching programme laid down for boys. This novel practice, especially promoted by Thomas More's circle, gave its benefits in the next generation to both Elizabeth and her sister Mary, and Lady Jane Grey. In 1562, when she was queen, Elizabeth spent time reading Latin and Greek with Roger Ascham every day. Thanks to the queen's example the practice grew. Lord John Russell, a scholar who taught Edward VI, announced his belief that 'sexes as well as souls are equal in capacity',[16] and taught his five daughters Latin and Greek. That, of course, was a conscious eccentricity, and Henry Peacham in *The Compleat Gentleman* (1622, p. 36) wrote of Russell's daughters as a rare marvel. Learning for women was the exception, though not entirely a rarity. When Joseph Swetnam published his notorious *Araignment of lewde, idle, and unconstant women* in 1615, three women issued pamphlets in reply, citing quite as many classical and biblical texts as he had. These were privileged women. Their kind could have supplied a far smaller proportion of playgoers than the generally illiterate housewives. Some could certainly write, many more could evidently read, supplying much of the market for the romances of knight-errantry which grew as light reading through the sixteenth century. Joan Alleyn, daughter of citizen Philip Henslowe, could write an easy letter to her husband Edward when his playing company was on its travels. A great appetite in women for reading and writing was certainly there. But time to read meant leisure, and leisure was usually a consequence of money. Magnates' wives would have been much more thoroughly literate than those attached to artisans.

Citizens' wives were a noteworthy presence in the playhouses. Respectable citizens treated women as a protected species, and their delight in plays became a worry. The restrictions on their range of activities and the assumption that their proper habitat was the home are attested by many writers besides the author of *A third blast of retrait from plaies and Theaters* (1580), who wrote about women playgoers that

Some citizens wives, upon whom the Lord for ensample to others hath laide his hands, have even on their death beds with teares confessed, that they have received at those spectacles such filthie infections, as have turned their minds from chast cogitations, and made them of honest women light huswives.

(2.6)

John Lane in 1600 wrote of 'light-taylde huswives' at the Bankside playhouses wearing masks – 'Though unseene to see those they faine would know' (2.44). Even Samuel Rowlands, a regular frequenter of plays himself, certainly saw playgoing as the mark of an immodest woman. In his *The Bride* (1617), he says of a 'good wife',

> At publike plays she never will be knowne,
> And to be taverne guest she ever hates,
> She scornes to be a streete-wife (Idle one,)
> Or field wife ranging with her walking mates.
> She knows how wise men censure of such dames . . .   (2.130)

although it should be noted that this poem appeared in the middle of the Swetnam controversy. Richard West made a similarly crass implication, in his epigram about a merchant's wife he thought he recognised, before concluding he had seen her picture in a brothel (2.82). Beaumont's Citizen's wife in 1607 and Peacham's in 1642 both imply that their husbands went to the playhouse more often than their wives did, and that was not because the wives were reluctant. In such a tame society it was obvious that most men expected only the wilder species of woman to be regular playgoers. The author of the *retrait* gave the motive as well as the character for such wild creatures:

Whosoever shal visit the chappel of Satan, I meane the Theater, shal finde there no want of yong ruffins, nor lacke of harlots, utterlie past al shame: who presse to the fore-front of the scaffoldes, to the end to showe their impudencie, and to be as an object to al mens eies.

(2.6)

But harlotry is an easy charge to lay where there is no foundation. Playgoing could be a family occasion. In November 1587 the Admiral's Men accidentally fired a loaded gun and 'killed a chyld, and a woman great with chyld', according to Philip Gawdy.[17] John Taylor the Water Poet wrote of a beggar getting his entire family into the playhouse, 'all in for one penny'.[18] The presence of women playgoers is much easier to establish than their motivation. Spenser's reference to 'a troublous noyes' of 'womens cries, and the shouts of boyes, / Such as the troubled Theaters oftimes annoyes' (2.26) suggests that women were certainly capable of reacting in numbers and vocally to what they saw on stage.

The prevalence of whores – perhaps, given their commercial motive in attending, we should say the availability of whores – at the playhouses is attested throughout the seventy-five years. But such testimonies need to be treated with even more caution than evidence about the literacy of women playgoers. Any meeting-place for large numbers of people was likely to be regarded as a market for their goods by most of London's itinerant whores. How much they went to playhouses in order to combine the pleasures of being a spectator with the business of marketing themselves there is no way of knowing. The suburban playhouses stood surrounded by brothels, and gallants tended to choose between them, like Davies's Fuscus, whose daily round varies only when

> . . . sometimes he comes not to the play
> But falls into a whore-house by the way. (2.20)

On the one hand many a brothel-worker might have taken a holiday from her work to become a genuine playgoer. On the other hand, the playhouses were the obvious place to solicit custom for the neighbouring brothels. According to Guilpin the plays themselves fired some playgoers to look for whores. He wrote in 1598 of 'an old graybearded Cittizen . . . Who comming from the Curtain sneaketh in, / To some odde garden noted house of sinne' (2.33). This of course suggests that brothel whores did not need to get work by attending the playhouses.

Women playgoers provide the hardest evidence for the social composition of Shakespearean playgoers. They were, as a whole, the least literate section of society. Their reasons for playgoing were most open to question and most subject to attack. And yet women from every section of society went to plays, from Queen Henrietta Maria to the most harlotry of vagrants. Evidence for a plentiful supply of women playgoers is there throughout the period, although few assertions, beyond the bare fact that women were present, can be trusted entirely. Hardly any view about such an emotive question as the morals of women play-goers tells as much about audiences as it does about the man making the statement. John Lane wrote of 'light-taylde huswives' at the Globe in 1600, but Francis Beaumont brought onto the Blackfriars stage in 1607 a citizen's wife of utter if comic respectability, who has been begging her husband for years to take her to a play. They were probably a more orthodox example of women playgoers than the whores, though both types were expected by Fitzgeoffery to be present at Blackfriars in 1617. *The Actors Remonstrance*, written in 1643 after the closure, acknowledges both too:

> . . . we shall for the future promise, never to admit into our sixpenny-roomes those unwholesome inticing Harlots, that sit there meerely to be taken up by Prentizes or Lawyers Clerks; nor any female of what degree soever, except they come lawfully with their husbands, or neere allies . . . (2.216)

Clearly women were presumed to be respectable so long as they were accompanied by a man, and to be whores if alone. Ann Halkett claimed that she was the first woman, in the 1630s, to organise a group of girls who paid for themselves and had no male escort. She started the custom

> for 3 or 4 of us going together withoutt any man, and everyone paying for themselves by giving the mony to the footman who waited on us, and he gave itt in the playhouse. And this I did first on hearing some gentleman telling what ladys they had waited on to plays, and how much itt had cost them.[19]

Several other women, including the sisters of Margaret Cavendish, did the same. Such a group still had a footman to escort them and hand over their money to the playhouse gatherer, the footman presumably attending them from their coach and waiting with the coachman to collect them after the performance. Ann Halkett's innovation needed its safeguards. Her motive was to free herself and her friends from laying financial obligations on their male escorts, but that was not to be bought at the cost of any doubts about their morality. There is no indication of which playhouses the group went to, but they were not likely to have been the outdoor amphitheatres.

That last statement is more an assumption than a deduction. The pattern of women's playgoing probably changed with time, but the principal change most likely came with the return of the halls in 1599. The admission price for the indoor playhouses meant that only the richest whores would have gone there seeking custom. All the private playhouse writers in the 1630s acknowledged the presence of 'ladies' as a large proportion of their audience, and ladies must by then have certainly predominated over the whores. That seems a reasonable assumption, but it has little tangible support from the hard evidence about who went to which playhouses, and in which decades. It is to this evidence, in a mildly despairing effort to establish something like a statistical basis for this analysis of the social composition of playgoers, that I turn now.

WHO WENT WHERE

Appendix 1 gives the name and a brief description of every person who can be identified as having seen a play in a commercial playhouse in London between 1567 and 1642. Appendix 2 lists the major references I have been able to locate about playgoers real or fictional, their social identity, and the general features of their playgoing. The first list amounts to no more than 250 names, the second a total of 224 quotations. Since on a conservative estimate the playhouses in their seventy-five years probably entertained their customers with close to 50 million visits, that is a very small sample for statistical purposes. Still, it is all we have, and treated with the right kind of scepticism it can be revealing. More than half of the 474 references are to real people, tangible if fortuitous evidence, and 32 of the 250 were women. Of the higher social ranks, 25 were foreign visitors, including 8 ambassadors, and 19 were nobles, including Queen Henrietta Maria, the dukes of Buckingham and Lennox, the earls of Dorset, Pembroke, Rutland and Southampton, and the Countess of Essex. Seven of the nobles were women.

Numerically, the distribution amongst the social classes provides a few surprises which modify some of the easier assumptions. Predictably most of the artisans are named from court cases and affrays, usually in gangs. Seven seamen, six feltmakers, five glovers, four butchers, three cordwainers, three victuallers, another half-dozen involved with clothing and drapery, and five house-servants, male and female, are listed from court cases of one sort or another, particularly from the Bridewell records. The Middlesex County Sessions likewise provide evidence of affrays or thefts at the Curtain, Fortune and Red Bull. Sadly, no similar records survive for Surrey. Gangs of seamen started a riot at the Fortune and feltmaking apprentices did the same at the Red Bull. Two gentlemen and an ironmonger were caught selling stolen drapery goods at the Fortune. Trades such as waterman (two, including John Taylor the Water Poet), a barber and a surgeon are in the lists, plus two haberdashers, a silkweaver, a bookbinder and a tailor at different times and playhouses.

Predictably the gentry were most conspicuous, with 144 real names and more than half the total number of references, but that apparent predominance is undermined by the paucity of references to affluent merchants. More than thirty-four writers, including Spenser and Milton, are there, some of them bridging the gap between citizens and gentry. Fewer than twenty freemen-citizens can be identified as playgoers amongst over sixty London commoners, and of them eleven were playwrights and three were players or impresarios. Of the remaining five, two went on the same occasion for a similar reason (Howe and Flaskett to Paul's in 1603), one was a regular playgoer in 1599 and 1611 (Simon Forman) and the fourth is known, like Howe and Flaskett, only because of his involvement in a notorious legal case (Dr Lambe in 1626). The fifth, Mrs Watton, was a citizen wife.

This number of affluent citizens is so small that we have to look for an explanation. Even including all the fictional and general comments on citizens at playhouses the total of references is still less than half the number for women or workingmen. Most oddly, in the decade 1590–99, when London had only the two amphitheatres for plays, there is barely more than a single reference to citizens as playgoers. The only clear-cut references from that decade are Guilpin's 'old gray-bearded Cittizen' at the Curtain (2.34), and Sir John Davies's to the non-selective gathering at the public playhouses, where 'A thousand townsemen, gentlemen, and whores, / Porters and serving-men together throng' (2.18). Either townsmen were notable absentees, or they were such constant buyers on the playhouse market that their presence was completely unremarkable. They were caught neither by references by their peers nor in the lawcourts.

Some evidence does exist to support the view that in the 1590s what Daborne called 'ignorant Cittizens' (2.104) were a standard presence, since the opposite seems to have happened later, when the poets of the indoor playhouses gave attention to citizens between 1636 and 1641 usually in the form of comments about their discomfort at such alien venues. Citizens were evidently a rare enough presence to be notable in the hall playhouses at that time. The inference is that citizens were the standard kind of playgoer in the 1590s, but that they were a distinctly less normal feature of the later indoor playhouse audiences. This is, regrettably, a fairly loose calculation. The evidence which names real playgoers is highly selective – almost the only names we know of real artisans who were playgoers, for instance, were recorded for their part in crimes or affrays – and needs careful scrutiny if it is to produce any valid inferences.

Women, whether because of the high proportion of illiterates among them, or because of the employment opportunities for whores, stood to gain a particularly advantageous return from playgoing, so it makes sense to examine the evidence for their presence first. Of the thirty-two real women known to have gone to playhouses, one was a queen (Henrietta Maria, who paid four visits to plays at the Blackfriars in the 1630s; Anne of Denmark was said to have enjoyed seeing plays mocking her husband, but these were not at a public playhouse), three were countesses, five others were titled, two were ambassadors' wives, ten were ladies, including the wife of the Dean of St Paul's, a celebrated eyelash-flutterer, three were playhouse gatherers, and one was a famous transvestite. Only two citizens' wives are named, but references to their presence appear as early as 1577, and are distributed fairly evenly throughout the whole period, in 1582, 1600, 1601, 1611, 1616, 1617, 1632, 1636, 1638, 1640 and 1643, for instance, as a look through Appendix 2 will indicate. Attendances by the known individuals listed in Appendix 1 strengthen the pattern suggested by the more general references. The assumption, or the accusation, that such wives went for harlotry or adultery belongs to the earlier period, up to about 1600, and some of the later references identify the women at the Fortune or Red Bull as fishwives or apple-wives, whereas the references to women playgoers at the indoor playhouses are almost exclusively, apart from Massinger's fictional City Madam and West's and Peacham's merchant wives, to ladies.

In all there are more references to ladies than to citizens, though most of them appear later than the references to the citizenry. Lyly addressed the ladies of his courtly audience in 1584, while Harington's lady of 'great birth, great reputation' is the first, in about 1595, to be mentioned at a public playhouse. Other references appear in 1599 (the epilogue of *As You Like It*), 1601, 1610, 1612 (Mrs Elizabeth Wybarn), 1614 (Mrs Elizabeth Williams, the married sister of Sir Dudley Carleton's wife, seeing a play at the rebuilt Globe), 1615, 1616, 1617, 1624, 1628, 1630, 1632, 1637, 1638, 1639, 1640 and 1641, besides a number of ladies, including the wife and sister-in-law whom Sir Humphrey Mildmay escorted to plays in the years between 1632 and 1640, and the parties of unmarried women whom Ann Halkett organised in the same decade.

As the novelty of playgoing settled down, the role of women in the audiences changed. In 1609 John Fletcher began to write plays aimed specifically at an audience that would be predominantly sympathetic to the female position, like his sequel to *The Taming of the Shrew*, *The Tamer Tamed*, written for the Blackfriars and the Globe in 1612.

The real takeover by women seems to have been at the Blackfriars and the Cockpit, where the boxes closest to the stage became the place where nobles and gentlemen took their ladies, and ladies took their pages to sit there on their own, as Peacham's citizen wife did with her husband's apprentice.

The status of the Blackfriars ladies and the effects of their status are not difficult to identify. Under Elizabeth, court ladies had little occasion to attend public playhouses. Under James, royal support for plays and playing made it more acceptable socially, and the King's Men playing at the Blackfriars through the winters when the court and the lawyers were all in town made their playhouse the best place for society to parade itself. The nobility like Elizabeth Cary and Lady Anne Clifford, for instance, were happy to go there. The latter was the only child of the third Earl of Cumberland, her father the massively rich landowner George Clifford, Elizabeth's official Champion. She championed a different cause. He debarred her from inheriting his vast estates in Yorkshire and Cumbria because she was female, bequeathing them instead to his brother.[20] From 1610, following her mother's example, she engaged in a struggle lasting more than thirty years to repossess what she considered her right. She did not succeed until 1643, when her father's last male relative died, leaving no other heir.

In 1601, aged eleven, she became a maid of honour at Elizabeth's court, and subsequently a lady-in-waiting to Queen Anne. She danced in several of Anne's court masques, including the *Masque of Beauty*, the *Masque of Queens*, where she represented Queen Berenice, and Daniel's *Tethys' Festival* in 1610. Daniel had been her tutor, and she later paid for his memorial. She married Richard Sackville, the Earl of Dorset, in 1609, and lived with him chiefly at Knole in Kent. Her feeling for her rights meant, understandably, that she ran into substantial male opposition. King James sympathised with her case, but ruled against her in 1617. She was alienated from her first husband, a gambler, spendthrift, masquer and tilter, by whom she had two surviving daughters and a son, born in 1620, who died of measles at six months. His father died in 1624 of what John Chamberlain notoriously said was a surfeit of potatoes. In 1630 after several years of reclusive widowhood she married Philip Herbert, younger brother of William, co-dedicatee of the Shakespeare First Folio and his successor as Lord Chamberlain. Through the next years she lived at Wilton in Hampshire, making the poet George Herbert her chaplain.

The second marital relationship was as strained, though for different reasons, as her first. When King Charles left London she supported him, whereas her husband became an active Parliamentarian. Her autobiography speaks of her unhappy life both at Knole and at Wilton. Her last thirty years were spent almost entirely in Yorkshire, when her castle at Skipton where she was born became a quasi-regal court. She outdid Bess of Hardwick in good works, making endless grants from her enormous wealth for restoration, including her seven castles, in each of which she lived for part of each year, and six churches and chapels. She paid for several remarkable monuments including Daniel's at his home in Somerset and Spenser's monument in Poets' Corner in Westminster Abbey. The extensive records of her eighty-six years survive, including her own note of a visit to *The Mad Lover* at the Blackfriars in 1617, though this was evidently by no means a unique event.

Visits by high society to the Blackfriars became easily the most noteworthy activity of the last twenty years of playing. The mind-set of at least some of its male visitors can be seen from an account of a playgoing experience there dating most likely from the 1620s or 1630s. By then the Blackfriars was notoriously offering young gallants the possibility of romantic meetings and sexual assignations. Not printed until 1657, T. M.'s *The Life of a Satyricall Puppy Called Nim* is a small book about a young and penniless gentleman seeking to make his fortune in London in the 1620s.[21] A picaresque tale, full of storytelling asides, Nim acquires £50 through his escapades with his servant Bung, and resolves to use it to get himself a rich lady who will keep him for his sexual agility. He spends his money on a splendid outfit and goes to the Blackfriars. He sits on a stool on the stage, greeting the gallants alongside him as if he knew them and flaunting his new cloak and his figure. He stands up at each interact to show off his elegant limbs, looking out for any ladies who might be watching him. He ignores the play, except to scorn a neighbour from the country who exclaims that he will revenge the boy playing a ravished lady. Eventually he sees a masked lady in the pit eyeing him, so he stretches his legs to show himself off to her. When she unmasks to speak to a friend he finds she is hideously ugly, but persuades himself that she is the more likely therefore to be sexually available. When the play ends he follows her down the stairs into the street, where he accosts her but she rejects him, assuming he thinks her a whore. Her brother slaps him across the face and reaches for his sword. He flees, and his servant, who had been standing in wait outside the playhouse to save his master the additional cost of his admission, later tells him the brother had sworn to kill him if he ever saw him again. That, the story concludes, stopped him from going to playhouses in case he might be recognised. The whole chapter is a fiction, but the incidental detail about the playhouse visit is exact, even the exclamation by his naive neighbour. Such stories depended heavily on the material details of their setting for their plausibility, so it must be an account of a recognisable playgoing experience.

It is notable that all of the known gatherers at the London playhouses were women. The only man known to have taken money at the door was a player, the leader of a travelling group of the King's Men, in 1627 at a Norwich inn. The presence of such working women suggests that women commonly determined audience manners and behaviour. A little surprisingly, the people and passages cited in the Appendices make much less note of whores than of either citizens' wives or ladies. The sensational nature of such identifications has possibly given them more prominence than their true number among playgoers really warrants. Even if we admit as whores the companions of soldiers, who Peter Heylyn in 1621 advised to 'fly to ye Globe or Curtaine with your trul' (2.142) or Richard Brathwait's ruffians identified in 1631 with their '*dainty Doxes*' (2.166), the total number of such references is still less than ten. Davies in *c.*1593, Platter in 1599, Dekker in 1608, Jonson in 1610, Heylyn in 1621, Brathwait in 1631 and the *Remonstrance* in 1643 are the chief instances, besides the few names listed in the Bridewell reports. The only real presence that men of the time thought belonged to this type, besides those noted by Platter, who as a traveller was only marginally less ready to write fictions than the others, was Marion Frith at the Fortune in 1611.

Marion Frith, or Moll Cutpurse as she was popularly known, is a special case which says more about the value of playgoing for publicity seekers than about the presence of likely whores. She was not a whore, although her behaviour led to her being treated as one. Pressed by the Bishop of London's court in 1612,

to declare whether she had not byn dishonest of her body & hath not also drawne other women to lewdnes by her perswasion & by carrying her selfe lyke a bawde, she absolutely denied yt she was chargeable with eyther of these imputations.[22]

Her misdemeanour was much less routine. The Ecclesiastical Court record reported that she had appeared on stage dressed as a man at a performance of a play, Dekker and Middleton's *The Roaring Girl*, in which her fictional persona was the central figure. The court record states:

This day & place the sayd Mary appeared personally & then & there voluntarily confessed yt she had long frequented all or most of the disorderly & licentious places in this Cittie as namely she hath usually in the habite of

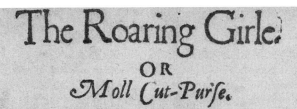

15. The titlepage of *The Roaring Girl*, showing Moll Frith.

a man resorted to alehowses Tavernes Tobacco shops & also to play howses there to see plaies & pryses & namely being at a play about three quarters of a yeare since at ye Fortune in man's apparel and in her boots and wth a sword at her syde, she told the company then present yt she thought many of them were of opinion that she was a man, but if any of them would come to her lodging they shoulde finde she is a woman and some other immodest and lascivious speaches she also used at yt time. And also sat upon the stage in the public viewe of all the people there presente in man's apparel & played upon her lute and sange a song.   (2.96)

Such bravado and such publicity created a major stir. The play itself, its publication in 1612 putting an accurate woodcut of Moll Cutpurse herself on the titlepage, references in other plays and pamphlets and an account by Chamberlain for Dudley Carleton, all testify to her notoriety. But a professional whore this twenty-six-year-old was not. She went to the playhouse for her own pleasure, not for profit. Her offences were partly the alleged lewdness of her display at the Fortune, but mainly a later affray in St Paul's Cathedral on the night of Christmas Day 1611, when her offence was openly to flaunt the fact that she was a woman in man's dress by showing her tucked-up petticoats under her cloak. The bishop remanded her in Bridewell for that pending further examination. She seems not to have been punished by anything more than the stay in Bridewell.

The chief general conclusion from this evidence must be that the wives of citizens were regular playgoers throughout the whole period, though with some social divergence in the later years which directed the poorer 'apell-wyfes' to the Fortune, and the wealthier 'Cheapside Dames' or city madams to the Blackfriars. Dekker mentions whole audiences of penny-paying fishwives at the Fortune in 1611 (2.101). Ladies went relatively rarely to the common playhouses before 1600, but were in numbers at the Globe from 1599 to 1614, and had become a major section of the audience at the indoor venues by Caroline times. References to the adulterous intentions of playgoing housewives faded with the quietening of the puritan protests by 1600, but the assumption that female playgoers were motivated by sex, whether for pleasure or money, remained a male prejudice throughout the period. There may well have been fewer professional whores looking for custom than there were 'trulls' or 'doxies' accompanying their menfolk for the pleasure of seeing a play. They clearly did not make so much of their presence that they deterred more respectable playgoers. Glapthorne, in the prologue to 'a Reviv'd Vacation Play' of about 1636, wrote urging citizens 'as you have done today, / To bring your Wives and Daughters to a play' (2.195).

Evidence for the presence of citizens' wives at plays confirms the inference that citizens themselves were likewise regular playgoers, since no respectable wife could easily attend a play without a male escort. I am inclined to believe that despite the infrequent reference to their presence citizens were the staple, at least of amphitheatre audiences, throughout the period. They attracted far less attention than the gallants, the Inns of Court students, or even the foreign visitors, who took in the playhouses much as they took in the river and a view of royalty, and noted their impressions accordingly. Given the number of citizens in London, their relative affluence, and their proximity to all the playhouse venues, it may not be wildly wrong to think of them and their lesser neighbours the prosperous artisan class as a kind of silent majority in the playhouses.

The artisan class and those socially below them were usually described by occupation rather than by name, except in court records about affrays. Gosson in 1582 identified tailors, tinkers, cordwainers (shoemakers or leather-workers) and sailors in a list intended to be more contemptuous than comprehensive. In 1589 Nashe wrote of 'every mechanical mate' as a would-be playwright, more ambitious in their urban setting than the rude mechanicals and their play in *A Midsummer Night's Dream* (2.12). Nashe also wrote of playgoing apprentices in 1592 (2.15). Davies wrote of porters and serving-men a year or two later (2.18), and in 1602 Philip Gawdy included serving-men in his conspectus of an audience at the amphitheatres (2.51). A drover features in a poem of 1605 by Rowlands about a playhouse incident (2.64), and in 1609 there is a reference to 'grooms', a dismissive term for the most lowly (2.87).

In this decade Dekker and others began to deride artisan garlic-chewing and the smellier occupations such as beer-brewing in their increasingly frequent references to audiences of 'stinkards'. In 1610 an affray at the Red Bull involved a butcher and four feltmakers. Two other butchers were in an affray at the Fortune in 1611, 'abusing certen gentlemen', in the same year that Dekker wrote about a 'Greasie-apron *Audience*' at the same playhouse (2.101). Heywood wrote of an 'unlettered' audience at the Red Bull in 1613 (2.105), the year of an eccentric visit by the Venetian ambassador to the Curtain where he stood in the yard amongst 'the gang of porters and carters' (2.110). A feltmaker's apprentice, Richard Gill, sitting on the edge of the stage, was wounded by a player at the Red Bull in 1622. In 1626 the Privy Council took action over an affray at the Fortune involving nine sailors and their associates from Stepney. In 1631 Brathwait wrote of ruffians and their '*Doxes*' (2.166). In 1632 Jonson in *The Magnetic Lady* scorned the 'sinful sixpenny mechanicks' and the ignorance of a 'Trewel, or a Hammer-man' (2.172), and Alexander Gill, joining the hostile chorus raised by Jonson's play, suggested that he would have done better 'If to the Fortune you had sent your ladye / Mongst prentizes and apell-wyfes' instead of to the Blackfriars with its 'silkes and plush', the garb reserved to the gentry by the sumptuary laws (2.173). A silkweaver was arrested for menaces at the Red Bull in 1638. In 1640 Tatham wrote dismissively of the '*Rables, Applewives* and Chimney-boyes' at the Fortune, in contrast to the 'Gentlemen' of the Red Bull (2.212). The gentlemen there had to be asked not to throw tiles and pears at the hangings, which suggests that the Red Bull's audience had not changed its habits, and therefore probably not its composition, as much as Tatham's flattery suggests. The *Remonstrance* of 1643 (2.216) names 'Prentizes' as still the most conspicuous element in the amphitheatre audiences at the closure.

Cony-catchers, and more specifically cutpurses, were also regular playgoers. It might be expected that the crowds in the yard gave them better pickings with less chance of detection than the ranks in the galleries seated on the 'degrees', or the playgoers on benches in the pit at the indoor playhouses. In fact, though, their favourite hunting ground seems to have been the amphitheatre galleries. There are signally few references to nips or cutpurses except at the amphitheatres, and the chief legal record relates to the Fortune, when the Middlesex magistrates invoked the presence of cutpurses together with the 'tumultes' at the end of plays as their reason for banning jigs there, in 1612.[23] This general allegation is supported in *The Roaring Girl* of 1611, where Moll Cutpurse identifies a well-dressed nip in the Fortune's twopenny galleries, although of course Peacham's wife was robbed at a hall playhouse. Apart from the general injunction about the Fortune the only legal records are about the theft of purses at the Curtain in 1600 and at the Red Bull in 1614.[24] Other allusions to cutpurses at playhouses, probably only marginally more reliable than allusions to the presence of whores, appeared in 1590 (2.13), c.1595 (Harington's 'great lady' and her cony-catchers, 2.25), 1600, 1605 and 1606. These all belong to the amphitheatres, including Rowlands's cutpurse who robbed a drover in the yard (2.64), although Moll's gentlemanly cutpurse also had fictional counterparts, and some factual support in a thief executed when seized at the Chapel Royal during a court performance for the Christmas festivities of 1611.[25] Nips evidently did not keep to the company of what Harrison saw as their proper class.

Until the revival of the boy companies and the hall playhouses in 1599 the artisan and servant classes joined with the citizens and gentry at playhouses. Those few descriptions which suggest that the full range of society was present at plays come from around the 1590s, when only the amphitheatres were open. Sir John Davies in about 1593 was clearly trying to include all comers in his epigram 'In Cosmum'. He uses the crowd struggling out of the playhouse at the end of a play as a metaphor describing the confusion of thoughts falling over one another when Cosmus struggles to express them all:

> For as we see at all the play house dores,
> When ended is the play, the daunce, and song:
> A thousand townsemen, gentlemen, and whores,
> Porters and serving-men together throng,
> So thoughts of drinking, thriving, wenching, war
> And borrowing money, raging in his minde,
> To issue all at once so forwarde are,
> As none at all can perfect passage finde. (2.18)

In the 1590s, at an amphitheatre play with its concluding jig, this is the range of society Davies thought characteristic among playgoers. Henry Chettle suggested a similar range in 1592: gentlemen, citizens, the servants of both classes, and apprentices (2.14). A slightly different story, though with similar implications, was told by Philip Gawdy in 1602. Gawdy, a lawyer of Clifford's Inn, wrote to his elder brother at Redenhall in Norfolk about the illegal impressment by the city authorities of soldiers for the war in the Low Countries. To Gawdy the Lord Mayor's mismanagement of the affair was a great joke because he took it as an opportunity to organise a raid on the playhouses. The outcome was a test for the annual complaint to the Privy Council that the amphitheatre playhouses were chiefly places where vagrants gathered together. Gawdy exulted in the spectacular failure of the test.

Ther hath bene great pressing of late, and straunge, as ever was knowen in England, only in London, and my L. Mayor and the rest of the Londiners have done so contrary to their Instructions from the Lordes of the councell as this last sondaye your good frend Mr Wade told me that their wer letters that day directed from the L. of the councell to Sr Jhon Payton, and Sr. Jerom Bowes, with others to examyne the Londiners indiscreat proceedinges, and all suche as had cause to complayne shold be hard, and their causes redressed. So that upon the Tuesday following their was a proclamation in London that no gentleman, or serving man should any more be impressed, for the weake before they did not only presse gentlemen, and sarvingmen, but Lawyers, Clarkes, country men that had lawe causes, aye the Quenes men, knightes, and as it was credibly reported one Earle, quight contrary to that the councell, and especyally my L. Cheif Justice intended. For their meaning was that they should take out of all ordinaryes all cheting companions, as suche as had no abylyty to lyve in suche places, all suche as they cold fynd in bawdy houses, and bowling allyes, wch they never went to any but only to the bowling allyes. All the playe howses wer beset in one daye and very many pressed from thence, so that in all ther ar pressed fowre thowsand besydes fyve hundred voluntaryes, and all for flaunders. Ther was a Cheshire gentleman called Mr Manwaring that hathe this three weekes expected to be a Knight, but both he, and all others besydes have myssed as yet their expectation.   (2.51)

Gawdy, as an Inns of Court man, evidently had no love for Guildhall and its citizen Lord Mayor. His account may therefore overemphasise the number of gentry and nobility rounded up at the playhouses to embarrass the Lord Mayor. But the numbers involved – four thousand impressed from three amphitheatres and a few bowling alleys– seem accurate, and his range, from serving-men to knights and other gentry, broadly matches the society described by Davies and Chettle. The only oddity is that the hall playhouses seem to have been exempted from the round-up. Gawdy's letter does not mention the Blackfriars and Paul's, and from his account of the Lord Mayor's expectation of rounding up vagrants and 'cheting companions' he seems to refer only to the amphitheatres. Since the boy companies performed only once a week while the adults played daily, and since the Guildhall complaints against vagrants were always aimed specifically at the suburban amphitheatres, it may have been that the raids took place when the boys were not on show, or else were directed only at the amphitheatres. The 'private' playhouses were both outside the city's control, one in the liberty of Blackfriars and the other inside the precinct of St Paul's, but so officially were the amphitheatres in the suburbs. In either case, it seems, the gentry, knights and earl were willing patrons of the adult players along with the serving-men.

Gawdy's evidence for 1602 casts doubt on the assumption, perhaps too easily made, that by 1600, on Rosencrantz's evidence, gentlemen had separated from the citizens and mechanicals and were going only to the hall playhouses. The question of a division between the popular and the privileged, when it came into existence and what playhouses it separated people into, is the most knotty item in this whole history of playgoing. The most reliable evidence comes not from rumour-mongers like Hamlet's fellow student but from the record of what real people went to which playhouses and in what years.

Inns of Court students were regular playgoers from the start, and a conspicuous presence at the amphitheatres from early on. Twice, in 1580 and 1581, gangs of students got into quarrels with players.

The Privy Council minutes for the summer of 1580 include an item concerning three of the Earl of Oxford's players, two of whom were imprisoned briefly 'for committing of disorders and affrays appon the gentlemen of the Innes of the Courte'.[26] The following summer it was Lord Berkeley's players who were attacked by 'a dysordered companye of gentlemen of the Innes of Courte & others'. This time both players and gentlemen were committed, possibly because it was not the Privy Council but the city authorities who now handled the affair. Lord Berkeley had to answer for his players. This hostility must have had a social origin, the common players facing the arrogant and idle young gentlemen in a hot summer.

Over the next twenty years affrays grew less, and the names of some youngsters who came to fame later can be found among the playgoers. Edmund Spenser and Gabriel Harvey were enthusiasts, along with more regular London residents such as Davies, Donne, Drayton, Joseph Hall, Marston, Henry Peacham and other Inns of Court students such as Everard Guilpin and Francis Meres. William Lambarde, Keeper of the Tower, and John Chamberlain, Sir Dudley Carleton's friend and correspondent, also went to the amphitheatres. One rather less eminent but literate man, James More, secretary to the country gentleman William Darrell of Littlecote, cost his master sixpence when he saw a play at Paul's in 1589. William Cavendish's servant cost him threepence at Blackfriars in 1601. The foreign visitors Samuel Kiechel in 1584, Prince Lewis of Anhalt-Cöthen and Johannes De Witt, both in 1596, and Thomas Platter in 1599, all went to the amphitheatres. After about 1610 all the gentry, and especially the Inns of Court students, went almost exclusively to the hall theatres, although Gondomar, the Spanish ambassador, went to a play at the Fortune in 1621 'with his whole train'.

In the 1590s while only the amphitheatres were open the gallant established himself as the most noteworthy playgoing presence. Within this broad category the three types Nashe distinguished in his account of 'afternoones men' followed different patterns of behaviour. Davies differentiated the courtier from the student, for instance:

> *Rufus* the Courtier, at the Theater,
> Leaving the best and most conspicuous place,
> Doth either to the stage himselfe transferre,
> Or through a grate, doth shew his double face,
> For that the clamorous fry of Innes of court
> Fills up the private roomes of greater price:
> And such a place where all may have resort,
> He in his singularity doth despise. (2.19)

Davies's point is that Rufus's singularity does not stop him from visiting 'common' whores. Samuel Rowlands linked the same activities in his book of satires in 1600, where one gallant says 'Speak gentlemen, what shall we do today? . . . / Or shall we to the Globe and see a play? / Or visit Shoreditch for a baudy house?' (2.42). The pattern of gallant behaviour was already something of a stereotype. And in 1600 the Globe was still a routine alternative to the bawdy houses in its neighbourhood and plays at the Blackfriars in the city.

Between the early 1580s, when the clamorous fry of law students fought with the common players, and the 1590s when Burbage and Alleyn were worshipped as models for gallant behaviour, playgoing for the students and gentry clearly transformed itself. By the end of the 1590s the amphitheatres became not only the market place for gallants to show their personal wares but even the models for such displays. From the depths of the Middle Temple Marston made fun of the apish behaviour of his contemporaries in 1597, as they copied the players:

> *Luscus* what's playd to day? faith now I know
> I set thy lips abroach, from whence doth flow
> Naught but pure *Juliat* and *Romio*.
> Say, who acts best? *Druscus*, or *Roscio?*
> Now I have him, that nere of ought did speake
> But when of playes or Plaiers he did treate.
> H'ath made a common-place booke out of plaies,
> And speakes in print, at least what ere he sayes,
> Is warranted by Curtaine *plaudeties*,
> If ere you heard him courting *Lesbias* eyes
> Say (Curteous Sir) speakes he not movingly
> From out some new pathetique Tragedie?   (2.31)

Alleyn at the Rose, Burbage at the Curtain playing Romeo (Drusus and Roscio), together with their suppliers Kyd, Marlowe and Shakespeare, by this time had evidently established more than just a financial footing in London society.

After 1599, when the boy players reopened, the numbers of gentry going to the amphitheatres probably shrank, since at least once a week they had other venues open to them and at the hall playhouses they ran less risk of being pasted to brewers' jackets. Most of the comments on audiences at this time, however, were made by interested parties, especially Marston writing for his employers at Paul's. The poets' reports are notably biased towards the 'select' hall playhouse clientele. The only real members of the gentry known to have attended playhouses in the decade up to 1610 divided themselves fairly equally, three at the Blackfriars and two at the Globe. Frederic Gerschow, a visitor to London in the Duke of Stettin-Pomerania's entourage, went to the Blackfriars on 18 September 1602. Like other foreigners with little English he was chiefly impressed by the preliminary concert and the singing, though he also commented on the 'many respectable women' present.[27] The heir of Chatsworth, Sir William Cavendish, made eight visits to one or the other of the hall playhouses between 1600 and 1602, but none to the adults at the amphitheatres. In 1603 Sir Richard Cholmley also went to the Blackfriars. A dashing twenty-three-year-old Catholic, who had been embroiled in the Essex conspiracy, he claimed to be a little embarrassed to find himself so late for the performance that the only seat available for him was a stool on the stage. He was still more embarrassed when at a pause between the acts he stood up to stretch his legs and another young gallant took his stool. Sir Richard by his own account behaved most properly, leading the other young man, some 'Lady's eldest son', out of the playhouse where he challenged him to a duel. When the young man said he had no sword, Sir Richard offered to buy him one, presumably an offer meant as an insult rather than to make the duel possible. The affray ended when the watch arrived and Sir Richard had to satisfy himself with 'two or three good blows' on his offender.[28] Cavendish's, Gerschow's and Cholmley's evidence confirms the genteel, though hardly gentle, attendance at the boy company performances at Blackfriars.

There is no evidence apart from Rosencrantz's 'little eyases' reference about how much the Globe players suffered while their intended playhouse at the Blackfriars was leased out to the boys. It is unlikely that the gallants gave up filling their commonplace books with lines from Shakespeare altogether, and in 1607–8 the Globe received one thoroughly distinguished visitation. Giorgio Giustinian, the Venetian ambassador in London from January 1606 to November 1608, made up a party, including as chief guests the French ambassador and his wife together with the Secretary of the Florentine embassy, to see *Pericles* at the Globe. The party took over the lords' rooms over the stage, at a cost to Giustinian of more than twenty crowns.[29] An entourage only slightly smaller went with Prince Frederick Lewis of Württemberg in 1610 to the Globe to see *Othello*.[30]

The practice of ambassadors going to the common amphitheatres seems to have begun at the Globe, but it carried on well beyond the time when Shakespeare's company repossessed the Blackfriars, and it extended to the other amphitheatres. Sir Robert Rich and Sir Henry

Wotton took the ambassador from Savoy, the Marchese di Villa, to an amphitheatre in May 1613. The Spanish ambassador Gondomar took his party to the Fortune in 1621 in a major act of self-display. With typical panache he feasted the players in the adjacent garden afterwards, a banquet unlikely to have been prompted by simple gratitude for the entertainment offered. Given the ignorance of English which most embassies enjoyed the most likely explanation is that Gondomar was flying the Spanish flag where the maximum number of people could see it. The position of the lords' rooms over the stage made the amphitheatres much better for this purpose than the halls with their discreet boxes, quite apart from the larger number of spectators the Fortune could take in.

There is another piece of evidence about ambassadorial ventures among amphitheatre audiences which suggests a second motive indirectly related to the first: spying on the crowds to discover popular sentiment. Unlikely though that would be for a grandee with no command of the language, it seems to have been the motive behind the eccentric behaviour of Foscarini, the Venetian ambassador, in 1613. Antimo Galli, a Florentine reporting home with caustic gusto about his neighbour, gives a startlingly vivid account of Foscarini's visit to the Curtain in August 1613.

. . . my Pantalone often goes out now all alone, though with a faithful interpreter who walks a little in front to show him the way. He goes about saying that he's travelling incognito, and goodness knows where he ends up. He often goes to the plays in these parts. Among others, he went the other day to a playhouse called the Curtain, which is out beyond his house. It is an infamous place in which no good citizen or gentleman would show his face. And what was worse, in order not to pay a royal, or a scudo, to go in one of the little rooms, nor even to sit in the degrees that are there, he insisted on standing in the middle down below among the gang of porters and carters, giving as his excuse that he was hard of hearing – as if he could have understood the language anyway! But it didn't end there because, at the end of the performance, having received permission from one of the actors, he invited the public to the play for the next day, and named one. But the people, who wanted a different one, began to call out 'Friars, Friars' because they wanted one that they called 'Friars'. Then, turning to his interpreter, my Tambalone asked what they were saying. The interpreter replied that it was the name of a play about friars. Then he, bursting out of his cloak, began to clap his hands as the people were doing and to yell 'Friars, Friars'. But at this racket the people turned on him, thinking him to be a Spaniard, and began to whistle at him in such a fashion that I don't think he'll ever want to go back there again. But that doesn't stop him frequenting the other theatres, and almost always with just one servant.

(2.110)

Galli's story reveals a number of things besides his own dislike of the audiences at the old Curtain. The clothing worn by this mixture of fool (*pantalone*) and Tamburlaine-like grandee (*Tambalone*) once he shed his cloak, for instance, was evidently as alien to the 'porters and carters' in the yard as his foreign speech and conduct. The yard was for working men and the unemployed poor only. Their hostility to Spain gives point to the display which Gondomar laid on at the Fortune in 1621, and suggests how predictable was the success of *A Game at Chesse* at the Globe in 1624. Galli also implies that the not so respectable citizens and gentlemen who did go to the Curtain paid their extra scudi to avoid the mechanicals and sit in the galleries, if they attended that amphitheatre at all. The Curtain was thirty-six years old in 1613, and the Prince Charles's Men playing there did not command the repertories available on Bankside or at the Red Bull and Fortune. Foscarini was venturing into the lowest reaches of playgoing in his incognito exploration of London's crowds.

DIFFERENT KINDS OF PLAYGOER

It has long been a standard assumption that the two decades from 1599 to 1619 saw major changes in playgoing. The records of gentlemanly playgoers give no direct indication of the nature of these changes, and since all the changes relate to the gentry, the privileged section of society, the other kinds of evidence need cautious analysis. In essence the standard assumption is that once the boy companies reopened at Paul's and the Blackfriars after 1599 some version of what Alfred Harbage called the rival traditions developed – rival repertoires, with distinct preferences for types of play and types of staging, and audiences from different sections of society. This view assumes that the boy companies drew their support from courtiers, gallants and law students, and were satirical about the city and citizens, while the amphitheatre companies drew their support chiefly from citizens and upheld the values of the city. The courtiers were served one kind of play, the citizens another. Once the boy companies fully established themselves at the hall playhouses in 1600 they developed a distinct repertoire of new plays while the amphitheatre companies in the main clung to the old favourites such as *The Spanish Tragedy* and *Faustus*. When Shakespeare's company acquired the Blackfriars from the boys in 1609 they gradually developed a courtier repertoire and perpetuated the division, so that the halls played for courtiers and the gentry while the amphitheatres played for citizens.[31]

There is no doubt that this is too simple a history. It is based partly on the intensely competitive publicity campaign which the boy company poets mounted in the early years of the seventeenth century, and partly from the fact that, because the chief buyers of playbooks were courtiers and law students, many more plays from the courtier end of the range have survived than have plays from the Red Bull and Fortune repertoire. Some of the features in this history do have a basis in fact, and confirm the broad assumption that from 1599 on the composition of audiences at different playhouses diverged quite markedly. But the divergences were more a branching out than a simple fork. Paul's boys differed from the Blackfriars boys. The Globe repertory differed from the Red Bull. The Cockpit differed from the King's Men at Blackfriars. None of these differences remained constant. The evidence needs sifting with care. It certainly infiltrates the history of changing play fashions which is the subject of chapter 5.

Poets writing for the boy companies, especially the boys at Blackfriars, went to great lengths to emphasise what a different clientele they enjoyed compared with the crowds at the Middlesex or Surrey playhouses. Marston started by calling the Paul's audience a 'choise selected influence' (2.46) in 1600, and brought in the point about freedom from the stench of garlic there which Dekker took up and repeated throughout the decade in his references to stinkards at the amphitheatres. In 1607 Beaumont's *Knight of the Burning Pestle* for the Blackfriars boys based itself entirely on exploitation of the indoor playhouse's gentlemanly affiliations to make fun of naive citizens. His Induction even made a game of exploiting the playhouse's reputation for mocking the city in its opening lines. The prologue begins

> From all that's neere the Court, from all that's great,
> Within the compasse of the Citty-wals
> We now have brought our Sceane.[32]

and is immediately interrupted by the angry Grocer who climbs on stage to voice his objection to the idea that city affairs are not great, giving it point by the nature of his objections. The boy prologue speaks of 'the noble City' and of the Grocer as 'an understanding man' without him grasping any inkling of the sarcasms:

CITIZEN. Hold your peace good-man boy.
PROLOGUE. What do you meane sir?
CITIZEN. That you have no good meaning: This seven yeares there hath beene playes at this house, I have observed it, you have still girds at Citizens; and now you call your play, *The London Marchant*. Downe with your Title boy, downe with your Title.

PROLOGUE. Are you a member of the noble Citty?

CITIZEN. I am.

PROLOGUE. And a Free-man?

CITIZEN. Yes, and a Grocer.

PROLOGUE. So Grocer, then by your sweet favour, we intend no abuse to the Citty.

CITIZEN. No sir, yes sir, if you were not resolv'd to play the Jacks, what need you study for new subjects, purposely to abuse your betters? why could not you be contented, as well as others, with the legend of *Whittington*, or the life and death of sir *Thomas Gresham?* with the building of the Royal Exchange? or the story of Queene *Elenor*, with the rearing of London bridge upon woolsackes?

PROLOGUE. You seeme to be an understanding man.

Beaumont certainly thought that the 'sweet favour', or face, of the sugar-selling Grocer was a sufficiently unfamiliar sight at the Blackfriars in 1607 to warrant introducing him as a stranger to the hall playhouses, and making him the butt of a Blackfriars audience. The play, however, did not succeed at its one performance because, according to its publisher in 1613, the audience 'not understanding the privy mark of *Ironie* about it . . . utterly rejected it'. From this it could be inferred that there were too many citizens present to enjoy such an anti-citizen joke, though other views are possible. Harbage thought that the mockery of citizens was not savage enough to satisfy an exclusively 'gentle' audience. More evidence is needed.

Some of the boy company plays certainly did have girds against citizens, but they also satirised gallants, lawyers and women. Tucca's recantation in the epilogue of *Satiromastix*, performed at both Paul's and the Globe, includes an apology for 'the opinion which I helde of Courtiers, Ladies, and Cittizens, when once (in an assembly of Friars) I railde upon them' (2.41). The Poetomachia or War of the Theatres, to which *Satiromastix* belongs, promoted a particular fashion for 'railing'. Railing flourished, especially in some of the city comedies of the whole period from 1599 to 1614, and its targets included many more types than citizens and their wives. They included the puritanical Mistress Purge of *The Family of Love* (1602), who complains,

> Hither I come from out the harmless fold
> To have my good name eaten up by wolves:
> See, how they grin! (2.53)

but these sheep-eating wolves were not courtiers deriding citizens. In the Induction to Day's *Isle of Gulls* a set of gallants whose taste is said to be for 'rayling, and invectives' ask of the play 'ist any thing Criticall?

Are Lawyers fees, and Cittizens wives laid open in it: I love to heare
vice anotomizd, & abuse let blood in the maister vaine, is there any
great mans life charactred in it?' The prologue-speaker of course denies
that there is any such material in his play, though the published text
suggests that the censor did not agree with him.

Jonson was the first promoter of the fashion for railing, as he
acknowledged in his prologue to *Volpone* in 1605. There he denies the
claim that 'All he writes, is rayling' while clinging to his disapproval
of the more common fashions:

> . . . thus much I can give you, as a token
> Of his PLAYES worth, No eggs are broken;
> Nor quaking Custards with feirce teeth affrighted,
> Wherewith your rout are so delighted.

Jonson was technically a citizen himself until 1619, and *Volpone* was
written for Shakespeare's company at the Globe. His contribution to
the divergence of playhouse repertoires was not a matter of simple
alignment with courtiers and gallants at the indoor playhouses.

The fashion for railing lost much of its impetus when the boy companies faded from the scene. Heywood gave it a valediction in his *Apology
for Actors*, and a similar disclaimer on behalf of the King's Men was
offered to the king in the epilogue to the revival of *Mucedorus* which
Shakespeare's company presented at Whitehall in February 1611.[33]
Railing was a fashion most visible in the written texts, and there is
not a great deal of evidence to show how closely it reflected audience
tastes or the social composition of playgoers. Since the poets railed at
courtiers and lawyers as well as at citizens it would be wrong to single
out 'girds at citizens' as a thorough confirmation of Beaumont's expectations about the non-citizen audience at Blackfriars. There is no firm
evidence in the repertory to show that citizens stayed away from the
boy company playhouses. It is true that while Jonson acknowledged
the likely presence of an artisan foreman in the remotest gallery at the
Blackfriars, the great majority of people identifiable as playgoers at
the Blackfriars, the Cockpit and Salisbury Court are gentry. Yet for all
the easily identified focus on Inns of Court men and other lawyers,
and gallants, their absence from these locations is as unlikely as their
absence from the amphitheatres. It is true that, with Peacham's fictional city madam excepted, amongst the large number of gallants
and nobles recorded as visiting these playhouse there are very few
named citizens. On the other hand, while the Blackfriars boys' plays
made fun of citizen tastes the Paul's company seems to have expected
a substantial citizen presence at their plays. At the Whitefriars, the

hall playhouse used for a while by the youths of the Blackfriars in 1610–11, a mix of gallants and citizens was openly acknowledged. Robert Daborne's Epistle 'To the Knowing Reader' prefixed to his *A Christian Turned Turk* in 1612 defended the play against 'the contempt is throwne upon it by silken gulls and ignorant Cittizens'. Foolish gallants in their privileged silks and ignorant citizens were equally guilty, in Daborne's view, of rejecting his work. The mix he ascribes this attitude to is significant, not just in their shared view of his play but in their predominant presence in the audience.

The strongest material basis for assuming that there must have been a divergence in the social composition of audiences at the different types of playhouse remains the price of admission. Galli's comments on the audience at the Curtain in 1613 indicate that single pennies were enough to divide the porters and carters in the yard from the citizens and gentry in the galleries. Such a division must have been far more acute when a playhouse had no standing-room at all and charged for the cheapest seat in the furthermost gallery the same price as could gain the best place at an amphitheatre. Merchants and wealthier citizens could afford the indoor playhouses (Beaumont's Grocer is tricked into paying more than £1 in all for his pleasure at the Blackfriars), but distinctly few of the apprentices and serving-men could. Circumstantial evidence presented below suggests that the mob of apprentices who smashed the Cockpit in 1617 were driven by the removal of its plays to a venue where they could no longer afford them. Jonson mentions a 'shop's foreman' paying sixpence at Blackfriars for a place in the top gallery, but this minimum price could bother even a gentleman. Ann Halkett's decision to arrange parties of ladies to go to the plays was spurred by her overhearing some gentlemen complain how much it cost them to escort ladies.

A link between the divergent repertories and divergent playgoers after Shakespeare's company began using the Blackfriars can be charted to some extent. It may not have been gentlemen whom Jonson particularly had in mind when he mocked the playgoers at the Hope who stayed loyal to *The Spanish Tragedy* and *Titus Andronicus* twenty-five or thirty years after their first success (2.112). On the other hand it was probably not a feeling that their social territory had been invaded that drew two butchers into trouble for 'abusing certen gentlemen' at the Fortune in 1611.[34] Shakespeare's company used both Blackfriars and the Globe alternately in winter and summer for thirty-three years up to the closure. Companies proved capable of moving from the Red Bull amphitheatre to the Cockpit's hall with no sign of social discomfort except perhaps to the apprentices who could not follow them.

The divergence was gradual and unemphatic. But it grew more and more distinct as the number of hall playhouses used by adult companies increased. The gentry who kept commonplace books with tags from plays and who paid the price of a bench at the Blackfriars or Cockpit certainly bought far more of the Blackfriars productions than Red Bull plays. Of the 500 or so plays published in Charles's reign, 150 name on the titlepage the playhouse at which the play was performed. Most frequently named was the Blackfriars. The Red Bull was named only six times, four of them for old plays from the period before 1619.[35]

Inns of Court students in particular seem to have confined themselves to the hall playhouses and their repertoire of playbooks. Of the few students who have left lists of their books, four had Jonson's folio *Works*. Francis Lenton's account of an idle law student asserted that

> Instead of *Perkins* pedlers French, he sayes
> He better loves Ben: Johnson's books of Playes.

The same young idler, according to Lenton, always kept to the expensive urban playhouses (2.157). Lenton's parodic account is confirmed with some precision by John Greene's diary for 1635, which records numerous visits by groups of students to the Blackfriars and the Cockpit, but no other playhouses.[36] Edward Heath's scrupulously kept accounts, which note the purchase of ten playbooks, and forty-nine visits to playhouses between 1629 and 1631, list sums never less than one shilling and sixpence or two shillings each time, which are hall prices.[37] Sir Humphrey Mildmay through the 1630s went to the Globe when the King's Men were playing there instead of the Blackfriars, but otherwise seems never to have gone to an amphitheatre. Amongst his fifty-seven visits he specifies eighteen visits to Blackfriars, four to the Globe and four to the Cockpit.[38]

The evidence consistently says that by 1630 – though not much before – the amphitheatres in the northern suburbs, the Red Bull and Fortune, served a distinctly less gentlemanly clientele than the hall playhouses in the city, the Blackfriars, Cockpit and Salisbury Court, and in summer the Globe on Bankside. The fact that the hall playhouses could perform plays taken from the amphitheatres, not only Globe plays at the Blackfriars but Red Bull plays at the Cockpit, suggests that the division was more of social class than audience taste. That in turn implies that the price of admission had more effect than any class loyalty shown for the specific repertoires.

16. An audience for William Alabaster's *Roxana*, 1632, from a set of boxes
on the titlepage containing small engravings. It probably depicts a hall
playhouse, possibly the Cockpit in Drury Lane (1616–64).

Evidence for the preferences of real playgoers such as Greene, Heath and Mildmay is backed by the resurgence in the 1630s of jibes at citizens and the Red Bull repertory. This resurgence, startlingly close to Beaumont's satire in *The Knight of the Burning Pestle*, which was itself revived and reprinted in 1635, may help to explain the new crop of references to citizen playgoers and their tastes in those years. The Red Bull in particular became a joke to the hall playhouse patrons for its old-fashioned repertoire of heroic military plays. Cowley's play *The Guardian*, written for performance at Cambridge as late as 1642, speaks of someone roaring 'like *Tamerlin* at the Bull' (1650, C3v). It was a distinct and vivid tradition, which Edward Howard remembered after the Restoration as a mark of 'the Red Bull writers, with their drums, Trumpets, Battels, and Hero's' (2.222). This was the fashion which repelled the erudite sons of Ben such as Jasper Mayne (2.196). A verse written in 1638 for Thomas Randolph's posthumous collection of his poems speaks of 'some vaine City gull' at the Red Bull, in contrast, like Massinger's city madam, to the court gulls who went to the Blackfriars and Cockpit. This too must have been socially inspired criticism rather than condemnation of a feeble repertoire, since the gentry at the Cockpit welcomed Red Bull plays such as *The Jew of Malta* and *The Rape of Lucrece*. This is a question to be examined more thoroughly in chapter 5.

Citizen and working-class playgoers by the 1630s had their own playhouses and their own repertoire with some distinctive features. It was predominantly masculine and heroic, though it was by no means entirely old-fashioned. Its favoured plays formed part of the nostalgic worship of Elizabethan glories which was rooted firmly in present troubles. The difference of this audience from those of the hall playhouses in social composition can be registered by setting against it Aston Cockayne's *Obstinate Lady*. This play was written before 1639, probably for the Salisbury Court playhouse (in 3.2 a character speaks of escorting a lady to the Blackfriars or Cockpit). Its prologue emphasises the contrast between amphitheatre plays and the fare for ladies and gentlemen which Cockayne's hall playhouse provides.

> Troth Gentlemen, we know that now adayes
> Some come to take up Wenches at our Playes;
> It is not in our power to please their sence,
> We wish they may go discontented hence.
> And many Gallants do come hither, we think
> To sleep and to digest there too much drink:
> We may please them: for we will not molest
> With Drums and Trumpets any of their rest.

If perfum'd Wantons do for eighteen pence,
Expect an Angel, and alone go hence;
We shall be glad with all our hearts: for we
Had rather have their Room then companie;
For many an honest Gentleman is gon
Away for want of place, as looke you yon!
We guess some of you Ladies, hither come
To meet your Servants, wh'are at dice at home.   (2.204)

By the time the playhouses were ordered to be closed the social range stretched from the boxes at Blackfriars, which might contain the Countess of Essex, the Duke of Lennox or the Lord Chamberlain (see 2.194), to the nameless chimney boys and apple-wives in the yard of the Fortune or Red Bull.

The available evidence does not give much help in fixing how early this division of playhouse clientele began, if only because the branching was gradual and intricate. The hall playhouses, notably Blackfriars, started high in the market and remained at the top when the King's Men took it over, though the company never changed its practice of closing the Blackfriars from May to September while the court was in the country and the lawcourts were not in session, and played instead to the broader spread of audience at the Globe. The amphitheatres which stayed in use through the winter enjoyed audiences more constant than the companies which played to them. Some plays, familiar as the typical fare of one particular playhouse, seem to have stayed at the playhouse even when the playing company changed.

In the 1630s the pattern that divided the three amphitheatres from the hall playhouses was not a simple one in terms of the companies that occupied them and therefore the plays they could offer. What the effect of that was on the social groupings of their audiences is unclear. The Fortune and Red Bull, playing through the year, had the reputation as 'citizen' playhouses, while the Blackfriars, the Cockpit and the Salisbury Court halls undoubtedly aimed at the richer clients. Where that left the Globe, playing for half the year when the fewest nobles and lawyers were in town, is equally unclear. Moreover, in the thirteen years between the opening of the Salisbury Court and the general closure, the companies on more than one occasion switched their playing not only between one amphitheatre and the other but between amphitheatre and hall playhouse. This table shows what happened to the four and later five companies that ran in addition to the King's Men through these years (QH = Queen Henrietta's Men; BB = Beeston's Boys; KR = King's Revels; PC2 = Prince Charles's (II) Men; Boh = Queen of Bohemia's Men; Rev = The Red Bull Revels Company):

Year	1629–31	1631–34	1634–37	1637–40	1640–42
Cockpit	QH	QH	QH	BB	BB
Salisbury Court	KR	PC2	KR	QH	QH
Fortune	Boh	KR	Rev	Rev	PC2
Red Bull	Rev	Rev	PC2	PC2	Rev

Four different companies used the Fortune, and three the Red Bull and the Salisbury Court, while two switched from hall to amphitheatre, and in one case later moved back again. Queen Henrietta's Men, almost equal to the King's in the early 1630s, shifted to the smaller hall playhouse during the massive plague epidemic of 1636–8, when Christopher Beeston replaced them with a company of six adult players and a gaggle of youths.

On the whole, the amphitheatre companies, however much they changed playhouses, seem to have settled as early as 1611 into the type of repertoire which they sustained until the closure and which fixed the identity of their audiences as consistent with the poorer working-class suburbs where they were lodged. They retained the traditional jig at the end of their plays, for instance, a practice the hall playhouses never indulged in and which the Globe company abandoned before 1614. That distinction belongs more to the history of audience tastes, which will be considered in chapter 5. This is only secondary evidence for the division of social classes between the playhouses.

4

Mental composition

Fixing the mental composition of the early playgoers in this period with any precision is not an easy or straightforward task. It is difficult first because individual responses, like the individuals themselves, can vary so widely from one another and from the collective emotions of an audience as playhouse crowd, and secondly because almost nobody bothers to put down in writing what they feel about a play while they experience it. Even the process of writing the memory of the event down is subsequent to, and therefore variable from, the immediate experience. Some recent critics have resisted the circular argument that finds audience response written into the plays, and makes easy assumptions from what it finds there. We have good reason to be grateful for the approach of scholars like Kent Cartwright, Thomas Cartelli and Jeremy Lopez who have carefully avoided the circular temptation that embraces the plays and their audiences. Analysis of some of the original responses by scholars such as Marion Trousdale and Charles Whitney (see Bibliography) have provided some handsome refinements to the broad perspectives offered in the first two editions of this book. A great deal, however, remains to be done to identify the original mindsets, and we can only hope that this third edition will help to generate further studies of the impact performances had on individual playgoers. We start here, though, with what tangible evidence there is about the context of the early mental constructs so far as we can see them differing from those of today.

The first point to make is the priority and the prevalence not just of aural memory but of the playgoer's ability to remember verse. Michael Drayton begins a verse epistle to his friend Henry Reynolds, written some time near the end of James's reign, with reminiscences of the long talks they used to enjoy by the fireside in winter. They would

> Now talk of this, and then discoursed of that,
> Spoke our own verses, 'twixt our selves, if not
> Other men's lines, which we by chance had got,

95

Or some Stage pieces famous long before,
Of which your happy memory had store. (2.121)

Drayton had written plays for Henslowe at the turn of the century.
Reynolds was the author of *Torquato Tasso's Aminta Englisht* (1628)
and other works in verse. Many other instances exist of gentry citing

17. Michael Drayton in 1599.

familiar quotations like John Harington's paraphrase of Jaques's seven ages of man stage piece to Cecil. Spoken verse was a feature in the literate memory.

This game of quoting verse from memory, whether of written texts or performed texts, was far more widespread and more far-reaching than in men like Drayton or Harington. Jonson had a formidable memory for poetry and drama. In *Discoveries* he claimed that 'I my selfe could in my youth, have repeated all, that ever I had made; and so continued, till I was past fortie: Since, it is much decay'd in me. Yet I can repeate whole books that I have read, and *Poems*, of some selected friends, which I have lik'd to charge my memory with.'[1]

Learning by rote was a widespread practice in schools, though not one uniformly recommended. It led to capacities of the kind that John Manningham recorded when visiting his cousin Richard, the squire of Bradbourne, in March 1602:

My cosen repeated *memoriter* almost the first Booke of Virg[ils] Æniads. And this day he rehersed without booke verry neere the whole 2[n]d booke of the Aeneads, viz. 630 verses without missing one word. A singular memory in a man of his age: 62.[2]

Possibly it is a measure of the mental capacity of Elizabethan playgoers that Manningham's cousin's feat should be thought 'singular', even with the impoverishment that Jonson acknowledged comes with age. If so, the feat of an Alleyn or Burbage, who had to memorise up to 800 lines for each play in a repertory used to presenting more than a dozen different plays each month must have been singular indeed.

What these feats of memory chiefly tell us about the early playgoers is their habitual assumption that poetry was words for speech rather than the page. The written word was no more than a means of making records of what was spoken. It was yet to acquire the authority that the last four hundred years of the printed word can now claim. Education and literacy were still rare enough and the price of books high enough to make the spoken word far more the central mode of communication than it is now. It was not just illiterate housewives who went to plays because they could hear stage fictions more easily than they could read them. The poets themselves wrote to be heard rather than to be read. The hearing of plays, implicit in the Latin origin of the word 'audience', was the basic expectation in the minds of all Shakespearean playgoers.

Yet even hearing and the capacity to memorise long passages of verse was a quality which varied across the social range of playgoers. Poets wrote to be heard by people like John Manningham, whose diary contains one brief reference to a play, *Twelfth Night* at Middle Temple

Hall in 1602, amongst forty-seven summaries of sermons he heard. The
summaries run to as much as two thousand words for each sermon,
giving the gist of the whole argument as Manningham remembered
it some time after the event, a notable feat both of concentration and
of memory. He clearly heard and thought about the sermons much
better than Lucius Cary, Lord Falkland, registered the plays that he
went to in Caroline times. Cary wrote to Thomas Carew thanking
him for the printed text of a play, the reading of which improved on
the performance because 'at the single hearing . . . mine eares could
not catch half the wordes'.[3] Both of these educated playgoers, whatever
their strength of memory or hearing, thought of the essential medium
as words spoken. That, perhaps, was one consequence of education.

There is no doubt that a basic division among playgoers was created
by differences in the level of education. At the less educated levels,
even as early as the 1570s, the eye prevailed over the ear and spectacle rivalled poetry as the main playhouse attraction. Tamburlaine
in his golden chariot being hauled by four kings was the most spectacular memory of the play for John Davies of Hereford (*Wittes
Pilgrimage*, I4v). The 'understanding' men of the yard and their preference for visual treats over wit or poetry became a familiar jibe amongst
the learned in the seventeenth century.

The mental composition of any individual playgoer must have varied according to a complex of factors ranging from the physical condition of the playgoer's feet or stomach, or the hat worn by the playgoer
in front, to the hearer's familiarity with Ovid or Holinshed. Education
and taste in reading, the contrasting social and political allegiances
of blue apron and flat cap culture against the court gallants and law
students, all influenced the kind of play written for the different playhouses and must to some extent therefore reflect at least the poets' and
players' expectations of their customers. It needed a fair degree of confidence about social distinctions, for instance, to allow the King's Men at
the Blackfriars under Charles to direct the final speech of Massinger's
The City Madam at the women in their audiences. In his conclusion,
Massinger bluntly underlined his moral that 'our city dames' should
learn the decorums of their modest social level and not try to imitate
the ladies of the court,

> . . . and willingly to confesse
> In their habits, manners, and their highest port,
> A distance 'twixt the City, and the Court.

Massinger's title, 'The City Madam', was coined as an antonym for a
species quite opposite to the court lady, and the play is in large part an

attempt to assert the more modest pattern of behaviour proper to the wife of a city merchant. She was, for instance, expected not to occupy a box at Blackfriars where she could be ogled by gallants. That was reserved for ladies of the court. It is not at all clear whether Massinger expected his moral to be registered by an audience made up of court ladies who would applaud his point, or alternatively to shame an audience of city madams, like Peacham's merchant wife with her apprentice, boxed in amongst the gallants with her nip or Nim. Probably he expected both. What is certain is that he did expect both kinds to accept his moralising. There were prejudices as well as influences in the Shakespearean playgoer's mind, as divergent as the playgoers themselves.

Unfortunately, social prejudices like Massinger's are more accessible in the plays than they are apparent in the playgoers. In consequence, apart from the anti-Spanish prejudice evident in Galli's account of the Curtain audience in 1613 and *A Game of Chesse* at the Globe in 1624, most of the evidence says more about the poets than their hearers. The range in education is far more tangible. It might be expected, for instance, that Webster's social allegiance as the crabbed citizen 'playwright-cartwright' held him among Henslowe's collaborative writers at first, and ensured that *The White Devil* appeared at the Red Bull in the winter of 1610–11. It may not have been just the poor conditions of its staging but its author's intellectual pretensions that brought his next play, *The Duchess of Malfi*, to the Blackfriars in 1614. His resentment over the amphitheatre performance in winter ('so open and black a theatre' 2.100) and its dull audience might have sent him to a hall playhouse for his next play in any case. But some features of *The Duchess*, and one learned echo in particular, suggest that he hoped to cater specifically for the more learned hearers at the Blackfriars.

Webster's plays are full of verbal echoes, ranging from such standard gentlemanly reading as Sidney's *Arcadia* through the slightly more esoteric philosophical musings of Montaigne to the decidedly intellectual rarity of William Alexander's *Four Monarchic Tragedies* published in 1607. He could have expected few of his quotations from these sources to be identified by even the most alert and well-read hearer. Even at Blackfriars where Fletcherian tragicomedy took much of its strength from that book most popular with gentlemanly hearers, *The Arcadia*, precise verbal echoes would not have been easy to catch. Fletcher, a great contriver of plots that tested moral extremes, depended on *The Arcadia* for features of his stories (men disguised as women, tyrants in love) for their moral crises rather than any verbal citations of Sidney. But Webster put one especially emphatic echo into the final couplet of *The Duchess of Malfi* which is distinct from all the others, and which he almost certainly did expect a few educated hearers at Blackfriars to understand.

Ostensibly the play's final couplet offers an epigrammatic summary of the play's moral:

> *Integrity of life is fame's best friend,*
> *Which nobly, beyond death, shall crown the end.*

The Duchess, in other words, will live on in human memory because her life had integrity, whereas the corrupted characters such as the Cardinal will be laid by and never thought on. The first quarto italicised the couplet as a moral apophthegm. As a moralising couplet it expresses the sentiment we find also in the Lord Mayor's pageant *Monuments of Honour* which Webster composed in 1624 and which includes this memorial for Prince Henry:

> Such was this prince, such are the noble hearts,
> Who when they dye, yet dye not in all parts:
> But from the *Integrety* of a Brave Mind,
> Leave a most Cleere and Eminent Fate behind.[4]

This, like the concluding couplet of *The Duchess*, alludes quite unambiguously to the opening of Horace's ode, Book 1, no. 22. The most famous of all the Horatian Odes, quoted twice by William Lily in his school grammar book *Brevissima Institutio*, 1570, it was referred to in *Titus Andronicus* 4.2.20–1, when Demetrius reads a scroll: '*Demetrius. Integer vitae, scelerisque purus,* / *Non eget Mauri iaculis, nec arcu.* / *Chiron.* O, 'tis a verse in Horace . . .' It was a tag familiar to anyone who had stayed at school until the sixth form under the Winchester syllabus or the fifth form of the Eton syllabus.[5] On its own the phrase would evoke Horace to any educated hearer. But a recollection of the original ode should also bring to mind a point which horribly complicates the epigram that rounds off the play. Beginning '*Integer vitae . . .*' the ode says that a pure life will keep a man immune from mortal harm since not even a wolf will attack a man recognised as possessing *integer vitae*. An audience which picked up that allusion might also recall that in the play Ferdinand, the brother who killed the Duchess, thought he was a wolf; he died of lycanthropy. When Horace was a familiar memory, that oddly macabre detail about crazy Ferdinand's death suddenly gained a new resonance. It is hard not to believe that Webster expected the more educated in his audience to pick up the context of his allusion to Horace and to realise that it reverses the ostensible point of the couplet. The Duchess killed by a wolf could hardly have been possessed of the true integrity of life which Horace praised. Her secret and morganatic marriage to her steward Antonio called her integrity into question. Webster clearly does seem to have been aiming at a split-level audience, offering one thing, the routine epigrammatic moral, for the bulk of the uneducated in his audience, and an oblique *lusus* for the learned to brood on.

Webster certainly found his element at Blackfriars. Burbage made Ferdinand one of his better-known parts, and Webster's own presence in the Blackfriars audiences became notable enough to get him included in Fitzgeoffery's *Notes from Blackfriars* in 1617. The problem is what we can make of the evidence that he deliberately wrote for two levels of education in the audiences there. When he reused the phrase from Horace on behalf of the London citizens in *Monuments of Honour* he intended it unambiguously, since in an elegy for Prince Henry he had no reason to do otherwise. Conceivably he meant to be equally unambiguous in *The Duchess*, though I think that unlikely.

On the whole, Webster aside, there is more evidence of playwrights making covert allusions to contemporary people and events than there is of allusions to passages or phrases from well-known books. The 'application' which Jonson called a menial trade was the characteristic style of the Poetomachia at the turn of the century, and made great use of familiar phrases from plays written by the contestants in the war. Such allusions were of course to current plays fresh in the memory of the playgoers, and expected no more education in the audience than frequent playgoing. The same applies to the echoes and parodies of famous plays like *Tamburlaine*, *The Spanish Tragedy* and *Hamlet*. Jonson's *The Alchemist* expects the spectators to know Kyd's play much better than the Broughton that Doll quotes in her mad fit or the writers on alchemy so lavishly quoted in the play. This kind of echo extends, at its farthest reaches, into the exploitation of familiar stage stereotypes like Touchstone's inversion of the country clown type in *As You Like It*, and the similar exchange of stereotypes between the simple soldier Othello and the blackhearted Machiavel Iago, or more broadly the adaptation of Shakespearean models of character and situation in the early Beaumont and Fletcher plays. Writers used far more allusion to the familiar stage repertoire than to even the most standard of the schoolbooks.

The wealth of allusion in Shakespearean drama, where it does not point to stage plays, has in all likelihood much more to say about the poets than their hearers, and probably more still about modern readers. To assess this likelihood it is necessary to scan the evidence, first about the conflict between hearers of the words and beholders of the spectacle, next about the minds of the learned few, and then about the very few detailed opinions of plays in performance which any of the Shakespearean playgoers actually did put on record.

AUDIENCES OR SPECTATORS

English lacks an adequate word for the feast of the senses which playgoing ought to provide, and the inadequacy is reflected in the words for playgoers. 'Audience' harks back to its judicial sense of giving a case a hearing. 'Spectators' belong at football matches where the eye takes in more information than the ear. There is no English term which acknowledges the full experience of both hearing and seeing the complete 'action' of a play. 'Audience' moreover implies a crowd, whereas a spectator is an individual. The emotional power shared by a crowd is more powerful but far less easily recorded than an individual's response to a play.

This distinction, between playgoers as a crowd and the individual spectator, is a simple consequence of the fact that all the relevant terms in Latin and English relate to specific senses. From the Latin *audire*, to listen, come *audiens*, hearing, *audientia*, an audience or the act of giving a hearing to something, and *auditor*, a hearer or student. From *specere*, to see, and *spectare*, to watch, come *spectaculum*, a show or play, or theatre, and *spectator*, a spectator or critic. English kept these Latin roots, despite a campaign for English alternatives waged in the later sixteenth century when the drama was beginning to demand a new vocabulary. Even then all that George Puttenham and the enemies of 'inkhorn terms' could come up with were 'hearers' and 'beholders'.[6] They never managed to evolve a term encompassing the feast of the conjoined senses which drama began to offer in Shakespeare's time. Their struggles to find a terminology appropriate to playgoing, and the triumph of the collective 'audience' over the individual 'spectator' tell us quite a lot about the mental equipment of the crowds at the Shakespearean playhouses.

The survival of 'audience' today as the nearest thing to an all-embracing term for playgoers became a Pyrrhic victory for the poets in the light of the new kind of two-dimensional operatic staging introduced to England at the Restoration and which has been dominant ever since. Understandably the writers valued their poetry more than the 'shows' of the common stage, and consequently rated hearing far above seeing as the vital sense for the playgoer. Every time Jonson called his audience 'spectators', as he almost invariably did, he was covertly sneering at the debased preference for stage spectacle rather than the poetic 'soul' of the play, which he claimed they could only find by listening to his words.

The idea of seeing rather than hearing men speak is a joke reiterated throughout *A Midsummer Night's Dream*. When Bottom as Pyramus declared 'I see a voice', he was renewing his own confusion when he awoke from his dream and misquoted the Bishops' Bible with 'the eye of man hath not heard, the ear of man hath not seen' (4.1). Shakespeare's play with its mockery of stage realism anticipated Jonson's more strident derision for those who use their eyes instead of their ears. The modern usage of what the poets, alert as they all were to the Latin terminology, felt was the respectable term, 'audience', conceals what Jonson thought was a heavy defeat for stage poetry at the hands of Inigo Jones with his spectacular masques and of the players with their mindless 'shows'. Hamlet's condemnation of dumbshows, an epitome of spectacle replacing speech, was buried by their continuing popularity through Stuart times.

Jonson's quarrel with Inigo Jones, who Jonson alleged served his royal master by reducing the secrets of universal harmony to mathematical tables, is deservedly well known. But his scorn for Jones's principles is soaked in the bitterness of a defeat which had set Jonson against the common stage even before he turned against the architect of the royal masques. His contempt, which led him in 1626 to hail Jones's work for the eye as mindless decoration – 'Oh, to make Boardes to speake! There is a taske / Painting & Carpentry are ye Soule of Masque'[7] – is implicit in the theory of art that he voiced as early as *Poetaster* and his prologue to *Cynthia's Revels* in 1600. The latter play, written as an exhibition of the new boy company's skills at Blackfriars, Jonson designed as an emphatic departure from the traditions the adult players of the Globe were catering for. He hoped that the wealthier audience filtered in at the Blackfriars through its higher admission prices might be more receptive to his poetry.

> . . . if gracious silence, sweet attention,
> Quicke sight, and quicker apprehension
> (The lights of judgements throne) shine any where;
> Our doubtful author hopes this is their sphere.
> And therefore opens he himselfe to those;
> To other weaker beames, his labours close:
> As loth to prostitute their virgin straine,
> To ev'ry vulgar, and adult'rate braine.
> In this alone, his MUSE her sweetnesse hath,
> Shee shunnes the print of any beaten path;

> And proves new wayes to come to learned eares:
> . . . his *poesie*, which (he knowes) affoords
> Words, above action: matter, above words.[8]

The vulgar and adulterate brains thronging the amphitheatres are debarred from judging the poetry which only learned ears can apprehend. The poet's hierarchy begins with 'action', which is all the 'weaker beames' see, ascends to the words which 'learned eares' can understand, and culminates in the 'matter', the idea which elsewhere he calls the 'soule' of his play.

By the time Jonson wrote *The Staple of News* in 1626 his view was less hopeful and more blunt. The two plays he wrote before he left playwriting for the ten-year silence which ended with *The Staple of News*, particularly *Bartholomew Fair*, gave the amphitheatre audiences a thoroughgoing test of their role as judges and predictably anticipated their failure. His prologue for *The Staple of News* ten years later has the near-despairing optimism of a writer who expects the worst but still feels obliged to make the effort.

> Would you were come to heare, not see a Play.
> Though we his *Actors* must provide for those,
> Who are our guests, here, in the way of showes,
> The maker hath not so; he'ld have you wise,
> Much rather by your eares, then by your eyes.[9]

The poet was at odds with his medium, and bluntly admitted it. Poetry was losing to shows on the public stages. Spectators were triumphing over listeners.

Jonson's was an extreme view, and he went against traditions both classical and modern to uphold it. Some of his contemporaries knew and approved his principle: Dekker and Heywood made the same point explicitly while Marston, Beaumont and others implied it. Shakespeare acknowledged it, but less emphatically. The issue developed in the 1570s and 1580s when the professional acting companies first set themselves up permanently in London. It grew into a question of the proper terminology for playgoing, usually as a choice between one sense and the other, and one term or another. A surprising range of terms was available, and the blanket word 'audience' did not predominate nearly so much it does now. The concept of huge and regular urban gatherings at plays was new enough to provoke a sensitive and discriminating variety of terms which only slowly narrowed down to the current usage. The shifts in terminology tell us something about the poets and their patrons in the playhouses.

The idea that poets wrote plays as poetry rather than spectacle and more as a treat of intellectual inventiveness than a traditional festival started early in the sixteenth century, mostly for the surviving court plays. A narrow concept, it generated plays like *Magnyfycence, King Johann* and *Gorboduc,* the staging of which kept close to the traditions of academic drama and the plays composed in Latin at the universities for audiences trained to listen intelligently. Their chief requirement was eloquent speech, not dramatic action or scenic extravagance. This tradition survived well into the seventeenth century in university drama and the Senecan closet plays of Kyd, Fulke Greville, Daniel and other poets who never bent so low as to be regular providers of plays for the public stages. Drama in education was customarily treated as an instrument for the teaching of rhetoric. It was a handmaiden of oratory, and its 'action' was technically only the gestures which should accompany the orator's 'pronunciation' of his speeches. Richard Edwardes, Master of the Chapel Children in the 1560s, in the prologue to *Damon and Pithias* written for the court in 1565, described the requirements for a stage play as no more than 'speeches well pronounste, with action lively framed'. Academic circles would have given strong backing to Jonson.

Support from the classics was decidedly mixed. The standard theories of human physiology deriving from Galen and ultimately Aristotle made sight the primary sense, more than hearing, and were quite unequivocal. Andreas Du Laurens, writing a treatise about vision, was understandably partial when he started his third chapter *'That the sight is the noblest of all the rest of the sences'*:

Amongst all the sences, that of the sight, in the common judgement of all the Philosophers, hath been accounted the most noble, perfect, and admirable. The excellencie thereof is to be perceived in an infinite sort of things: but more principally in foure: as first, in respect of the varietie of the objects which it representeth unto the soule: secondly, in respect of the meanes of his operation, which is (as it were) altogether spirituall: thirdly, in respect of his particular object, which is the light, which is the most noble and perfect qualitie that ever God created: and lastly, in respect of the certaintie of his action.

(*A Discourse of the Preservation of the Sight,* trans. Richard Surphlet, 1599, pp. 12–13)

Du Laurens was giving his subject a puff. Yet Robert Burton in *The Anatomy of Melancholy,* also basing his case on the classics and always keen to record any disagreements among his sources, was equally positive about the superiority of sight over hearing. Sight 'sees the whole body at once; by it we learn and discern all things' and consequently it 'is held to be most precious, and the best'. Hearing is 'a most excellent outward sense, *by which we learn and get knowledge'*, but it is less precious than sight.[10]

The only support that Elizabethan physiology gave Jonson was the concept that sight could have a special role in enslaving the reason. As Du Laurens put it,

Yea, tell me, how many soules have lost their libertie through the sight of the eyes? Doe not men say that that little wanton, that blind archer doth enter into our hearts by this doore, and that love is shaped by the glittering glimces which issue out of the eyes, or rather by a certaine subtile and thin spirits, which passe from the heart to the eye through a straite and narrow way very secretly, and having deceived this porter, doe place love within, which by little and little doth make it selfe Lord of the house, and casteth reason out of the doores? (*A Discourse of the Preservation of the Sight*, p. 12)

Jonson might well have reckoned that the seductions of love and the seductions of stage action did the same job of deceiving the rational porter.

Classical drama gave little more support to the poets than classical physiology. To the students and others who came to hear philosophical lectures their Latin name was 'auditor'. Plautus, however, the best-known of the Latin playwrights to Elizabethans, called his audiences watchers rather than hearers. In the prologue to *Amphitruo* and in the final line of the play when he urges them to applaud he names them *spectatores*. The Romans do not seem to have had a settled idea of what name should belong to playgoers. St Augustine, writing in the fourth century in his *Confessions* about the plays he saw as a young man used both *spectator* and *auditor*. His subject was the falsity inherent in the fictions of the '*spectacula theatrica*', where playgoers got pleasure from the fictional miseries of the stage characters. He thought that eyes and ears could be equally deceitful.

The uncertainty of the Latin terminology is not unimportant, because every Elizabethan poet knew the classical writers, and when Puttenham was composing his *Arte of English Poesie*, at the beginnings of commercial London theatre, writers were seriously trying to find exact English equivalents for the Latin terms. Eventually the anti-Catholic prejudice against the use of Latin faded, but it left its mark, and it clarifies the denotations which became interchangeable. 'Plays' and 'players', for instance, gained in credibility and definition by their exact equivalence to '*interludes*' and '*lusores*'. 'Actors' entered only later, muted by the qualification 'stage-actor', because of the place that 'action' held in oratory. Similarly 'shows' stood in for spectacles.

Puttenham translated '*redeunt spectacula mane*' as 'early the shewes returne'.[11]

Although the stages became concerned to offer 'shows' to the 'beholder' who gradually became a 'spectator', the English 'hearer' and its Latin equivalent 'auditor' held on with surprising strength. With the advantage of hindsight we might feel that the contest between speech and spectacle was a foregone conclusion. Long before the proscenium arch's two-dimensional staging and fixed sets the eye was bound to overcome the ear. In 1616 Thomas Gainsford pointed out that 'as an Orator was most forcible in his ellocution; so was an actor in his gesture and personated action',[12] showing which came first in each of the existing two versions of public speech. In the epistle to *The Fawn*, 1606, Marston put 'action' as the poet's main objective. Apologising for the play's appearance in print, he acknowledged that '*Comedies* are writ to be spoken, not read: Remember the life of these things consists in action'. Puttenham had already acknowledged how much at odds 'action' could be with careful listening. The common people, he wrote,

rejoyse much to be at playes and enterludes, and besides their naturall ignorance, have at all such times their eares so attentive to the matter, and their eyes upon the shewes of the stage, that they take little heede to the cunning of the rime, and therefore be as well satisfied with that which is grosse, as with any other finer and more delicate.   (*The Arte of English Poesie*, p. 82)

In the 1570s he was presumably contrasting the poulter's rhyme used by the stage clown with the less thumping rhythms of an orator's prose.

The actor's resources all assumed that the eye was a stronger sense than the ear. Action was visible, role-playing, movement and interplay between characters, the costumes and the standard stage properties, let alone the more openly exhibitionistic 'shows' of swordplay, fireworks and 'discovered' set-pieces, were all designed to hold the eye. So the spectator should have replaced the auditor with ease. But if we make such an assumption we have to ignore not only the survival of 'audience' as the standard word but the vastly greater readiness of Elizabethans to use their ears for all forms of learning. Varro's use of the term 'auditor' for a reader should remind us how normal it was to read aloud. Hamlet, who enters before his 'To be or not to be' speech reading silently, was exceptional in this as in so many of his other habits. The written word was no more than a means of recording speech. Both the collective 'audience' and the singular 'auditor' enjoyed a much longer currency in English than 'spectator', and in Shakespeare's time the competition was on fairly even terms.

The *Oxford English Dictionary* records 'audience' and 'auditory' from the 1370s, and 'auditor' from the 1380s, when Chaucer used it.[13] While 'audience' tended to hold the judicial connotation of a hearing, in the king's court and in the lesser lawcourts, 'auditor' meant simply a listener. The modern number-crunching auditor uses an only mildly perverted form of the original meaning. We have to look beyond *OED* to locate the terms used specifically for playgoers.

In about 1533 a stage direction in the closet interlude *Love* described a stage trick with fireworks which survived for more than a century:

Here the vyse cometh in ronnynge sodenly aboute the place among the audiens with a hye copyn tank on his hed full of squybs fyred.[14]

I have found no other applications of the judicial term to playhouse audiences in the earlier sixteenth century. The anti-Latinate Edwardes wrote of the 'lookers on' in his prologue to *Damon and Pithias* in 1565 and Puttenham favoured 'hearers and beholders', as a kind of doublet. In about 1580, though, Nathaniel Woodes emphatically used the term for hearing which seems to have run parallel to 'spectator' up to at least 1642. The prologue to his morality interlude *The Conflict of Conscience* gives as its author's objective 'to refresh the myndes of them that be the Auditors'. For a while 'auditor' was more current than 'audience', in usage by Gosson and other academically trained writers. Shakespeare used the word exclusively through the 1590s. In *A Midsummer Night's Dream* 3.1.79–80 Puck exclaims 'What, a play toward? I'll be an auditor, / An actor too perhaps'. In *Love's Labours Lost* 5.1.138 and *A Midsummer Night's Dream* 1.2.26 the royal playgoers are quite properly called the 'audience', in a combination of their judicial and playgoing functions. Hall in his satire *Virgidemiarum II* (1597) wrote of a playhouse with a 'dead stroke audience' (2.29), and Marston in his satire *The Scourge of Villainy* a year later registered the influence of university Latin when he described a Cambridge student actor as 'Yon Athens Ape (that can but simperingly / Yaule *auditores humanissimi*' (2.31). He called the playgoers at Paul's for *Antonio and Mellida* (1600) 'select, and most respected Auditours'. In 1603 Middleton wrote in *Father Hubburds Tale* of 'a dull Audience of Stinkards sitting in the Penny Galleries of a Theater' (2.58), and Chapman, retaining the distinction of singular from plural, referred to 'many a moist auditor' in *The Widow's Tears* 4.1.42 (1605). Even Jonson began with an 'auditory' in *The Case is Altered* (1597), and a respectful 'auditors' in *Every Man Out*.

By early in the new century, though, Jonson's point about poetry being for the ear registered, and a more self-conscious usage developed.

Poets said they wrote for ears whereas players merely offered shows. Jonson expected the Blackfriars audience of 1600 to display its superiority by using its ears. In the Induction to *The Isle of Gulls* (1606) Day made a character react in mock horror to the idea of a claque amongst the playgoers, using the exact terminology: 'Doe Poets use to bespeake their Auditory?' (2.66). In 3.2 a foolish gallant speaks of fashioning his discourse 'fit to the ears of my auditorie', and in the prologue Day emphasises the alleged gentility of his audience by pretending to disclaim any 'bawdy and scurrill jests, which neither becomes his modestie to write, nor the eare of a generous Auditory to heare'. Bawdy jokes of course were the antithesis of what a poetically inclined audience would wish to hear. The evidence indicates that the opening of the Blackfriars along with Paul's sprang the social divide amongst playgoers, making the different kinds of fare on offer more distinct than they had been before. There was now such variety that the choice between hearing and seeing became an issue, carrying with it the whole range of options between the different repertories.

Curiously the first writer to use the term 'spectator' appears to have been that most critical of educated and gentlemanly playgoers, Philip Sidney. The first use *OED* records is in the revised *Arcadia*, in an account of a character concerned to watch an 'action':

Plexirtus (so was the bastard called) came thether with fortie horse, onely of purpose to murder this brother; of whose comming he had some advertisement, and thought no eyes of sufficient credite in such a matter, but his owne; and therefore came him selfe to be actor, and spectator.

(*Prose Works*, ed. Feuillerat, I.210–11)

Plexirtus wished to observe in his singular person the fratricide he wished to enact. Sidney made his revision in 1584. The word 'spectator' does not occur in the earlier version of 1580, nor in the *Apologie for Poetry*, written 1581–3. Nonetheless in the *Apologie*, writing of comedy, Sidney uses 'beholder', the same term Puttenham was using a few years earlier, and assumes that playgoing is more for the eye than the ear:

And litle reason hath any man to say, that men learne the evill by seeing it so set out, since as I said before, there is no man living, but by the force truth hath in nature, no sooner seeth these men play their parts, but wisheth them in *Pistrinum*. (III.23)

Sidney goes on to mention the anecdote of the tyrant Alexander Pheraeus who was moved to tears by 'hearkening' to a tragedy, but broadly his assumption is that the eye is the principal instrument at a play. On stage illusion, possibly referring back to his initial translation of Aristotle's *mimesis* as 'a speaking picture', he declares 'the *Poets* persons and dooings, are but pictures, what should be'.

Edmund Spenser was not far from Sidney in these years, and in his youth in London he was a keen playgoer. He too, despite his academic training, accepted the primacy of the eye. In *The Faerie Queene* II.iv.27 he inserted the new word into the dramatic experience with the phrase 'the sad spectator of my Tragedy'. At about the same time Nashe in *Pierce Penilesse* (1592) described the fourth of the standard leisure activities for young men in London as '*seeing* a Playe', and adopted the Latinism in his description of brave Talbot 'newe embalmed with the teares of ten thousand spectators' (2.15). Perhaps it was the arrival of the new term which stimulated awareness in the 1590s of what the alternatives implied. Certainly John Weever chose the right one when he wrote a characteristically crabbed epigram about Hieronymo in *The Spanish Tragedy* biting out his tongue and continuing to speak.

> *Ruffinus* lost his tongue on stage,
> And wot ye how he made it knowne?
> He spittes it out in bloudy rage,
> And told the people he had none:
> The fond spectators said, he acted wrong,
> The dumbest man may say, he hath no tongue.[15]

By 1599 when this was written the difference between hearing and seeing an actor or an action had registered itself firmly. Shakespeare changed his own terminology in 1600 in *Hamlet*, with his first use of the word 'spectator'.

In *Coriolanus* (1608) Volumnia gives patrician instructions to her son on how to perform his second attempt at winning the plebeian votes, in these terms:

> Thy knee bussing the stone (for in such business
> Action is eloquence, and the eyes of th' ignorant
> More learned than the ears).

Arrogant Volumnia claims that it is ignorance that relies more on eyes than ears. The same patrician assumption sat in Hamlet's mind when he warned the players against giving their clowns too much licence, 'that will themselves laugh to set on some quantity of barren spectators to laugh, too'. With the boy companies competing for the more educated audiences, as the educated Hamlet sees it the populist clowns attracted merely spectators, observers of spectacle designed for the eyes of the ignorant. Modern viewers of Shakespeare on screen ought to note Hamlet's contempt, along with his invention of the word 'groundling' for the gaping fish at his feet.

From 1600 onwards Shakespeare abandoned the idea of an auditory and called his customers spectators. In *The Winter's Tale*, where theatre illusion is precisely set out to deceive the eye with a bear on stage and a statue that comes to life,[16] Hermione uses the term for seeing a play as the appropriate one for deception. Her life, she says, was a happy tale and is now sad, 'which is more / Than history can pattern, though devis'd / And play'd to take spectators'.[17] The same kind of 'taking' is present again shortly after, in Time's invitation to the credulous:

> . . . Imagine me,
> Gentle spectators, that I now may be
> In fair Bohemia.

The ease with which sight can be confused by mere appearance, affirmed in Paulina's claim about the moving statue, 'It *appears* she lives', was anticipated by the gentleman of the preceding scene when he described the reunion of Leontes and Camillo:

A notable passion of wonder appear'd in them; but the wisest beholder, that knew no more but seeing, could not say if th'importance were for joy or sorrow.
(5.2.15–18)

Shakespeare evidently gave some ear to Jonson's grievance against thoughtless spectators.

The poets who openly adopted Jonson's view about going to see voices chiefly expressed their opinion in the first two decades of the seventeenth century. It is hardly surprising that the poets should speak out for hearing but it is noteworthy that the complaints about spectators can be found across the whole range, from poets writing university plays to Heywood with his Red Bull spectacles. Curiously, in view of the reputation the Red Bull eventually gained for spectacle, it seems through the period 1610–14 to have become more of an issue there and at the Hope than anywhere else.

All the poets agreed that there were two kinds of playgoer divided according to the priority of eye or ear, but they did not always agree over who represented which. Jonson's differentiation between the 'Schollers, that can judge and faire report / The sense they heare' and the 'vulgar sort / Of nutcrackers, that onely come for sight' in his 'prologue for the court' of *The Staple of News*, was naming the educational basis for the divide. On the other hand Thomas Tomkis, writing for Cambridge scholars in 1602, suggested that at the university it was not only groundlings cracking nuts but women who came to admire the bodies more than the voices. After a display of *'the olde kinde of Pantomimick action'*, Communis Sensus comments that such acting is absurd 'unless we should come to see a Comedy, as gentlewomen to the commencement, only to see men speak' (*Lingua*, 4.2). University orators may not have been quite as unwavering in their concern to put elocution before action as Thomas Gainford assumed.

Patriarchal prejudice expected women to react to bodies more than to voices. John Earle and Aston Cockayne both used the word 'spectator' specifically of women. The Character 'Of a Player' in Earle's *Microcosmographie* of 1628 claimed 'The waiting-women Spectators are over-eares in love with him' (2.155). Cockayne wrote of 'spectator ladies' in his *Masque* of 1639. Marston, writing for Paul's boys at about the same time as Tomkis was writing in Cambridge, was equally sceptical about the capacity of gentlewomen to listen while they watched. The Induction to *What You Will* (1601) brings on three gallants carefully described as 'three of the most to be fear'd *Auditors*' of the poet's verses. When the Prologue finally gets to his prepared opening they tell him to address it to 'the kinde Gentlemen, and most respected Auditors'. But in the meantime some ladies have been noticed, and for them the word is 'we straine the spectators patience'. Like Earle, Marston implies that only the respected gentlemen will listen more than look.

However much the hall playhouses raised Jonson's hopes for a full and understanding auditory they did not live up to his expectation. Day wrote of an 'auditory' at Blackfriars in *The Isle of Gulls*, but the same playhouse disappointed Jonson's followers Beaumont and Fletcher with their hostile reception for Fletcher's *Faithful Shepherdess* in 1608. Beaumont, who knew Jonson intimately enough to have read his plays in manuscript and to write commendatory verses for their publication, made use of Jonson's complaint in verses he wrote for the publication of Fletcher's play. Printing it as a 'second publication' after its staging, he wrote, would allow the original playgoers 'to see the thing they scorn'd', although half of them were clearly illiterate to start with. Their brains were in their eyes.

> . . . It was thy happe to throw away,
> Much wit, for which the people did not pay,
> Because they saw it not . . .   (2.91)

The joke was Bottom's and Tomkis's, about seeing men speak, but the inspiration here was Jonson.

Writing for the more pretentious clientele of the boy company at the Blackfriars, poets might reasonably be irked if their wit was misunderstood, although Fletcher had better grounds for grief than most, since the playgoers at his play seem to have expected a traditional kind of show with May-games and rural clowns, not the usual Blackfriars provision. But the same thing happened to Webster's *White Devil* in 1610 at the Red Bull, and he combined with Dekker to voice the same grievance as Fletcher over amphitheatre audiences. Webster's epistle written for the play's publication complained that it failed on stage because the playhouse in winter was dark, and the play therefore 'wanted (that which is the only grace and setting out of a tragedy) a full and understanding auditory' (2.100). This seems to argue that the Red Bull might have had a more attentive auditory if the weather had been less hostile, but the same incapacity to hear verse was Dekker's target not much later, in the dedication to his *If This Be Not a Good Play, the Devil Is In It*, which appeared not long after, in 1612. He dedicated his play to the Queen's Men at the Red Bull, apparently because they took it after the Prince's Men at the Fortune had rejected it. He was careful first to wish them 'a *Faire* and *Fortunate Day*' for their next new play, and went on to express the hope that 'my *Worthy Friends Muse* . . . deserve a *Theater* full of very *Muses* themselves to be *Spectators*. To that Faire Day I wish a *Full*, *Free*, and *Knowing Auditor*' (2.102). In the prologue to the play itself he implied that poetry had been made to suffer in conflict with other priorities, and hoped that the '*Banished* Auditor' might be recalled from his exile by poetry, to enforce '*Rare silence*' on the multitude. The Red Bull poets were beginning to regret its name for spectacle. Heywood, the Red Bull's resident player-playwright, presumably knew the trend he was confronting when he half-heartedly proclaimed in the prologue to the first of his four stage spectaculars, *The Brazen Age*, that 'more then sight / We seek to please' (2.105).

The central text in this dispute is the set of Articles which Jonson drew up to present his audience with at the Hope in 1614 in the Induction to *Bartholomew Fair*. Essentially a parodic exhibition of the duty of wise judging that Jonson wanted all playgoers to accept, the 'ARTICLES of Agreement' named all the varieties of audience:

. . . The said *Spectators*, and *Hearers*, as well the curious and envious, as the favouring and judicious, as also the grounded Judgements and understandings . . .

Apart from the very early *The Case is Altered* and *Every Man Out*, this was the only occasion when Jonson used more than the contemptuous

'Spectators' as a term for his audiences. The hearers are 'favouring and judicious' while the spectators are merely 'curious and envious', and everyone knew how much could be expected of the understanding men, the groundlings at the Hope. Since legalistic language always prefers two terms where one will do, Jonson added 'hearers' to his usual 'spectators', expanding the oxymoronic and self-contradictory 'judicious Spectators' to whom he had sarcastically appealed in the prologue to *The Alchemist* at the Blackfriars in 1610 (2.94).

Shakespeare of course was always precise in his uses. His 'audience' was always a hearer, usually in the legal sense. The watchers who are 'mutes or audience' to Hamlet's tragedy (5.2.337) are legal witnesses. Polonius spying on Hamlet in Gertrude's closet plans to make himself 'some more audience than a mother' by listening to what Hamlet may say. In *King Lear* the blinded Gloster is literally Lear's audience or 'hearer' as a witness in the mock-trial of Lear's daughters. Spectators were the groundlings that Hamlet looked down on.

The distinction between hearers and spectators gradually lost its clarity from the time of *The Alchemist* onwards, though by no means in a graceful downward slide. The last Master of the Revels, Henry Herbert, used Jonson's phrase from *The Alchemist* without the least awareness of its teeth in 1633, when recording his admiration for Shirley's *The Young Admiral*. If other poets imitated Shirley, he wrote, it 'shall speak them masters in their art, at the first sight, to all judicious spectators'.[18] Such an injudicious echo belies the care with which the poets used the term in those decades. Heywood, who had used 'spectators' and 'Audients' indifferently in his *Apology for Actors* before 1610, showed discomfort in *The Brazen Age*, and openly recognised the divide in the same year that Herbert wrote his comment on *The Young Admiral*. Preparing *Londini Emporia*, an account of his city pageants, Heywood wrote that the third show

is a model devised to humour the throng, who come rather to see than to heare: and without some such intruded anti-maske, many who carry their ears in their eyes, will not sticke to say, I will not give a pinne for the Show.

(*Dramatic Works*, IV.324)

Writing of his *Iron Age* in 1632 he again used the poet's word, 'auditories'. Richard Flecknoe even took the point into the Restoration, when two-dimensional scene-changing was in its first bloom. Stage decorations, he noted,

now for cost and ornament are arriv'd to the height of Magnificence, but that which makes our Stage the better makes our Playes the worse perhaps, they

striving now to make them more for sight than hearing, whence that solid joy
of the interior is lost.   (*A Short Treatise of the Stage*, 1664, G7v)

Flecknoe was heralding the scenic and operatic staging which paradoxically went with the triumph of the term 'audience', the more
paradoxical in that its triumph was never certain before the Restoration. Perhaps the real mark of change was the loss of awareness in
the Restoration that allowed 'audience' to become the standard term
against the thrust of its etymological bias.

In the last three decades before the London playhouses were closed,
the whole range of terms remained current, usually employed with
knowing precision. Gainsford in *A Rich Cabinet* wrote of a player that
'if there be not a facility in his deliverance, and as it were a naturall
dexteritie, it must needes sound harsh to the auditour' (see 2.124).
The publisher of the 1620 text of *The Two Merry Milkmaids* used it
of the poet's audience. John Gee, writing in 1624 of the late Richard
Burbage's speaking, claimed that he was 'the *Loadstone* of the Auditory' (*New Shreds of the Old Snare*, 1624, p. 21). He used 'auditory'
for orators and lawyers, but specified that the Jesuits beguiling young
girls with ghostly apparitions made them a 'spectator', and once (p. 19)
a 'Spectatrix'. On the other hand, a funeral elegy for Burbage in 1619
put the sight of him first:

> Oft have I seene him, play this part in jeast,
> Soe livly, that Spectators, and the rest
> Of his sad Crew, whilst he but seem'd to bleed,
> Amazed, thought even then hee dyed in deed.   (2.134)

At that moment in the play, of course, the corpse was silent, so the
term was the right one. An equally emphatic writer commenting on
the 'shows' at the Red Bull in 1615 also used the apt word. Thomas
Greene, the company clown, he wrote, used to 'flash choaking squibbes
of absurd vanities into the nosthrils of your spectatours'.[19] Presumably
the gunpowder flashed in people's noses rather than banged in their
ears. On the other hand Richard Baker, replying to William Prynne's
attack on plays of 1633, *Histromastix*, was an unashamed beholder.
He used the term 'spectator' regularly, along with 'beholders' and 'the
seeing of plays'. He also claimed that 'a Play *read*, hath not half the
pleasure of a Play *Acted*: for though it have the pleasure of *ingenious
Speeches*, yet it wants the pleasure of *Gracefull action*' (*Theatrum
Redivivum*, 1662, p. 33).

For all its gradual de-prioritisation, the term 'audience' seems to
have served as the fall-back term throughout the period. Marston

used it in *Antonio's Revenge* (1600) and *Jack Drum's Entertainment* (1602). John Stephens used it of the Blackfriars playgoers in 1617,[20] and Leonard Digges used it of the Shakespeare faithful in his verses for the First Folio. Brome applied it to an amphitheatre audience (called 'Audients) in 1638 (2.201). Later in the century Christopher Wren spoke of the 'vast Auditory' that was to gather under the circular dome of his new St Paul's, listening to what was spoken from the central pulpit. But more often writers used the kind of word available for a crowd, 'assembly', 'throng', or in the more lordly mouths, 'multitude'.[21] The most congenial and commonplace word between 1594 and 1640 was 'company'. The paradoxical triumph of 'audience' after the Restoration was certainly not a tribute to the majority's judging role or its sensitive ear for poetry. The chief feature of a 'spectator' marking out modern playgoers from Elizabethan thanks to three-and-a-half centuries of theatre redesign is the word's assumption of individualism. The Elizabethan 'company' has gradually become a set of isolated watchers, their minds set in the two dimensions of scenic staging rather than the Elizabethan three.

LEARNED EARS

In a little treatise he wrote in 1598 Sir John Harington considered three kinds of 'Playe': devotional, wanton, and recreational. He counted playgoing in the second category, and underscored the correctness of its inclusion among the wanton pastimes. Still, he added,

For my part . . . I thinke in stage-playes may bee much good, in well-penned comedies, and specially tragedies; and I remember, in Cambridge, howsoever the presyser sort have banisht them, the wiser sort did, and still doe mayntayn them.[22]

The wiser sort were more broad-minded than the puritan precisians. A few years later he echoed one particularly well-penned comedy in a way that says something about the use of familiar allusions amongst courtiers. By 1605, under King James, he was much nearer the rim of the court circle than he had been under Elizabeth. On 20 April of that year he wrote to Cecil, the Lord Treasurer, asking for his help securing the posts of Archbishop of Dublin and Chancellor of Ireland. Both Harington and Cecil were keen playgoers, so the principal allusion in Harington's letter was a memory familiar to both. On the verge of rural exile, Harington in 1605 made an excellent melancholy Jaques:

the world is a stage and that we that live in it are all stage players . . . I playd my chyldes part happily, the scholler and students part to neglygently, the sowldyer and cowrtyer faythfully, the husband lovingly, the contryman not basely nor corruptly . . . Now I desyre to act a Chawncellors part hollylly.[23]

As You Like It did not get into print until 1623, so both men remembered the play from stage performances. However modest Harington was here in confessing his negligence as a student, however reluctant his scholarship had been in translating Ariosto and however tongue-in-cheek he was when he invoked so many sources to make his *Metamorphosis of Ajax* seem respectable, his use of *As You Like It* to Cecil shows his facility with allusion. More to the point, he indicates that a begging letter from the queen's cousin to her Lord Treasurer could allude to contemporary plays as easily as to Horace or the other well-known classics. Allusion to well-known lines from stage plays is in part a matter of accessibility. If learned courtiers like Harington and Cecil could refer so familiarly to poems from the common stage, how readily might they pick up more scholarly allusions like the beginning of Horace's Ode 22 when they heard them on stage? How far could a poet go to exploit the common ground of education and reading, and how many playgoers could he expect to share such common ground?

Horace is one author whom the learned would certainly recognise. Access to such a major author in the schools, though, was a privilege granted by the grace of education and mastery of Latin. As such it would have been available to relatively few of the penny-payers in an amphitheatre audience. If Webster used Horace in a consciously divisive way to differentiate the learned elite from the many-headed commoners as he seems to have done at the end of *The Duchess of Malfi*, the likelihood is that every allusion to a classical author and every one of the Latin quotations that abound in *The White Devil* would have been designed on the one hand to flatter the educated and on the other to distinguish those few from the many, hearers from spectators. Some such boastful appeal to the learned must have been Shakespeare's intention when he flaunted the same phrase in *Titus Andronicus* in the early 1590s. He may have been reacting to Robert Greene's jibe about the upstart crow stealing the university men's bright feathers.

Such a differentiative attitude to audiences might be expected in Jonson, so ardent to confine his appeal to the attentive and informed ear, but it is not evident in many other writers, including the later

Shakespeare. Allusions have to be recognisable if they are not to be confined to the restricted circle of the writer's own private conception. If we are to be sure that an allusion, particularly a learned *lusus*, was designed to appeal to the most intellectually alert in a Shakespearean audience we have also to be sure that the current sensibilities had the capacity and disposition to receive it.

Most notably among analysts of the ironic mode of allusion in Shakespearean drama, Richard Levin has compiled a daunting body of evidence about contemporary audience responses.[24] All of it casts doubt on the existence of a predominantly allegorical or allusive disposition in early mind-sets. Some consideration of this evidence, depressingly restrictive as its implications are, will follow in the next section of this chapter. An alternative kind of evidence, possibly more helpful, is the capacity of early scholars to pick up echoes or allusions in their reading. Reading being a more leisured form of assimilation than playgoing, the quiet of a study ought to provide a high-water mark for the Shakespearean capacities at this learned game. So we start with that.

A little evidence does exist in at least one location for this high tidemark. The personal library of William Drummond of Hawthornden gives an insight into the character of closet learning in the early seventeenth century. Most of it has survived intact and bears evidence for his careful reading in the marginal jottings he made in many of his 800 books. After graduating from Edinburgh University in law, Drummond, like many gentlemanly Scots, went on to continue his studies in France. On the way he spent some time in London. He was there in 1606 during the visit of the king's brother-in-law Christian of Denmark, and reported home that 'there is nothing to be heard at Court but soundings of Trumpets, Haut-boys, Musick, Revelling, and Comedies'. While enjoying these soundings and playgoings he read *The Courtier*, *The Mirror of Knighthood* and *A Midsummer Night's Dream* among other publications, and bought a copy of Lodge's *Phyllis* to take with him to France. In 1610 he was back in Britain again, with the beginnings of his handsome library of literary works. After his father died in 1611 he settled as the laird of Hawthornden and became the major book collector and minor poet we know, possibly most famous for the breathless report he made of Jonson's outpourings to him on his travels north in 1619. He was a gentleman of leisure and learning. The marginalia in his surviving books and papers reveal some of the effects of a gentlemanly playgoer's reading.

Thanks only in part to his years in France, Drummond was learned in several languages. He could manage Greek as well as Latin, in which he read Virgil and Horace, Volpi, Zanchi and Castiglione. In French he read the works of Passerat, Desportes, Ronsard, Pontus de Tyard, Tabourot, Pasquier and Jodelle. In Spanish he read Boscan and Garcibasco, in Italian Petrarch, Bembo, Groto, Sannazaro, Paterno, Guarini, Bonardo, Belli, Guazzo, Tasso, Marino, Moro and others. Principally he was a master of the Romance languages, French, Italian and Spanish, on the basis of his excellent knowledge of Latin vocabulary. His English books reflect his reading in the Romance languages, including first and foremost Sidney and Watson, plus Daniel, Drayton, Spenser, Peele, and plays by Shakespeare and the Scottish William Alexander. From the Arcadian tradition he read Montemayor and Gil Polo in English and French as well as the original Spanish. His favourite Shakespeare plays were, not surprisingly, *A Midsummer Night's Dream*, *Love's Labours Lost* and *Romeo and Juliet*, though he knew another four or five, including *Hamlet*, pretty well.[25]

A test of how his learning affected his reading and probably his hearing of plays can be found in his copy of William Alexander's *Four Monarchic Tragedies*, now in the National Library of Scotland (MS 1692). It contains an autograph sonnet to Alexander dated about 1614, and a good few marginalia also in Drummond's hand. The book has been cropped at some point, losing some of the annotations, but they are clearly all citations of verbal parallels which Drummond found in Alexander's verses. Most of the parallels are with Sidney's *Arcadia*, and they vary from simple points of vocabulary to broad parallels of rhetorical conceits. At sig. F3 in Alexander's *Tragedie of Darius* 3.2, for instance, where a couplet reads

> And from the height of Honour to digresse,
> To womanise with courtly vain delights . . .

Drummond picked up the verb, and noted in the margin 'S.P.S. Lib. I [i.e, Book I of *Arcadia*] this effeminate Loving of a woman doth womanize a man'. Sidney's point was well known in Jacobean times. It is the basis for Donne's epigram 'Manliness'. Drummond, however, was simply concerned to note the specific word and its context. Besides this and other echoes of Sidney he picked up words from du Bartas, citing the parallels in French, Montemayor in Spanish, Ariosto in Italian and specifically in *The Tragedie of Darius*, 'Jacques de la Taille, who wrote Darius tragedie in french'. He was tracing deliberate utilisations of the sources, not any kind of plagiarism. He had a copy of Jean de la Taille's poem in his library, and probably checked it to verify the echoes he found. But he quoted at least the Sidney parallels from his memory.

18. William Drummond of Hawthornden in his youth, from a painting.

Alexander's tragedies were closet dramas, just as Drummond was a closet audience. The circumstances at the Blackfriars or at a court performance could hardly have afforded anyone the leisure to make connections with the detail and precision of Drummond's marginalia. I think he stands as an extreme, the most well-read, multilingual and undistracted corner-sitter in a potential Jacobean audience. His reading, if not his hearing of plays, allowed him to detect a high number of literary echoes, deliberate or not.

How common the Drummonds with their *Arcadia* and their Alexander in their memories might have been in any of the playhouses we cannot tell. Gabriel Harvey, another playgoer, had a similar library and wrote similar marginalia in it, but like Drummond he never lived regularly in London. It is not likely that such scholarly minds existed in large numbers, and they would certainly not have been among the more verbally active members of any audience. Even Jonson's hopeful expectation of Haringtons and Cecils in a courtly audience cannot have been much more than an unavailing hope, to judge from accounts of the behaviour that was customary at court masques. Jonson, Dekker and the other professional poets had to use print to ensure that the elaborate ceremonial allegories in their masques became accessible to the enlightened few for whom they were composed. Dudley Carleton and Orazio Busino have left accounts of masques at which the rush for food and the consequent collapse of the banquet tables seem to have been the most memorable features of each occasion.[26] Webster's bifocal allusion to Horace in *The Duchess of Malfi* assumed that the learned who would pick it up were few, even at the most select of the playhouses in 1614. Since he seems to have written the play specifically for the King's Men at Blackfriars it was aimed at the clientele at the only indoor playhouse then operating, the top of the market. And because the allusion only works by swimming against the current of its ostensible meaning, he evidently expected most playgoers even at Blackfriars to understand the couplet only at its superficial level.

Understandably enough in situations where emotion rather than intellect was used to drive the stories, there is more evidence for divisions between audiences in their social and cultural character than in their learning or intellect. Unless he held a distinctive and distinctly old-fashioned view of the moral force of plays on his audiences, Massinger probably assumed that the women at Blackfriars near the end of the 1620s would be predominantly ladies of the court rather than rich merchants' wives, taking pleasure in their social superiority rather than shame from seeing their pretensions exposed on stage. In 1607, close to the middle of the seventy-five years of Shakespearean playgoing, Beaumont made a similar assumption, apparently with rather less justification, at the same playhouse for its then boy company. The comic Grocer and his wife in *The Knight of the Burning Pestle* were set up as objects of ridicule for the 'Gentlemen' among whom they sit on stage.

The play thus serves as the most extreme mark of the division, real or at least assumed to be so by Beaumont, between crass citizen tastes and the superior gentlemanly values. The gentlemanly Beaumont set his marker down in a mood of elitist satire and genial contempt for citizens, and yet in 1607 the audience missed his point completely. The portrait of the silly citizens may therefore be not merely over-coloured satirically but overstated to the extent that there were too few gentlemen present at Blackfriars who were willing to dominate the audience response by openly relishing Beaumont's joke. The on-stage gentlemen to whom the wife speaks in the interact following Act 3 and at the epilogue evidently did not play along with Beaumont's comedy.

The performance opened with Citizen George, an employer member of the Guild of Grocers, climbing on stage to stop the play, called *The London Merchant*, that the company advertised on its playbills and had hung up on a board on the *frons scenae*. He expected a play flaunting such a title, echoing amphitheatre plays like *The London Prodigal*, printed in 1605 as a King's Men's play at the Globe, to renew the boy company's notorious 'girds at citizens' that he claims they have been running for the last seven years. The Prologue's first lines, announcing a switch from all that's great at court into the city, confirmed his suspicion. In fact the *London Merchant* play when the boys finally get to stage it does prove to be a burlesque of *The London Prodigal* and its like. Both plays have a heroine called Luce. The Globe play emphasised the mercantile interpretation of the prodigal son parable customary in citizen thinking, moralising the errant son's reform and his return to the ways of financial prudence. Beaumont's play reverses the moral by forcing the miserly characters to convert themselves into the ways of prodigality. Instead of a prodigal son *The London Merchant* has a prodigal father. Its hero is a penniless son who wins the fair Luce from her own grasping father, who at the end is forced to forgive and accept his new son-in-law along with the principle of prodigality. The play the boys officially announced directly challenged the mercantilist interpretation of the biblical parable of the prodigal, offering 'mirth' as a better principle in life than miserliness.

By his contributions to the performance the citizen Grocer shows how mercantilist values were embodied in citizen literary tastes. He objects to the boy players' policy of plays with 'new subjects, pur-posely to abuse your betters', proposing the old favourites instead, such as the story of the industrious apprentice Dick Whittington, which had grown into a London legend at the end of the sixteenth century, or Heywood's *2 If You Know Not Me* (1606), which celebrated Sir Thomas Gresham, builder of the Royal Exchange. What the Grocer wants is something 'notably in honour of the Commons of the Citty', like the Royal Exchange or the feats of apprentice gallantry staged in Heywood's *Four Prentices of London* and Day and Wilkins's *The Travels of the Three English Brothers*. Beaumont, loyally following

Jonson and his own evident tastes, was holding the repertory of the pro-citizen amphitheatres up to ridicule. The boy Prologue's opinion of these recent amphitheatre successes is indicated by his mock-proposal to stage 'the life and death of fat *Drake*', not Sir Francis but a citizen's dinner, or 'the repairing of Fleet-privies', one of the city's current preoccupations. In 1607 citizens were being levied for contributions to build several new waterworks, notably Sir Hugh Middleton's New River project.

The Grocer's assumptions about middle-class honour and pro-citizen plays were by no means Beaumont's only targets. The Grocer's wife and apprentice join him on stage, and each of them reveals a distinct taste in contemporary drama. The wife favours escapist romances about characters like Jane Shore, the citizen wife loved by Edward IV, who featured in *King Edward IV*, a play in Henslowe's records. Nell the wife wants the apprentice, Rafe, to take the romantic lead as a knight-errant in the *Burning Pestle* play, in imitation of the Palmerin stories which Rafe enters quoting at length and almost verbatim, except where Beaumont changes the horse Palmerin rides into an elephant. She wants Rafe to kill a lion with his grocer's pestle, in the fashion of *The Travels of the Three English Brothers*. Rafe shows his acting mettle by reciting Hotspur's huffing speech (*1 Henry IV* 1.3.201ff), and his master claims that he had starred in a version of *Mucedorus*, another Globe play, and *Jeronimo*. In the *Burning Pestle* play itself Rafe appears as an apprentice errant, performing deeds of gallantry like those in the Red Bull's *Travels*. In the fourth Interact he appears as a Maylord dressed in scarves and bells and carrying a gilded staff. In the final Act he becomes the leader of a town band of citizen militia.

Besides this mockery of citizen ambitions and spectacle the boy players make sure that the Grocer himself and his understanding of the play-making business are thoroughly guyed. He completely misses the boy Prologue's sarcasm about 'the noble Citty' and fat Drake, just as his wife Nell misses all the bawdy jokes she innocently broaches. Both display a Dogberry-like ignorance. Through Interact III Nell asks George if the picture on the hangings shows 'the confutation of Saint *Paul*', and he corrects her by declaring it to be '*Raph* and *Lucrece*'. In 3.2 she refers to the biblical story of '*Jone* and the Wall'. Their capacity for understanding spectacle is as defective as their hearing. In both *The London Merchant* and the play that Rafe tries to perform, *The Grocers' Honor*, George and Nell invariably mistake the fiction for reality. She asks Rafe if he has slept well after a night is supposed to have passed, and both speculate about the progress of the lovers as they wander through Waltham Forest. They accept Rafe's adventures as true events, and are disappointed at the boys' refusal to adopt their proposals for spectacular Red Bull-type shows on stage. Just as they innocently identify themselves with the mercantile values guyed in the main play and as a result misconstrue everything they see, so they accept Rafe's ludicrous knight-errantry as stage realism.

If there is any degree of truth in Beaumont's picture of citizen play-goers at the Globe and the Red Bull, the only surprise is that Jonson should have left the boy company's playhouse to give *Sejanus* and *Volpone* to the Globe. Beaumont's picture certainly reflects the pressure to favour spectacle over verse which Jonson fought against from the Blackfriars stage in 1600 and 1601.

Such evidence for socially divided playhouse audiences says a lot about social prejudice, but little about how learned were the ears that Beaumont wrote for. The failure of *The Knight of the Burning Pestle* in 1607 speaks much better for Beaumont's sophistication in metadrama than his expectations of his hall playhouse audience. The process from writer's initial concept through its renegotiation by the players into the product that interacts with the audience's expectations and preconceptions is, to put it mildly, a complex one. Many factors of varying degrees of marginality intervene on the intellectual capacity and momentary alertness of a single playgoer. Not many of these factors can be identified, let alone isolated as causal features of the experience of a play. On the evidence of *The Knight* alone we can see that the levels of audience sophistication varied enormously, and that the elegant complexity of Beaumont's metatheatrical games was not a regular feature of the collective audience responses. It certainly did not develop consistently while the drama of the time gradually learned to make new ways of enlivening the still novel experience of playgoing. Differentiating the degrees of sophistication by playhouse is an unreliable procedure, if we credit the initial rejection of *The Knight*. Nor was there a consistent progress from the plays like *The Spanish Tragedy* and *Titus Andronicus* that Jonson hailed as the old tradition to the sophistication of Beaumont's metadrama. Levels of metatheatrical awareness varied in audiences throughout the period.

LEVELS OF AWARENESS

For all the willingness of the early spectators to submit to the illusions offered them, one substantial difference of playgoers then from cinemagoers and television spectators now was their awareness of the game of illusion that was in constant play on the early stages. With most current entertainment media the chief object is to remove self-awareness and make spectators believe momentarily that what they see is real. That strongest of prerequisites for cinematic realism stands in contrast with early playgoing, where it was a feature thought to appeal only to the weakest intellects. Stage illusion was a regressive feature in the early plays. Starting from the assumption that audiences were grouped in three dimensions, clustering as closely as possible to the speakers, the players set up a number of deliberately unrealistic features in their staging practices that should have impeded George's and Nell's credulity. Shakespearean drama has many elements that deny illusionism. Speaking in verse rather than prose, delivering your mind in soliloquy as a person in solitude yet speaking directly to the immediately accessible listeners at your feet, using boys to play women, allowing clowns to ad-lib with their hecklers, the very fact that three-dimensional playing meant half the audience was visible on the other side of the players, these features of early theatre abounded with deliberate inhibitions against the easier kinds of illusionism. The high status of plays performed by boys rather than adults was itself a feature of anti-illusionism. When it was boys pretending to be adults the effect removed the unease the superior classes felt at seeing the stronger forms of stage illusion when adults played adults, since the boys were more obviously play-acting the adult emotions.

Anti-illusionist practices were in part a reaction to the pulpit diatribes which claimed any deliberate illusion to be Satan's work. The pulpits made it likely that the players knew only too well how the pleasure of believing in the truth of what you saw that overtook so many innocent spectators was potentially dangerous, especially in excess. Playgoers like Nim (2.160) who mocked their neighbours for believing what they saw on stage to be real were not alone with Beaumont in their feeling of superiority. The writers certainly divided their positions between the Heywoods who went openly for spectacle and illusionism and the Jonsons who derided the more credulous of their patrons. The Elizabethan discomforts of standing or even sitting for hours in a closely packed crowd always offset any enchantment in the spectacle. Spectacle was always relatively parsimonious, with players even in new plays seen wearing the same dress they had walked in for different roles on previous days. That made the event's overt theatricality much more conspicuous than what we undergo in modern cinemas. By company rules players normally supplied their own clothing if nothing special was needed, so it was not just the familiar faces that renewed themselves for each new play.

One of the main things working against the relative novelty of playgoing for Londoners in the 1580s, and more especially after, was this close familiarity most playgoers acquired with the players. From the time the duopoly started in 1594 for six years barely more than the two companies with the same two groups of fifteen players appeared in every play. Even before that people had begun to go to plays to see Tarlton or Alleyn rather than the roles they played. The book of Tarlton's 'Jests' has several anecdotes about people going just to see him and enjoy his jokes, his backchat with the audience and his extemporising. The attraction of the players rather than their plays is affirmed by the story about the innkeeper who remembered Richard Burbage playing Richard III. Bishop Corbet's verse about the man who 'mistook a player for a King', and 'when he would have sayd, King Richard dyed, / And call'd – A horse! a horse! – he, Burbidge cry'de' (2.133), is only one of many indications that the players were more familiar to their audiences as themselves, star players, than as the characters they portrayed.

The same concept is apparent in the metatheatrical games that Shakespeare and Jonson regularly played. Shakespeare clearly expected his audience attending the Globe in 1600 for *Hamlet* to know that the player now playing Polonius, probably John Hemminges, had been Caesar in the previous year's play, as Polonius tells Hamlet he did at university. Since Hamlet had been Brutus, the reminder foreshadowed the same player as Hamlet killing the same player as Polonius in the scene that followed this nudge to playgoers' memories. To the regulars at the Globe it made a neat theatrical in-joke. More recent awareness of metatheatrical games, growing out of postmodernism with Brecht's *Verfremdungseffekt* and Pirandello's *Six Characters*, was routine in London plays of the late 1590s. It reflects the writers' knowledge that their audiences were fully aware of their environs, and that the fictions were to be seen as overt mimicry whose pretences at creating illusions had to be obvious.

There are many reasons why such ostentatious theatricality became the normal attitude at this time, besides the difficulty of persuading people to ignore the elbows and the smells of their neighbours in the crowd. Puritan objections to playgoing largely stemmed from the evident dishonesty of players who pretended to be what they were not, and the telling of lies by their counterfeiting, an ominous term Shakespeare used regularly in his earlier years, of personalities quite distinct from the players' own. In fact Burbage was the first player to be acclaimed for the success of his art of 'personation'. Before that, Marlovian language and the grand gestures of an Alleyn were the model for tragic playing. It was Shakespeare who created parts for Burbage that allowed him to differentiate himself from Alleyn's characteristically verbose style.

The scale of Burbage's success helped to quieten the often-voiced view that all players were con men and tricksters who depended on deceit for their success, but so long as playhouses could draw the gullible and credulous it never died. When Jonson held his mirror in *The Alchemist* up to the residents of Blackfriars at their local playhouse, he took care to represent not just the gulls on the audience side but the tricksters and con men on the stage side. Face, Subtle and Doll were players conning the Blackfriars gulls. Lovewit, the house owner who returns in time to reap all the profits from the con tricks, was probably Jonson's jibe at Shakespeare, now retired from playing but since 1608 an owner of the Blackfriars playhouse, still prepared to don a disguise to profit from the tricks played on the local gulls.

If we adopt a broader perspective than this close focus on regular playgoers, another factor that cannot be discounted is the wide publicity given to all players as tricksters. This was laid against them not only by the precisians, puritan preachers, but by the learned. A likely reason why the superior classes in the late sixteenth century preferred companies of boy players for so long against the professional adults must have been a consequence of the boys' smaller size and therefore the overt imperfections in their art of illusion playing adults. On the other side, the adult company boys with unbroken voices who cross-dressed in order to play the women's parts were frequently condemned as ingles or catamites for their masters.[27] Spectacle, illusionism and self-display attracted hostility because they looked like the Devil's work. Cross-dressing provoked biblical and moral injunctions against the boys' deceits, with an inevitable extension into their masters' sexual sinning. Dens of iniquity such as playhouses must invite pederasty as well as the more usual sins. To anyone looking for ammunition the adult company boys' youth made them vulnerable to exploitation by their con-men masters. It is striking that in contrast to those allegations against the adult players the boy companies rarely suffered from the catamite label so heavily laid on the adult company boys. Boy companies were rarely condemned except for occasional cross-dressing and their share in the generally noxious practices of playing.

To the squeamish the boy companies were more acceptable because their counterfeiting was less deceitful. Concern over counterfeiting and illusionism was widespread, and ranged from the fierce scepticism of Reginald Scot's *Discovery of Witchcraft*, or Samuel Harsnett and his mentor Bishop Bancroft, to the academic attacks on playing and the publication of William Perkins's sermons. Perkins stated baldly that 'an illusion is the work of Satan, whereby he deludeth or deceiveth man'.[28] A very similar preoccupation generated the cony-catching pamphlets exposing criminal deceptions. In their distinctive ways the scepticism of Scot, Robert Greene and Sidney matched the anti-theatre diatribes of Northbrook, Gosson and Munday.

Such concerns appear to intensify the depth of the division between credulous beholders of stage spectacles and attentive hearers of the poetry. This might overstate the significance of the metatheatrical mind-set as a safety factor in the playgoing experience. The writers are not necessarily the best informers about the likely metatheatrical awareness of the minds they were composing their plays for. Given the known range of playgoing thinking, one of the least accessible elements in the experience is the inevitable competition between the mind concentrating on the play and the distractions suffered by the body it was housed in. Hamlet's reiteration of that word ('this distracted globe', and 'the distracted multitude') echoes when he lectures the players about the spectacle-minded element in their audience. His author was certainly prepared to use it in the same scene in the exchange between Hamlet/Brutus and Polonius/Caesar. We cannot know whether the first audiences for *Hamlet* were expected to be distracted from the play or by the play, or perhaps both at different moments in the process. Nonetheless, there must have been some reason for the high expectations that Jonson and Shakespeare both entertained when they composed their metatheatrical tricks, at least about each other's responses. That must have gone further abroad. To begin a play on a hot autumn afternoon in 1600 and immediately tell the audience that the time is past midnight and it is bitterly cold suggests they had some confidence in the audience's active capacity to piece out the imperfections with their thoughts.

PLAYGOER REACTIONS

Having metatheatre in mind as a priority for audiences helps us to identify a mind-set in ourselves that can distort our understanding. We find it difficult, for instance, to accept the instant mood-switch that was then familiar to all whenever a profound tragedy like *Julius Caesar* concluded with a jig, as Thomas Platter observed at the Globe in 1599 (2.37). This was a feature of playgoing that Dudley Carleton invoked in a letter to John Chamberlain written four years after *Hamlet* first appeared on stage. After telling his friend about the rather ridiculous but unfortunate death of a mutual acquaintance, he went on to make a rather heavy-handed joke, and introduced it as 'a jig after this tragedy'.[29] Usually such shifts of mood are easier when the mind is not fully absorbed in the story, as we are with cinema. The insertion of comic scenes into tragedies bothered the purists even then for their own reasons, but what Lyly called 'gallimaufrey' plays of mixed moods were a feature of almost all the plays of the time. If we accept the publisher's claim that he cut comic scenes from the 1590 text of *Tamburlaine*, that leaves us with *Richard II* as almost the sole exception to the pattern of rapid mood-switching.

A readiness to relish mood switches might explain the almost unique closure of *Hamlet*, which leaves three major figures dead on stage and no means set down for removing them. The bodies of Denmark's king and queen and a major courtier were left on stage once Prince Hamlet's body has been carried off. He gets the standard funeral procession for soldiers, carried by four captains like the bodies of Brutus and Coriolanus. The absence of any word for the removal of the three other bodies signifies, however cryptically in our readings, a close that would have been much easier for Elizabethans to accept than moderns. It is more than tempting to ask whether, after Fortinbras has 'embraced my fortune' and marched off, the three corpses might not have sprung back to life to dance a final jig. The then-standard practice of ending the day with a jig is the easiest way of explaining the otherwise rare awkwardness of leaving bodies onstage at the 'plaudite'. It is of course a particularly delicious sidelong irony that a play in which the prince characterises 'a jig or a tale of bawdry' as to the taste only of 'tedious old fools' like Polonius should be what brings it to an end.

As the preceding sections of this chapter have shown, it is easier to identify the length and breadth of audience tastes than the height of their mental capacity or the exact shape of the mental constructs they took into the playhouses. The plays which lasted in the various company repertories, the most popular and characteristic products, define the audience tastes that chose them. These tastes, of which there is more to be said in chapter 5, by their nature remained passively receptive. With some companies they allowed the attractions of *Faustus* and *The Spanish Tragedy* to stay constant for fifty years in the northern amphitheatres. Using that kind of evidence to identify what audiences liked in the mass as passive tasters of what was set before them is, allowing for the patchy nature of all the testimonies, a fairly straightforward exercise. On the other hand the poets by their nature had more active appetites, always on edge to find novelty. It is hardly surprising that all the contemporary commentators who found occasion to mock ageing tastes in playgoing were stage poets – Dekker and Middleton (2.97), Dekker (2.101), Jonson (2.112), Massinger (2.159), Carew (2.163) and Brome (2.201). While playgoers certainly did vote with their feet as they followed the poets' activities in particular directions, thus revealing the development of preferences in audience tastes on a very broad perspective, reactions by individual voices to the novelties which poets kept offering are markers of a more localised kind.

Sadly, very few accounts of playgoing by Elizabethans exist, and the writers of those few accounts did not feel obliged to make much more than a few jottings about the plays they saw. There were neither theatre reviews nor journals to publish them in, so the best accounts are either from personal diaries written to remind the writer what he or she witnessed, or letters about a current stage sensation sent to entertain their recipients. These accounts dwell on the plot rather than features such as character, poetry or staging, and in consequence have led modern commentators such as Richard Levin to use them as evidence that Shakespearean playgoers took their plays literal-mindedly and for the story alone. This is too dismissive. Taken altogether, there are many more quotations of famous lines of verse, praises for particular players' characterisations, comments on that trade so hotly pursued, 'application', and accounts of spectacle than there are summaries of plots. A comprehensive survey of audience reactions to the plays of this period suggests a complex and wide-ranging responsiveness, each in its own way representative, which makes the few eye-witness accounts of performances seem almost simple-minded. The major accounts need to be examined rather as normative and anecdotal stories than as expert analyses made from the top end of the playgoing range.

Before looking at some of these accounts of plays seen in performance, we need to contextualise the period's most celebrated critique of plays, Sidney's extended condemnation of stage realism in the *Apology for Poetry*. Written in about 1582, and widely circulated in manuscript (Lyly seems to have been familiar with it), Sidney's little treatise did not appear in print until 1595. Between the writing and the publication much had changed. Strikingly, though, little that Sidney objected to had altered, and even more strikingly little notice was taken of his criticisms either in 1582 or in the years following its 1595 publication, except possibly by Ben Jonson. The players and their writers swept Sidney's criticisms aside not so much because they seemed out of date as because they lacked popular support in their audiences. His condemnation of stage realism and his objections to clowning have a place in the history of audience taste, but being aristocratic and academic it was evidently marginal to the flow of the main currents. He was attacking something too strong to be touched by his objections.

There is no direct evidence that Sidney went to the public playhouses. The only play he mentions specifically, *Gorboduc*, was first staged in the hall of the Inner Temple in 1561, and may never have appeared on the amphitheatre stages, though Sidney's familiarity with it suggests that it was performed through the 1570s. The characteristics of the other plays he condemned might also have been visible at court or the Inns of Court as readily as at the Theatre or Curtain or a city inn. On the other hand his knowledge of staged plays shows the sort of everyday ease which can hardly have been cultivated exclusively by the irregular seasonal offerings by the law students or at Elizabeth's court. His dislike of clowns, paper dragons breathing fire and smoke, and four swordsmen representing two armies suggests either weariness at the debased level of popular choice or a more personal contempt for what satisfied the court. The former is the more likely. Sidney's critique therefore stands as the expression of a sophisticated and learned courtier's distaste for the standards of popular dramaturgy in the early years of London's commercial playgoing.

Sidney objected principally to three things. The first was doggerel rhyming, which allowed him to register the differences between printed and stage poetry in 1582. Secondly he objected to stage poets flouting the classical rules for the unities of time and place, a fault he found even in the one play he regarded as well written.

> But if it bee so in *Gorboducke*, howe much more in all the rest, where you shall have *Asia* of the one side, and *Affricke* of the other, and so manie other under Kingdomes, that the Player when he comes in, must ever begin with telling where he is, or else the tale will not be conceived. Now you will have three Ladies walke to gather flowers, and then we must beleeve the stage to be a garden. By and by we heare newes of shipwrack in the same place, then we are too blame if we accept it not for a Rock. Upon the back of that, comes out a hideous monster with fire and smoke, and then the miserable beholders are bound to take it for a Cave: while in the meane time two Armies flie in, represented with foure swords & bucklers, and then what hard hart wil not receive it for a pitched field. (*Prose Works*, III.38)

The plays misuse time as violently as place. Sidney the hard-hearted realist derides the credulous, clearing himself from them over non-realistic staging and the implausibility of the fictions. He finds Aristotle's three unities affirmed by the need for realism. Sidney's criticism is not so much about the poets flouting classical precedents as the players' feeble challenges to human credulity. He objects equally to the flouting of other kinds of classical decorum, notably putting clowns in company with kings. This last point brings out Sidney's major grievance, the use of clowns to generate mindless laughter. Comedy is mixed into tragedy, and debases it.

Laughter almost ever commeth of thinges most disproportioned to our selves, and nature. Delight hath a joy in it either permanent or present. Laughter hath onely a scornfull tickling . . . For what is it to make folkes gape at a wretched begger, and a beggerly Clowne: or against lawe of hospitalitie, to jeast at strangers, because they speake not English so well as we do?

Sidney hated the sound of communal laughter. Individual delight is not the same thing, and stage poets abuse the nature of poetry by aiming at the cruder forms of pleasure.

Sidney ended his diatribe by apologising for spending so many words on stage poetry. His explanation was that 'as they are excelling parts of *Poesie*, so is there none so much used in England, and none can be more pitifully abused'. Even as early as 1582, it seems, stage plays had become the pre-eminent vehicle for Tudor poetry. Sidney wanted to raise the standard of stage poetry. His criticisms never did anything to alter the liberality with which the poets treated time and place, and only in one later company do his strictures against clowns seem to have struck a sympathetic chord, as the next chapter will show.

The four major accounts of performances by playgoers are spread across thirty-two years, and two of them deal with performances of Shakespeare. Two are in personal diaries and two in letters. John Manningham, a law student at the Middle Temple, wrote a diary in which he described a Shakespeare company performance of *Twelfth Night*, not an afternoon at the Globe but an evening show at Middle Temple Hall in February 1602. Although it was not at the usual amphitheatre, the performance must have been by Shakespeare's company, bought by the lawyers for their evening's entertainment. Manningham's entry reads:

At our feast wee had a play called 'twelve Night, or what you will'; much like the comedy of errores, or Menechmi in Plautus, but most like and neere to that in Italian called *Inganni*. A good practise in it to make the Steward beleeve his Lady widdowe was in Love with him, by counterfayting a letter, as from his Lady, in generall termes, telling him what shee liked best in him, and prescribing his gesture in smiling, his apparaile, &c., and then when he came to practise, making him beleeve they tooke him to be mad.   (2.50)

Manningham's knowledge of Italian drama seems to have been less solid than his studies of Plautus at school. The play closest to *Twelfth Night* is the *Ingannati*, not any of the group known as the *Inganni*. The plot device of identical twins seems to have prompted the comparison, although the different sexes of *Twelfth Night*'s twins evoked no comment. The most noteworthy feature of the story was clearly the gulling of Malvolio. Apart from that, a quite reasonable observation, the entry shows Manningham missing the point that Olivia was mourning for her brother, not a husband, and understood the play in the more conventional shape of a widow being wooed by her servant. Widows were commonly thought to be vulnerable, and several popular ballads tell tales of rich widows being seduced by their cook or their steward, like the Duchess of Malfi. Manningham read the play as a stereotypical situation for male jokes, where for once the villain is tricked in a way that satisfied conventional morality. It is a version of the play at some distance from modern readings.

Simon Forman, the fortune-telling quack who kept extended diaries of his activities through his last years, went to four plays in April and May 1611, making a detailed note about each of them. He headed the paper 'The Booke of plaies and Notes hereof per formans for Common pollicie', which is an apt summary of his reason for making the notes. The four plays were *Macbeth* on 20 April, *Cymbeline*, a play about Richard II (not Shakespeare's) on 30 April, and *The Winter's Tale* on 15 May. All four were at the Globe, not the Blackfriars, since Forman actually marked three 'at the Glob', and the fourth in the same early summer period was *Cymbeline*.[30] He summarised the plot of what he witnessed in fewer than 500 words, fairly accurately so far as we can tell from the extant texts. Some indication of his reason for making the summaries 'for Common pollicie' is given by the brief moral drawn at the end of the last two. After his account of the third, the Richard II play, he gave an example of John of Gaunt's double-dealing and concluded, 'Beware by this Example of noble men, and of their fair wordes, & sai lyttel to them, lest they doe the like by thee for thy good will.' At the end of his briefer account of *The Winter's Tale* he described Autolycus, listing his cozening devices, and concluded, 'Beware of trustinge feined beggars or fawninge fellouss.'

Varying conclusions have been derived from recent analyses of his summary of the first play, *Macbeth*. It is accurate down to the details of the witches' prophecies to Macbeth and Banquo, the aftermath of Duncan's murder, and Banquo's ghost at the feast. No moral is drawn. Forman tells *Cymbeline's* story like a narrative from the old romances that Beaumont burlesqued. Again the plot is summarised accurately and no moral is drawn. All four plays are treated similarly except for the morals that conclude the last two. Both are based in details from the play and drawn from single characters whose 'pollicie' might prove dangerous to the innocent.

All we can deduce from these four accounts is that Forman thought of each play as if it were a dramatised romance narrative, with incidental lessons that could be drawn by a naive individual from the activities of tricky characters. The idea that plays were educative was hardly new. It underlies Sidney's critique, and Heywood makes it his strongest point in *An Apology for Actors*, published very soon after the time Forman was writing his summaries. Forman was attentive to the narrative sequence and picked up the details with nearly complete accuracy. His moralisings seem to have been afterthoughts. He may be typical of one fairly ordinary type of playgoer, more absorbed in the story than the verse or characterisations, not at all interested in symbols or their application, inclined to moralise only in the conventional way as a response to the depiction of villainy at work.

The third major account of a play is of a performance again at the Globe, this time in August 1624 while King James and his court were out of town. *A Game at Chesse* was quite literally a nine-day wonder, because the King's Men kept it running for that many days before the Spanish ambassador heard of it and complained to James, who had it stopped. The Master of the Revels who had approved it in July seems to have escaped through the protection of his master, the Lord Chamberlain, William Herbert. Blatant propaganda designed to ride on the current wave of anti-Spanish feeling, it was rightly a sensation. Several people wrote about it. The report written by John Holles, Lord Haughton, to the Earl of Somerset on 11 August, was easily the most graphic.

My Lo. though from Mr. Whittakers, or others, this vulgar pasquin may cum to your eares, yet whether he, or thei saw it, I know not, muche beeing the difference between ey-sight, & hear-say: when I returned from your Lordship hither uppon munday, I was saluted with a report of a facetious comedy, allreddy thryce acted with extraordinary applause: a representation of all our spannishe traffike, where Gundomar his litter, his open chayre for the ease of that fistulated part, Spalato &ca. appeared uppon the stage. I was invited by the reporter Sr Edward Gorge (whose balance gives all things waight to the advantage) to be allso an auditor therof, & accordingly yesterday to the globe I rowed, which hows I found so thronged, that by scores thei came away for want of space, though as yet little past one; nevertheless lothe to check the appetite, which came so seldome to me (not having been in a playhouse thes io. years) & suche a daynty not every day to be found, I marched on, & heard the pasquin, for no other it was which had been the more complete, had the poet been a better states-man: the descant was built uppon the popular opinion, that the Jesuits mark is to bring all the christian world under Rome for the spirituality, & under Spayn for the temporalty: heeruppon, as a precept, or legacy left those disciples from their first founder Ignatius Loyola, this their father serves for the prologue, who admiring no speedier operation of his drugg, is inraged, & desperate, till cumforted by one of his disciples, the plott is revealed him, prosperously advanced by their designe uppon England: with this he vanisheth, leaving his benediction over the work. The whole play is a chess board, England the whyt hows, Spayn the black: one of the white pawns, wth an under black dubblett, signifying a Spanish hart, betrays his party to their advantage, advanceth Gundomars propositions, works under hand the Princes cumming into Spayn: which pawn so discovered, the whyt King revyles him, objects his raising him in wealth, in honor, from meane condition, next classis to a labouring man: this by the charaxcter is supposed Bristow: yet it is hard, players should judge him in jest, before the State in ernest. Gundomar makes a large account of all his great feates heer, descrybes in scorne our vanities in dyet, in apparell, in every other excess, (the symptomes of a falling state) how many Ladyes brybed him to be groome of the stoole to the Infanta, how many to be mother of the mayds, with muche suche trashe, letters. from the nunnry in Drury Lane, from those in Bloomsbury &ca. how many Jesuites, & priests he loosed out of prison, & putt agayn into their necessary work of seducing how he sett the Kings affayrs as a clock, backward & forward, made him believe, & unbelieve as stood best with his busines, be the caws never so cleere: how he covered the roguery of the Jesuits in abusing wemen licensiously: how he befooled Spalato with a counterfeit lettre. from the Cardinall Paolo his kinsman, promising to leave his Cardinals hatt to him, himself then being elected Pope: with muche suche like stuff, more wittily penned, then wysely staged: but at last the Prince making a full discovery of all their knaveries, Olivares, Gundomar, Spalato, Iesuite, spannish bishop, & a spannish evenuke ar by the Prince putt into the bagg, & so the play ends . . . surely thes gamsters must have a good retrayte, else dared thei not to charge thus Princes actions, & ministers, nay their intents: a foule injury to Spayn, no great honor to England, rebus sic stantibus: every particular will beare a large paraphrase, which I submit to your better judgment.[31]

Again, the report summarises the play that was performed clearly and accurately (several manuscripts containing staging variants survive, some of them Middleton's own), and Holles recognised the play's 'applications' pretty firmly. What is least clear is how much of his scepticism about the play came from his own reactions and how much from the scandal about its performance.

The fourth account is again of a performance in August at the Globe. Ten years after *A Game at Chesse*, it seems to have been brought to life by another set of back-stage manoeuvres by the King's Men's backers, notably the Earl of Pembroke, successor to his brother William as Lord Chamberlain, and co-dedicatee with him of the Shakespeare First Folio. The account appears in a letter written from London by Nathaniel Tomkyns to his friend the landowning politician Sir Robert Phelips in Somerset. Tomkyns had done some business in London over a legal case involving some men living on a royal manor which Phelips was responsible for. The first third of the letter covers the business

Tomkyns had done for Phelips, and the remainder deals with London's current gossip. The last item Tomkyns offers as 'some merriment' to soften his sad news of a friend's death, like Carleton's jig after the tragedy.

Here hath bin lately a newe comedie at the globe called *The Witches of Lancasheir,* acted by reason of ye great concourse of people 3 dayes togither: the 3rd day I went with a friend to see it, and found a greater apparence of fine folke gentmen and gentweomen then I thought had bin in town in the vacation. The subject was of the slights and passages done or supposed to be done by these witches sent from thence hither and other witches and their familiars; Of ther nightly meetings in several places: their banqueting with all sorts of meat and drinke conveyed unto them by their familiars upon the pulling of a cord: the walking of pailes of milke by themselvers and (as they say of children) a highlone: the transforming of men and weomen into the shapes of severall creatures and especially of horses by putting an inchaunted bridle into ther mouths: their posting to and from places farre distant in an incredible short time: the cutting off a witch-gentwoman's hand in the forme of a catt, by a soldier turned miller, known to her husband by a ring thereon, (the onely tragicall part of the storie:) the representing of wrong and putative fathers in the shape of meane persons to gentmen by way of derision: the tying of a knott at a mariage (after the French manner) to cassate masculine abili-tie, and the conveying away of the good cheere and bringing in a mock feast of bones and stones steed thereof and the filling of pies with living birds and yong catts &c: And though there be not in it (to my understanding) any poeticall Genius, or art, or language, or judgement to state our tenet of witches (which I expected,) or application to vertue but full of ribaldrie and of things improbable and impossible; yet in respect of the newnesse of the subject (the witches being still visible and in prison here) and in regard it consisteth from the beginning to the ende of odd passages and fopperies to provoke laughter, and is mixed with divers songs and dances, it passeth for a merrie and excellent new play.[32]

The play was Heywood and Brome's *The Late Lancashire Witches.* It seems to have been commissioned to influence judgement in the retrial of four women from Pendle and the family who accused them of witchcraft. They had been brought to London because some Privy Councillors, notably Laud, the Archbishop of Canterbury, had well-justified doubts about the case. The play sensationalised the accusations by taking the accusers' side, though judging from Tomkyns's account not very seriously. Its use of details from the Lancaster hear-ings makes it likely that Brome and Heywood were supplied with copies of the major depositions against the accused, probably by Pem-broke, Laud's enemy on the Privy Council. The play was designed to be a rabble-rousing case for the prosecution.

The Earl of Pembroke, Philip Herbert, had ready access to the King's Men, as his brother had ten years before, and also access to the papers Brome and Heywood used for their play. The Master of the Revels, Herbert's deputy, stopped another play about witches from being performed at the Salisbury Court playhouse until the Globe play had finished its run. Tomkyns's account suggests that neither writers nor players took their propagandising duty very seriously. His own scepticism, completely ignorant as he was of the backstage manoeuvres, seems as deep as Laud's. All the play showed of witchcraft was 'things improbable and impossible', mere clowning about a piece of topical news.

Tomkyns preserved his judgement as an independent witness more worthily than the cheerfully credulous clowns among the players or the profoundly divided feelings of the Privy Councillors. The allegations of witchcraft were left as untouched by the event as the Privy Councillors. In spite of the falsity of the charges, the women were returned to prison in Lancashire. Three of them were still there three years later. Tomkyns's regret at the play's lack of 'poetical Genius, or art, or language' puts him in the Sidney class of playgoer, valuing poetry above 'ribaldrie' and 'fopperies to provoke laughter'. Such a delicate judgement may or may not have been shared amongst the other 'fine folke gentmen and gentweomen' who came to view the sensation.

None of these four accounts of plays in performance offers anything truly distinct as a characteristic crowd response. Manningham thought of *Twelfth Night* in stereotyped terms, Forman concentrated on the story-lines, and Tomkyns watched the witchcraft trickery from a standpoint which left him wishing he had been to something with more poetry. Holles went to the Globe because it was a political sensation, and saw enough to confirm his expectation.

To these distinctive accounts we should add the kinds of audience response noted by Richard Levin, which he finds favoured 'the portrayal of intrinsically interesting personalities and their actions', with an expectation that their actions can be viewed as real and that they should evoke the appropriate emotions with tears or laughter. These responses led Levin to sum up Shakespearean audiences as expecting chiefly 'a literal representation of individual characters and actions that were meant to be interesting and moving in their own right, and to embody the primary significance of the play'.[33] None of the evidence considered in this chapter runs seriously counter to that conclusion, though one important reservation should be noted. This is that the normative way of describing a play need not have been particularly close to a normative response to it in performance. Descriptions of plays quickly became conventional, obeying familiar prescriptions. The plays were summarised as a whole, registering their most distinctive features. These descriptions, especially those of Manningham and Forman, reflect the convention of describing plays much more exactly than they indicate the writer's complete response to the experience.

The best evidence for the convention is on the earlier titlepages of plays in quarto. From the early 1590s booksellers routinely pasted titlepages on posts in the city to advertise their latest products. Very likely some of them echoed the text set up for the printed playbills posted to advertise the day's performance, issued by specially licensed stationers like James Roberts. Roberts himself issued many of the early quartos, and could easily have copied their titlepage wording from his own playbills. Judging from some of the extant wording, play quartos were advertised in terms not unlike John Manningham's description of *Twelfth Night*. This is how *Richard III* was described on its first publication in 1597:

The Tragedy of King Richard the Third. Containing his treacherous Plots against his brother Clarence: the pittiefull murther of his innocent nephews: his tyrannicall usurpation: with the course of his whole detested life, and most deserved death. As it hath beene lately acted by the Right honourable the Lord Chamberlaine his servants.

Whoever wrote that had seen the play in performance and registered the emotions appropriate to the main incidents in the plot. Similarly, if more crudely, Roberts's issue of the first quarto of *The Merchant of Venice* in 1600 announced it as:

The most excellent Historie of the *Merchant of Venice*. With the extreame crueltie of *Shylocke* the Jewe towards the sayd Merchant, in cutting a just pound of his flesh: and the obtaining of Portia by the choyse of three chests.

Roberts was advertising a colourful show here, in the hint that Shylock gets his pound of bloody flesh. He chose the trial scene and the casket scene as the play's most memorable events. In a similarly spectacle-minded way he also issued *A Larum for London* for the same company in 1600, advertising it as 'A LARUM FOR LONDON, OR THE SIEDGE OF ANTWERPE. With the ventrous actes and valorous deeds of the lame Soldier'.

Playbills and play titlepages must have made their mark on people's idea of how to describe a play. The most lurid of all, rivalled only by a similar story from Holinshed played by the Chamberlain's Men in the mid-1590s, *A Warning for Fair Women*, was issued as early as 1592. It was *Arden of Faversham*, its titlepage declaring not only the story but its moral:

The Lamentable and True Tragedie of M. Arden of Feversham in Kent. Who was most wickedlye murdered, by the meanes of his disloyall and wanton wyfe, who for the love she bare to one Mosbie, hyred two desperate ruffins Blackwill and Shakbag, to kill him. Wherein is shewed the great mallice and discimulation of a wicked woman, the unsatiable desire of filthie lust and the shamefull end of all murderers.

However gruesomely this story was sensationalised, the similarity of such tabloid newspeak to Manningham's and Forman's descriptions supplies grounds for two suspicions. First, these accounts all followed a familiar and standardising pattern. Second, such a pattern gives us only a small part of the full range of possible responses by playgoers to what they experienced. A great deal is left out, not least any memorable poetry or Jonsonian 'application'. In the hinterland of audience response, too, they say nothing about the way the collective feeling augmented and intensified individual reactions to the story and its key moments. We read few comments on that even now.

One last distinguishing feature of early attitudes to playing deserves some attention. Pepys in 1661 confessed to himself to be 'troubled in mind that I cannot bring myself to mind my business, but to be so much in love with plays'.[34] In 1662 he congratulated himself over how well his work was now progressing in the absence of wine and playgoing. Perhaps rightly, most early playgoers did think of plays as just an entertainment, a distraction from the serious things of life. On 29 October 1630 Sir Thomas Roe wrote about the value of plays to Elizabeth of Bohemia, King Charles's sister, during a long closure for the plague. He told her:

Your Majesty will give me leave to tell you another general calamity; we have had no plays this six months, and that makes our statesmen see the good use of them, by the want: for if our heads had been filled with the loves of Pyramus and Thisbe, or the various fortunes of Don Quixote, we should never have cared who had made peace or war, but on the stage. But now every fool is enquiring what the French do in Italy, and what they treat in Germany.[35]

One of the underrated differences between playgoing then and seeing or reading the plays now is that we take them far more seriously. Locked as they are into education systems and into the commercial business of public entertainment, they have developed a status and a cachet in face of or because of the popular competition from movies, musicals and television Shakespeare that they never enjoyed in their own times. Probably the biggest single difference of playgoing then from now is the everyday nature of the plays they experienced.

Yet before leaving this territory, where in a sense the 'serious' study of Shakespearean stage poetry should begin, I should like to sketch in just one line of speculation about the serious impact of plays on these rarely privileged playgoers. By 1600 stage plays had turned into such a dominant feature of London's culture that it is impossible their stories should not have affected the society which harboured them in innumerable ways. Intangible though they are, these effects were part of the mental equipment playgoers took to the plays they saw. The repertory's intimate familiarity to the most frequent play-goers has been touched on already. A significant extension of that study turns up a few symptoms of a more pervasive impact. Since the minds and actions of monarchs have been most closely studied in recent years, I shall confine my speculations to two of them, plus one other incident that shows the complex interaction between life and fiction.

This last was a public scandal under King James that has already undergone book-length analyses of the interconnections between public news and contemporary use of the news and its 'application' in plays and masques.[36] That scandal was the tribulations and the trials of Frances, Lady Howard, over her divorce from the Earl of Essex. They were married when young, and Essex promptly went off on a grand tour for some years, allowing her to claim that the marriage was never consummated. After the divorce her remarriage was negotiated to her new lover, one of the king's favourites, and was followed by the charge that in 1615 she poisoned Sir Thomas Overbury in order to strengthen her position. Both lovers were disgraced, and forced by a reluctant monarch to live in retirement from the court. It was the biggest of many scandals at the Jacobean court, and was reflected in the plots of several plays written at the time. But on the other side of the same coin it might be argued that plays like Webster's *The White Devil* of 1611, with its portrayal of a woman using sex and poison to boost her career, helped to shape the public's view of the scandal if not that of its protagonists. As David Lindley has suggested, a patriarchal and fiction-derived reading of the case is analogous with other instances where fact and fiction are inextricably bonded together. Many other inscriptions of events shown on stage and thus shaping audience responses must have influenced the documentation about them that survives to generate the standard views of history.

Two other incidents hint at complex subterranean interactions between fiction and fact in this period. When the Essex rebels asked for *Richard II* to be staged on the afternoon before their attempted coup against Elizabeth they revealed some of the misconceptions which showed their rebellion to be such a sickly miscalculation of London's mood. Censorship had cut some of the scene in which Bullingbrook takes the crown from Richard out of all three of the quartos printed in Elizabeth's lifetime. After the coup failed, she herself acknowledged the point of the analogy which the Essex rebels tried to draw between Richard and herself, and commented on the frequent performances on the public stages. Since Elizabeth saw herself as Richard it was not surprising that the rebels saw Essex as Bullingbrook. He was after all a descendant of the Duke of Gloucester whose murder is held against Richard at the opening of the play, so he had a dynastic claim standing at no great distance from Bullingbrook's. Only a faith in stage fictions as political realities amongst the Essex followers can explain the romantic impracticalities underlying their plot.

Some comparably romantic notion of princes living in an Arcadian world and riding gallantly into histrionic action to seal international peace through human love must have sent Prince Charles and Buckingham, thinly disguised and swashbucklingly athletic as they rode through France, to confront the reluctant Spanish Infanta and conclude the long-drawn-out negotiations over their marriage. It had long been the ambition of Charles's father to create by the marriages of his children a union which would finally bring to an end the religious wars and particularly the exhausting hostilities between the two great empire-building kingdoms of England and Spain. Charles's adventures in their extravagant impulsiveness have the exact mode of Fletcherian tragicomedy. Thwarted love, disguise, princely knight-errantry and the happy ending necessary to love dramas were essential features of the mental constructs out of which Charles and Buckingham devised their political adventure. Its painfully ridiculous outcome, like the more plainly tragic result of the Essex rebellion, marks the remoteness of the protagonists from political reality. On arrival at the Spanish court Charles was refused access to the Infanta, so one morning he climbed the wall of her private garden, hid, and then sprang out in front of her. Not being so well versed in Arcadian romances, she screamed and fled, and he never saw her again. The old truism that, after Charles became king two years later, court displays of masques and dramas helped to conceal from him the knowledge of his real position was already there in the misconceptions that prompted the Spanish marriage adventure.

From that perspective Sir Thomas Roe was seriously underrating the power of drama.

Essex and his followers, like Charles and Buckingham, confused fictions with realities. Their minds were made suggestible by the stories the players supplied to them and their advisers. The minds of men in company, as Bacon put it (2.151), can easily be swayed by the sight of great actions on stage. We will probably never know with much precision how far the playhouse repertories might have influenced social and political thinking, but it was by far the most substantial form of social intercommunication available, the only kind of popular journalism and the only occasion when large numbers of people gathered together except for sermons and executions. It was certainly not cast in a minor role.

The shadowing in fiction of affairs of state, in a city trained and devoted to the arts of 'application', is a much sharper guide to popular and even to governing modes of thought about politics and society in Shakespearean times than the drama and films of today. The fictions of the stage were certainly far less marginal to affairs of state, not least because imaginative thought had few other outlets, and none which possessed the coerciveness of the minds of men in company. So it seems appropriate, as a final step in this outline history, to trace the sequence of playgoing tastes, the fashions that developed, ruled, changed and diversified between 1567 and 1642.

5

The evolution of tastes

THE FIRST PAYING PLAYGOERS (1567–87)

Once it took on a plainly commercial function, as it did when the Red Lion was built in 1567 and the Theatre came into use in 1576, London playgoing quickly became a settled institution. Its settled place in London's commerce, however, paradoxically meant that it became subject to rapid and incessant change. Regular attendances at a fixed venue required the impresarios to offer a constant supply of novelty. Whereas when travelling the players could sustain themselves with the same plays repeated in constantly changing venues, once the venue was fixed the repertory had to keep changing. As the chief determinant of this change there had to be an intimate interaction between the settled appetites of the playgoers and the food they were given. The result was constant, pressurised evolution in the players' repertoire of plays, a kind of cultural Darwinism, with the poets and their audiences as parents and the plays as their offspring. Henslowe's *Diary*, which records the financial labours of half of London's theatrical parentage at the peak of evolution in the 1590s, is above all an account of how intimate the interaction was between what the playgoers enjoyed and what the companies gave them. Between 1592 and 1600 Henslowe processed more than three hundred plays to feed London's new appetite. The history of Shakespearean playgoing has to start with the repertories which are the principal fossil record of this evolutionary process.

Most of the evidence about the repertory that James Burbage planted in his playhouses through the 1570s suggests that it had little new to offer at first. The amazing changes which took place at the end of the first twenty years, around 1588, look like a belated response by the impresarios and poets to the new demands the London venues were stimulating. No stock of the plays already in existence before the 1580s could have satisfied the tastes that revealed themselves in 1587 and 1588. Plays like *Common Conditions* (printed in 1576), *The Conflict of Conscience* (c.1572) and *Clyomon and Clamydes* (c.1570) all share a distinctly ungainly medley of moral teaching and romantic escapism, as if the bare commercial motive for entertainment could not walk out comfortably if it lacked the overcoat of morally instructive pretensions. Plays such as these were what the Queen's Men took around the country in 1583.[1]

The release from this moral overcoat which the professional London playhouses began to provide must have been due principally to the way the new playhouses created the first captive audiences. Only when plays could be offered to a crowd which had gathered and paid exclusively to enjoy a play were the poets freed to create offerings like *The Spanish Tragedy* and *Tamburlaine*. Audiences in country halls and at markets gathered for reasons either more weighty or more casual than seeing a play. Plays staged in banqueting halls were a garnish to the feast supplied by a generous host. The commercial playhouses set up for the first time a regular means for every playgoer to buy precisely and only the garnish of his or her own entertainment. The plays designed to feed such a well-focussed hunger followed.

In the 1560s use of an open market place or a banqueting hall meant that authority's frown was a recurrent danger. Once that was nationalised in 1578 with the appointment of a single censor, the Master of the Revels, the players had an easier time getting their plays licensed, although of course they now had to start with their new plays in London before taking them on tour. Romantic narratives or 'gallimaufreys' as Lyly called them, plays familiar on the travel circuit like *Clyomon and Clamydes*, were evidently the staple of the amphitheatre playhouses at first, and their popularity evoked enough protests from the more educated end of the audience range to give early notice of a social division in tastes. George Whetstone in 1578 and in the 1580s Gosson, Sidney and Lyly all objected to these medleys of romantic fantasy staged with cardboard monsters and knockabout clowns. The vigour of the protests might be taken as an acknowledgement of the hold on popular taste such plays had, and also of the players' now-evident aim to attract a mass rather than a select audience.

Brayne and Burbage's playhouses were built to supply an appetite they well knew already existed. The medleys or 'hybrid plays', as Anne Barton has called them, were based on assumptions about theatrical illusion which had grown to accompany a gradual swing in the mid-century from the didactic to the entertaining.[2] Burbage could probably tell from his gatherers by the 1580s that a new market was developing. A new middle zone of public taste, fixed in London, offered fresh possibilities to an urban audience. It was positioned somewhere between the taste of the court and the knockabout moralising of the country market places. The 'hybrid plays', Sidney's 'mungrell Tragycomedie', developed in the gap that opened near the beginning of the century between the community play of medieval religious drama and the 'self-contained play' of banqueting hall and court entertainment. Now there was a new body of urban playgoers who could begin to impose their presence and their preferences on their suppliers. Gosson in 1582 objected to the new community:

the common people which resorte to Theatres being but an assemblie of Tailors, Tinkers, Cordwayners, Saylers, olde Men, yong Men, Women, Boyes, Girles, and such like.   (2.8)

Everyone, that is, other than the gentry. Ordinary citizens, Gosson felt, needed protection from corrupting experiences like playgoing. But such citizens, even boys and girls, had the pennies to pay for their corruption, and money was power.

There was another reason for starting captive playgoing in London besides the growth of an urban body capable of paying for admission. This second reason might well be credited more directly to the poets than to the companies or the swell of social change. In the 1570s presenting plays at court was a conspicuous sign of the power and influence of the nobles whose companies presented them. The Earl of Leicester and the then Lord Chamberlain, the Earl of Sussex, played no small part in the sponsorship of the new playhouses and their London playgoers. J. Leeds Barroll has produced evidence to show that the status at court of major members of the Privy Council between 1573 and 1583 determined which companies were employed to perform the Christmas entertainments each year.[3] The plays and players must have proved entertaining enough to reflect the status of their sponsors at court to everyone's satisfaction. That mutual benefit no doubt helps to explain why Leicester got his company a royal patent in 1574, and why the position of Master of the Revels as the chief organiser of court entertainment was regularised in 1578. The potential tensions in such rival displays of ostentatious nobility may also explain why when Lord Chamberlain Sussex died in April 1583 the Master of the Revels, acting on Walsingham's orders for the Privy Council, immediately set up the Queen's company by making a clean sweep of all the star players from the leading nobles' companies, as if to check the rivalry by creating a royal monopoly.

Underlying these courtly manoeuvrings is the point that theatre had now become baldly a matter of secular entertainment, and a conspicuous one. The religious and folk rituals of Easter and May-games across the country were a distant memory, and the transitional didacticism of 'morality' plays was also going fast. Playgoers, now paying directly for their entertainment, were motivated exclusively by the pleasure they expected for their pennies. At this point their taste in pleasure meant that they now preferred to swallow fantasies of romantic knight-errantry on stage which were already familiar in print. The comic Vice of the morality plays riding to Hell on the Devil's back turned into a clown making his living by foolery. The moral requirement faded as the commercial incentive grew.

One factor which promoted the development of plays was fortuitous so far as the playing companies were concerned, but massive in its effect on the playmakers. When the queen took the best of the professional players for a company of which she made herself the patron, she galvanised London playing in two ways. First, her authority secured the new company better access to the city's own central venues, the inns, than could the companies patronised by lesser grandees. Secondly, the large size of the new company, with twelve sharers instead of the six or eight of Leicester's or Sussex's Men, gave the writers much better scope for plays that called for a bigger number of players. That sort of play was possible in London, where there were hundreds of would-be players on hand. This earliest period of development came to an end when, between about 1587 and 1594, the writers created an inflow of what might be called 'large' plays which made unique demands on the size of casts. They began to write plays specifically for London audiences.

From the ambitious period between 1587 and 1594 it is possible to identify at least fifteen plays which, even with thorough doubling of the lesser parts, required more players than did those written before or after. They include *The Wounds of Civil War, Edward I, Edward II, Edward III, 1 Henry VI, 2 Henry VI, 3 Henry VI, Sir Thomas More, Titus Andronicus, The True Tragedy of Richard III, The Famous Victories of Henry V, Friar Bacon and Friar Bungay, The Massacre at Paris, The Taming of the Shrew*, and the plot of *2 Seven Deadly Sins*. All four of the companies that began to dominate London playing from 1588 performed some of them: the Queen's, the Admiral's, Strange's and Pembroke's. When the Lord Chamberlain intervened officially in May 1594 and set up two new companies with even better privileges than the one royally patronised company of 1583, his action, or the circumstances prompting his creation of the new duopoly that replaced the Queen's Men's monopoly, seems to have cut back on this ambitious growth. From then on the London companies took in plays that routinely needed casts of little more than eleven men and four boys, a pattern that continued until 1642.

From May 1594 the new duopoly stabilised the position of the professional companies. London playgoing became for the first time a durable and settled activity. The duopoly companies stopped thinking of themselves as travelling groups who occasionally played in London, and became wholly London-based. The Privy Council actually assigned them to two suburban playhouses, the Rose and the Theatre, at the same time making a concession to the Lord Mayor by banning all future playing at the city's inns.

Like all evolutionary trends, many factors combined to alter the fare which playgoers consumed through the 1580s. Commercial security made larger companies and longer plays seem possible. The Queen's Men's plays like *Clyomon and Clamydes* show the state of growth in the 1580s. At 2,220 lines it was a consequence of the growth of the standard company from the five who played Skelton's *Magnyfycence* in the 1520s or the eight in *Cambyses* (c.1561) to the eleven men and four boys of *Tamburlaine* (1587) and the later plays.

The greatest stimulus to change was the fact that playing for any length of time at the one fixed venue created a hugely enlarged demand for new plays. So long as the companies travelled through the country they needed barely three or four scripts to satisfy their geographically dispersed clients. In London by the mid-1590s Henslowe's companies had to perform as many as thirty-five different plays in a year. Whether or not the playgoers truly needed constant novelty, a repertory that was committed to staging a different play every day of the week ensured that they got it. A third factor which must have influenced what playgoers saw was the poets' recognition, given a constant flow of the same kinds of playgoer, with what they could expect of such regular customers, and (more directly useful) with the companies for which they wrote their new plays. The fact that *Tamburlaine* included the number of parts which with doubling could be handled by a company of precisely the standard London size was no accident. With that size went quality. *Tamburlaine*'s verse was also written for players who had shown something of what could be done on a stage once poulter's measure and rhyming fourteeners were supplanted by decasyllabic blank verse. The Queen's company in 1583 had in Knell and Bentley as well as in Tarlton players who had developed a level of professional expertise well capable of encouraging other kinds of development.

Who were the paying playgoers at the first public playhouses in London? The outcry against them from the pulpits and Guildhall, which ran as a campaign with city funding from 1580 to 1584 and only stopped when the Privy Council set up the Queen's Men as a monopoly, makes it likely that it included few clerics or aldermen of the city, and certainly not the more puritanical of either group. In 1580, 1581 and 1584 there were 'affrays' which give rather more positive evidence, as well as indicating some of the tensions which the playhouses and the outcry against them generated.

Three Privy Council minutes of April to July 1580 dictate the action required over a scuffle which took place at a playhouse between men of Oxford's company and some law students. In April two players from Oxford's, Robert Leveson and Lawrence Dutton, were lodged in the Marshalsea prison 'for committing of disorders and frayes appon the gentlemen of the Innes of the Courte'. In July a letter ordered a bond for a year's good behaviour to be taken from Thomas Chesson, a former Oxford's player, to secure his release from prison.[4] This and the next incident are the only records of players actually coming to blows with playgoers in the entire history of the stage up to 1642, except for the attack by apprentices on Beeston's playhouse in 1617, which had a special cause, as we shall see. The 1580 affray was repeated the following summer, when once again a band of law students came to blows with a playing company. A City of London order of 11 July 1581 marked down

Parr Stafferton gentleman of Grayes Inne for that he that daye brought a dysordered companye of gentlemen of the Innes of Courte & others, to assalte Arthur Kynge, Thomas Goodale, and others, servauntes to the Lord Barkley, & players of Enterludes within the Cyttye. (2.7)

Despite the fact that Stafferton evidently took the initiative, the players were detained along with the gentlemen. Lord Berkeley himself intervened, asking the Lord Mayor to release his players and making himself answerable for their conduct. Players were now a mark of status, and needed the kind of care which valued possessions usually receive. We know nothing of the reasons for either of these summer affrays between the players and their customers, but it is unlikely to be related to the hostility either of the pulpit or Guildhall. It might have been a distant reflection of the rivalry between the noble patrons at court, or it may simply reflect at some remove the excitement generated by this major novelty in London's society. The Inns of Court students who made such a conspicuous section of later audiences must have joined the crowds at the new amphitheatres early on, and the affrays might have been little more than crude ways of making their presence felt. Certainly the documents about the affrays of 1580 and 1581 indicate that law students made their presence in the first audiences well known.

The third affray was gang warfare, between a serving-man and a group of handicraft apprentices at the Theatre in 1584. A few years later Henry Chettle commented that house servants and apprentices formed rival gangs in playhouses. Handicraft boys were usually the poorest apprentices. Elizabeth's chief minister, Lord Burghley, received a vivid report of the 1584 affray from William Fleetwood, who told it as a tale of gangland bravado. Again, it happened in the heat of summer.

Uppon Weddensdaye one Browne, a serving man in a blew coat, a shifting fellowe having a perrelous witt of his owne, entending a spoile if he cold have browght it to passe, did at Theatre doore querell with certen poore boyes, handicraft prentises, and strook some of theym, and lastlie he with his sword wonded and maymed one of the boyes upon the left hand; where upon there assembled nere a ml people.

. . . This Browne is a common cossiner, a thieff, & a horse stealer, and colloreth all his doynges here about this towne with a sute that he haithe in the lawe agaynst a brother of his in Staffordshire. He resteth now in Newgate . . .

(2.9)

Fleetwood went on to report that the Lord Mayor had issued an order to suppress the playhouses, and that James Burbage, owner of the Theatre, had resisted, claiming immunity as Lord Hunsdon's man. Hunsdon, Henry Carey, was the new Vice-Chamberlain, and Burbage was evidently hoping that his master's power at court would protect him against the city. Such disturbances would hardly have eased the Lord Mayor's displeasure against the amphitheatres, which technically were outside his jurisdiction in the suburbs, even though the Privy Council held him responsible for civil disorders in their vicinity, on the grounds that all citizen workers came from his territory.

Concern over the disorderly behaviour of the crowds at the public amphitheatres might have been intensified by the apparently contrasting docility of the gentlemen and ladies who attended the indoor playhouses in Paul's and the Blackfriars, which opened in 1575 and 1576. A plea in the prologue to *Sapho and Phao* (*c*.1584) suggests that Lyly wanted to remind his listeners that an audience made up exclusively of gentry should not behave in the same rough way as amphitheatre audiences. A gathering of gentlemen and ladies (the epilogue to *Gallathea* of the same period is addressed to 'You Ladies') ought not to give voice to any disapproval. The artfully diffident prologue for *Midas* (1589) suggests that true gentlemen would never actually hiss at what they disliked. Serving-men, apprentices and Inns of Court students at the Theatre and Curtain evidently did not behave like gentlemen.

Lyly's concern to differentiate the behaviour of the playgoers attending boy company plays from the crowds at the amphitheatres is to some extent a reflection of the narrowness of his ambitions. As will be seen below, his eye was always on the court rather than the commercial theatre. For years he manoeuvred to obtain the post of Master of the Revels, which Edmund Tilney secured in 1578. His plays at the first Blackfriars playhouse in 1583–4 and later at Paul's through 1587–90 were aimed precisely at courtiers and the gentry who were familiar with the court's major preoccupations. *Endimion* (1588) and *The Woman in the Moon* (c.1590), for instance, both make use of the stock courtier image of Elizabeth as Cynthia, the moon, and exploit the dogma of the king's two bodies as phases of the moon. Partly Lyly did this because the traditional identity of the boy companies as choristers who acted only for the improvement of their education and the incidental recreation of their betters gave him a claim to the top end of the market. Partly he did it as a means of holding the regular patronage of the courtiers through this specialised set of interests. The boy companies had specific but limited talents. They had a social cachet adult companies lacked. They could speak his lucid prose and exploit his wit-play but they would be an obvious second best to the adults at playing romantic heroics or the clowning of a Tarlton. These limitations made him offer decidedly different fare from the rumbustious popularism of the amphitheatres, and cater openly for more selective appetites. That the boy companies did not outlive the 1580s, that the Privy Council itself ordered them to be suppressed, and that Lyly died in penury is perhaps as much a measure of the growing strength of the competition as of his hazardous gamble.

TARLTON'S FOLLOWERS (1576–88)

'Rumbustious popularism' is a tendentious phrase which, however evocatively designed, needs some definition. 'Popularism' is an overused term when applied baldly to the Shakespearean repertory. For Harbage the chief distinction of the Globe was its artisan audience, which he called 'popular' as distinct from the 'select' or elite audiences of the indoor playhouses. Some Elizabethan writers gave him a precedent for this with their equally tendentious habit of distinguishing the 'private' halls from the 'public' amphitheatres. I would prefer to rescue the term 'popular' from the associations Ancient Pistol gave it ('base, common, and popular')[5] and keep it for those few phenomena like Tarlton and *Hamlet* which seem to have been truly popular in their capacity to 'please all'[6] at every level of English society.

Tarlton's fame, which made him a legend for sixty years after his death, is significant more for the phenomenon he represented than for any jokes he actually created. It is hardly too much to say that, as much as the Virgin Queen herself, he became the chief emblem of the emerging national consciousness towards the end of the sixteenth century. What Gabriel Harvey in a typically inventive doublet called 'piperly extemporising and *Tarletonising*'[7] became the hallmark of success as a professional entertainer. There had been professional jesters and fools before, both at court and in the May-games of peasant and artisan holidays. But Tarlton was the first to become a national figure, and most significantly his fame was equally potent at court, in the playhouse and in provincial towns. As a Queen's comedian he travelled the country more extensively and systematically than any player did before or after. The book of *Tarlton's Jests*, produced posthumously and including some chestnuts which Tarlton himself certainly never invented, marks the range of his popularity by dividing its stories about him into three categories. The titlepage records them as

1. His Court-witty Jests
2. His sound City Jests
3. His Countrey-pretty Jests.[8]

His popularity ran through the whole nation and through every social rank.

What probably says more than anything else about the leading adult players and their clients in the 1570s and 1580s is the relationship between Tarlton and Sir Philip Sidney. Tarlton was a Londoner, born in Ilford, almost within sound of Bow Bells, and first came to general notice as a comedian in the 1570s in the playing company of the then Lord Chamberlain, the Earl of Sussex. In 1576 he gave the press a serious poem, *Tarlton's Tragical Treatises*, which he dedicated to Frances Mildmay, Sussex's daughter, in an epistle describing himself as the Lord Chamberlain's servant. The intriguing thing about the fragment of this poem which survives is that it is a defence of poetry. As such it is a far cry from the arguments Sidney was to compose a few years later:

> Seth verse and I so different are,
> I'll press with ragged rhyme
> To manifest the mere goodwill
> That I to learning owe,
> No painted words but perfect deeds
> Shall my invention shew.[9]

Tarltons Ieſts.

Drawne into theſe three parts.

{ 1 *His Court-wittie Ieſts*
{ 2 *His found Cittie Ieſts.*
{ 3 *His Country prettie Ieſts.*

Full of Delight, Wit, and honeſt Myrth.

LONDON,
Printed for *Iohn Budge*, and are to be ſold at his ſhop, at the
great South doore of Paules. 1613.

19. Richard Tarlton with his stage trappings, pipe and tabor, from a woodcut on the titlepage of *Tarlton's Jests* (1613). John Astington (*Shakespeare Survey* 50, p. 163) considers the woodcut an earlier and more reliable reproduction than the celebrated drawing in Harleian MS 3885, f.19.

It is curious that a player and ballad-maker (his first ballad appeared in 1570) should spring to the defence not of playing but of poetry, just when the new public playhouses started stirring the city's animus. Perhaps it is accidental that Sidney should have written his *Apology* only three or four years later, under the prompting of Gosson's misapplied dedication of his anti-player *School of Abuse* to him in 1579. It is certainly odd that Sidney should have been so dismissive in the *Apology* of plays which mingled clowns and kings when he knew Tarlton so well that in the year he wrote the *Apology*, 1582, he agreed to be godfather to Tarlton's son.

Sidney's links with popular theatre and particularly with Tarlton are something of a mystery. Sidney evidently was a playgoer, and knew enough of London's current repertory in 1580 to incorporate in the *Apology* an extended condemnation of the 'gallimaufrey' plays. But the attitude he adopted in the essay clearly did not extend into his friendships in life. Like Whetstone, from whose *Promos and Cassandra* he probably took his attack on clowns consorting with kings, his position was ambivalent. Whetstone's prefatory epistle for the publication of his play in 1578 objected to the adult companies using clowns:

not waying, so the people laugh, though they laugh them (for theyr folleys) to scorne: Manye tymes (to make mirthe) they make a Clowne companion with a Kinge; in theyr grave Counsels, they allow the advise of fooles . . .

And yet in *Promos and Cassandra* itself a character, John Adroynes, is the 'clown' of the subplot and plays a rustic fool at court in exactly the mode of Tarlton. Sidney, whether he met Tarlton in the amphitheatres or at court, was no more consistent than Whetstone.

Tarlton's link with Sidney was by no means his only access to court circles. When he was dying in 1588 he appealed to the queen's most powerful factotum, Sir Francis Walsingham, to protect his six-year-old son, whose godfather Sidney had died two years before. Walsingham was Sidney's father-in-law. Like all the material relating to social patterns at this time the evidence for Tarlton's links with the aristocracy is more plentiful than his links with the rest of the nation. But all three categories in the *Jest Book* say the same thing. His capacity to inspire laughter was universal, and his fame as a comedian guaranteed his welcome at all social levels.

His comedy was rumbustious in degrees which varied according to his venue. At court and in his extemporising in the playhouses his act seems to have been more witty than knockabout, though wit survives more readily in print than knockabout does, and that assessment must be partly conditioned by the fact that the only surviving evidence is in print. The anecdotes in the *Jest Book* which report his extempore verses, especially two which he produced when apples were thrown at him by spectators, seem to be dependent on his reputation for their humour rather than to be justifications for it. A better mark of his rapport with his audiences is a pair of accounts about how the first sight of his face alone, peeping through the hangings at the back of the stage, could start people laughing. His stocky figure, peculiar squint and flat nose could set an audience off even without the pipe and tabor which announced his routine. Henry Peacham has a verse which speaks from first-hand experience:

> Tarlton when his head was onely seene,
> The Tirehouse dore and Tapistrie betweene,
> Set all the multitude in such a laughter,
> They could not hold for scarse an houre after.

Nashe in *Pierce Penilesse* (1592) tells how when Tarlton was with the Queen's Men on tour he reduced a country audience similarly, much to the annoyance of a local magistrate who felt the queen's servants deserved more respect than to be laughed at.[10]

His rumbustious knockabout and his exploitation of the comedy inherent in separating the clown from his stage parts in plays can be seen in Tarlton's first entry as a Kentish mechanick in the Queen's Men's play *The Famous Victories of Henry V*. The first scene presents Henry and various courtiers, and the second scene introduces the watch, four London citizens. They chat about what a peaceful night it is, until Tarlton breaks in on them. The stage direction reads '*Enter Dericke roving*'. He shouts 'Who there, who there?' and gallops off, re-entering a few moments later in the same manner.

DERICKE. Who there, who there, who there?
COBLER. Why what ailst thou? here is no horses.
DERICKE. I alas man, I am robd, who there, who there?
ROBIN. Hold him neighbor *Cobler*.
ROBIN. Why I see thou art a plaine Clowne.
DERICKE. Am I a Clowne, sownes maisters,
   Do Clownes go in silke apparrell?
   I am sure all the gentleman Clownes in Kent go so
   Well: Sownes you know clownes very well:
   Heare you, are you maister Constable, and you be speake?
   For I will not take it at his hands.

The comedy starts with Dericke charging past the four members of the watch while calling out for the watch to come because he has been robbed. It progresses into a joke about his rustic dress and the stock comedy of a countryman in the city. Between Robin's two speeches there must have been some wrestling, since the last line of this passage indicates Dericke's hostility to Robin. Broad comedy of this kind – physical knockabout, incongruous dress, comic stereotypes – warrants the term 'rumbustious'.

Playgoers could engage in this kind of comedy, with its extra-dramatic tactics of direct address to the audience with the clown speaking out of character or playing like Dcricke a part claiming not to be a clown. It depends largely on the audience knowing Tarlton as himself, and his special act after the play when he versified extempore on subjects given him by the audience. This familiar practice of backchat might easily spill into the play itself, as two of the *Jest Book* anecdotes indicate. Because both of them give some sense of the intimate kinship which existed between players and audience, they are worth quoting at length.

How *Tarlton* and one in the Gallery fell out.

It chanced that in the midst of a Play, after long expectation for *Tarlton*, being much desired of the people, at length hee came forth. Where (at his entrance) one in the Gallerie pointed his finger at him, saying to a friend that he had never seene him, That is he. *Tarlton*, to make sport at the least occasion given him, and seeing the man point with one finger, he in love againe held up two fingers: the captious fellow, jealous of his wife (for he was married) and because a Player did it, took the matter more hainously, and asked him why he made hornes at him? No (quoth *Tarlton*) they be fingers:

For there is no man, which in love to me,
Lends me one finger, but he shall have three,

No, no, sayes the fellow, you gave me the hornes. True (sayes *Tarlton*) for my fingers are tipt with nailes, which are like hornes, and I must make a shew of that which you are sure of. This matter grew so, that the more he medled the more it was for his disgrace; wherefore the standers by counselled him to depart, both hee and his hornes, lest his cause grow desperate. So the poore felow, plucking his hat over his eyes, went his wayes.

An excellent jest of *Tarlton* suddenly spoken.

At the Bul at Bishops-gate was a Play of Henry the 5 wherein the Judge was to take a box on the eare: & because he was absent that should take the blow, *Tarlton* himself (ever forward to please) took upon him to play the same Judge, besides his own part of the Clowne: and Knel then playing *Henry* the 5 hit *Tarlton* a sound boxe indeed, which made the people laugh the more, because it was he: but anon the Judge goes in, and immediately Tarlton (in his Clownes cloathes) comes out, and askes the Actors what newes? I (saith one) hadst thou been here, thou shouldst have seene Prince Henry hit the Judge a terrible box on the eare. What, man, said *Tarlton*, strike a Judge? It is true y faith, said the other. No other like, said *Tarlton* and it could not be but terrible to the Judge when the report so terrifies me, that me thinkes the blow remaines still on my cheek, that it burnes againe. The people laught at this mightily: and to this day I have heard it commended for rare.

The first of these anecdotes suggests something of the crowd psychology in such gatherings. If Tarlton picked on an individual it became a contest of wit where the crowd cheered the winner and jeered the loser, as they might in a physical struggle. Several of the 'sound City jests' have this outcome, mostly during a bout of extemporising in the playhouse. The crowd felt itself to be homogeneous, a gathering of like-minded pleasure-seekers out to enjoy their pennyworth. Possibly the men in the galleries took more part in the extemporising backchat than the crowd in the yard. Certainly the gallery was a more conspicuous place from which to conduct an exchange with the player. But there does not seem to have been any firm sense of social division between the standers in the yard and the sitters in the galleries of the kind which is shown later by the derisive references to 'understanders'. Tarlton made his audiences a single unit through the cohesion of shared laughter.

More than any other player in this history Tarlton seems to have been a positive influence on the evolution of his medium and the development of audience tastes. He probably invented, and certainly made famous, the figure of the cunning rustic clown. The word 'clown' first appears in English in the 1560s. Related to the Low German for a farmhand ('yokel' is probably the nearest equivalent} and perhaps helped by the courtly pastorals of the 1570s which used 'Colin' as a shepherd's name, it meant a country fool or cunning innocent. Tarlton put the stereotype on stage, dressing himself in country clothes, a buttoned cap, baggy slops in russet, a bag at his side and the pipe and tabor (a small side-drum) commonly used in country May-games. Chettle in *Kind-Harts Dreame* identifies Tarlton's ghost by 'his suit of russet, his buttond cap, his tabor, his standing on the toe, and other tricks' (2.14).

If it were not for Tarlton's use of it, very possibly the word 'clown' would now be no more in use than the alternative word 'swad', which also meant a yokel. Gabriel Harvey writes at the beginning of his commonplace book of being 'drowsely or swaddishly affected' (*Gabriel Harvey's Marginalia*, p. 87), and Sir John Davies has an epigram about a 'countrey swadd' whose behaviour to his lady is more direct than a courtier's. 'The Courtier first came lepping in, / And tooke the Lady by the chin, / The cuntry swadd as he was blunt / Came tooke the lady by the elbow.'[11] The currency Tarlton gave to 'clown' as the word for a stage yokel might have promoted 'swad' as an alternative that avoided the stage associations of the other word. The new term 'clown' was distinct enough for Jonson to invent an etymology for it, describing a clown in *A Tale of a Tub* 1.3.40–1 as a rustic, the Roman 'colonus', a colonist or farmer. '*Colonus* is an Inhabitant: / A Clowne originall.'

Tarlton thus had a persona, the innocent abroad whose guileless front makes him the butt who always wins in the end. As Dericke in *The Famous Victories* he is a countryman from Kent who copes with the affairs of London and the court by virtue of his native wit. He made the stereotype of the guileless rustic so popular that several commentators after his death claimed that real countrymen were imitating Tarlton.[12] Touchstone in *As You Like It*, the urbane court fool entering Arden's country world of rustics, performs his part as a very self-conscious opposite to Tarlton, and enjoys a sophisticated game of reversed clowning against the stereotype which his audience clearly knew well, even though by the time *As You Like It* came to the stage its originator had been dead for eleven years.

In one sense Tarlton was old-fashioned even in the 1580s. He based his act on direct address to the audience and exploited the gap between the player and his play-role at a time when plays were generally moving towards the more illusionistic mode of the self-contained play. Comedy seems always to have been slower to take on new fashions than tragedy. Captive audiences encourage illusion, which separates the stage spectacle from its beholders and the consequent identification of players with their roles. As a trend this never went so far as cinematic realism makes possible today. Richard Burbage as Hamlet could still step outside his role to joke about Polonius having previously played Caesar and his killer playing the 'brute' part. That kind of in-joke aside, though, Burbage evidently did convince his audiences of the reality of the roles he played. His elegist's account in 1619 tells of him playing the death of Hamlet in so lifelike a way that not only the spectators but his fellow players thought he was truly dying (2.134). This is an exaggeration, but the terms the elegist chose for praising Burbage were echoed by Thomas May and others and show how fully the power of dramatic illusion in the self-contained play had by 1620 taken over from Tarltonising. In the 1590s the word 'personation' came into the language of playing for the first time. Tarlton's kind of audience, drawn by his fame and united by comedy into intimacy with the players, did not long outlast the 1580s. Will Kemp of the Chamberlain's Men copied his roles, but his style did not last long in the new century.

Tarlton himself was by no means the only star of his company. Traditionally the clown had his special extra-dramatic act, which could easily force its way into the play itself as it did when Tarlton took the Chief Justice's role in *The Famous Victories*, but he was also a member of the team. He took smallish parts in such plays as *King Leir* and *The Troublesome Raigne of King John,* both of which the Queen's Men were playing in 1588. All three plays, however, were closer to being star vehicles for the tragedians than for Tarlton or his fellow comic Robert Wilson. Nashe called Tarlton a king, and the ruler of traditional and popular audience taste he certainly was. But his successors as clowns or fools found the scope of their acts narrowing and by Tarlton's death the tragedians were recognised as the chief drawcard. Marlowe's Tamburlaine was ready to replace Tarlton when he died in 1588. In that year the shift in audience priorities from knockabout to tragic poetry was voiced with all its author's arrogance as a direct thrust against the clown. Marlowe's prologue to *Tamburlaine* announced his stage's withdrawal

> From jigging veins of rhyming mother wits
> And such conceits as clownage keeps in pay.

In 1590 Marlowe's publisher followed his author's preference by omitting the 'fond and frivolous gestures' which despite what the prologue claimed did still accompany the play in performance.[13] Whetstone and Sidney's protests, objecting to mindless laughter ('mother wits' means moithering or fuddling the wits), now had something from Marlowe to put against them. The paucity of evidence about audience attitudes in this period, and *Tamburlaine*'s publisher's note, should make us careful not to read too much into Marlowe's prologue. In the long run, though, there is no doubt that by 1588 audiences were beginning to follow where Marlowe led.

LYLY'S SPECIAL APPEAL (1580–90)

The social breadth of Tarlton's popularity has to be set against the continuing competition between the adult companies and the boy choristers. Tarlton and the Queen's Men secured a near-monopoly of adult playing in 1583, but the adults still had rivals in Paul's School and the Chapel Children playing at Richard Farrant's hall in the Blackfriars precinct. In the years between 1575 when Paul's Boys got their playhouse and the establishment of the Queen's Men when Sussex died in 1583 the honour of performance in the holiday seasons at court went mostly to the adults. But the child companies were by no means forgotten. Even Richard Mulcaster's boys at the Merchant Taylors' School performed seven or eight times at court in the decade up to 1583. A Privy Council edict of 1578 lumped boy companies in with adults as professional entertainers.

Unlike the adults, who on the whole spent more time in the country than in London, the boys performed exclusively in London. The relative infrequency of their performances – one a week at most compared with the almost daily plays at the amphitheatres – together with their more exclusive venues inevitably meant that their audiences came from a narrower and higher social range than went to the amphitheatres. Halls, admitting smaller numbers, all seated, using artificial light, more intimate in scale and proximity to the stage, also had the superior social cachet of the banqueting hall environment which helped to maintain the fiction that the boys played not for money but to demonstrate their educational skills. In practice the boys did get some schooling, two or three hours daily for the Paul's choristers, and their voices were certainly trained for singing. Since the education curriculum in Elizabethan schools targeted the art of good speaking, performing plays was a logical extension of that aim, and one which an educated audience would have been well trained to appreciate. Inherently the boy chorister performances were far removed from Tarlton's popularism.

Playgoers, however, were demanding paymasters. The Guild of Merchant Taylors stopped performances by their boys in 1574, on the grounds of wounded dignity.

... every lewd persone thinketh himself (for his penny) worthye of the chiefe and most comodious place withoute respecte of any other either for age or estimation in the comon weale, whiche bringeth the youthe to such an impudente familiaritie with their betters that often tymes greite contempte of maisters, parents, and magistrats foloweth thereof, as experience of late in this our comon hall hath sufficiently declared.[14]

Disrespectful crowds of Londoners jostling the worshipful masters who were their official hosts marked the end of the banqueting hall tradition. They also promised a better reception for large and loud adult players than for boys.

The most outstanding feature of the boy company repertory in the 1580s was the drama of John Lyly. As with Marlowe's work for the adult players in the same decade it is difficult to see exactly how much Lyly's work was original, in that sense of imaginative creation which Coleridge identified with and for his poetry, or how much it was an intelligent and sensitive writer's response to the theatrical opportunities his time offered him. Certainly the style of *Euphues*, set in dialogue, was a novelty to the boys of Paul's, whose plays till then had been a mixture of morality and romance. But its measured, wittily elegant prose was well suited to a company of ten boys trained in elocution rather than swordplay. Lyly's activities, carefully designed and wholly distinctive in the audience they aimed at, though ultimately not commercial successes, carry some intriguing implications about playgoing in the 1580s.

Lyly was almost certainly drawn to write for the theatre by the manoeuvres at court in the early 1580s when Leicester, Sussex, Oxford and other nobles began using companies of players to exhibit their power and influence. When Walsingham destroyed the rival companies in April 1583 by taking their leaders for the Queen's Men, Oxford moved quickly to monopolise the boy players, who Walsingham had not touched. In June he took a lease of the Blackfriars playhouse and hired Lyly to write for an amalgamated company of the Blackfriars and Paul's boys. The Paul's master, Sebastian Westcott, had died in 1582 and his successor, Thomas Gyles, was not a producer of plays.[15] Oxford sponsored the amalgamated company at court in the next two Christmas seasons, where they played Lyly's *Campaspe* and *Sapho and Phao*. In mid-1584, however, the owner revoked the lease of the Blackfriars playhouse and Lyly had to wait three years before resuming at Paul's, where he produced plays from 1587 to 1590. An ironic letter written in 1585 by Jack Roberts says that 'my Lord of Oxenfordes man called Lyllie' would be sure to put anything personal or satirical into the mouths of the Paul's boys if he could.[16] Lyly made the boy company cater for the intimate world of courtiers and court gossips.

Campaspe was evidently not a success on stage, judging from the prologue written for the Blackfriars performances of its successor, *Sapho and Phao*. It set out to offer a distinct contrast with the adult repertory through its elegant prose repartee. It also sought to exploit the distinctive nature of the boys' talents, for instance in 5.1, where successively one boy performs a dance, another '*tumbleth*' and a third '*singeth*'. The prologue for Blackfriars of *Sapho and Phao* is defensive, clearly signalling Lyly's hopes of a distinctly quiet set of playgoers:

Our intent was at this time to move inward delight, not outward lightnesse, and to breede, (if it might bee) soft smiling, not loude laughing.

(*Complete Works*, II.371)

There is no doubt here to whom Lyly is appealing for approval. Sidney had completed his *Apology* only a year or two before Lyly wrote *Sapho and Phao*, and it was evidently circulating in manuscript around the court and the gentry to whom Lyly addressed this prologue. Soft smiling is the gentlemanly alternative to the loud laughter evoked by the clowns, and which Sidney attacked in the *Apology* as an 'extreme show of doltishnesse . . . fit to lift up a loud laughter and nothing else'. Lyly's plays are a direct response to Sidney's condemnation of the 'mungrell Tragy-comedie' which mingled clowns with kings. His prologue invited the Blackfriars audience to share Sidney's preference.

This appeal was not heard with universal sympathy. Lyly had stressed the gentlemanly composition of the Blackfriars audience and pleaded for gentlemanly restraint if not positive approval of his Sidneian offering in his first Blackfriars prologue, for *Campaspe*.

Onelie this doeth encourage us, that presenting our studies before Gentlemen, though they receive an inward mislike, wee shall not be hist with an open disgrace.   (2.11)

Gentlemen will surely be courteous towards boys. It is a weakly defensive assumption of good behaviour, and does not sound entirely confident that it will prove well justified.

If Lyly did get such audiences they did not bring him great profit. In 1589 he tangled himself in the Marprelate controversy, writing pamphlets and possibly plays for the church establishment, with the result that once the government had captured the Marprelate printing press and tried to clamp down on all the controversy it stopped plays at Paul's altogether. Tarlton had also been involved in anti-Marprelate propaganda with the Queen's Men, but they survived. Only Lyly and the sole surviving boy company suffered directly. The gentlemanly appeal of Lyly's plays was not strong enough to gain them any favour in competition with rumbustious popularism, which to the government began to seem like bread and circuses. Playgoers were too fond of loud laughter to sustain a gentlemanly repertoire beyond the 1580s.

MASS EMOTION AND THE ARMADA (1588–99)

What seduced playgoers between 1587 and the end of the century was more than anything else an increase in the emotional immediacy of the plays' subject matter. England fought with Spain not only at sea facing the Armada but on land across the North Sea for the Dutch fighting Spanish imperialism. Militarism and hostility to Spain and Spain's Catholicism amongst London audiences was mirrored on stage. For more than ten years wars and stories of wars became the main meal on the broad platforms of the amphitheatres. There were no hall playhouses available through these years to offer more intimate fare, but the mood was in any case right for the drums, swordplay and noise which suited the larger stages and natural daylight of the open-air playhouses.

The success of swordplay on stage in the 1590s may have been partly a cause and partly an effect of the disappearance of the halls. The evidence is complex and inconclusive. The adults appear to have had access to large rooms at city inns in Gracechurch Street through the winter,[17] and when the Privy Council finally bowed to the Lord Mayor and blocked that outlet in 1594 James Burbage built an indoor playhouse at Blackfriars for the first of the duopoly companies. The divide between halls for boys and amphitheatres for adults was maintained for the next fourteen years against the will at least of Burbage, first by the final ban on playing at city inns in 1594, and then by the ban on his new playhouse in 1596. Largely by accident authority connived at maintaining the adults in the open-air playhouses and their battle displays which developed with the Armada in 1588. The stages built for crowds standing in daylight were much safer for battle scenes and swordfighting than candle-lit stages in enclosed halls.

Swordplay was already a standard offering on the amphitheatre platforms of the 1580s in exhibition bouts and prize fights. It was a simple matter to add it to the plays. Tarlton became a Master of Fence in 1587 by fighting seven other masters, so he for one had the skill to entertain in this fashion. Others clearly had it too. In *Orlando Furioso* the hero, played by Edward Alleyn, engages in a duel on stage which the quarto text scores with the stage direction '*they fight a good while and then breathe*'. At the Red Bull, where Alleyn's swashbuckling tradition survived right up to the closure, a feltmaker's apprentice in 1623 sitting on the edge of the stage was hurt by a player during a stage swordfight. His pride was more injured than his body, and he held to the spirit of the playgoing occasion by issuing a challenge to the player who wounded him.[18] The duel which concludes *Hamlet* was conceived for the open-air stages used for fencing displays.

Playgoing became a uniform custom in the 1590s for a variety of reasons. The only playhouses available were amphitheatres, which limited one kind of choice. Helped by a long closure for the plague in 1593 and the deaths of several playing company patrons, which freed their 'servants', in May 1594 the government licensed two new companies. They thrived in the prosperous years which followed: Shakespeare and Burbage's company patronised by the Lord Chamberlain himself, and Alleyn's company under the Chamberlain's son-in-law the Lord Admiral. The so-called 'duopoly' dominated playing for the next thirty years, and in one case right to the closure of 1642.

Henslowe's accounts of the Admiral's Men's activities in these years are the most vivid record we have for the way players and their poets struggled to satisfy playgoers' tastes. Unfortunately the accounts are primarily financial, and only secondarily about the plays which were fed to the playgoers. More than half the plays named in Henslowe's records have vanished, and the only direct evidence he provides about playgoers is the frequency with which some kinds of play were fed to them.

The uniformity of playgoing through this period, when only the two companies shared a monopoly of playing in London, suggests that the playgoers came from all the social strata. What little other evidence there is tends to support this supposition. It says nothing about whether some playgoers might have preferred other kinds of fare or other kinds of playhouse. The impresarios who reopened the hall playhouses in 1599 and 1600 clearly thought they would. Nonetheless, a total of two licensed amphitheatres in the suburbs was the sole official provision from 1594 till 1600. The comments of Sir John Davies and others indicate that the full range of society accepted amphitheatre playgoing in this period, courtiers, the 'clamorous fry' of law students, citizens, whores, porters and house-servants, ladies and the city's womenfolk.

Nashe did a little sociological delving in *Pierce Penilesse* to identify the kind of people who might be free to attend a play on a working afternoon.

. . . the after-noone beeing the idlest time of the day; wherein men that are their owne masters (as Gentlemen of the Court, the Innes of the Courte, and the number of Captaines and Souldiers about *London*) do wholy bestow themselves upon pleasure, and that pleasure they devide (howe vertuously it skils not) either into gameing, following of harlots, drinking, or seeing a Playe . . .

The players themselves were blameless:

Whereas some Petitioners of the Counsaile against them object, they corrupt the youth of the Cittie, and withdrawe Prentises from their worke; they heartily wishe they might bee troubled with none of their youth nor their prentises; for some of them (I meane the ruder handicrafts servants) never come abroade, but they are in danger of undoing . . .   (2.15)

A comparatively innocent use of leisure. The other side of that picture should be set alongside Nashe's, because it goes some way towards explaining why the authorities, especially the city fathers whose function was to control civil and criminal trouble, were so concerned about the new institution.

Playhouses are designed to attract crowds, and crowds attract criminals and civil disorders. In a city with no police force and minimal ways of enforcing the law, that design created a major headache for the

London authorities. The playhouses were in the suburbs where the justices of Middlesex and Surrey ruled, but the Privy Council expected the London authorities to control any riots by Londoners whether in the city or its suburbs. Robert Greene's second cony-catching pamphlet records how playgoers were fair game for criminals in 1591.

At plaies, the Nip standeth there leaning like some manerly gentleman against the doore as men go in, and there finding talke with some of his companions, spieth what everie man hath in his purse, and where, in what place, and in which sleeve or pocket he puts the boung and according to that so he worketh either where the thrust is great within, or else as they come out at the dores.

(2.13)

When Francis Langley proposed building a new playhouse, the Swan, the Lord Mayor, Sir John Spencer, who was the most insistent antitheatrical mayor of them all, wrote to Lord Burghley on 3 November 1594 asking that all of London's playhouses should be pulled down.

... the quality of such as frequent the sayed playes, beeing the ordinary places of meeting for all vagrant persons and maisterles men that hang about the Citie, theeves, horsestealers, whoremoongers, coozeners, connycatching persones, practizers of treason, and other such lyke.   (2.22)

He used the same terms in his petition to ban all plays sent to the Privy Council on 28 July 1597. The city authorities were particularly frustrated by the location of the amphitheatres in the suburbs, where disorders by gangs of apprentices were most likely to break out. Both Shoreditch and the Bankside supported thieves' kitchens and brothels as well as the bear-baiting and playing amphitheatres. When Davies wrote about 'free' Fuscus, or Rowlands joked about gallants choosing between a play and a bawdy house (2.20, 42), they were lumping together the main activities of London's haunts of pleasure. Even if we ignore the outcry from the pulpits it seems reasonable to assume that most playgoers were the 'free' in whose view of life pleasure rated a high priority.

The forms playgoing took changed quite emphatically by the end of the decade. One of the consequences of having only the one kind of venue seems to have been an intensified pressure to evolve new forms. That pressure affected the evolution of audience likes and dislikes in distinct ways, one of the more striking being a development in the sense of reality in the subjects portrayed on stage.

Reality on stage in the 1590s is a complex thing. It was not simply stage realism, though that went with it, but something more like an emotional response to staged events which depended for its strength on a conviction that the display was a form of truth. There is a resounding sense of its power in Francis Bacon's recognition of it in his comment on the minds of men in company (2.151), though when he wrote in 1625 it was still a new phenomenon.

Whatever the reason – the new poets, the evolution of playgoing, and the national shock of the Armada all had a little to do with it – the minds of men in company at plays in the 1590s needed stronger meat for their affections than the 1580s had given them. The 1590s made a great evolutionary leap from the fantastic images so handsomely derided by Gosson in 1582:

Sometime you shall see nothing but the adventures of an amorous knight, passing from countrie to countrie for the love of his lady, encountring many a terrible monster made of broune paper, & at his retorne, is so wonderfully changed, that he can not be knowne but by some posie in his tablet, or by a broken ring, or a hankircher or a piece of a cockle shell [19]

The leap was towards what Nashe described in the audience for Shakespeare's *1 Henry VI* in 1592, the common response to a realistic evocation of a real event:

How would it have joyed brave *Talbot* (the terror of the French) to thinke that after he had lyne two hundred yeares in his Tombe, hee should triumphe againe on the Stage, and have his bones newe embalmed with the teares of ten thousand spectators at least (at severall times) who, in the Tragedian that represents his person, imagine they behold him fresh bleeding. (2.15)

This is the first description of a mass emotion other than laughter in any London playhouse. If, as is likely, Shakespeare's play about military disasters across the Channel was the 'harey the 6' of Henslowe's *Diary*, then the receipts for its performance at the Rose on Bankside suggest that Nashe underestimated the numbers so moved by at least a half. It was Henslowe's most profitable play after *The Wise Men of Westchester*, a knockabout comedy. Serious matters with an immediate gut appeal to the militarism which set sail in England against the Armada soon took a grip on the repertory. They gave playgoers the tears of conviction. What the players had to supply in supplement to that was plausible impersonation. That, with Shakespeare's development of 'personation' in the interactions between characters on stage, replacing the domineering emotionalism of Marlowe's mighty line, was what grew from the evolutionary leap of the 1590s.

The great stage figures of Marlowe's period, Tamburlaine, Faustus and the hero of *The Spanish Tragedy*, share several features. They are all historical or quasi-historical figures with no great claim to a place in the history books. They all speak great verse. They all have powerfully individual personalities, and they all face immense personal challenges. Their verse was mocked by the more advanced tastes as early as 1597 (see 2.29), and it was chiefly their individuality which gave them all such enduring lives on the stage up to 1642, while stereotypes like Tarlton's clown retreated to the fringes or disappeared altogether. Mass emotion in playgoers and powerful 'personation' on stage grew together at the end of the 1580s.

Marlowe's mighty line has been analysed thoroughly, usually as an innovation in the development of spoken verse, which it certainly was. I would add to that analysis two other reasons for its fame, both of them likely consequences of the growth of London playgoing. In varying degrees they are both conjectural, but they fit the other evidence and have strong implications. The first is the extent to which Marlowe's verse was designed to work on the audience's emotions. Marlowe was one of the first university wits to grasp the new opportunities which the willing captives in the London amphitheatres gave poets. He must have recognised his own power to sway audiences with words, that great secret in nature which Bacon saw as the susceptibility of the minds of men in company. Poets had never before been able to take the opportunity to move the 'affections' of three thousand packed and willing hearers at one time. Marlowe was the first poet to grasp that chance.

The second reason is the part played by Tamburlaine, Faustus and Hieronymo in the growth of 'personation'. The term first came into use in the 1590s, signalling not only the concept of a player pretending to be a real human being (as distinct from Magnificence or a king like Cambyses) but the arrival of stage heroes through whom many of the spectators could identify themselves and their wants. Each of the three characters drew his force from one of the three deepest wells of emotion in the Elizabethan mind. Tamburlaine the shepherd turned conqueror embodied militarism and earthly power. Faustus the sceptic embodied religious doubt. Hieronymo the revenger constructed a model for earthly justice in a corrupt world. Three such potent embodiments of Elizabethan emotions did not evolve and thrive on the stage without strong support from their audiences.

These three wells will be drawn on in the next section. One feature of the 1590s which is missing from them should be noted first: all three were peculiarly masculine preoccupations. In all the seventy-five years between 1567 and 1642 no other decade supplied so little of what was expected to please the women in the audiences. Shakespeare did produce his romantic comedies, and a few domestic dramas (considered in a later section) may have been designed to attract women. But the masculine affairs of war and military history, and the bawdy clownings which pervade the repertories of the 1590s show less concern for the women playgoers than any plays before or after.

RULE, RELIGION AND REVENGE (1588–99)

Tamburlaine launched a fashion which Nashe in 1589 unkindly called 'the swelling bumbast of a bragging blanke verse' (2.12). Appropriately enough Nashe took his metaphor from the fashion in dress favoured by the Spanish enemy, padded or bombasted sleeves and fustian doublets, clothing both exhibitionistic and (by association) militaristic. Alvin Kernan's phrase for Marlowe's style, 'the pathetic fallacy in the imperative mood',[20] nicely captures the assumptions about earthly sympathy and human aggression which Tamburlaine represented to the original playgoers. The imperiousness of his 'stalking and roaring', which half a dozen commentators mention in the 1590s, opened a rich vein for Henslowe and the poets to suck.

A plethora of imitations soon showed its value. *Selimus, Alphonsus of Aragon, The Wars of Cyrus*, the two parts of *Tamar Cham*, probably the lost *Cutlack* and *Muly Molloco* which feature as two of Henslowe's more popular plays, plus *The Battle of Alcazar* and plays about English soldiers abroad such as *Sir Thomas Stukeley*, besides the less battle-ridden plays of political isolationism such as *Friar Bacon and Friar Bungay* all share the narrow nationalism and militancy which Marlowe first gave voice to.

Few of these imitations outlasted the decade in the playwriting fashion, though playgoers proved more durable. *Tamburlaine* itself drew mockery among some playgoers both for its verse and for Alleyn's strutting in the title role. He was universally seen as a mighty conqueror, and some commentators emphasised his rise from Scythian shepherd to great king. Donne in *The Calme* (1597), Rowlands in 1605 and Middleton in a city pageant of 1623 all emphasised his social climb. In time his stage presence became a joke. Beside Joseph Hall, other sarcastic references to *Tamburlaine* include Marston's in *Histriomastix* (c.1597, G1r) and *Antonio and Mellida* (1599, Induction), E. S. in *The Discovery of the Knights of the Post* (1597, C2v); Dekker (*The Wonderfull Yeare*, 1603, C4v); T. M. (*The Blacke Booke*, 1604, D1r), and of course Ancient Pistol.[21] The mockery makes it tempting to assume an evolution in audience taste away from bombast and battle heroics, and certainly some parts of playgoing society went in that direction. It is even more tempting to trace the development in Shakespeare from

Talbot to Henry V as a more central line of evolution. In the Queen's Men's *Famous Victories* Henry is transformed from dissolute prince to all-conquering king by nothing identifiable in human psychology other than the prodigal son's redemption, whereas the companion of Falstaff in Eastcheap undergoes a complex process of entirely human adaptation. But to fall for such temptations is easy and unhelpful. There were certainly developments in the complexity of character psychology before *Hamlet* broached it as a new interest in 1600, but almost all of them were Shakespeare's own. With the marginal exception of Marlowe in *Edward II* the principal developer of 'personation' besides Shakespeare was Kyd with his mad Hieronymo.

No one feature will explain the unique and lasting popularity of *The Spanish Tragedy* on the Shakespearean stage. Throughout the seventeenth century it was quoted and burlesqued more than any other play, even *Hamlet*. Claude Dudrap[22] has identified quotations from it in fifty-nine plays performed between 1591 and 1642, a startlingly powerful measure of its quotability and its enduring familiarity with playgoers. Such popularity was not due to its verse alone, and there may well be some cogency in Muriel Bradbrook's suggestion that the play is a 'projection of deep fears, the exorcism of guilt which the actors and audience shared'.[23] Revenge is a complex phenomenon psychologically as well as morally, and the conclusion to the play, doing earthly justice through the enactment of a masque by the characters on stage, may as Bradbrook suggests be an oblique form of response to the long-lasting assault by the church against the theatre.

No Elizabethan could have taken lightly Hieronymo's debate with himself over the morality of revenge in 3.13, in which he weighs Seneca, ten of whose revenge plays had appeared in English in 1581, against God's word in Genesis that earthly revenge is wrong and justice sits only in heaven. Hieronymo's choice of Seneca resounded in many people's minds as justice, however rough. Bradbrook identifies a Christian context for the play's appeal: 'The figure of the human Revenger represents assimilation and mastery of fear evoked by such a work as Dr Thomas Beard's *Theatre of God's Judgement* (1597), where, upon the stage of the whole universe, God is seen as the supreme Revenger.' Beard's citation of figures well known in the playhouse, such as Tamburlaine, Arden of Faversham, Richard III and Antony and Cleopatra, probably echoed the fears of not a few playgoers. Like Hamlet, Hieronymo appealed because he was hero and victim at once. He enjoyed his revenge and he paid God's price for his pleasure. The play's popularity must have struck chords somewhere in the depths of ambivalent Elizabethan psyches.

On the face of it *Faustus* served a much more straightforward religious purpose. Its displays of devilry at work were said to be capable of provoking reactions of mass hysteria in both audience and actors. It was staged in religious technicolour, between the understage area, traditionally the hell which lay beneath the earth of the stage platform itself, and the heavens of the zodiac-painted stage cover. A description written in 1620 shows that Alleyn's playhouse kept these traditions unchanged for many years.

> . . . men goe to the *Fortune* in *Golding-Lane*, to see the Tragedie of Doctor *Faustus*. There indeede a man may behold shagge-hayr'd Devills runne roaring over the Stage with Squibs in their mouthes, while Drummers make Thunder in the Tyring-house, and the twelve-penny Hirelings make artificiall Lightning in their Heavens.   (2.137)

For all that roaring and flashing, the play generated plenty of tension. One reference, which has a ring of truth in its offhand delivery, tells of a man with 'a head of hayre like one of my Divells in Doctor *Faustus*, when the olde Theater crackt and frighted the Audience'.[24] There is probably more truth in that account of audience tension than the story of the players who suddenly noticed during a performance that there was one devil too many in the company, and fled, spending the night in prayer and repentance.[25] A similar fright was generated by a cracking noise from the timbers in the courtroom during the trial of an alleged witch over the Overbury murder.

However fanciful such stories seem, the religious power of *Faustus* should not be underestimated. Alleyn played the role in a surplice with a cross stitched on the front, according to a verse by Samuel Rowlands.[26] It is not unlikely that in wearing such a costume he was taking precautions against his own premature damnation. The play was certainly seen as a morality of intellectual pride suffering the pains of hell, just as *Tamburlaine* was seen as its converse, to judge from all the references to 'that Atheist *Tamburlan*'.[27] When Marlowe died so spectacularly in a tavern brawl in 1593, whether or not the knife thrust was aimed by a Privy Council spy, his fate was hailed from the pulpits as God's judgement in exactly the form his play seemed to depict. Its popularity very largely depended on audiences viewing the stage spectacle as moralistic and personal.

Henslowe's records confirm what contemporary references would have suggested anyway, that these three plays along with Shakespeare's were the staple fare that excited playgoers, guaranteed the players' prosperity up to 1600 and indeed fixed the basic lines of taste in plays for generations to come. But there is evidence for other tastes as well, and the full banquet must include a lot more than these main dishes. Comedy also changed rapidly and its changes show signs of a divergence in audience tastes towards the end of the decade. Perhaps the most illuminating change of all, though, was the arrival of contemporary events openly reproduced on the stages.

CURRENT AFFAIRS (1588–1603)

In the 1590s the popular playhouses began to tap that reservoir of curiosity about the real lives of living people which is now the chief refreshment in newspapers. Newsworthy people and events, the quotidian gossip of journalism, turned up as stage fare for a wide range of audience appetites. Thomas Platter described Londoners as 'learning at the play what is happening abroad; indeed men and womenfolk visit such places without scruple, since the English for the most part do not travel much, but prefer to learn foreign matters and take their pleasures at home'.[28] The much-travelled Platter might regard this as insularity, but he was also identifying the first great market for daily journalism. The depiction of contemporary affairs in the playhouses, although the evidence is patchy and fragile, does offer a testimony to the increasingly day-by-day ordinariness of playgoing, and its shifts offer some testimony about the social dispositions of the people at whom the players aimed.

Lyly's covert allusions to contemporary affairs were plainly (almost the only plain thing about them) in-jokes for the tightly cohesive gossips of the court and its associated gentlefolk. Jack Roberts's reference in 1585 to Lyly's use of Paul's boys was to his publication on stage of the sort of tattle and scandal which professional letter-writers like Whyte and Chamberlain included in their reports. Early in the seventeenth century newspapers were invented to feed this appetite, as Jonson's *Staple of News* very strongly registers. The aristocracy had professional letter-writers to keep them informed. Roland Whyte for the Sidney family and John Chamberlain for Dudley Carleton are the best known. Pamphlets of 'News' became common from the 1590s. Their appeal was the same as a tattle-sheet with, in the playhouse, the bonus of well-being which comes from feeling part of a crowd collectively deriding its scapegoats. That is always an enticement to a massed audience. But in small and powerful coteries like Elizabeth's court it was a difficult game to play if you did not have the control and the consequent licence of a Tarlton. The players' involvement in the Marprelate controversy after Tarlton's death burned a few fingers and showed how quickly the licence could be withdrawn.

The Martin Marprelate pamphlets, with their splendidly cutting mockery of the Bishops of London and Winchester and of 'John of Cant' were thoroughly scandalous, and the players must have been drawn to the controversy for its own sake, without any sponsorship by the authorities, though all their efforts seem to have been on the government side. The utter failure of Elizabeth's officers to track down the Martinists' secret press, and the implicit challenge the controversy set up against political as well as ecclesiastical authority, kept it a sensation for nearly eighteen months. Anti-Martinists, freed to participate by the fact that they were defending the established church and state, poured out pamphlets and stage works in a self-augmenting frenzy, much as the journalistic media have always done to drum up work for themselves. John Laneham wrote pieces for the Queen's Men at the Theatre which formalised Tarlton's jibes and ballads. Lyly and Nashe both wrote of 'old Lanam', a player in the Queen's Men, writing 'Jigges and Rimes' against Martin.[29] An anti-Martinist pamphlet of October 1589 describes an allegorical adaptation of the traditional folk-play May-games against Martin. It is a new

worke . . . intituled . . . *The May-game of Martinisme.* Verie defflie set out, with Pompes, Pagents, Motions, Maskes, Scutchions, Emblems, Impreases, strange trickes, and devices, between the Ape and the Owle, the like was never yet seene in Paris-garden. Penry the welchman is the foregallant of the Morrice, with the treble belles, shot through the wit with a Woodcocks bill . . . *Martin* himselfe is the Mayd-Marian, trimlie drest uppe in a caste Gowne, and a Kercher of Dame Lawsons, his face handsomlie muffled with a Diapernapkin to cover his beard, and a great Nosegay in his hande . . . *Wiggenton* daunces round about him in a Cotten-coate to court him with a Leatherne pudding, and a woodden Ladle . . .

> (*The Returne of the renowned Cavaliero Pasquill of England,*
> Nashe, *Works,* I.83)

Whether this reports a genuine burlesque staging about the Martinists or is the pamphleteer's fantasy it reflects the terms in which the players chose to represent their audiences' interest in the Marprelate arguments. In a later pamphlet Nashe stressed the traditional May-game framework *(Vetus Comoedia)* and the allegorising:

Me thought *Vetus Comoedia* beganne to pricke him at London in the right vaine, when shee brought foorth *Divinite* wyth a scratcht face, holding of her hart as if she were sicke, because *Martin* would have forced her.

> (*Works,* I.92)

What is also significant, whether or not it reflects the burlesque traditions of the May-games, is the physical representation of the Martinists

John Penry and Giles Wiggington on stage.[30] It was a relatively short
step from such parodic allegorising to more realistic portrayals of newsworthy figures on the popular stage, especially the simple portrayal of
battle heroes.

Covert and sometimes open allusions to contemporary people and
events have a history almost as long as the stage itself. Nashe's dis-
arming prologue to *Summer's Last Will and Testament*, presented by
Paul's boys to the Archbishop of Canterbury after he had closed Paul's
playhouse, was not the first to suggest that allusion-hunters can find
more than is there. He advised 'Moralisers, you that wrest a never
meant meaning out of everything, applying all things to the present
time' to turn their attention from his play to the 'common stage'.
Early in the 1590s, though, the common stages were elaborating the
urge to moralise their spectacles by introducing direct representations
of famous or scandalworthy figures. *Arden of Faversham* is a strange
play in many respects. Its stage provenance is unknown, though it can
be dated close to *Tamburlaine* at the end of the 1580s. Its author is
equally unknown, though its theatrical quality is high enough to have
produced claims that it must be early Shakespeare. It is also the first
play to stage a major domestic scandal. The murder of Arden by his wife
and her lover took place forty years earlier, but it was a famous story,
and Holinshed's 1587 edition gave four pages of the *Chronicles* to it.[31]
Called 'a naked tragedy' in its epilogue, the play is a straightforward
dramatisation of Holinshed's account, with some pathos, some ser-
monising and considerable psychological insight. What is most striking about it is the utter contrast with *Tamburlaine* and its imitations.
The emotional force derives from its familiar domestic setting, its
claim to be true, the very ordinariness of its world. Even in later years
few writers were so willing to let the story speak for itself. If there
were any evidence for its impact on contemporary playgoers it would
be tempting to call it superlative journalism. Without that, it must
stand only as evidence for one writer's sense of what his market would
bear. When in the later 1590s the Chamberlain's Men staged an imitation, *A Warning for Fair Women*, also based on a wife-murder reported
in Holinshed, its Induction claimed that it was a wholly new kind of
tragedy distinct from the stock materials of revenge tragedy. This does
suggest that *Arden* was not widely known.

The taste which evoked *Arden* of *Faversham*, *A Warning* and plays
like *A Yorkshire Tragedy* (1606) was possibly satisfied earlier and
more often than the evidence in surviving plays can tell us. When
the Lord Treasurer sarcastically told Star Chamber in 1596 that he
would like to see the playmakers make a comedy out of a case in front

of the Chamber and 'to act it with those names',[32] he was presumably acknowledging a well-known practice. Domestic scandals were certainly put on stage in remarkably faithful versions of the known events in two later cases, Chapman's *The Old Joiner* of *Aldgate* (1602) and a play by Dekker and others, *Keep the Widow Waking* (1624). Neither play text has survived, but court records say enough about them to make it likely that both plays came close to modern newspaper reportage. C. J. Sisson analysed the circumstances in detail, and while his reconstruction of the plays necessarily owes more to what the courts said actually happened than to what Chapman and Dekker wrote, it seems certain that the appeal of the plays for their audiences was meant to lie in the assumption that they were faithful accounts of the events.

Chapman wrote his play for Paul's boys, about a group of people living and working in the immediate neighbourhood of Paul's, who in 1600 became embroiled in manoeuvres which went to litigation over who should marry a wealthy young girl. One of the suitors, a bookbinder named John Flaskett with a shop in Paul's yard, commissioned the play in order to present his version of the quarrel and so influence the court in his favour. In the subsequent court proceedings it was alleged against Flaskett that the play was his idea:

that a stage play should be made and was made by one George Chapman upon a plott given unto him concerning . . . Agnes Howe . . . (her cause and sutes then depending) & the same under coulorable & fayned names personated, so made & contryved was sold to Thomas Woodford & Edward Pearce for xx markes to be played upon the open stages in divers play houses within the citie of London to resemble and publish the dealing of her father towards her concerning his practize with several sutors to bestow her in marriage with one that might forgoe her portion & that therbie she might shutt up & conclude a match with . . . Flaskett rather than to suffer her name to be so traduced in every play house as it was lyke to be.[33]

Flaskett himself took Howe, the girl's father, to see the play at Paul's. Howe protested in court that he did not realise what the play was about until he was sitting there and heard people around him say it was about the case.

. . . this defendant thinketh that the same Play was meant by this defendant & his daughter & Mris Sharles John Flaskett & others, att which Play he did once sitt together with Flaskett & sawe the same, being unawares unto him brought to sitt by Flaskett to see the Play. And further he hath heard manie say that the Play was made of this defendant & his daughter & also of others.

(2.54)

Howe, who finally won the legal contest against Flaskett, did not take great offence. He seems to have enjoyed the publicity.

Dekker's play was rather different, although its occurrence in 1624 is good evidence for the durability of the journalistic function that the stages established in the 1590s. He worked with Rowley, Ford and Webster to dramatise two sensational cases of felony and murder for the Red Bull players. The play's subplot was again the story of a young woman being exploited for her money, but the main plot was the murder of a widow by her son. The subplot was the subject of a suit in Star Chamber, and the main plot, based on a murder in Whitechapel in April 1624, prompted the publication of ballads and a play by Thomas Drue as well as Dekker's play.[34] The links between broadsheet ballads and the stage were not confined to the clowns with their jigs and endpieces. What they shared was their newsworthy subject matter.

The same newsworthiness led to the conflict between the King's Men and another company in 1634, over the current fuss about the Lancashire witches. This dispute seems to have followed an attempt by the other company, probably at Salisbury Court, to cash in on the fuss over the witches by inserting some extra material in another play. The Master of the Revels, who must have been an ally of the King's Men in publicising one side of the Privy Council's quarrel over the witches, noted

A peticion of the Kings Players about ye Witches complayning of intermingleing some passages of witches in old playes to ye prejudice of their designed Comedy of the Lancashire witches, and desiring a prohibition of any other till theirs bee allowed and Acted.[35]

The King's Men wanted their scoop. The target of the ban was probably a revival of another newsworthy play, *Dr Lambe and the Witches*, telling the story of the man notorious enough to be noticed by apprentices at a play at the Fortune in 1628. They chased him through the streets and stoned him to death. If the second witches play was staged at Salisbury Court, sensational news of this kind evidently appealed to hall playhouse audiences as much as to those who went to the amphitheatres. Paul's and Salisbury Court used the same material as the Red Bull and the Globe, appealing to the same taste for seeing ordinary people doing extraordinary things.

William Crashaw preached a sermon at Paul's Cross on 14 February 1608 in which he protested at giving puritans the names of their churches in *The Puritan*, played at Paul's and recently published. '. . . now they bring religion and holy things upon the stage . . . Two hypocrites must be brought foorth; and how shall they be described but by these names, *Nicholas S. Antlings, Simon S. Maryoveries* . . . by these miscreants thus dishonoured, and that not on the stage only, but even in print' (2.81). Crashaw had the support of the 1606 Statute against profanity on stage. Possibly Paul's was in Henry Parrott's mind, along with the Blackfriars boys who evoked the French ambassador's protest, when he noted in his epistle to *The More the Merrier* (1608) how much there had been of 'satiric inveighing at any mans private person (a kind of writing which of late seems to have been very familiar among our pocts and players, to their cost)' (2.79). The 'railing' vein which opened with the boy companies at the turn of the century was running fairly dry by that time.

John Howe, the barber surgeon who saw himself staged at Paul's in 1602, was bland about his experience. He was reported to have told the Paul's manager that 'he had no reason to take it to himself for that Kings had been presented on the stage and therefore Barbers might'.[36] Of course a barber who was winning his case could afford to be less sensitive than a king about how the stage portrayed him. The more aristocratic the victim the less complaisant he was likely to be. The letter-writer Roland Whyte reported on 26 October 1599 to Sir Robert Sidney that his recent military exploits were in the public eye.

Two daies agoe, the overthrow of *Turnholt* was acted upon a Stage, and all your names used that were at yt; especially *Sir Fra. Veres*, and he that plaid that Part gott a Beard resembling his, and a Watchett Sattin Doublett, with Hose trimmed with Silver Lace. You was also introduced, killing, slaying, and overthrowing the *Spaniards*, and honorable Mention made of your Service, in seconding Sir Francis Vere, being engaged.[37]

There is nothing in Henslowe which indicates responsibility for this, so it may have been put on at the Globe. A few years later it was certainly the Globe players who exploited the interest in Scottish affairs generated by England's new king with an account of the Gowry conspiracy of 1600. As John Chamberlain reported on 18 December 1604,

the tragedie of Gowrie with all the action and actors hath ben twise represented by the Kings players, with exceeding concourse of all sortes of people, but whether the matter or manner be not well handled, or that yt be thought unfit that princes should be plaide on the stage in theyre life time, I heare that some great counsaillors are much displeased with yt: and so is thought shalbe forbidden.   (2.60)

A full set of the 'actors' in the Gowry conspiracy must have included King James himself. Displeasure by the great at the portrayal of living people on stage was demonstrated on several other occasions, notably over a play at the Curtain in 1601, the portrayal of the French king in Chapman's *The Conspiracy of Byron*, which exercised the French ambassador in 1608, and of course Middleton's *A Game at Chesse*.[38]

The greatest sensation of this period was of course the Essex conspiracy of February 1601. Essex himself when being tried in 1600 for the failure of his Irish expedition complained to Elizabeth, 'shortly they will play me in what forms they list upon the stage'.[39] The relations between Essex and Elizabeth were a notable temptation. In 1604 the Privy Council punished Daniel for representing Essex in *Philotas*, a charge to which the poet gave a wounded and plausible denial, though not many seem to have believed him. The trouble was what Nashe called the common stage habit of moralising, which led to Jonson's derisive assertion in the dedication to *Volpone* that 'Application is grown a trade'. Elizabeth herself not only applied Shakespeare's *Richard II* to her own position in relation to Essex but complained to Lambarde that the applicable story had been acted forty times in the public playhouses and streets. In the 1590s Everard Guilpin and an enemy of Raleigh both wrote verses applying the Bullingbrook of Shakespeare's play to Essex,[40] like the Essex conspirators when they commissioned Shakespeare's company to perform *Richard II* on the eve of the rebellion. The 'common stages' were the only vehicle for current comment, and they readily supplied the need.

Sadly, though, the supply is not often easily identifiable. Even today we can argue over whether Jonson was moralising the Gunpowder Plot in *Catiline*. The closer such sensations came to the pains of possible censorship, the more covert the presentation and consequently the wider the application was likely to be. Events like *A Game at Chesse*, running at the Globe to packed audiences for nine days of August before the authorities got to hear of it, were thoroughly exceptional (2.148). What stands out most clearly is the enthusiasm of London audiences for this kind of journalistic news and topical comment, whether heroic accounts of battle as with Vere and Robert Sidney in 1599 or satirical in the years that followed.

CITIZEN STAPLES AND JULIET'S REBELLION
(1588–1605)

In the five years 1594–9, when the only food for playgoers was supplied by the two adult companies playing at the amphitheatres to the north and south of the city, the provision was strikingly similar and surprisingly narrow in its range. The years before had been changeable and far less prosperous. The years after, from 1599 to 1605, show a noticeable divergence between the playhouse south of the river and the northern playhouses. But in the central years when Davies and others thought that the amphitheatres contained the whole range of society the surviving plays from the two repertories seem to have catered more for citizen than for gentry appetites. As many as 145 plays, more than at any other time, were written for the stage in each of the two five-year periods 1594–9 and 1599–1604,[41] and all the plays of the first of these periods reflected citizen tastes. Robin Hood stories, popular in May-games and traditional festivals, were revamped for the London stage. Maid Marion turns up in Henslowe's *John a Kent and John a Cumber*, which was (if, as seems likely, it is the play known in his *Diary* as *The Wise Men of Westchester*) the most popular play in the Rose playhouse repertory after *1 Henry VI*. Henslowe later employed Munday to write a two-part life of Robin Hood, *The Downfall of Robert Earl of Huntingdon* and *The Death of Robert Earl of Huntingdon*, which are complex elaborations for an urban audience of the traditional folk tales evolved in the country areas.[42] Plays about English history were a staple throughout, though their most popular feature by far was Falstaff in Eastcheap. The values most characteristically expressed were those of citizen Simon Eyre in *The Shoemaker's Holiday*. As the Dick Whittington story grew into a legend in prose tales so the citizen values embodied in such topics as the prodigal son story and the fantasies of apprentice heroics dominated the stages.

Identifying what has been called the 'rival' repertories that belonged to the duopoly of companies offering London playing through these years is made difficult by the varying character of the evidence. For the Chamberlain's Men little has survived besides the works of two writers, Shakespeare and Jonson. Between 1594 and 1599 Shakespeare's plays were largely confined to English histories and love comedies. Besides that distinctly narrow range, Jonson brought his 'humours' comedies to the company from the Admiral's, which started the fashion at the Rose in 1597. Our knowledge of the Rose repertory is much wider, at least in its play-titles, with over eighty names of plays compared with the fifteen or so from Shakespeare's company.[43] Both companies staged similar stories from English history, and only mildly divergent kinds of comedy. It is from the latter, though, that different affinities may become apparent.

The surviving Rose plays represent the work of at least seventeen writers. Between 1596 and 1599 the men Henslowe paid included Chapman, Chettle, Day, Dekker, Drayton, Hathaway, Haughton, Heywood, Jonson, Lee, Marston – who did not deliver – Munday, Porter, Rankins and Wilson, often working in collaboration. Marlowe,

Kyd and others of the older writers were already in the repertory. The variety of plays at the Rose was large, and they may have been more innovative than the Shakespeare company. They certainly seem to have initiated 'humours' comedy with Chapman's *An Humorous Day's Mirth* in 1597, a fashion which Jonson quickly took up and exported to Shakespeare's company. The novelty of that new fashion is shown in Henslowe's record of the early takings for *An Humorous Day's Mirth*, which grew bigger on every day of its first six performances. Gossip about it is affirmed by John Chamberlain's report that he was drawn to go to it by all the talk (2.30). The Admiral's Men also appear to have started the fashion for citizen comedy, based on contemporary London life. Shakespeare dipped no more than a toe into that pool, with *The Merry Wives of Windsor*, which in most respects is a model citizen play about virtuous wives resisting lecherous advances from gentlemen (Falstaff), and marriage across the classes between a citizen daughter and a gentleman's son. It possibly exploited and in its title certainly competed with Henry Porter's *Two Angry Women of Abingdon*, written for the Rose company. So far as we know, the nearest the Chamberlain's came to a play set in London through these years was *A Warning for Fair Women*. There is not really enough evidence to tell how much else either company introduced in the way of new fashions.

Speaking in broad terms, and contrasting this repertory with what came after it, it can be said that the two companies which operated from 1594 ran a similar repertory of plays. The militancy which Alleyn's company reflected with *Tamburlaine* and its imitations while Burbage's company used it with English history had a similar appeal. Each company was well aware of its rival's offerings, and both companies staged plays about Henry V, Owen Tudor, Hieronymo, Jack Straw, King John, Richard III and Troilus and Cressida. Both companies offered heroic romances, prodigal plays and citizen comedies such as *Fair Em*, *The Shoemaker's Holiday*, *An Englishman for my Money* and *The Merry Wives of Windsor*. Only in one fairly minor way did the interests of the two companies diverge at this time. It was a divergence which intensified quite markedly in the following five years, however, after 1599. This warrants careful attention.

Charles Howard, the Lord Admiral, hugely enriched by the profits he made from English piracy during the war, and patron of the Henslowe company, was a powerful figure at court. Henslowe's and Alleyn's awareness of his political position may well explain the distinctive allegiances which can be seen in the later repertoire of the Henslowe companies, and may have been an influence earlier. The Burbage company committed a political as well as a social error in making Sir John Oldcastle, the original Falstaff, a figure of vice. Undoubtedly affected by the other company's action in switching their playhouse from Shoreditch to a site on Bankside barely fifty yards from the Rose, their rivals did not hesitate to capitalise on the error with their own *Sir John Oldcastle*. The play used the fact that Oldcastle was distinguished as a Protestant martyr in Foxe's *Acts and Monuments*. Foxe was available for reading in churches by government order along with the Bible, and had the status almost of hagiography for the Protestant apologists. The Catholics contrariwise made capital out of the Falstaff version. In 1603 Robert Parsons (the Jesuit propagandist Doleman) wrote a pamphlet, *The Third Part of a Treatise, Intituled: of three Conversions of England*, in which he applauded the Falstaffian version of the Protestant martyr: 'Syr John Oldcastle, a Ruffian-knight as all England knoweth, & commonly brought in by comediants on their stages'. So spoke the enemies of the government. Possibly the staging of the Oldcastle play or possibly the influence of Lord Howard prompted the Henslowe companies at the turn of the century to mount a whole series of plays about Protestant heroes. The 'Elect Nation' plays,[44] and the accompanying celebrations of the heyday of Elizabethan England which Henslowe produced in 1603–5, notably Rowley's *When You See Me You Know Me* (1604?), Dekker and Webster's *Sir Thomas Wyatt* (c.1604), Heywood's *If You Know Not Me* (1605), and other plays by the Henslowe collaborators amount to a small campaign for citizen values. They shed the military heroics of the 1590s, as James's peaceable kingdom of diplomatic saintliness took hold of English politics, but the values they upheld were expressly Protestant and Elizabethan. How much these plays were produced under stimulus from the company's patron and how much they indicate an allegiance to a particular kind of audience and its values is not clear.

There is little sign that the Shakespeare company followed far along the course of the Henslowe companies after 1600 in upholding such distinctive London values. They burlesqued the speech of Tamburlaine in *2 Henry IV* and *Henry V* as a mark of their divergence from Alleyn's style. Perhaps more to the point they accepted another divergence once they settled on Bankside and the Henslowe companies moved to the northern suburbs. Like the 'Elect Nation' plays this second divergence may have been designed by the Henslowe writers to establish a clearly different identity of the Fortune in the north from the players newly arrived on Bankside. It crystallised as a decidedly conservative citizen attitude to love and marriage. That was not at all the attitude the Chamberlain's Men fostered.

In the 1590s the Shakespeare company became notably popular with the Inns of Court students for its plays about love. Marston's Luscus and his fellows kept commonplace books of verse from Shakespeare's comedies, quoting Romeo and the 'new pathetique Tragedie' the company was then staging at the Curtain. Francis Meres and other young gallants delighted in this attention to love by the author of their favourite *Venus and Adonis*. The Henslowe playwrights made no attempt to copy this newly popular taste. After 1600 they actively opposed it and the romantic challenge to citizen views about marriage which it embodied.

Shakespeare's presentation of marriage was relatively new in that his plays upheld the power of love over parental authority. For Juliet to rebel against the Capulets' insistence that she marry the man of her parents' choice was an act of disloyalty which few of the richer London citizens were ready to applaud. Ex-Lord Mayor Sir John Spencer, a notoriously affluent skinflint, disowned his only child in 1599 when she ran away and married a lord. To citizens Shakespeare's heroines were an alarming novelty. When Beatrice challenged the convention of women undergoing arranged marriages (*Much Ado*, 2.1.42–7) and the young lovers in *A Midsummer Night's Dream* rebelled against the harsh Athenian laws they were voicing kinship with Juliet. Even *The Taming of the Shrew*'s marvellously complex reshuffling of the traditional love story, contemplating life after marriage and setting Bianca's conventional posturing in contrast to honest Katherine, was in its own way a sensational contribution to the debate between young love and parental authority. Heywood's *A Woman Killed with Kindness*, which took the other side in the debate on behalf of the Henslowe companies, probably found its title in Petruchio's derisive use of the proverb about killing a wife with kindness (4.1.195).

Exactly when the companies began to diverge over this question is not clear, because so much of the Admiral's Company's repertoire has been lost like the Chamberlain's. Possibly some of the lost plays recorded in Henslowe's lists, such as *Wonder of a Woman* (1595), *The Chaste Lady* (1595–6), and *A Woman Hard to Please* (1597), may have expressed a view hostile to love, but *The Two Angry Women of Abingdon* ends happily enough in a love-match, as does Haughton's *An Englishman for my Money*. The distinction is not really evident before 1600.

Conflict with Shakespeare's company after it settled at the Globe in 1599 was certainly pushed by the second Henslowe company, Worcester's, which began playing, with Shakespeare's former fellow the clown Will Kemp in the company, first at the Rose on Bankside and then at the Boar's Head in 1601. Dekker's lost *Medicine for a Curst Wife* was written for them, followed by *How a Man May Choose a Good Wife from a Bad* and *A Woman Killed with Kindness*. The contention, if that is what it was, ran on into the reign of James, when the Globe staged Wilkins's *The Miseries of Enforced Marriage* based on pamphlets about the life of Walter Calverley which were printed in 1605. If it was a genuine contention over attitudes to marriage it seems unlikely to have been inspired by the political bias of the Elect Nation plays. These later elements in the Henslowe repertoire seem to have been mainly inspired by its citizen and conservative allegiance.

The modern assumption that art and commerce are naturally polarised has done a disfavour to Henslowe and his playmakers. His records indicate the constant pressure he was under to acquire new plays as fast as possible. Viewed from the commercial pole the collaborative writing which produced most of his plays can easily seem to be hackwork catering for established and familiar tastes, providing what audiences wanted. That this is not the case is evident both in the narrow political bias of the Elect Nation plays and in the sides taken over the marriage debate. On both issues the Henslowe writers chose to take a conservative line supporting Elizabethan values. It was a conservatism which knew what it was doing and which deliberately set the northern playhouses in closer sympathy with predominant citizen interests, so far as we know them, than did the plays of the Globe players. Shakespeare's plays already had a particular appeal for law students and gallants in the 1590s. In the new century the Globe company's allegiance to the specific tastes of the London citizenry drained away.

This divergence between the Henslowe playhouses and the Globe is important, but it is not easily explained. The return of the boy players at Paul's and the Blackfriars in 1599 may have sharpened the sense of loyalty to citizen values in the Henslowe writers. As law students and all the wealthier playgoers began flocking to the new hall playhouses it would be natural for the amphitheatres to narrow their focus onto the citizens who stayed loyal to them. Certainly 1599 can be seen as the beginning of the long run which the Fortune and Red Bull enjoyed up to the Caroline period when they became explicitly known as 'citizen' playhouses. James Wright gave them that name in 1699, from a fairly distant historical perspective, but it was not inaccurate (2.224). They sustained the repertoire of the 1590s right through to the closure in 1642, with Marlowe at its core throughout. In the 1630s the 'majestic' acting and military trappings of the Red Bull plays, the style set by Alleyn in the 1590s, became a standing joke to the sophisticated, although the plays themselves were occasionally also staged at the indoor Cockpit. The durability of the Marlowe style and repertoire is a testimony to the strength of the citizen enthusiasm for the playhouses most accessible to London's working population.

Even less easily explained through this time of unprecedented competition at the beginning of the century is the position of the Globe company. Situated next to the Bankside baiting houses and whorehouses and not much further away from the city across London Bridge, it had every reason to expect the same clientele as favoured the northern playhouses. It would probably have expected to lose more of its clientele of Romeo-quoting law students to the boy companies than Henslowe, and Shakespeare did stop writing love comedies after 1600 once the hall playhouses were competing with the Globe. It is true that James Burbage once thought to provide adult fare at the Blackfriars for the playgoers who now went to the boys there, but in 1600 the Globe players had no reason to expect that they could ever take that playhouse back from the boys. They must have faced a choice, between going the Henslowe way and catering for the conservative citizen taste or competing with the boys and their new fashions. With hindsight the wisdom of their preference for a new kind of repertoire seems obvious. It could not have been so then, though, and until *Hamlet* arrived to, in An. Sc.'s phrase, 'please all' and secure their independent role, they must have had grave doubts about the commercial practicability of their chosen course.

Very likely the crux of the matter, and possibly the trigger for their choice, lay in the question of the company's clown. Will Kemp's departure from the Shakespeare company in 1599 was one of a complex series of adjustments which started the company on a road leading firmly away from the jigs and knockabout clowning that were citizen staples at the northern playhouses until the 1640s. In 1599, when they were just starting in a costly new playhouse, Kemp's departure left the company hazardously poised for a new beginning in conditions of unprecedented competition.

Kemp's 'applauded Merymentes', as they were called on the titlepage of *A Knack to Know a Knave*, were a celebrated feature of the Shakespearean company's repertory in the 1590s. Dogberry was written for him, and probably Falstaff. The parts of Launce in *Two Gentlemen of Verona* and Peter in *Romeo and Juliet* were probably added to the original texts to augment Kemp's contribution to the company of which he and Shakespeare became shareholders in 1594. But whether or not he was the first Falstaff, Kemp's real fame lay less in his comic roles in the plays than in his jigs. He was a singing and dancing clown whose talent is probably seen most distinctly in the script for the jig *Singing Simkin*, a piece of knockabout bawdy clowning in rhyming doggerel whose virtue lies more in its energy than its wit.[45] The song and dance jig or endpiece seems to have disappeared from the Globe stage not long after Kemp left the company, unless Feste's last song in *Twelfth Night* is a kind of singing endpiece. Thomas Platter, seeing *Julius Caesar* at the Globe in September 1599, mentioned the jig which followed the play, but a reference in 1613 to John Shanke leaving the Fortune for the Globe suggests that he stopped performing jigs when he joined his new company (2.106). The abandonment of jigs may have been an expression of choice by the company as much as a necessity following Kemp's departure. Shakespeare's fellows may well have shared Hamlet's view about clowns who extemporised.

The circumstances of Kemp's departure are obscure, though some hints of his own indicate that he may not have gone altogether willingly. On his return from his epic morris dances to Norwich and over the Alps he joined Worcester's Men, working for Henslowe, who approved of jigs, in the winter of 1602–3. Robert Armin, who took Kemp's place in the Shakespeare company, was a singing or court fool, not a knockabout clown in the Kemp tradition, though he must have taken over Kemp's old parts such as Dogberry and Peter. His acquisition of Kemp's place is a token of the divergent line the Globe company took in 1599 from its northern rivals, over clowning as well as the priorities of marriage. Jigs were always a feature of the northern playhouses, but the Globe seems not to have returned to that kind of clowning perhaps until the 1630s, when its reputation began to make it a more plebeian playhouse than the Blackfriars. More will be said about that below.

The years from 1588 to 1605 provide a central focus for playgoing in the whole of the Shakespearean period. Marlowe's and Kyd's first success helped to create the taste which both companies satisfied in their divergent ways through the middle years. Those years also created the tradition which sustained the 'citizen' playhouses for another forty years. The same years prompted Shakespeare's company to move on, partly under their own impetus and no doubt partly also under the stimulus of the boy companies and the fresh appetites which they identified. What appears between 1594 and 1599 to have been a homogeneous, all-inclusive social range from gallants to grooms and from citizens' wives to whores, in the next years quickly became a stratified social scale divided amongst different playhouses. The northern playhouses then supplied the wants of the lower social levels, and carried on along the same road for forty years. The Globe players and the boy companies had different aspirations.

THE WAR OF RAILING (1599–1609)

Captivating spectacle, the 'theatre of enchantment', as Neil Carson has called it, became the predominant mode in the central five years while the citizen staples ran in the amphitheatres. Towards the end of the period, though, a new mode entered, which Carson calls 'theatre of estrangement'.[46] Emphasis on the metatheatrical element in playgoing was not new in 1599, but it soon became a routine acknowledgement of the 'junior' and non-realistic role-playing of boys in the plays written by their new writers. Playwrights writing for the citizen repertory ordinarily spoke of audiences as 'bewitched', believers, however momentary, in the players' impersonations, sharing a collective '*charmd* soule' which could be subdued to the magic of the stage show. Heywood wrote of bewitched spectators in his *Apology*, Dekker of the 'charmd soule' in the prologue to *If This Be Not a Good Play* (2.101). Carson sees this as a characteristic of the 1590s, when as he puts it 'the popular-theatre playwrights had been moving fairly consistently in the direction of what I would call naive illusionism' (p. 79). Well before 1605 this enchantment was being challenged by the sophisticated artifice of the boy companies, making audiences self-conscious, flaunting the artificiality of stage pretence with metatheatre, and insisting that audiences became not spell-bound believers but sceptical judges. Jonson's insistence that audiences should function as judges made its mark.

This new anti-mimetic mode in theatre was natural for boy companies, whose 'juniority' made them only approximate physical imitations of adult reality. The new mode also granted them the superior appeal of an obviously more sophisticated concept of drama to set above the adult players' naive illusionism. Its development however is complicated by Jonson's and Shakespeare's contributions to the Globe company. The 'humours' plays were making a mark with audiences as early as 1597, when John Chamberlain found the first of them to have been overpraised. Jonson's two 'humours' plays were first staged by Shakespeare's company, introducing not only the comedy of humours but, in *Every Man Out of his Humour*, a new expectation of critical alertness in the audience and consequently a new tone of acerbity in stage comedy. This 'satire', which Joseph Hall and John Weever derived by a false but apt etymology from *sat irae*, full of anger,[47] started as an Inns of Court fashion well calculated to appeal to the audiences already happy to mock their fellows quoting Romeo. Jonson's transfer from his early work with Henslowe to the Chamberlain's Men was dictated more by his killing of Henslowe's player Gabriel Spencer than by any sense that the other company would supply a more welcoming audience for his plays, but *Every Man in his Humour* does suggest that he knew what he was doing when he made the transfer. Opening his play with a father lamenting the way his student son dreams away his time with 'idle *Poetrie*' was a sure way to catch the interest of Marston's gull Luscus and other would-be Romeos, as well as their mockers. The ridicule both of the father and of the student son with his friends which follows is in the vein of Marston and his fellow satirists. Jonson's play gave Shakespeare's company their first opportunity to put Inns of Court satire on stage and to broach the practice of 'railing', as it came to be called.

Railing became the chief and most conspicuous alternative to the naive illusionism of the heroics of Marlowe and the citizen repertory. It was taken up quickly by the boy companies which formed soon after Jonson's first success. They had strong incentives. As Marston put it, writing for Paul's in 1601,

> This is the straine that chokes the theaters:
> That makes them crack with full stuff't audience,
> This is your humor onely in request
> Forsooth to raile . . .   (2.49)

The boys and their liking for railing may have provoked the so-called War of the Theatres, which localised the battlefield for railing by turning the device against the playwrights themselves. The War was a curious little fracas, a wonderful quarry for the trade of application amongst intimates of the playhouses. Whether it really had much to do with competition for audiences or not, it was clearly designed to satisfy the new taste for railing. It certainly did have a great deal to do with some poets' animosity towards Jonson and the acerbic tone his railing brought into comedy. Dekker's *Satiromastix*, using Jonson's tone of sat-ire against him, reads like the protest of a writer who feels himself to have been unfairly provoked by a savage mode which he was quite capable of adopting himself for his retaliation.

The boy companies evidently had an interest in fostering satirical comedy, since it became their most characteristic mode, seen at its best in *Eastward Ho!*, *The Isle of Gulls*, and *The Knight of the Burning Pestle*, though all three of these date from the last phase of the Blackfriars boys, and Paul's never went so far as the Blackfriars. The intensification of Blackfriars railing in their last years brought down

James's fury on them for their *Byron* plays in 1608. Heywood's disavowal of the mode, written at about that time, has the air of revulsion against something whose time has passed.

Nowe to speake of some abuse lately crept into the quality, as an inveighing against the State, the Court, the Law, the Citty, and their governments, with the particularising of private mens humours (yet alive) Noble-men, & others. I knowe it distastes many; neither do I any way approve it, nor dare I by any meanes excuse it. The liberty, which some arrogate to themselves, committing their bitternesse, and liberall invectives against all estates, to the mouthes of Children, supposing their juniority to be a priviledge for any rayling, be it never so violent, I could advise all such, to curbe and limit this presumed liberty . . .[48]

Heywood was not himself given to railing and his rejection of it here was composed in the heart of the citizen repertory. He was partly commenting on an alternative theatrical tradition to his own and partly on a fashion whose time was now up.

The fashion for railing tried chiefly to appeal to the gallants and law students whose enthusiasm for doing it in print was halted by the bishops and their book-burning in 1599.[49] Jonson's transfer of railing to the Shakespeare company's stage is one of the pieces of evidence linking them more with gallant and law student playgoers than with the Henslowe clientele. The company did, along with Paul's boys, stage *Satiromastix* as an attack on Jonson after he left them (and Henslowe) for the Blackfriars boys. There is some point in the connection Brian Gibbons makes between the Globe repertory and that of the boy companies.

Towards the end of Elizabeth's reign, plays at Blackfriars, Paul's and, increasingly, the Globe, register a note of discontent with public affairs, while the other adult companies at the Red Bull, Swan, Rose and Hope largely continue to evoke an air of cheerful patriotism and national self-satisfaction. It has been surmised that this divergence in attitudes to government and monarchy reflects a progressive split in the political attitudes of the two audiences: the first included lawyers, members of the Commons, merchants and Inns of Court students, nobility and gentry, the second more predominantly tradesmen, citizens, labourers, carriers, apprentices, serving-men.[50] Such a surmise is well supported by available evidence, both about the social divergence of the boy company audiences from the amphitheatre audiences, and about the divergent repertories. But there are hints in the evidence which indicate that it is not really sufficient to put the Globe company precisely into the same category as the boy companies, or indeed to put the two boy companies together. The position of Shakespeare's company might more fairly be seen as a neutral one between the polarised Blackfriars and the citizen companies, with Paul's uneasily balanced somewhere between the other hall company and Shakespeare's, and shifting more towards the citizen side as time went on.

One problem in identifying the kind of playgoer for whom the Shakespeare company prepared itself is the limited evidence about the allegiances implied in its plays. Shakespeare himself wrote more than two-thirds of the plays that survive from his company's repertory between 1599 and 1609, and neither his nor any of the few other plays uphold the Protestant patriotism of the Elect Nation plays on the one hand or the acerbic railing of the Blackfriars on the other. The company staged Jonson's two humours plays before the boys came back on the scene, yet Jonson did not hesitate to include them with the other adult companies in his attack in *Poetaster* on the hypocrisy of adult players. He accused them of deploring the '*humours, revells* and *satyres,* that girde, and fart at the time', but of still corrupting morals with their ribaldry. The player in *Poetaster* proudly boasts that his fellows on Bankside 'have as much ribaldrie in our plaies, as can bee, as you would wish . . . All the sinners, i' the suburbs come, and applaud our action, daily' (*Poetaster,* 3.4). The Globe as well as Henslowe's Rose was included in this condemnation of Bankside plays catering for the poor of London's suburbs, 'your tabernacles, . . . your *Globes,* and your Triumphs' (3.4.201). This reference is followed by an extended burlesque of the Player's speech and other passages in *Hamlet,* and concludes with the player lamenting the loss of his audience to the boys: 'No bodie comes at us; not a gentleman, nor a –' (329–30).

What heed the Globe company paid to Jonson's strictures it is not easy to see. They had been mocking fustian plays from the rival adult repertoire with Ancient Pistol since 1597. They did not hesitate to stage *Satiromastix* as Dekker's counterattack against Jonson and the Blackfriars boys in the War of the Theatres. Shakespeare, possibly mindful of Jonson's criticism of romantic comedy in *Every Man Out,* also needled him quietly in *Twelfth Night.* But he then stopped writing in the genre.[51] He also dropped his plan for a new series of history plays, this time about Rome, starting with *Julius Caesar.* And yet the plays he wrote instead of these staples were certainly not railing satires. If anything they harked back to the amphitheatre plays of the previous decade. *Hamlet* probably and *King Lear* certainly were rewritings of old Queen's company plays from 1590 or earlier, that the company probably inherited in 1594. None of the company's other plays – *The*

Devil's Charter and *The Merry Devil of Edmonton*, for instance – show the least influence from the boy company repertory or the targeted playgoers. By the time Jonson returned to them with *Sejanus* in late 1603 and *Volpone* in 1605 the company's neutrality must have long outweighed the staging of *Satiromastix* as a mark of their position.[52]

By 1605 the Globe company was not just neutral between the northern amphitheatres and the halls but pre-eminent. In 1603 the court had recognised their lead when James made himself their patron while giving the two Henslowe companies to his wife and son. The boys' campaign to distinguish themselves from the citizen and artisan tastes of the Henslowe companies had the effect of polarising the repertories if not their audiences. Remaining neutral, Shakespeare's company avoided the 'public' or popular tag which clung to Henslowe's companies and also the risks of being outrageous which the Blackfriars boys ran to get their 'private' or 'select' playgoers into their seats. The taste for railing was shortlived – it did not even last so long as the ten years of the boy companies – partly because satire is by its nature not a durable fashion. Apart from *Satiromastix*, its polarising effect does not seem to have had any impact on the Shakespeare company's repertory. What is less clear is whether it affected the social composition of the Globe's audiences, and brought back the upper social echelons from the halls to the Bankside.

Marston, Jonson and the other playwrights who praised the select nature of the hall playhouse audiences in 1600 and 1601 all had their reasons. Marston's role as poet-in-chief for Paul's boys made him strident in his insistence on the intimate and clubbable atmosphere at Paul's. Freed not just from the sticky jerkins of artisan brewers but from 'drunken *Censure*' and choked more with tobacco than the smell of garlic (2.46, 49), his audiences could be persuaded to make the smaller size of the Paul's gatherings, no more than two hundred heads at a sitting, into a special mark of superiority. The tobacco-smoking and card-playing gallants now conspicuous at the hall playhouses had previously been noted at the Theatre, Curtain and Globe, so it is more likely that the hundred or so at Paul's and the seven hundred or so at Blackfriars would have come from the Globe than from the Fortune, Rose or Boar's Head. That seems to be confirmed by the Player's lament in *Hamlet* at losing custom to the boys, and Jonson's derisive echo of it in *Poetaster*. The lament need not be taken too seriously, since Richard Burbage the player of Hamlet who was told that the boys were usurping the men was in fact, as owner of the Blackfriars playhouse, their landlord. The statement may have been a company in-joke. The Henslowe players never made any complaints about the boy companies.

How long any transfer of allegiance to the boys might have lasted and how costly it was to the adults there is no way of telling. The boy companies were never as healthy a commercial operation as the adult companies, and they performed far less frequently. As early as 1604 the Blackfriars impresario was trying to revoke his lease and return the hall to Burbage. By 1605, when Paul's closed finally and the Blackfriars boys were in trouble with the authorities, it seems reasonable to conclude that the Globe company must have resumed its tradition of catering for all tastes, and that all social ranks were again represented among the playgoers at the Globe. It must be admitted, though, that the evidence is circumstantial. Probably the strongest confirmation is the company's immediate success when they took over the Blackfriars in 1609, as we shall see below.

The humours plays and their railing satire are tightly linked with the varieties of city comedy which flourished from 1599 onwards and reached their apogee with *Bartholomew Fair* in 1614. City comedy was a variable thing, and to some extent it should be distinguished from the satirical railing of the first years of the boy companies. The development of city comedy is a feature of the ten-year history of the boy companies from 1599 to 1608, but it appeared on every type of stage, and its different manifestations are as varied as the different types of repertory. Before those differences are considered, it is worth looking more closely at what the targets of the specifically railing types of comedy were.

Girds at citizens, as Beaumont's Citizen called them, remained a feature exclusively of the boy company plays. Girds or jibes are mentioned by Day, Beaumont, Field, Fletcher and others as the basis for a more or less legitimate if amusing grievance on the part of the wealthier citizens and merchants. Girds at puritans also evoked complaint from the pulpits. Since plays were seen as a corrupting alternative to sermons, some sermons by the more puritanical preachers in the decade up to 1609 not surprisingly contain violent expressions of hostility to plays (2.55, 81). Puritanism however was a political question. The satirical play *The Family of Love* was implicitly endorsed by an attack on that sect which James wrote for the republication of *Basilikon Doron* in 1603. Girding at citizens was a smaller matter, a declaration of social groupings and consequent social alliances. The most distinctive feature about the citizen girds was that they did rouse explicit objections. Equally derisive satire against gallants and lawyers can be found in the railing plays, but only merchants seem to have felt themselves vulnerable enough to warrant a protest. Possibly they felt too far outside the game, too alien in the intimate and wealthy society of the boy company playhouses, whereas gallants and law students could enjoy the jokes against their kind. Beaumont's *Knight of the Burning Pestle* was certainly written on some such presumption.

The extent to which the targets for railing were social rather than political is most clearly demonstrated in the satire against James himself. It was inevitable that any successor to Elizabeth would have appeared a lesser, more fallible human being. Certainly it is to his credit, in a way, that most of the satire he attracted was directed at fairly trivial and easily recognisable things like his love of hunting and his Scottish followers. Beside the jibes about the 'few industrious Scots' and the 'thirty pound knights', in *Eastward Ho!*, a letter of Sir Thomas Edmondes (February 1606) testifies to the satirical basis and particularly the Scottish accents which Day exploited in 1606. 'At this time there was much speech of a play in the Black Friars, where in the "Isle of Gulls", from the highest to the lowest, all men's parts were acted of two diverse nations: as I understand sundry were committed to Bridewell.' This satire was not so much directed at James's policy of union between the two countries which he ruled as at the introduction of his Scottish followers into the court and positions of power.[53] Concern over corruption at court was a later phenomenon.

Satire against James appeared mostly in the period from 1603 (when the queen was said to be enjoying stage parodies of her husband) to 1608. Henry Crosse complained that 'there is no passion wherwith the soveraigne majestie of the Realme was possest, but is amplified, and openly sported with, and made a May-game to all the beholders' (*Vertues Commonwealth*, 1603, P3). Anne of Denmark was reported by the French ambassador in 1604 to have attended plays in order to enjoy their mockery of her husband. Possibly the gift of her patronage to the Blackfriars boys so that they could, however briefly, be called the Children of the Queen's Revels means that they were the company who provided her with that kind of pleasure. This fashion in fact coincided with a rising tide of hostility to railing and to some degree marks its furthest extension. The playwrights began increasingly to disclaim railing as a mode – Chapman in 1604, Jonson in 1605, Day and Marston in 1606, Beaumont in 1607 and Barry in 1608 – though by no means all the disclaimers were sincere.[54]

Railing plays were almost exclusively a feature of the boy company repertories, all but twelve of whose fifty-five surviving plays were satirical.[55] Much of the raillery appears in city comedies, for which it was well suited. *Eastward Ho!*, probably the best in the genre, is a sophisticated burlesque of the citizen playhouse repertory and its prodigal son plays, though the fact that its satire against James led to a protest by one of his Scotsmen and punishment for its poets should remind us that the genre was not just a weapon of social class allegiance. It was a fashion, a mode of cynical and acerbic talking, presumably characteristic of the gallant and law student audiences to whom Jonson first appealed with *Every Man In.* The railing plays launched the Blackfriars boys on their brief career and supported the growth of city comedy. The comedies, however, reflect a larger phenomenon, the staging of London life. City comedy gives a broader perspective than railing for the wide range of the London playhouses between 1599 and 1614.

CITY COMEDY (1599–1614)

Domestic drama came to the London stages as early as *Arden of Faversham*, before 1592, although the Induction to its main successor, *A Warning for Fair Women*, later in the 1590s proclaimed its own originality. The strengthening of urban comedy is indicated by the change of clowning in about 1590 from rustics to rude mechanicals. In 1597 the citizens of Windsor and Abingdon were put on stage in romantic comedies, one by each of the duopoly companies. A mode of what Alexander Leggatt calls specifically citizen comedy existed before Jonson transformed it with his humours plays and their Roman New Comedy models. What took over after Jonson's success came out of a mixture of three influences. Romantic comedy about citizens was one. The drama of Plautus, familiar to the university-educated literate in the audiences, was the second. Jonson's own ambition to beat a new path into satire was the third. All three mingled but kept parts of their separate identities in the years that followed. All three seem to have influenced, and no doubt were influenced by, the divergent repertories of the various playhouses and their social allegiances.

Leggatt defines 'citizen comedy' as plays about citizens, not necessarily plays written for them or upholding their kind of values.[56] The main interest of citizen plays was money and marriage. Much of their incidental comedy lies in the presentation of city types, exaggerated either indulgently (as in Dekker's Simon Eyre) or satirically (as in most of the Blackfriars boys' plays). The social allegiance is obviously important, but easily capable of being misread. Leggatt points out that the Paul's boys' *Westward Ho!* has been taken as an anti-citizen play by modern critics, presumably because it was a boy company play, whereas its fifth act is, like *Merry Wives*, a triumph for the virtuous citizen women and therefore (presumably) at some remove from other boy company anti-citizen plays.[57] Leggatt's point about *Westward Ho!*

emphasises the need to avoid a circular argument and to be cautious both in identifying allegiances in the plays themselves and in deducing from them the bias of the audiences at particular playhouses.

A look at the plays staged by any one company does suggest some conclusions, but most of them are complicated by Jonson's special contribution to city comedy and his fluctuations from one company to another. After his start with Henslowe he launched his humours plays, including the first truly railing comedy, *Every Man Out*, with Shakespeare's company. Their developments in *Poetaster* and *Cynthia's Revels*, the first of which is certainly a city comedy although, like the early version of *Every Man In*, its setting was ostensibly Rome, were written for Blackfriars boys and develop the acerbic mode of railing to an unprecedented level. For *Volpone*, set in Venice, he returned to Shakespeare's company. *Epicene* with its satire on citizen rapaciousness was written for the Blackfriars boys, and then *The Alchemist* for Shakespeare's company after it repossessed the Blackfriars. Its jokey realism depended on its performance 'here in the *friers*', a neighbourhood known for its wealthy Mammons and its puritans as well as its playhouse, and so mocked all its residents, who by then included Jonson himself. Since he laid such intense demands on his audiences, insisting that they should be as acute and judging as Asper, Cordatus and Mitis in *Every Man Out*, it is tempting to see the differences between his plays written for the different companies as at least partly shaped by his expectations of the intellect and capacity of their audiences. *Every Man In* as performed by Shakespeare's company had elements of traditional knockabout and other comic features Jonson knew from his years writing for Henslowe. *Every Man Out* abandoned any such physical comedy, and might well have gone to the boy players if they had been operational by then. What Anne Barton calls 'the insupportable weight of its self-commentary',[58] quite apart from its assault on the bases of Shakespearean comedy, looks at least in part like a deliberate test of what the Shakespeare company and presumably its audiences could bear.

Jonson's first play for the Blackfriars boys, *Cynthia's Revels*, was composed in the tradition of Lyly's court plays which had been the staples of the earlier Blackfriars boy company. By contrast his next play, *Poetaster*, besides developing the railing mode, was written fast as a pre-emptive strike in the War of the Theatres and offers criticism rather than social allegiance, though it did include another parody of *Romeo and Juliet*'s balcony scene. It is the next three comedies, two of them for Shakespeare's company, which show the clearest signs of Jonson's adaptation to suit the traditions of particular companies.

Volpone was a wholly new departure in comedy for Jonson. Dealing with crimes more than follies, it eschews any specifically London
social characterisation except for the gullible English travellers. Its target is human greed, which can only be linked with social divisions in
the large-scale terms of L. C. Knights's analysis of economic change
and its social consequences.[59] It is completely devoid of any local
'application', at least of the kind which provoked Dekker and Marston
in *Poetaster*. The virtuous Celia remains loyal to her citizen husband
against Volpone's seductions and her husband's own gross corruption.
The virtuous Bonario refuses to flout the authority of his equally corrupt father. In social and theatrical content it has little which might
not have been welcomed at one of the northern playhouses. Its social
neutrality may very well reflect Jonson's awareness of the neutral position of the Globe repertory.

When he wrote his next comedy, *Epicene*, for the Blackfriars boys
(now banished, in 1609, to the new Whitefriars hall) he allowed the
play to present a much more extreme position. The first play which
he openly set in London, it was written entirely in the prose that the
boy companies always favoured, and, with some evident reservations,
it adopts the New Comedy mode of plays like Middleton's *A Trick to
Catch the Old One*. Its heroes are a trio of gallants short of money,
and the plot turns on their scheme to extract a healthy income from
the reluctant uncle of one of them. It is no wonder that Dryden praised
it as Jonson's finest comedy, since it anticipates so many features that
became typical of Restoration comedy. Young 'fashionable men' gull
the foolish and trick the knavish in order to secure for themselves
the style of living – wit allied with money – which was beginning
to show itself in the drama as the sole ambition of young gallants
about town. The chief gull, Morose, like Hoord in Middleton's play,
is a born gentleman turned merchant whose grasping attitude over
money poses a direct threat to the liberality which gives the gallants
their standard of conduct. Less extreme in its polarisation of attitudes
between frugality and prodigality than Beaumont's in *The Knight of
the Burning Pestle*, which puts up prodigal 'mirth' as preferable to
mercantile frugality, it still stands a long way from *Volpone*'s moral
rigour.

If Jonson was at all concerned about the kind of playgoer at particular playhouses, *The Alchemist* must have bothered him more than his
other plays. Written like *Volpone* for Shakespeare's company, it was
also explicitly composed for their newly acquired hall playhouse and
its wealthier clientele. He expected the audience to resemble the one
for which he had written *Poetaster*, but the players were the company

he had condemned in that play. Times had evidently moved on. No
doubt he had many reasons for choosing the kind of play he wrote for
this new mixture, and no single reason can explain any one of its features. But a poet so sensitive to the interaction between performance
and audience and so demanding of his audiences cannot have chosen
his setting or his plot without careful calculation.

To fix the action on either side of the main door of a private house
in the Blackfriars district, to people the play with a full spectrum
of London citizenry from Sir Epicure Mammon to Abel Drugger and
Jeremy the manservant, was to extend citizen-play realism to parodic
length, almost as much as the carefully checked-off hours of the day
and the location seem to parody the unities of time and place. Like
Volpone it was written in verse, and like *Volpone* it pillories greed.
Unlike *Epicene* it takes no sides, and it gives little more concession to
the liberal preferences of the gallant mentality than the name of the
character who comes off best in the end, Lovewit. For all the precision
of its London locality, it seems as calculatedly neutral in its social
allegiance as *Volpone*, certainly far more than *Epicene*. It is a London
play for an audience of Londoners, specifically those likely to go to the
Blackfriars. They mirror its clientele as precisely as its setting in the
'friers'.

The effect on Shakespeare's company of their long-delayed acquisition of the Blackfriars playhouse in 1609 is a matter for the next section. Here we need only note how comprehensively Jonson put *The
Alchemist*'s social allegiance into neutral compared with the alignment he gave *Epicene* the year before. The allowances he made in
Epicene for the expectation that the Blackfriars boys would appeal to a
specifically 'gallant' set of values may throw some light on the differences which appeared earlier in the decade between the two boy companies, which he helped to exploit in *Eastward Ho!* Paul's boys, with
much the smaller playhouse, were always a more shaky commercial
proposition than the occupants of Blackfriars. From the outset, though,
they depended on a similar social cachet as a 'private' playhouse with
a 'select' audience and young players. They also seem to have seen
the Blackfriars boys as more serious rivals than the adult players. That
must be why they staged *Satiromastix* in the War of the Theatres.

Yet they also seem to have tried to develop a local citizen audience, staging Chapman's version of a minor piece of neighbourhood
gossip and using two 'citizen' playwrights with citizen antecedents
from the Henslowe stable, Dekker and Webster, for the *Ho!* plays in
the years immediately before they closed. These citizen interests and
the comprehensive burlesque of the *Ho!* plays that the Blackfriars boys

mounted with *Eastward Ho!* suggest that Paul's boys lacked the narrowness of the 'select' social allegiance for which the Blackfriars boys consistently catered. Apprentice Quicksilver in *Eastward Ho!* resembles apprentice Ralph of Beaumont's gird at citizens for the same company in his enthusiasm for the old citizen repertory, quoting *Tamburlaine* and *The Spanish Tragedy* much as Ralph quotes Hotspur's huffing speech and the Red Bull repertoire of plays. Shakespeare's company had got in first at that game with Pistol in *2 Henry IV*, of course, but in *Eastward Ho!* Jonson, Marston and Chapman lumped all their rivals, Henslowe's companies, Shakespeare and Paul's boys, together with their mockery of the prodigal tradition. Their particular trademark was anti-citizen burlesque. Paul's may have started with similar material, but they soon parted company from their boy rivals.

When the Blackfriars boys left the Blackfriars playhouse the fashion for railing and burlesque was dying. The 'salt' had lost its savour. In Brian Gibbons's summary,

as the Jacobean age proceeds, Court corruption and political tyranny cease to be treated in comedy and become increasingly the province of satiric tragedy and tragi-comic romance. Meanwhile in a parallel development, critical comedy concentrates on the city as a setting, depicting the tensions between commercial and social pressures and moral values.[60]

As *Measure for Measure*'s Duke said piously early in the decade, 'Novelty is only in request' (3.2.210). Fashions were under such constant pressure to change that they were several times compared to fashions in clothing, and it is difficult to see how much of the change was a consequence of tastes evolving and how much was due to more material factors such as the changes in playhouse conditions. Certainly the Blackfriars boys took their railing off with them when they handed their hall over to Shakespeare's company. Such audiences as stayed with or returned to the Blackfriars under their new management do not seem to have forced many changes in the repertoire of the adult company after 1609. Their most substantial change was the replacement of Shakespeare by Fletcher, though even that adjustment did not take away their staple, the Shakespeare canon.

AFTER 1609: THE SETTLED HIERARCHY

If we choose to think of the decade from 1599 to 1609 as a period of rivalry between the boy companies and the adult players, 1609 can easily be seen to mark total victory for the adults. After the King's Men took back the lease of the Blackfriars and its shares were allocated to the holders of shares in the Globe, it was never again possible to use the social cachet of boy players and their 'private' accommodation as a temptation to the wealthier playgoers. Shakespeare's company with their kingly title and their unique repertoire of Shakespeare's plays became the outstanding company in every way, whichever of their playhouses they were using. That is a rather narrow perspective, though. The acquisition of the Blackfriars as their winter playhouse should more properly be seen not as a victory over the boy tenants but as a belated fulfilment of the plan that the company originally hatched in 1594.

Part of what the Blackfriars boys indirectly accomplished was the renewal by the adults of their old preference for a place to play in winter inside the city. The intervening years had weakened Guildhall's opposition by giving the company its royal title, and the presence of the boys silenced the residents of the Blackfriars neighbourhood. Pre-eminence as the King's Men must also have encouraged the Shakespeare company to undertake the extravagance of maintaining two playhouses, something no other company ever did, and indeed to rebuild the Globe richly when the false economy of thatching the original building burned it to the ground in 1613.

The culmination of a series of fortunate accidents – fortune more than globe – in 1609 gave the company the three things on which their uniquely long and successful career was based. First, they were the only company in a position to follow the early practice of using an amphitheatre in summer weather and a hall in the winter. Secondly, by the accident of the Burbages being short of cash to build the Globe in 1599 the leading players of the playing company became shareholders in the two playhouses, and presumably took a large part in the decision to operate in the new mode. The success of this new management system, a uniquely democratic organisation of conjoint landlords and tenants, was the envy of the later companies who worked for landlord impresarios.[61] Thirdly, their possession of the Blackfriars gave them the playhouse situated closest to the Inns of Court, familiar over the ten preceding years as the venue for a repertory aimed pretty precisely at law students and gallants. No other adult company had that resource in 1609, and no hall playhouse came into existence to rival the Blackfriars for another seven years.

Those seven years fixed the different species of repertory distinctly and permanently. At the northern playhouses the plays were more and more designed for citizens and the 'porters and carters' whom Galli described at the Curtain in 1613 (2.110). The Elect Nation plays in the Fortune repertory were reprinted in 1612–13, *Sir Thomas Wyatt* first in 1607 and then in 1612, *When You See Me* in 1605 and 1613, and *If You Know Not Me* in 1605, 1608, 1610 and 1613. That suggests a series of revivals in 1612 or so by the Fortune company. The Middlesex magistrates complained in 1611 about the tumults which accompanied the jigs still in use to end the day's performances there. Heywood's celebrated plays and displays of the Four Ages for the Red Bull were variations on what the annual city pageants sponsored by the mayor and guilds offered each year. The allegiance is evident. Inhabitants of the suburbs to the north and east of the city, where the Fortune, Curtain and Red Bull operated, were the poorest in London while the Blackfriars was the wealthiest district. The social identity of the different neighbourhoods influenced the reputations of their playhouses.

In 1616 the Blackfriars playhouse, located alongside the Inns of Court and halfway between the City of London and the new aristocratic housing developments of the City of Westminster, was joined by Beeston's Cockpit in Drury Lane half a mile away, just to the west of the City of London boundary. The Cockpit soon began to share the Blackfriars' superior reputation along with its superior neighbourhood, and became the only alternative to the Blackfriars in term time for student playgoers such as Edward Heath and John Greene, who regularly went to both. Gentry like Sir Humphrey Mildmay went primarily to the Blackfriars, secondly to the Cockpit. Unlike the law students, whose terms coincided with the period when the King's Men were using their hall playhouse, Mildmay also went to the Globe in the summer months. His loyalty to the company was greater than to its neighbourhood. Gondomar's visit to the Fortune in 1621 when he gave a banquet for the players seems in the broad context of this growing social polarisation to have been a calculated piece of political slumming. The King's Men drew gentry to the Globe every year, but there is less and less evidence that people of Mildmay's social status visited the northern playhouses after 1609.

More obviously than any other change, the King's Men's takeover of the Blackfriars altered the pattern of playgoing into a socially stratified distribution. But they altered far more than just their venue, and the effects on playgoing were complex. Most substantially they increased the supply of Blackfriars performances sixfold. The boys kept to one performance a week in spite of the commercial incentives they had to increase their revenue. Even in 1606 the epilogue to *Eastward Ho!* still voiced the modest hope that its pleasures might 'attract you hither once a week'. No bar was placed on the King's Men using Blackfriars for their customary six afternoons a week. Despite that increase in the availability of performances at the most gentrified playhouse, how-ever, the transfer did cut off the King's Men's performances for more than half the year from most of the playgoers who had visited them on the Bankside.

The sixfold increase in the price of admission at Blackfriars over the Globe minimum plus the reduction in the capacity of its auditorium by two thousand or more places altered at a stroke the nature of the audience for whom Shakespeare's company performed through seven months of the year. And those were only the material changes. For a playing company to be allowed to use Blackfriars daily marks a pro-found change in the status of the players. In 1596 the Lord Chamberlain himself, Lord Cobham, supported the petition blocking the players from using their new playhouse. In 1609 nothing was said. The lib-erty of the Blackfriars had long been popular with the aristocracy not just as a handsome residential area but because of its church services. Stephen Egerton's sermons at St Anne's, for instance, were extremely popular, especially with ladies. Margaret Hoby, a puritan lady, daugh-ter of one of the signatories of the 1596 petition, recorded in her diary for 30 November 1600 that 'after I was come home and had dined, I went to the blake friers, from whence I returned home and set downe in my testement the chieffe notes delivered by Mr. Egertone'.[62] She was writing about the church, not the new playhouse.

In the circumstances it is a little surprising that the escalation of playgoing in 1609 in competition with churchgoing did not provoke another petition until the adult players had been there for all of ten years. Only the prestige of the King's Men in society at large can explain the painless acquisition of their new playhouse. That prestige, based principally on Shakespeare's plays written for the Globe, set the other companies their standard.[63] The northern companies now more openly kept clear of the privileged in the centre of the city, leaving them to the King's Men. Records of performances at court confirm the Blackfriars players' ascendancy. Not until 1616 did Christopher Beeston mount any challenge for that end of the market.

The King's Men's repertoire of plays from 1609 onwards aspired to satisfy the top of the social hierarchy, but it still based itself centrally on the plays of Shakespeare. His major plays remained staples for the next thirty years, if the lists of plays offered at court are any indica-tor. Only in the Caroline period did Fletcher's even larger run of plays for the company overtake Shakespeare's as favourites at court. The flow of new plays initiated by the success of Beaumont and Fletcher once they transferred from the boy company repertory secured its head of pressure largely by redeploying Shakespearean elements. *Philaster,*

The Maid's Tragedy and *A King and No King* came to rival *Pericles* as the characteristic style of the King's Men, and all three plays are infused with Shakespearean situations and characters to a degree which shows not just their authors' but their audiences' familiarity with the originals. Playgoers at both the Blackfriars and the Globe took enthusiastically to the Arcadian style of the so-called 'Beaumont and Fletcher' canon produced by the team of writers led by John Fletcher (one of whose collaborators was Shakespeare) as an outgrowth of its Shakespearean base.

The nature of Fletcher's changes to the King's Men's repertory reflects the arrival of the company's plays at the Blackfriars in two distinct ways. One was the arrival of the fashion for tragicomedy, a mode for which the writers invented tragic/romantic stories that might end either in death or in happy unions. The central feature of Fletcher's tragicomedies was the ingenuity of plotting used to test moral and political issues in extreme situations. The other major and almost unique feature was Fletcher's focus on women as the focal members of his audiences. From 1611 when he produced *The Tamer Tamed*, a sequel to Shakespeare's *Taming of the Shrew* in which the women take complete control of Petruchio and the play's other husbands, the female characters were given less passive roles and enhanced plot-functions. That priority in the repertory remained consistent through the second and third decades of the century.

From about 1620 the influence of women in the audiences grew wider and extended to other repertories. Middleton's *Women Beware Women* and Middleton and Rowley's *The Changeling*, while retaining a touch of the moralism over wives apparent in Heywood's *A Woman Killed with Kindness*, show a new level of concern for female independence. The two plots of *The Changeling*, while emphasising the degradation of Beatrice Joanna in the main plot, take care to hand the secondary plot's wife, after she has ridiculed the disguised gentry who try to seduce her while pretending to be madmen, absolute control over them and over her foolish husband. In the Red Bull's *Two Noble Ladies* of 1620 one heroine uses her piety like Marina in *Pericles* to convert a pagan conjuror to Christianity, while the other dresses as an Amazon warrior to conquer her lover and with him the rival kingdom (to which, following the rules of the new tragicomic mode initiated by *Philaster*, she is the heir).

Fletcher's plays were not so much a new playgoing fashion as an extension of the supremely popular one starting with Shakespeare's own last plays at the Globe. The company did not radically alter any of its repertory when it moved into Blackfriars. Gerald Bentley's idea that Shakespeare's last plays differ from their predecessors because they were written for the newly acquired hall playhouse and its new clientele, and that the company hired Beaumont and Fletcher to write for them because the younger men had experience writing for the previous tenants, has not had a prosperous life.[64] He ignored the fact that *Pericles*, certainly a play in Shakespeare's late style, was on stage at the Globe in 1607, before the company had any reason to expect that they might repossess the Blackfriars, and that *The Winter's Tale* and *Cymbeline* were staged at the Globe in 1611 when Simon Forman saw them. Shakespeare's first and only play obviously written for the Blackfriars was *The Tempest* in 1610.[65] Bentley also overlooked the fact that Beaumont and Fletcher, whether writing together or separately, were noted chiefly for plays which failed when performed by the boys. More likely in 1609 Shakespeare, preparing for his retirement to Stratford, left an opening for a new contracted playwright which the company did not want to entrust to Jonson and which Fletcher eventually filled. *Philaster*, the first play Beaumont and Fletcher wrote for the King's Men at Blackfriars, opens with what looks like an uneasily self-conscious joke about the audience for the old company in its new venue.

CLE. Here's nor lords, nor ladies.
DION. Credit me, gentlemen, I wonder at it. They received strict charge from the King to attend here . . .

Possibly when Fletcher penned this opening for his new employers he was unsure whether the top of the social range would come to see the adults in the boys' playhouse.

Jonson, writing *The Alchemist* for the same venue a little later, had fewer doubts. He expected his Blackfriars audience to be familiar with *The Spanish Tragedy* and with the Globe repertoire, and indeed to be largely the same as the King's Men had always entertained. *Philaster*, which is a rewriting of *Cupid's Revenge*, a boy company play, eliminating its gods and simplifying its staging, may reflect Fletcher's uncertainty about the readiness of the Blackfriars audience to receive the King's Men's offerings. Its echoes of *Hamlet* and *Othello* may well have been emphasised for the sake of the former Globe audience which they hoped would stay loyal to the company at its new venue, as Jonson expected. Fletcher's uncertainty was probably ill-advised.

The next Beaumont and Fletcher play, *The Maid's Tragedy*, shifted in the other direction far enough to include a masque, in explicit imitation of the court's most distinctive pastime. Shakespeare's late plays in any case made far more extravagant demands of the company in staging and of the audience in suspending their disbelief at the sur-real events on stage. He definitely was happy to accept the challenge of a Blackfriars audience long accustomed to the sophisticated games of the 'theatre of estrangement'. Still, that was a minor change from his previous practices. His Globe plays transplanted to the Blackfriars unchanged, as his Blackfriars plays transplanted to the Globe.[66] Audi-ence expectations seem largely to have been transplanted with them. The Fletcher team's nearly fifty plays written for the King's Men exploited a fashion first created by Shakespeare for the Globe. Adding the Blackfriars playhouse to the company's resources may have helped the development of the fashion but it can hardly be said to have created it. The company had in effect announced its concept of a separate and roofed indoor playhouse when they persuaded Henry Carey to ask for the Cross Keys in October 1594. In a real sense acquiring the Blackfri-ars in 1608 merely reaffirmed the wish they had entertained from the outset.

This is not the place to examine the nature of the fashion which Shakespeare's last plays generated (much more is offered in *The Shakespeare Company, 1594–1642*). Its closest affinities are to Sidney's *Arcadia*, the favourite reading of young gallants and university men. That affinity together with the availability of the plays at the venue most convenient for the Inns of Court no doubt helped to confirm the King's Men in their grip on the upper sections of the playgoing market. It does not, however, tell anything like the whole story of the King's Men's audiences after 1609.

The huge sum, between £1,000 and £1,400, that the King's Men's housekeepers chose to spend rebuilding the Globe in 1614 was not merely a display of their affluence. A financial commitment of that magnitude showed their determination to continue the tradition they had established through the previous decade. *Henry VIII*, the play which caused the Globe to burn, has distinct affinities with the plays of nostalgia for Elizabeth's England that the square amphitheatres of the northern suburbs were reviving in 1613. Its epilogue condemns the practice of girding at citizens. To some extent the company did see the Globe as a citizen playhouse. But the amphitheatre also offered Blackfriars plays, and there is no evidence before the late 1630s to sug-gest that the company chose to stage some plays at one venue and not the other. Even *Hamlet*'s duel must have been accommodated indoors somehow.

Nothing in the available evidence suggests that the King's Men's pre-eminence and their possession of the playhouse most frequented by the privileged altered in any way their assumption that they catered for the whole range of society. Standing at the top of the hierarchy of players they could still revive an old citizen favourite, *Mucedorus*, to offer the king for the Christmas revels of 1610. Their appeal was wider than any of their rivals, and their repertory more wide-ranging. Under James they kept a stable formula sustained by the input from the Beaumont and Fletcher canon. The only evidence for change turns up under Charles, when the company seems to have begun to acknowledge a difference in tastes between the Blackfriars gentry and the Globe's citizenry, though even that may be rather more a matter of adapting styles between the hall and the open amphitheatre than of catering to a different clientele. Before the 1630s, and certainly in the years from 1609 till Richard Burbage died in 1619, the company saw itself as catering for the whole of society, and it offered the same fare at both playhouses.

BEESTON'S COCK AND BULL (1616–30)

Christopher Beeston was London's cleverest innovator in theatre affairs between 1609 and his death in 1638. He began as a player apprenticed to Augustine Phillips in the Lord Chamberlain's Men, appearing in *Every Man in his Humour* in 1597. He transferred to the Henslowe enterprises by 1602 and became financial controller of Queen Anne's Men, taking over management of its business affairs in 1612 when its leading player Thomas Greene died. He lived in Clerkenwell near the Red Bull where his company performed, and was a friend as well as a colleague of Heywood, who wrote his pageant plays for him. The citizen repertory however did not satisfy Beeston. An adroit manager, he saw the way forward as an upward shift to match the King's Men in their use of the Blackfriars. By 1616 he had the resources to take a thirty-one-year lease on a property in Drury Lane, half a mile north-west of the Blackfriars, north-east of Whitehall Palace, and very close to the Inns of Court. The property was 'All that edifices or building called the Cockpits, and the Cockhouses and shed thereunto adjoining'.[67]

The original cock-fighting pit had its own circular auditorium, which Beeston probably retained as the basic structure for the new hall playhouse while extending one end of the circle to add a square stage and boxes, with a tiring house behind the extension. King James had forbidden new building in the district, or the enlargement of existing buildings by more than one-third, so Beeston calculated his development nicely. If, as seems very likely, he did use the surviving Inigo

Jones drawings of an adapted cockpit for his new playhouse, its auditorium would have resembled the curved galleries of the Blackfriars, though it had only two levels of galleries, so its seating capacity would have been smaller.[68] Restricted though the income was, Beeston evidently felt there would be more profit from imitating the Blackfriars than he could get at the Red Bull. He kept his financial interest in the Red Bull, but transferred its company to the Cockpit, where it would play all the year round, unlike the King's at Blackfriars. He evidently expected to profit from the fact that his would be the only hall playhouse operating through the summer months.

Beeston's subsequent career does not impinge directly on the question of audience composition and allegiances, though the link he maintained in the 1620s between the Red Bull and Cockpit raises some intriguing questions which will be considered below. The immediate question is how he succeeded with his attempt to rival the Blackfriars, and what effect it might have had on the range of London repertories.

From the time Beeston's new playhouse opened when the law term had commenced late in 1616, the Revels Office allowed four companies to work in London. The King's Men as the leading company were followed by the Queen's at the Cockpit, the Palsgrave's at the Fortune and Prince Charles's, who took over at the Red Bull when Beeston transferred the Queen's Men to the Cockpit. The Queen's company's transfer to the Cockpit was not quite the same as the King's Men's transfer from the Globe to the Blackfriars. Beeston's company, much less prosperous than the King's Men,[69] did not copy them by retaining an amphitheatre for the summer season, and they paid a peculiar price for not doing so. The Queen's company had a drum and trumpet repertory designed for the 'fishwives' and artisans of the city. When they left the Red Bull they took those plays with them to the Cockpit. Although a new company started playing at the Red Bull, its plays were different.

The apprentices and fishwives could hardly make the same transfer to the Cockpit as the players, because its prices were a lot higher. That meant they lost their favourite repertory. Consequently it is something less than a coincidence that on the following Shrove Tuesday holiday early in 1617 a gang of apprentices went to the Cockpit and wrecked it. The fact that they chose to attack the Cockpit ahead of the northern amphitheatres and the Blackfriars, and that they also destroyed Beeston's new house next door, suggests that they were taking revenge for the loss of their plays. John Chamberlain's colourful account confirms that the riot was a show of animus against the newly installed Cockpit company. Although the players defended their playhouse and shot some of the attackers, 'yet they entered the house and defaced yt, cutting the players apparell all to pieces, and all other theyre furniture, and burnt theyre play bookes and did what other mischeife they could'.[70] Playbooks and apparel were a playing company's most valuable possessions. We know the attack was pointedly against the company rather than against playhouses in general, because on Shrove Tuesday the following year they tried again. Their plan this time was to assemble at the Fortune and to attack both the Cockpit and the Red Bull, but the Privy Council was forewarned and stopped them. Since they used the Fortune as their assembly point their animus was evidently not against playhouses in general but against the two which had disrupted their pleasures. It can only have been Beeston and his removal of the Red Bull repertoire to the more expensive Cockpit which stirred these acts of revenge.

There is regrettably little direct evidence about the plays that Beeston took to the Cockpit. Webster had been writing for the Queen's Men at the Red Bull, and after the success of his *Duchess of Malfi* at the Blackfriars *The White Devil* and *The Devil's Law-Case* might have seemed useful hall-playhouse fodder. More surprisingly Heywood, who wrote regularly for the Cockpit in the 1620s, may also have gone to Beeston's new hall with his pageant plays. *The Iron Age*, dealing with the Trojan War and originally composed for the Queen's Men at the Red Bull, might have been one that made the transfer, since the epistle which accompanied its publication in 1632 claimed that at different times it had 'thronged three severall Theaters, with numerous and mighty Auditories'. The Red Bull was certainly one of the three. The Curtain may have been a second, and it is difficult to ignore the circumstantial evidence of the Red Bull company's transfer and Heywood's subsequent association with the Cockpit to conclude that it must have been the third.

Almost nothing is known for certain about the early Cockpit repertoire, but since play-texts were a major part of a playing company's assets, and since the Red Bull company did make the transfer, it seems likely that the first years there saw the performance of plays originally written for the Red Bull. Some plays which had belonged to Henslowe before Beeston joined the Queen's Men do turn up later in the Cockpit repertoire. The most notable of these is Marlowe's *Jew of Malta*, which was printed in 1633 with an epistle by Heywood and a prologue for the Cockpit revival praising Richard Perkins, the Cockpit's leading man, in the title role. Perhaps with other Marlowe plays such as *Edward II* it moved to the Cockpit when the Queen's Men opened there in 1616. Heywood's *If You Know Not Me* also transferred there at some point. So the second hall playhouse, at least through its early years, sustained an older and more openly citizen repertoire than its rival at Blackfriars.

Beeston's enterprise at the Cockpit was in some respects a rather shady operation. He was accused by the Queen's Men after he ejected them from the Cockpit in 1619 of milking their funds to feed his own interests. There was a good deal of acrimony over the Cockpit, which may have blocked his return to the Red Bull after the Shrove Tuesday riot destroyed his new house. In the event he rebuilt the damaged Cockpit – evoking its alternative name, the Phoenix – and ran it with the Queen's Men until their patron died in 1619. He then introduced Prince Charles's Men, who had taken the Queen's Men's place at the Red Bull, to the Cockpit. Once again a Red Bull company supplied the wants of the Cockpit audiences. No plays from the Prince Charles's first Red Bull period have survived, though Middleton and Rowley appear to have written for them at about this time.[71] On the evidence of his readiness to use Red Bull players and repertoires Beeston himself felt that the King's Men's seasonal transfers between the Globe and Blackfriars could be imitated. If he was wrong, it was not because of the repertoire of plays but because his kind of transfer was for an indefinite period. The apprentices in 1617 were objecting to the removal of a Red Bull repertoire wholly and durably beyond their reach.

From 1616 onwards the supply of new plays to the four repertories slowed down markedly. Many of the new plays never reached print and have been lost, particularly those belonging to the Red Bull and Fortune companies. From this time on neither of the northern amphitheatre companies was invited to perform at court. By the 1630s the King's Men were taking only four new plays a year, when more than 80 per cent of the plays offered at court were old favourites. Consequently it becomes more and more difficult to identify a particular repertoire at a particular playhouse. To some extent the repertories were particular, and playhouses did have distinct reputations, based chiefly on their stock of old plays which attracted particular types of audience. The Red Bull players strengthened their reputation as what Edmund Gayton called 'terrible teare-throats', speaking and strutting more vigorously than their rivals. The Bull played the man while the Globe and Blackfriars told tricks of love (2.106). From 1616 onwards the reputations of the different playhouses are more revealing than their repertoires, conceivably more because of the different playing styles that the Red Bull's reputation for noise suggests than distinct kinds of play. It is this possibility which makes the continuing series of transfers from the Red Bull to the Cockpit so intriguing.

From the time when Beeston's reborn Phoenix started performing regularly in 1617 until at least 1630 the repertoires of the two playhouses were similar, however much their reputations diverged. The Red Bull staged *Swetnam the Woman Hater* in 1617, a play designed in part to please the sort of ladies who wrote pamphlets challenging Joseph Swetnam's misogyny. Like Middleton and Rowley's *A Fair Quarrel* the Swetnam play was entirely suitable for the ladies in the boxes at the Cockpit. Such plays did not deserve the jibe Thomas Tomkis levelled against the citizen playhouses in 1614 in his Cambridge play *Albumazar*, an imitation of *The Alchemist* and *The Tempest*, that at 'the Plaies I see at the Fortune and Red Bull . . . I learne all the words I speake and understand not' (2.120). Tomkis wrote academic plays which expected his audiences to be familiar with London playgoing and current reputations. In *Lingua* (1607), for instance, he commented on the abuse to be expected in boy company plays, 'when Boys dare traduce men in authority' (*Lingua*, D3v). The Red Bull's reputation for overdoing it was evidently current well before Beeston found its company a new home. And odd though it seems, that reputation stayed with the Red Bull tenants even though its actual players transferred every few years to the Cockpit. Whether that had anything to do with the open-air acoustics of the amphitheatres in contrast with the volume required indoors in the hall playhouses is an issue the King's Men must have confronted twice every year, but to which we have no clear answer.

In 1625 when the companies resumed playing under the new king Beeston reopened the Cockpit with a new group, called Queen Henrietta's Men. Following what had by now become his standard practice he acquired for his new company Richard Perkins and other leading players who had been notable at the Red Bull. They did well, if the fact that Beeston kept them together much longer at the Cockpit than he did his other companies is anything to go by. In August 1628 the Duke of Buckingham, greatest grandee in the country and soon to be assassinated, visited the Cockpit to see Heywood's *Rape of Lucrece*, a play originally written for the Red Bull. The Cockpit company performed ten times at court over Christmas 1629, while the Blackfriars company played twelve. In the following season they played sixteen times.

Not very surprisingly, in 1630 a group of Blackfriars poets complained that they were losing customers to the rival hall. Thomas Carew condemned the alternative attraction for its rowdiness and the declining standards of recent audiences in a verse epistle for a play, *The Just Italian*, that William Davenant had recently written for the

20. The Duke of Buckingham, from a painting.

Blackfriars. Carew lumped the Cockpit and Red Bull tastes together, in a complaint clearly designed to be offensive to the Cockpit.

> I have beheld, when pearched on the smooth brow
> Of a fayre modest troope, thou didst allow
> Applause to slighter workes; but then the weake
> Spectator gave the knowing leave to speake.
> Now noyse prevayles, and he is taxed for drowth
> Of wit, that with the crie, spends not his mouth.
> Yet aske him, reason why he did not like;
> Him, why he did; their ignorance will strike
> Thy soule with scorne, and Pity: marke the places
> Provoke their smiles, frownes, or distorted faces,
> When, they admire, nod, shake the head: they'le be
> A scene of myrth, a double Comedie.
> But thy strong fancies (raptures of the brayne,
> Drest in Poetique flames) they entertayne
> As a bold, impious reach; for they'l still slight
> All that exceeds Red Bull, and Cockpit flight.   (2.163)

Perched on the 'smooth brow', presumably a bench flanking the music room on the stage balcony at the Blackfriars, Carew claimed that the 'weake Spectator' used to concede authority to the opinions of the 'knowing'. Implicit in this is his belief that the new poetry and wit of the Blackfriars writers was superior to the old-fashioned noise and 'double Comedie' shared by the citizen and the Cockpit repertories. The Cockpit's supporters promptly challenged this accusation, calling it 'a discourse of cock and bull', and Heywood a little later also spoke out for his friend's company against Carew.

Modern commentators have found it harder to accept this lumping together of the tear-throats at the Red Bull with the Cockpit than writers of the time did.[72] Beeston was evidently not so ready to accept innovation as the Blackfriars, and yet while the volume and overdoing for which the Red Bull was notorious could not have adjusted easily to the Cockpit the plays and even the players clearly did. The number of companies that moved through the 1630s between one type of playhouse and the other, identified above in the table at the end of chapter 3, also argues that the players were as adaptable as their plays, whatever their audiences made of them. This suggests that the two playhouses became distinct in the social identity of their audiences more through their prices and their locality than their repertoire. Printers named the Cockpit nearly as often as they proclaimed the Blackfriars as the place of first publication for plays, often concealing their origin as Red Bull products. If printers thought the social status of the playhouse mattered, so presumably did audiences.

THE BLACKFRIARS IN THE 1630s

The Blackfriars scaled the heights of social respectability in the 1630s, a level marked most singularly by Queen Henrietta Maria's four visits, and more routinely yet notoriously by the Lord Chamberlain, Philip Herbert, in his sordid squabble with the king's cousin over a key to a box at Blackfriars. The story of Nim on his stool ogling the masked ladies sitting in the pit facing the stage (2.160) in pursuit of a financial lifeline says as much about the social eminence of the playhouse as it does about the hoops that penniless gentry put themselves through to get attention while playgoing. Under Charles the King's Men had taken playing a long way since 1594 when they secured the first licence to perform in London's suburbs in an eighteen-year-old amphitheatre.

In the last twelve years before the closure the social prestige of particular playhouses settled into a distinct hierarchy. The Blackfriars pre-eminence was never shaken after 1630, though for different reasons the Cockpit and the Globe served as respectable alternatives in summer. The third hall playhouse, the Salisbury Court in Whitefriars, which opened in 1629, was smaller than the two older halls, and remained self-consciously inferior to them in status if not in what its stage offered. Bankside continued to be the resort for bear-baiting and brothels throughout the year, but kept its attraction for playgoers as the suburb where the Blackfriars players held their summer season. The Swan, the still-extant Curtain, and the Hope after its first year of staging both bears and players never gave the Globe any competition, so in a way the King's Men were as distinct on the southern Bankside as they were in central Blackfriars. The two square amphitheatres in the northern suburbs strengthened their identity as popular venues catering primarily for the masses, artisans, apprentices and the lowest levels of the hierarchy of wealth. Some evidence links the Fortune and Red Bull with the Globe up to 1642 as providers of vigorous drum and trumpet plays of a simpler make than the halls provided – or could provide, given their smaller size and enclosed shape with the consequent acoustic constraints. How consistently the amphitheatres aimed to supply heartier appetites than those of the ladies and their escorts in the boxes at the hall playhouses to some extent remains an assumption based on the physical conditions of the different venues.

It is hardly surprising that most comment in these later years focussed on the Blackfriars. Francis Lenton's cheerful verses about the rise and fall of a young prodigal gallant coming as an Inns of Court student to London, written in 1629, show like Nim's story how closely social standing and the choice of playhouse went together. Lenton's young man initially goes to the Cockpit. Soon though, in

'silken garments, and . . . sattin robe' he starts attending the Blackfriars and, staying in town out of term, the Globe. With his copy of
Jonson's 'booke of Playes' he seems to ally social pretensions with
intellectual as he ascends from the Cockpit repertory to that of the
King's Men.

> The Cockpit heretofore would serve his wit,
> But now upon the Fryers stage hee'll sit. (2.157)

No doubt both his progress and his pretensions were characteristic of
the time, though in 1629 it may have been his intellectual pretensions
to 'wit' that drew him to the Blackfriars rather than the social ladder.
In that he may vaguely reflect the dispute over the divergent repertoire
of plays which sparked Carew and the Cockpit writers.

Despite Lenton's demotion of the Cockpit below the Blackfriars, in
the years from the late 1620s to 1636 the two playhouses were almost
equal in social standing. Shackerley Marmion, writing for the smaller
Salisbury Court hall in 1631, praised them equally.

> . . . on each hand
> To over-top us, two great Lawrels stand;
> The one, when she shall please to spread her traine,
> The vastnesse of the Globe cannot containe;
> Th'other so high, the Phoenix does aspire
> To build in . . . (2.169)

Ladies in this period went as readily to the Cockpit as the Blackfriars,
and both repertories began to run plays aimed specifically at what were
thought to be female tastes. This equivalence, which led Inns of Court
gentry like John Ford to write for both playhouses, lasted until the long
plague closure of 1636–7, when the ten-year run of Beeston's company
came to an end and he replaced them with the group of youngsters
known as 'Beeston's Boys'. The Blackfriars then ran unchallenged till
all playing was stopped.

In the 1630s prologues written for the Blackfriars and the Cockpit
began to develop a language of their own. Addressing themselves to
any or all of the four categories they identified in the hall audiences,
gentry, ladies, wealthy merchant citizens and 'wity young masters o'
the *Innes o' Court*',[73] they indicate that a new currency of judicious
criticism was being minted.

> Let some say *This was flat*; Some here *the Sceane*
> *Fell from its height*; Another that the Meane
> Was *ill observ'd*, in such a growing passion.[74]

All these new prologues and epilogues were probably themselves a consequence of the settled sense which audiences now had of themselves as judges. This, sadly though understandably, came too late for Jonson. He attacked the Blackfriars audiences in 1635 bitterly for being no better than the 'understanders' at the amphitheatres:

> . . . those deepe-grounded, understanding men,
> That sit to censure *Playes*, yet know not when,
> Or why to likc . . .[75]

But Alexander Gill mocked Jonson for sending his *Magnetic Lady* to the Blackfriars instead of the Fortune and its apple-wives.

> . . . when as silkes and plush, and all the witts
> Are calde to see, and censure as befitts,
> And yff your follye take not, they, perchance,
> Must here themselfes stilde, gentle ignorance. (2.173)

The self-conscious function of gentle audiences at the hall playhouses was to 'censure'. For the first time plays had become respectable matter for serious discussion. The king himself made critical notes in the margins of his playbooks and more than once interceded on a matter of critical judgement with the Master of the Revels. It became a mode of the town.

On the whole, audiences at the Blackfriars and Cockpit seem to have bccn much more akin than their repertoires. In some respects both playhouses shaped their offerings to suit the new Caroline respectability and showed a new respect for the ladies in the boxes. The main shifts in taste reflected the female presence and called for refinements in the verbal crudities of the older repertory. The Master of the Revels, Sir Henry Herbert, was himself a clumsily insistent censor, taking a narrow line over oaths and profanity and demanding that revivals of old plays like *The Taming of the Shrew* and Fletcher's sequel *The Tamer Tamed* should be freshly 'purged' before they could be performed. His well-known objection to Charles's more liberal idea of what constituted an oath shows that he was not just led to this stand by his nced of the fee for reading the playbooks. He gave unctuous praise to Shirley's innocuous *Young Admiral*, a play slickly adapted from Lope de Vega's *Don Lope de Cardona*, and urged other playwrights to copy Shirley's verbal moderation (2.178). Abraham Wright also liked *The Young Admiral*, so what prompted Herbert's judgement was not just his officious idea of censorship.[76]

A large contribution to this shift in taste came from the circle of gallants who attended Henrietta Maria and wrote for the Blackfriars.

The courtier poet Lodowick Carlell, who wrote for court performance but passed his work on to the King's Men, along with the pushing young gallants Davenant, Suckling and Rutter, did most to fix the concept of 'wit' as the test of quality in the Blackfriars repertoire. Their exhibitionistic style generated controversy with other poets, making enemies of Massinger and Shirley who wrote in the older tradition. Two of Massinger's plays written for the Blackfriars failed between 1630 and 1633, at least one of them because it was decried by a faction of gallants in the audience. Massinger did not enjoy Carew's verses in 1630 attacking the Cockpit and Red Bull. One of Carew's supporters in turn condemned him for bringing

> ... his flat
> dull dialogues frought with insipit chatt
> Into the scale with thy Sweet Muse, which sings
> ditties fit only for the eares of Kings.[77]

Shirley, chief victim of the Carew attack, was appointed to Henrietta Maria's household in 1632, and may have felt that he was joining not so much the opposition as a superior and select company. But in November of that year Herbert censured him severely for *The Ball*, played at the Cockpit, where 'ther were divers personated so naturally, both of lords and others of the court, that I took it ill'.[78] Shirley never again ventured into the intimate satire which this charge implies. He fell out of favour as Davenant rose. A sharp comment in *The Bird in a Cage* (1633) about 'the flattering tribe of courtiers . . . glow worms' indicates his uneasiness in such company.

It may be too simple to see Davenant and his allies making a concerted attempt to displace Massinger from the Blackfriars and make him join Shirley at the Cockpit, where a less innovative repertoire was more welcome, but the circumstantial evidence does suggest that a campaign aimed at some such change did run for a while at the Blackfriars. The transfer of writers like Ford from the Blackfriars to the Cockpit, the failure of several Massinger plays and Shirley's difficulties in the period from 1629 to 1633, including his brief transfer from the Cockpit to Salisbury Court, offer confirmation that some upheavals in taste did take place when Davenant and his allies established themselves at the Blackfriars.

Conservatism in the playgoing tastes of the gentry was probably one factor which kept the Cockpit in strong competition with the Black-friars up to 1636. Traditional preferences lingered on, sustained by the quality of the old repertoire which made it good policy to mount such revivals as Shakespeare's and Fletcher's *Shrew* plays in 1633. In explicit contrast to this pleasure in the old plays, and possibly to emphasise their own originality, Davenant and his allies distanced themselves carefully from them. In the prologue to his *Unfortunate Lovers* at Blackfriars Davenant characterised the habits of amphitheatre audiences, dominated by citizens, as out of date.

> Good easy judging souls, with what delight
> They would expect a jig, or target fight.   (2.197)

The Blackfriars audiences of 1638 were required to be more severe judges, and to enjoy not swordplay but wit-play.

There is a good deal of evidence suggesting that the Cockpit plays were a lot more traditional and less innovatory than the Blackfriars throughout this period. The plays which Beeston took from the Red Bull to the Cockpit stayed in the hall playhouse's repertoire. As late as 1639 Beeston's son had quite a number of Red Bull plays protected for his Cockpit company. This protection, which took the form of an edict issued on 10 August 1639 by the Lord Chamberlain, was designed to stop illegal performance or publication of plays in the Cockpit repertoire. The old plays were still valuable commodities to the Cockpit.

It also seems that at least some of the gentry visiting the Cockpit maintained citizen-like preferences for the knockabout comedy of jigs. So Shirley claimed in *The Changes*, in 1631:

> Many gentlemen
> Are not, as in the days of understanding,
> Now satisfied without a Jig, which since
> They cannot, with their honour, call for after
> The play, they look to be serv'd up in the middle.   (2.168)

In other words gentry in the halls (or that combination of gallants, country squires and merchants who expected by the 1630s to be called gentlemen) still yearned for the amphitheatre practice of jigs performed as afterpieces for the 'understanders', and hoped to see them revived in Cockpit plays respectably disguised as a play-within-the-play or dance. Heywood expressed a version of that sentiment himself when he grumbled about the passing of the Red Bull tradition and the history plays of the 1590s in favour of the lesser things which the Blackfriars now offered.

> . . . where before great Patriots, Dukes and Kings
> Presented for some hie facinorious things,
> Were the Stage-Subject; now we strive to flie
> In their low pitch, who never could soare hie:
> For now the common argument intreats,
> Of puling Lovers, craftie Bawdes or cheates.   (2.185)

Heywood did not like the new Blackfriars plays, including the pastorals and the Platonic love interest which the queen's circle fostered.

The new Blackfriars fashion was not itself entirely new. It really rested on elements of the Fletcher canon. The terms in which Marmion praised the King's Men in 1634 for their revival of Fletcher's early play *The Faithful Shepherdess* indicate both a source for the new taste and the self-conscious pride in critical judgement which nurtured it. Addressing the company's chief player, Joseph Taylor, Marmion wrote:

> When this smooth Pastorall was first brought forth,
> The Age twas borne in, did not know it's worth.
> Since by thy cost, and industry reviv'd,
> It hath a new fame, and new birth atchiv'd.   (2.181)

The play appeared at court at the end of the Christmas festivities in January 1634. Rutter wrote an imitation of it for the Blackfriars. A careful combing of the old repertoire, knowing the queen's liking for romantic and pastoral drama, was all to the good for the company's status. Novelty, not in the plays but in taste, was the new requirement at Blackfriars.

The early Beaumont and Fletchers matched the new critical sense nicely. *The Knight of the Burning Pestle*, revived in 1635–6 and performed at court, now got a much better reception for its mockery of the old tastes than it received in 1607. This kind of mockery, some of which will be considered in the next section, was an important feature of the attitudes voiced at the hall playhouses in these last years. Even the smallest of the three, Salisbury Court, which also took in citizen companies and their plays, was happy to signal the gulf in tastes between a gallant on the one hand and a country gentleman and a merchant on the other. The Praeludium to Goffe's *The Careless Shepherdess*,[79] written for a revival in about 1638 which probably tried to cash in on the Blackfriars fashion for pastorals, makes fun of three such stereotypes in its audiences. A money-conscious citizen named Thrift, a courtier named Spruce and a 'landlord' from the country come on stage to discuss their preferences as playgoers. The citizen finally decides to retrieve his shilling and instead 'go to th' Bull or Fortune, and there see / A Play for two pence, with a Jig to boot'. The 'landlord', although he does stay to watch the pastoral, has a similar preference. He and Thrift exchange reminiscences of clowns they have enjoyed, especially Timothy Reade, who was the Salisbury Court's clown at the time and probably played one of the speakers. 'I would have the Fool in every Act, / Be't Comedy, or Tragedy', says the country landowner. Insistent mockery of this kind, aimed at the debased standards of playgoing amongst the wealthier citizenry and lesser gentry, is a feature of the hall playhouses in the last years. Partly it grew out of the self-consciously judgemental role which audiences starting with Charles himself felt to be their proper function. Partly it was an effect of the long divergence in tastes which began in 1600.

CITIZENS IN THE LAST YEARS (1630–42)

In a section of *The Jacobean and Caroline Stage* entitled 'The Reputation of the Red Bull Theatre',[80] G. E. Bentley lists twenty jibes about the low theatrical standards of the Red Bull and its various companies. 'As the Curtain falls into disuse,' he concludes, 'the Red Bull reigns supreme in ignominy.' This view takes too readily as an absolute the dismissive statements made by gentlemanly commentators. It ignores the fact that in numbers if not in revenue the northern playhouses did more business than the halls. It certainly ignores the close association which Beeston maintained between the Cockpit and the Red Bull. Bentley's twenty jibes need to be set in the context of a vigorous and far from mindlessly traditional city-related repertory. The principal question is how far the social polarisation between halls and amphitheatres in the 1630s evoked a similar polarisation of social and political allegiances in the repertories.

The jibes against the Red Bull fall into three categories. Mostly, like Tomkis in *Albumazar*, Carew in his defence of Davenant's *Just Italian*, and the Praeludium to *The Careless Shepherdess*, they voiced derision at its debased standards of literary sophistication. These jibes began as early as 1614 and ran for more than half a century, mocking its 'musty phrases' and old-fashioned clowning. A second charge was noisy overacting. Jonson in *Timber* (1632) scorned the '*Tamerlanes*, and *Tamer-chams* of the late Age, which had nothing in them but the *scenicall* strutting, and furious vociferation, to warrant them to the ignorant gapers'. Critics claimed its players were 'terrible tearethroats', its clown a 'roaring Rimer', and its tragedians created a simile for roaring 'like *Tamerlin* at the Bull'.[81] Its kings and queens spoke 'in a *Majestick tone*' of exaggerated loftiness.[82] The third charge, a little more neutral, concerned its repertoire of plays about war. Its audiences were 'Turmoyl'd with Battailes'. 'Drums, Trumpets, Battels, and Hero's' were the trappings of '*Red-Bull* wars', with their 'sieges laid to the *Musique-Roome*'. Davenant claimed that citizen audiences for Heywood's *The Iron Age* were happy with 'a furious Tale of *Troy* which they ne're thought / Was weakly Writ, if it were strongly *Fought*'.[83]

All these claims about exaggeration and battles were laid down in the last fifteen years of the Red Bull, after Beeston had taken his last contingent of players from it. The tradition of playing Tamburlaine loudly and vigorously had started however with Alleyn, the original player of the part. Marlowe's opus and the tradition of playing it with 'furious vociferation' stayed in the Red Bull's repertoire and seems to have become identified as its most typical offering, particularly in the last years. The very fact that *Tamburlaine* stayed on as Red Bull fare when the companies themselves moved elsewhere and other Marlowe plays like *The Jew of Malta* were transferred to the Cockpit implies that, however the ownership of the playbook may have changed hands, the play itself was thought to belong at that particular playhouse. The fact that the Cockpit used so much from the Red Bull repertory in the 1630s implies that it was the style of playing, and probably the plays with battles in them, which most distinguished the Red Bull.

As *Tamburlaine* became a feature at the Red Bull, so *The Spanish Tragedy* seems to have been identified with the Fortune, in ways suggesting there was a broadly similar style of acting at those two playhouses. At the end of the decade the two companies developed some hostility to one another. Their proximity of shape and location may have turned them into rivals. The animosity blew up when the Prince's Men exchanged playhouses with the Red Bull King's company at Easter 1640. If we can judge from John Tatham's prologue written for the Prince's company when it was displaced from the Fortune, the Red Bull was the less prestigious playhouse. He complained that the Fortune's owners had 'thrust us out of doore / For some peculiar profit', and voiced his angry contempt for the debased following which the former Red Bull company would leave behind them at the Fortune.

> . . . shee has t'ane
> A course to banish Modesty, and retaine
> More dinn, and *incivility* than hath been
> Knowne in the *Bearward Court*, the *Beargarden*.					(2.212)

The Fortune audience, not its actors, are here accused of being more noisy and barbaric than the bears. Apparently such a reputation was not shared by the Red Bull.

Tatham, of course, may well have been exaggerating, since a reverse exchange had taken place with no acrimony six years earlier.[84] Curiously, that exchange may have taken the Red Bull style of overacting to the Fortune, because in 1639 the Red Bull players themselves accused the Fortune players and especially their leading player, Richard Fowler, of overdoing *The Spanish Tragedy*. A clownish tailor in Thomas Rawlins's *The Rebellion* insists on acting Jeronimo, declaring, 'Marke if I doe not gape wider than the widest / Mouth'd Fowler of them all.'[85] Fowler, who was known for his 'Conquering parts',[86] cannot have used an acting style widely different from the tear-throat fashion attributed to the Red Bull.

This kinship, even in hostility, between the two northern amphitheatres provides some justification for James Wright's statement in *Historia Histrionica* that the Fortune and Red Bull were 'mostly frequented by Citizens, and the meaner sort of people' (2.224). Wright must have been at least a little influenced by the frequent jibes against their old-fashioned repertories. It is difficult to ignore their implication that the meaner sort of audience was poor not only in financial resources but in its tastes, and it is not clear which form of poverty influenced Wright. The coexistence of Red Bull plays at the Cockpit does suggest that the differences in the types of playhouse were beginning to alter the image which the public had of their repertories. The Red Bull's name for plays with battles in them signals the extent to which they exploited the open conditions of a large stage and daylight for sword-fighting, which the Cockpit, staging former Red Bull plays, could not. There is no serious swordfight in *The Jew of Malta*, although *The Rape of Lucrece* could well be counted as one of Heywood's 'spectacle' plays. If so, the Fortune's open stage would naturally have put it nearer to the Red Bull than to the hall playhouses.

The continued liking for the repertoire of the 1590s at the northern playhouses has several possible causes. One is the recurrent waves of militarism which swept London at fairly regular intervals. Another is a similar recurrence of nostalgia for the golden age of Elizabeth, which ran strongly through the 1630s.[87] This was certainly not a feeling shared by the Blackfriars poets. Each of these possible causes for the apparent conservatism of citizen taste emphasises the extent to which audiences became polarised socially between the different kinds of playhouse. The trouble is that this argument is almost circular. Battle plays belonged on open stages which, being cheaper, were attended by the poorer sort. Which chose which? The fact that the amphitheatres played mainly older plays, texts that apart from being cheaper to produce can offer little clear evidence about how tastes were evolving, is no help. The best evidence about the division between the two kinds of repertoire probably lies in what, in a time of growing political strain, was picked out for censorship.

Herbert did not like satirical in-jokes about courtiers, or profane language, but little else sent him by the King's Men or Beeston gave him concern. Charles intervened occasionally, once with his rather more benign ruling than Herbert's about what constituted an oath, and once objecting to a rash declaration in a Massinger play about unjust taxation. Herbert insisted that Massinger change the setting of *Believe As You List* from contemporary Portugal to ancient Carthage on the grounds that current issues overseas might be offensive to foreign ambassadors. The poets writing for gallants and courtiers knew how to be cautious over affairs of state.[88]

On the other hand two major misfortunes visited by censorship on the northern playhouses in 1639 suggest that by comparison they were far less cautious. These two incidents are not matched by any comparable cases in the whole of the previous seventy years, so far as records show, except for *The Isle of Dogs* in 1597 and *A Game at Chesse* in 1624. Both of those events also happened at amphitheatres, though only the Middleton play, with its onslaught on the government's foreign policy, bears any relation to the two incidents of 1639. Middleton's play, in any case, seems to have had the connivance of people in high places, a privilege which the northern playhouses certainly did not enjoy. Their offences have something specific to say about playgoing at the citizen places of this last phase.

The first offence occurred in May, in the performance of a lost play, *The Cardinal's Conspiracy*, at the Fortune. The players evidently used it to attack the high-church Arminianism of the court establishment. In a letter reporting the case, Edmond Rossingham wrote:

Thursday last the players of the Fortune were fined 1,000£. for setting up an altar, a bason, and two candlesticks, and bowing down before it upon the stage, and although they allege it was an old play revived, and an altar to the heathen gods, yet it was apparent that this play was revived on purpose in contempt of the ceremonies of the church.   (2.205)

Application was still, up to a point, a profitable trade. The company evaded the censor by using an old play, and applied it to a current cause for anger in the city.[89] The intention was to feed popular hatred of Romanism.

The second event came in September, when the Red Bull players staged another cause for anger, this time about the city's own affairs. *The Whore New Vamped*, the text of which is also understandably lost, attacked the city's mercantile interests savagely. It attacked the new duty on wines, called the monopolist Sir William Abell, a city alderman, a knave and drunkard, and showed the proctors of the probate court as dishonest. The play was extremely popular and had a run of 'many days together' before the Privy Council intervened on 29 September. The Council's minutes report that complaint was this day made to his Majestie sitting in Councell, that the Stage Players of the Red Bull have lately for many days to gether acted a scandalous and Libellous play wherein they have audaciously reproached, and in a Libellous manner traduced and personated some persons of quality, and scandalised, and defamed the whole profession of Proctors belonging to the Court of the Civill Lawe, and reflected upon the present Government.   (2.206)

The author, the players and the Master of the Revels were all examined to see whose fault it was that the offensive play appeared on stage. Hostility to government practices over monopolies and the city figures and their agents who made profitable use of the monopolies was a popular and populist feeling. It came naturally to the 'meaner sort' of citizens.

These were both local matters, of religious prejudice and city misgovernment. They differ radically from the matters which drew censure on the hall playhouse companies by their distance from the affairs of the court. Beeston's company at the Cockpit suffered in 1640, charged over a much more direct political comment than those at the Fortune and Red Bull. The Cockpit's offending play, as Herbert reported, 'had relation to the passages of the K.s journey into the Northe, and was complayned of by his Majestye to mee, with commande to punishe the offenders'.[90] The royal conduct of government was not a central subject in the citizen playhouses. Their repertory generally shows hostility to the counsellors of government and its city agents rather than to the king himself. But by 1640 politics and royalty were central to everyone's thinking, and staging views on the subject was as inevitable as it was sensitive.

Finally in this far from strange but not uneventful history, its acts being seven decades, comes the question of the closing years at the Globe. Its repertory differed from the Fortune and Red Bull as the Blackfriars differed from the Cockpit. When the company moved to it for the summer it enjoyed the continued custom of the Mildmays and gallants who stayed in town out of term, but its locality was no more respectable than the Red Bull's, and its open stage still invited performances of the battle plays which had financed its original construction in 1599. What is not clear is how long the company loyalty to its tradition of using the Globe in an equal partnership with the hall playhouse lasted, and whether some years or even decades after its reconstruction in 1614 the Globe altered its repertoire of plays from the Blackfriars range to satisfy the larger numbers of playgoers paying lower prices through the summer. The key question is whether the lower prices at the Globe did or did not significantly alter the social or mental composition of its audiences.

Contemporary comment on the Globe's playgoers indicates little change from the Blackfriars clientele, either in gallants or ladies. Nicholas Goodman in 1632 wrote of the Globe that 'halfe the yeere a World of *Beauties* and brave *Spirits* resorted unto it' (2.170). A few references do suggest that citizens were preponderant in the summer, but they belong to the fashion of witty contempt for slow and old-fashioned citizen tastes, and say little about the real composition of the audiences or about the favoured repertoire of plays. Henry Glapthorne's poem 'To a Reviv'd Vacation Play' carries in its title the implication that summer was the season for the older style of play. The poem, written as a prologue, probably for the Cockpit, ironically praises citizen wit and begs the citizens present to forget their business cares.

> And now we hope you've leisure in the Citie
> To give the World cause to suspect you witty.   (2.195)

Such mockery had been customary in the hall playhouses for forty years.

Possibly more revealing than the gentry's usual prejudice is a point implied by Lovelace, who wrote only for the Blackfriars, about the divisions within the hall audiences. The epilogue to his lost play *The Scholars* that was printed with his poems in 1649 notes how distinct was the division made by money even inside the hall playhouse. The gentry in the Blackfriars pit want different things from the cheaper beings in the upper gallery.

> His *Schollars* school'd, sayd if he had been wise,
> He should have wove in one two comedies.
> The first for th' gallery, in which the throne
> To their amazement should descend alone,
> The rosin-lightning flash and monster spire
> Squibs, and words hotter than his fire.
> Th'other for the gentlemen of the pit
> Like to themselves all spirit, fancy, wit.   (2.215)

The upper gallery, he claims, the sixpence-payers, prefer exactly the same visual spectacles and hot words for which the amphitheatre playhouses were noted. This implies that the seasonal transfer of gentry from the Blackfriars to the Globe and back might have been accompanied by more of the Globe clients than the prejudice of the Blackfriars writers normally allowed them to admit. If so, it calls into question the one truly explicit piece of evidence from a King's Men's playwright which suggests that the Globe playgoers were treated to a repertoire of the King's Men's plays distinct from those the Blackfriars playgoers enjoyed.

Shirley's *The Doubtful Heir* was written in Dublin, where Shirley went during the long closure because of plague in 1636–7. It was performed in Dublin in about 1638. In April 1640, when Shirley returned to London, he offered it to the Blackfriars. Massinger had just died, and it was probably the company that summoned Shirley back from Ireland. In May, as usual, they transferred their performances to the Globe, and it was there that Shirley's play appeared next, soon after Herbert licensed it on 1 June. Shirley, it is thought, was upset by the change in venue. For more than a decade until his return to Dublin he had written two plays a year for Beeston at the Cockpit. He had been away from London for four years. Now he had secured London's outstanding playhouse for his work, only to find himself overtaken by the seasonal switch to the Globe. In his 'distress', as Bentley calls it,[91] he wrote a seemingly sarcastic prologue telling the Globe playgoers what not to expect in a play that had been designed for a hall playhouse.

This prologue was published with his poems in 1646, under the title '*A Prologue at the Globe to his Comedy call'd* The Doubtful Heire, *which should have been presented at the Black-Friers*'. The text is worth quoting in full.

> *Gentlemen*, I am onely sent to say,
> Our Author did not calculate his Play
> For this Meridian; The Bank-Side he knowes
> Is far more skilful at the ebbes and flowes
> Of water then of Wit: He did not mean
> For the elevation of your Poles this Scene.
> No shews, no frisk, and what you most delight in,
> (Grave understanders) here's no Target fighting
> Upon the Stage, all work for cutlers barrd,
> No Bawd'ry, nor no Ballads; this goes hard.
> The wit is clean, and (what affects you not)
> Without impossibilities the plot;
> No Clown, no squibs, no Divells in't; oh now
> You Squirrels that want nuts, what will ye do?
> Pray do not crack the benches, and we may
> Hereafter fit your palats with a Play.
> But you that can contract your selves, and fit
> As you were now in the *Black-Friers* pit,
> And will not deaf us with lewd noise, or tongues,
> Because we have no heart to break our lungs,
> Will pardon our vast Scene, and not disgrace
> This Play, meant for your persons, not the place.   (2.211)

This, I think, does not have the note of distress that Bentley hears in it. The 'meridian' of the Globe was remote not from the Blackfriars but from Dublin. Most of the elements contained in the jibes at the Red Bull are there, even an allusion to overloud speaking. We players, says Shirley, being used to playing at the Blackfriars, will not 'break our lungs' in the 'vast Scene' of the Globe's much larger stage. He implies that a good proportion of the Globe audience must be familiars of the Blackfriars, and that the play is meant for their persons, not the Globe place. It is the open amphitheatre which generates the 'understanders' who crack nuts and make lewd noises because the players are not speaking loudly and providing them with bawdy song-and-dance jigs, fireworks and sword-fighting. Kathleen McLuskie hears no distress and calls the prologue 'reverse flattery',[92] telling the audience what good taste it has approving a play which lacks the stigma of the traditional amphitheatre plays.

Shirley prepared this prologue only a month or so after returning from his four-year absence. When he wrote it he had probably not yet encountered a Globe audience. Therefore it makes rather tenuous evidence to hang much weight on, especially when its tone can be interpreted as variously as Bentley and McLuskie do. Nonetheless it does carry implications about the Globe audience, especially in its closing lines, which neither Bentley nor McLuskie quotes. The arch tone of the opening may well be ironically amusing flattery, enough to indicate that Shirley did really expect the Globe audience to enjoy the prologue's exaggerated apprehension over the nutcrackers' anger at receiving food prepared for different appetites. The final appeal to 'you that can contract your selves, and fit / As you were now in the *Black-Friers* pit', the equivalent position in the hall to the Globe's standers, is confident. He expects that the Blackfriars 'persons', presumably even the wealthy persons of the pit, will after all be at the Globe 'place'. The only difficulty seems to be the different style of acting and the old-fashioned repertoire to be expected at an amphitheatre.

From Shirley's concern about the 'vast Scene' and the extra noise the players were expected to generate on it we might conclude that the style of acting did differ enough between the two types of venue to require different types of play. Perhaps the fact that the Red Bull and Cockpit used the same plays while only the Red Bull developed a reputation for its players tearing their throats can be put down to the same effect on playing style, not from the repertoire of plays but from the types of playhouse. If so, the King's Men must have developed two distinct acting styles, one for winter and the other for summer. The only evidence for that is Shirley's prologue, and this, given his years away in Dublin and the arch tone, may not be entirely trustworthy.

If it has any truth in it, though, it might help to explain the rather heavy-handed byplay in the epilogue to Davenant's *News from Plymouth*. The play was licensed on 1 August 1635, and the epilogue was printed in the 1673 edition of Davenant's poems under the title 'To a Vacation Play at the Globe'. The speaker, renewing his part as a comic country gentleman from the play itself, enters holding a heavy old longsword, and threatens to 'mowe you off' if the audience, 'Yeo'man and Squire, Knight, Lady, and her Lord', do not pay their respects to the king by respecting the King's Men. This kind of sword or 'fox' was typical of Globe plays according to Shirley, and was swung by Ancient Pistol in *Henry V*. Davenant expected this audience to have made the transfer from Blackfriars to the Globe. No friend of Shirley to judge from the 1630 cock and bull quarrel, he appears to have taken a rather similar view of the summer clientele at the Globe.

The only conclusion I would draw from Shirley's verses is that he expected the Globe's playgoers to include a substantial number from the Blackfriars, and that he did not expect them to take offence at the kind of jibe which was voiced in the halls against the amphitheatres. The latter suggests that a preference for drum and trumpet plays and jigs was not a major element in the chemistry of Globe tastes. As always the Globe, its offerings and its playgoers stood midway between the extremes of low amphitheatre reputation and hall playhouse snobbery which first began to show themselves in the year the Globe was built.

Playgoers 1567–1642

Abdy, Sir Christopher. Brother-in-law to Humphrey Mildmay, recorded as accompanying him to a play. His family were merchants in the Cloth-workers' Guild.

Alderson, Thomas. Sailor, of Stepney. On 16 May 1626 he was bound over for the sum of 100 marks (£33) for leading an affray at the Fortune. The gang, chiefly of seamen, besides Alderson included Carver, Collison, Davige, Foster, Francke, Gilbye, Gray, Herringe, Kerbye, Margrave and Smyth. The charge was 'a daungerous and great ryott committed in Whitecrossstreete at the Fortune Playhouse and especially for strikinge beatinge and assault-ing Francis Foster the constable and Thomas Faulkner, an inhabitant at the Fortune Playhouse'. Alderson was said to have threatened to bring the whole (unpaid) navy to 'pull downe the playhouse'.

Alleyn, Edward. Actor and impresario. After he left acting in 1602 and went fully into theatre management with the Fortune and the Hope, he still attended other playhouses. On 1 October 1617 he made a note: 'I came to London in ye coach & went to ye red bull. 0.0.2.' (i.e. for twopence).

Archdall, Sarah. Wooed by Simon Forman as a possible bride, they met twice at the Curtain playhouse, on 19 and 22 April 1599, the second time in the company of her uncle (Barbara Traister, *The Notorious Astrological Physician of London*, pp. 153, 169). The Shakespeare company was using the Curtain while they waited for the completion of the Globe.

Baker, Father Augustine. In 1596–9, when he was a student at Clifford's Inn, his relaxation was first to read Latin comedies and Erasmus. 'His 2d sort of recreation was to resort to playes; whither yet he never went without a pocket book of the law, which he did read when the play or any sort of it pleased him not' (*Memorials*, ed. J. MacCann, 1933, p. 66).

Baker, Sir Richard. Author of an answer to Prynne's *Histriomastix*, called *Theatrum Redivivum* when published in 1662. Baker died in 1643, and his reply to Prynne, citing several playgoing experiences, obviously dates from before 1642.

Banfield, Mr. A lawyer, who accompanied Mildmay to a play in November 1639.

Beaumont, Francis. His *Knight of the Burning Pestle* shows familiarity with the amphitheatre repertory of plays such as *1 Henry IV*, *The Four Prentices of London*, *Mucedorus* and *The Travels of the Four English Brothers*.

Beeston, Christopher. Theatre manager and impresario. He wrote a poem for Heywood's *Apology for Actors* which says 'of playes I make best use . . . Two hours well spent'.

Bestney, Nicholas. A 'junior gentleman' stabbed at the Fortune in 1614.

Blether, Christopher. A yeoman, charged along with William Frend 'for making an affray and tumult at the Fortune playhouse' in February 1614.

Blount, Sir Christopher. Younger brother of the Earl of Devonshire, he fought in the Netherlands, and at Cadiz and in Ireland with the Earl of Essex, whose stepfather he was. He went with other conspirators to the Globe on 7 February 1601 to see *Richard II*. He was executed on 18 March of that year.

Borne, Gilbert. A butcher charged with making an affray at the Fortune in 1611 with Ralph Brewyn and others.

Boteler, or Butler, Ned. Accompanied Mildmay and a group of others on 21 May 1634 to a play by the King's Men, probably *Cleander*, which he called *The Lover's Progress*.

Boyle, Elizabeth, née Killigrew. Sister-in-law of Mary Rich, with whom she frequently went to plays in about 1640.

Bradford, Joseph. A glover charged with making an affray at the Fortune in 1611 with Ralph Brewyn and others.

Bradley, Richard. Yeoman who knifed Nicholas Bestney at the Fortune in 1614.

Brathwait, Richard. Author of fifty or more publications, many pseudonymous, between 1611 and 1662. A student of Oriel College Oxford and Gray's Inn, he claimed in 1614 that Thomas Heywood was his friend. References in his writings show him to be a frequenter of playhouses, and in his account of his life he claimed to have stopped writing for the stage because writing for money was beneath him.

Brewyn, Ralph. A butcher in an affray at the Fortune in 1611, charged at Middlesex Sessions along with Shaw, Borne and Lynsey, butchers, and Gillingham, Bradford and Collins, glovers. The charge was 'abusinge certen gentlemen at the playhouse called the Fortune', on a complaint by 'the officers of the Fortune playhouse'.

Brian, Edward. A feltmaker involved with four others (Fryne, Jenckes, Mason and Oldbury) in an affray at the Red Bull in May 1610.

Brown, R. Mentioned in a letter by James Howell as a keen playgoer at the Blackfriars and Cockpit in the early 1620s.

Browne, Thomas. A 'serving man in a blew coat' accused of stirring trouble amongst some 'handicraft prentises' at the door of the Theatre in 1584.

Browne, Valentine. An Inns of Court student, admitted to Gray's Inn in 1639. In 1642 at a play he took offence over a mistaken piece of horseplay by the MP Peter Legh, and subsequently killed him in a duel. He was a nephew of the Herbert brothers.

Brunswick, Duke of. A visitor to London in December 1624, when he went to a play at the Blackfriars.

Bryan, Luke. A sixty-year-old member of the king's guard. At a play at the Red Bull in 1607, he quarrelled with the gatherer, Joan Hewes. According to the lawsuit, 'Well quoth Joan Hewes . . . if you will paie me for your admittance, paie quoth the said Luce Bryan replyeinge said unto . . . Joane Hewes thou art an arrant whore and a theefe' (Laura Gowing, *Domestic Dangers*, p. 118).

Buckingham, Duke of. In August 1628, shortly before he was assassinated, he went to the Globe to see *Henry VIII*. The next day he saw Heywood's *Rape of Lucrece* at the Cockpit.

Bushell, Edward. Accompanied other Essex conspirators to the Globe on 7 February 1601.

Busino, Orazio. Chaplain to the embassy of Venice. He visited the Fortune with his ambassador in 1617.

Butler, James, twelfth Earl, first Duke of Ormond. As Lord Thurles, became involved in an affray with Charles Essex at the Blackfriars in January 1632, when he was standing on stage in front of one of the boxes. His biographer described him as 'a great admirer of plays, and acquainted with all the good actors of the stage. He took such delight in the theatre, that it scarce ever wanted his presence' (Carte, I.17). His education was in the hands of the Archbishop of Canterbury, who, according to the same biographer, was a man 'who, whatever learning he had himself, shewed very little concern to encourage it in others' (Carte, I.12). In the 1640s Ormond commanded the king's army.

Buxton, John. A student of Gray's Inn in the 1620s, his account book specifies almost fifty playbooks bought in quarto, and payments for his attendance at indoor plays (David McKitterick, '"Ovid with a Littleton": The Cost of English Books in the Early Seventeenth Century', *Transactions of the Cambridge Bibliographical Society*, 11th ser. 2, 1997, 184–234).

Caldwell, Mary, of Essex. Attended a play with George Evelyn, brother of the diarist, and some ladies, in November 1639.

Carleton, Sir Dudley. Ambassador to Venice and The Hague, and Secretary of State under Charles. His letters to John Chamberlain show his attendance at court masques, at a student play in Leiden, and a general familiarity with London playing.

Carver, James. Sailor, of Shadwell. Bound over for 100 marks (£33) on 16 May 1626 with a gang mostly of seamen including Thomas Alderson for an affray at the Fortune.

Cary, Elizabeth. Author of *Mariam*, her daughter's biography states that she was a frequent playgoer in her earlier years.

Cary, Lucius, Lord Falkland. He was cited in the publisher's address in the Folio edition of Henry Killigrew's *The Conspiracy* as attending the first performance of the play at the Blackfriars, probably in 1630 or 1631. Writing to Thomas Carew returning a playbook, he asked for a copy on the grounds that 'if I valued it so high at the single hearing, when myne eares could not catch half the wordes, what must I do now, in the reading when I may pause uppon it' (Kurt Weber, *Lucius Cary*, 1940, p. 63).

Cavendish, Margaret, née Lucas, Duchess of Newcastle. With her sisters she was used 'in winter time to go sometimes to plays, or to ride in their coaches about the streets to see the concourse and recourse of people' (*The Life of William Cavendish* . . . , ed. C. H. Firth, 1886, p. 285).

Cavendish, Sir William. The Cavendish household books at Chatsworth in Derbyshire record several payments for his going to see the boy players in 1600–3. They record on 3 November 1600: 'My master his going to a play at paules 18d'; similarly in October 1601, with a servant: 'Hallams going into the plea 3d'; in the same month a play at Blackfriars cost 12 pence; 1s 6d on 26 November 1601; three visits in March 1602, costing between 1s 6d and 3s, plus on 2 April 1603 'goinge into a play 9d a stoole to sitt downe on 2d'; another visit in April 1603; and on 26 June 1602 a play at Paul's for 4s 6d (John M. Wasson and Barbara D. Palmer, ed. Reed, *Derbyshire and the West Riding*, forthcoming). The variable sums paid suggest that on some visits he may have taken guests with him.

Chamberlain, John. Professional letter-writer. He saw 'a new play of humors' in midsummer 1597, 'drawne alonge to yt by the common applause', but was not impressed (*Letters*, ed. McClure, I.32).

Chambers, Edmund. A waterman, fined 'for an assault and battery on Martin Slater [the player] gent at Hallowell St at the Curtayne Dore' in July 1613, and for 'making an affray and a tumult'. Slater was bound over for 'beating and wounding the said Edmund'.

Charles, Prince of the Palatinate. Accompanied the queen to a performance at Blackfriars, 5 May 1636. This may have been a special evening performance rather than a normal commercial afternoon. Charles's mother had been patron of the Lady Elizabeth's Men.

Cholmley, Sir Richard. In 1603, aged 23, he went to a play at Blackfriars, where being late he had to take a stool on the stage. When, 'as the custom was', he 'stood up to refresh himself', a young gallant took over his stool. Cholmley led the young man outside and challenged him. When the youngster said he had no sword Sir Richard offered to buy him one. A constable appeared, and Sir Richard had to be content with giving the gallant 'two or three good blows'. The young man was 'my Lady's eldest son' according to his manservant, who fetched the constable.

Clifford, Lady Anne. Lady Anne Clifford Sackville, daughter of the third Earl of Cumberland, Countess of Dorset, later Countess of Pembroke. A court lady who performed in several masques, her papers say that she went to a performance of *The Mad Lover* in 1617. Her library included a copy of Jonson's 1616 Folio. (See *The Diary of Anne Clifford, 1616–1619*, and above, pp. 72–3).

Collins, Thomas. A glover charged with making an affray at the Fortune in 1611 with Ralph Brewyn and others.

21. Lady Anne Clifford aged fifteen. The photograph shows the left-hand
panel of a triptych painted to show her personal history, now in the Abbot
Hall Art Gallery, Kendal. The portraits behind her are of Samuel Daniel and
Anne Taylor, her tutors, and the books are those she read under their
tutelage.

Collison, William. Sailor, of Blackwall in Stepney. He was bound over for £50 on 16 May 1626 for his part in an affray at the Fortune along with Thomas Alderson and others.

Constable, Sir William. Fought in Ireland with Essex, who knighted him there. On 7 February 1601 went to the Globe with other Essex conspirators. In the 1640s he fought on the Parliamentary side, and sat as a regicide in 1648.

Cotton, John. Possibly the speculator who tried to build an amphitheatre for shows in 1620, and an officer of the royal household as Keeper of the Standing Wardrobe of Westminster. In 1599 he regularly escorted Elizabeth Reignoldes to playhouses.

Cranfield, Lionel, first Earl of Middlesex. His account books include an entry dated 28 January 1610: 'laid out at your going into the play, 7s.' (*HMC Sackville: Cranfield Papers, 1551–1612*, Historic Manuscripts Commission, 80, London, 1940).

Crofts, Will. A gentleman involved in an affray with Lord Digby at the Blackfriars in 1635. His father, Henry Crofts, was Humphrey Mildmay's brother-in-law. His mother was sister to Francis Wortley, a minor poet, 'son of Ben' and nephew to Mildmay's wife.

Curle, Francis. A gentleman who was said on 3 January 1610 in the London Consistory Court to have escorted Mrs Watton to a play.

Davies, Sir John. Gallant and Inns of Court man. His epigrams indicate that he was a frequent playgoer in the 1590s.

Davies, Sir John, of Oxford. He held office in the Tower, and was known as a necromancer. Accompanied other Essex conspirators to the Globe on 7 February 1601. He was sentenced to death for his part in the plot, but pardoned.

Davies, John, of Hereford. An epigram in his *Scourge of Folly* hails Shakespeare's playing of kingly roles, and in *Wittes Pilgrimage*, 1605, I4v, he recalled seeing Tamburlaine 'encoacht in burnisht Gold, / Raigning his drawers, who of late did Raigne').

Davige, Lawrence. Gentleman of St Andrew's, Holborn. He was bound over on 16 May 1696 for £5 over his part with Thomas Alderson and others, mainly seamen, in an affray at the Fortune.

Dekker, Thomas. Playwright. In 1624 in a lawsuit over a play of his, *Keep the Widow Waking*, performed at the Red Bull, he deposed that he 'did often see the said play or part thereof acted but how often he cannot depose'.

Dering, Sir Edward. Author of the first adaptation of Shakespeare's *Henry IV* plays, a regular playgoer in the 1620s according to his diary. In December 1623 he attended six plays in seven days. He was MP for Kent in 1640–2 and introduced the Root and Branch Bill into Parliament.

Dering, Sir John. He paid one shilling and sixpence at the indoor playhouses, probably for a place on a bench in the pit.

De Witt, Johannes. A Dutch visitor to London in 1596. He described the play-houses and sketched the Swan, then the most newly built of the amphitheatres.

Digby, John. Younger brother of Sir Kenelm Digby. He was waylaid by Suckling as he left a play at the Blackfriars in November 1634, and involved in an affray which injured both parties.

Digges, Leonard. In his verses published in 1640 but probably written for the First Folio of Shakespeare's works in 1623 (he died in 1635) he claims familiarity with *Julius Caesar, Othello*, Falstaff, *Much Ado* and *Twelfth Night*.

Donne, John. Poet, known as 'a great frequenter of Playes' (Baker, *Chronicle*, 1696, p. 450). He wrote of *Tamburlaine* in *The Calme*, and a letter in Latin to Jonson about *Volpone*.

Doricla (Dorislaus), Isaac. A Dutch historian resident in England from 1628, friend of Kenelm Digby and Selden, an anti-monarchist. He accompanied Mildmay to playhouses in November 1634, November 1635, February 1638, February 1639 and February 1640.

Drake, Joan. A spiritual biography of Mrs Drake, a reformed high-lifer, published in 1647, reports that Dr John Dod lodged in her house in an attempt to reform her, but she 'would laugh and jest at all he said in derision: In her thoughts likening him unto *Ananias*, one whom at a play in the Black-Friers shee saw scoft at, for a holy brother of *Amsterdam*' (Alan Pritchard, 'Puritans and the Blackfriars Theater: the Cases of Mistresses Duck and Drake', *SQ* 45, 1994, 92–5, p. 94). She must have seen *The Alchemist* by 1618.

Drayton, Michael. Poet. In *Idea*, Sonnet 47 speaks of attending his own plays in 'thronged Theaters'. He wrote for Henslowe at the turn of the century.

Ellice, Thomas. Possibly related to Robert Ellice, of Gray's Inn, a friend of John Ford and a dedicatee of Ford's *Lover's Melancholy* (1629). Thomas wrote a verse for the publication of *'Tis Pity She's a Whore* (1633) indicating he had seen the play in performance.

Essex, Captain Charles. In a brawl with James Butler, Lord Thurles, at the Blackfriars in 1632.

Essex, Countess of. In a box at Blackfriars in 1632 when her escort was in a brawl.

Essex, Robert Devereux, second Earl of. The accounts of his trial state that he went to 'the playing' of Hayward's story of Henry IV (E. K. Chambers, *William Shakespeare*, 2 vols., Oxford, 1930, II.323). This must have been Shakespeare's play, although the earl himself was not named in the account of the visit made by Merrick and others.

Evelyn, George. Brother of the diarist. He attended his beloved, Mary Caldwell, and other ladies to the playhouses in November 1639.

Faulkner, Thomas. Described as 'an inhabitant at the Fortune playhouse', assaulted by a gang of seamen and others (Alderson, Carter, Collison,

Davige, Foster, Francke, Gilbye, Gray, Herringe, Kerbye, Margrave, Smyth)
at the Fortune in May 1626.

Fennor, William. In *Fennors Descriptions* (1616) he indicates familiarity with
the Fortune playhouse.

Fitzgeoffery, Henry. Inns of Court student. He describes an audience at the
Blackfriars in *Satyres and Satyricall Epigrams*, 1617.

Flaskett, John. A bookbinder. He visited Paul's Boys in 1603 to see himself
portrayed as Touchbox the suitor in Chapman's *The Old Joiner of Aldgate*.

Fletcher, John. Lowin and Taylor's dedication to the 1652 edition of his *Wild
Goose Chase* (1621?) says that he attended its performance: 'The Play was
of so Generall a receiv'd Acceptance, that (he *Himself a Spectator*) we
have known him un-concern'd, and to have wisht it had been none of His;
He, as well as the *throng'd Theatre* (in despight of his innate Modesty)
Applauding this *rare issue of his Brain*.'

Florio, John. In his *First Fruites*, an English–Italian conversation book, he has
a dialogue inviting a lady to see a play at the Bull Inn or other playhouse.

Forman, Simon. Physician and necromancer. He went to the Curtain on 19
and 22 April 1599, and to the same company at the Globe in the summer
of 1611 where he saw four plays, including *Macbeth*, *The Winter's Tale*
and *Cymbeline*.

Foscarini, Antonio. Ambassador of Venice up to 1615. Recorded as visiting the
Curtain, the Fortune and possibly other playhouses three or four times.

Foster, William. Cordwainer of Stepney. Bound over on 16 May 1626 for £50
for his part in a gang mainly of seamen such as Thomas Alderson who set
up an affray at the Fortune.

Francke, Robert. Sailor, of Blackwall in Stepney, bound over on 16 May 1626 for
£50 along with Thomas Alderson and other seamen for an affray outside
the Fortune.

Franke, Margaret. Niece to William Wybarn. Either she or another niece Mary
Windsor was in a family group of her aunt's at a play at the Globe in August
1612. (See entry for Elizabeth Wybarn.)

Frend, William. An alebrewer, charged along with Christopher Blether for
'making an affray and tumult at the Fortune playhouse' in February 1614.

Frith, Marion. Transvestite, who attended a performance of a play about her,
The Roaring Girl, at the Fortune in 1611.

Fryne, John. A feltmaker involved with four others (Brian, Jenckes, Mason and
Oldbury) in an affray at the Red Bull in May 1610.

Fulsis, Alexander. Stole a purse containing £3 from Alexander Sweet at the
Red Bull in 1614.

Gayton, Edmund. An Oxford don, he wrote *Pleasant Notes upon Don Quixot*
after the closure, publishing it in 1654 with ample if questionable evidence
in it (see Appendix 2) of his first-hand experience of the repertory of plays
at the Red Bull and elsewhere. He refers to at least twenty-two plays, and
praises in particular Taylor and Swanston of the King's Men.

Gee, John. A student of Brasenose College, Oxford, in 1613, briefly a Roman Catholic in the early 1620s. In *New Shreds of the Old Snare* (1624) he writes of Burbage having been the 'lodestone' of his audience. He also refers familiarly to the Fortune, Red Bull, Cockpit and Globe, and knew the ghosts in *The Spanish Tragedy* and *Hamlet*, and Moonshine with his lantern in *A Midsummer Night's Dream* as well as *The Alchemist*.

George, William. His purse containing ten shillings was picked by Harrison, Holdaye and Staple 'att the Curten' in August 1613.

Gerschow, Frederic. In the train of the Duke of Stettin-Pomerania, and attended a play at the Blackfriars on 18 September 1602, about which he commented on the exquisite singing and the hour-long concert before the play (*Transactions of the Royal Historical Society* n.s. 6 (1892), pp. 26–8).

Gilbye, John. A purser, of Blackwall in Stepney. Bound over on 16 May 1626 with a gang chiefly of seamen including Thomas Alderson for his part in an affray at the Fortune.

Gill, Alexander. Wrote hostile verses about Jonson's *Magnetic Lady* at Blackfriars in 1632.

Gill, John or Richard. An apprentice, injured at the Red Bull by the player Richard Baxter during a performance in March 1622. He sent a challenge to Baxter, saying, 'Mr Blackster So it is that uppon Monday last it . . . to be uppon your stage intending noe hurt to anyone, Wheere I was greevously wounded in the head as may appeare, And in the sugeons handes who is to have xs. for the cure, . . . I desire you to give me satisfaccion seeing I was wounded by your owne hand . . . weapon. If you refuse then looke to your selfe and avoyde the daunger which shall this day ensure upon your Company and House. For . . . I am a Feltmakers prentice and have made it knowne to at the least one hundred and fortye of our . . . who are all here present readie to take revenge uppon you unles willingly you will give present satisfaction.'

Gillingham, Henry. A glover charged with making an affray at the Fortune in 1611 with Ralph Brewyn and others.

Giustinian, Giorgio, ambassador of Venice. Together with the Secretary of Florence and the French ambassador and his wife he saw *Pericles* at the Globe in 1607–8 (*Calendar of State Papers Venetian* XIV, p. 600).

Gondomar, Sarmiento de Acuna, ambassador of Spain. He went with his train to the Fortune in 1621, and subsequently banqueted with the players (Chamberlain, *Letters*, II.391).

Gorge, Sir Edward. John Holles reported in 1624 that he had been urged to see *A Game at Chesse* by Gorge, who told him about the play's scandals.

Gosson, Stephen. A playwright turned puritan attacker of plays in *Playes Confuted in Five Actions*, 1582.

Gray, Patrick. Sailor, of Blackwall in Stepney. Bound over on 16 May 1626 along with Thomas Alderson and other seamen to answer charges for an affray at the Fortune.

Greene, John. Student of Lincoln's Inn. His diary records numerous visits to plays, including on 8 November 1635 a day when all 'ther batchelors' went either to the Cockpit to see *The Lady of Pleasure* or to the Blackfriars to see *The Conspiracy*. Amongst the plays he records seeing are *Rule a Wife and Have a Wife*, *The Elder Brother* (both Blackfriars plays), *Truth's Triumphs*, *The Malcontent*, *The Changeling*, *The Inconstant Lady*, *'Ffalstafe'*, *Wit Without Money*, *The Lady of Pleasure* and *The Conspiracy*, all Blackfriars or Cockpit plays.

Greene, Katherine. Possibly arrested as a prostitute, since no husband is mentioned, she was freed because she was pregnant. The Bridewell records for 5 August 1631 state that she was arrested 'by Constable Lewis Fleete streete taken att a play in Salsburye Courte she being with childe is delivered'.

Guilpin, Everard. Satire V in *Skialetheia* (1598) mentions going to the Rose or Curtain. Other satires and epigrams echo plays such as *Richard II*.

Habington, William. In verses prefixed to Davenant's *Madagascar* (1638) he claimed that he was 'mongst the first, to see the Stage / (Inspired by thee) strike wonder to our Age' (Davenant, *Shorter Poems*, ed. Gibbs, p. 8).

Halkett, Anne, Lady. Born 1622. In her *Autobiography* she states that she never disobeyed her parents before 1644: 'so scrupulous I was of giving any occasion to speake of mee, as I know they did of others, that though I loved well to see plays and to walke in the Spring Garden sometimes (before itt grew something scandalous by ye abuse of some), yett I cannot remember 3 times that ever I wentt with any man besides my brothers; and if I did, my sisters or others better than myselfe was with mee. And I was the first that proposed and practised itt for 3 or 4 of us going together withoutt any man, and every one paying for themselves by giving the mony to the footman who waited on us, and he gave itt to the play-house, And this I did first upon hearing some gentlemen telling what ladys they had waited on to plays, and how much itt had cost them; upon which I resolved none should say the same of mee.'

Hall, Dr Joseph, later Bishop. In *Virgidemiarum* he indicates that he had seen *Tamburlaine*.

Hallam, – Servant to Sir William Cavendish. He accompanied his master to Paul's in October 1601, paying threepence.

Harington, Henry. His verses written for the preliminaries of the Beaumont and Fletcher Folio (1647) show that he knew the plays in performance.

Harington, Sir John. He quoted Jaques's speech from *As You Like It* in 1604, long before it was published.

Harrison, John. A cordwainer accused along with Staple and Holdaye of picking William George's purse at the Curtain in August 1613.

Harvey, Dorothy. The Bridewell records for 8 December 1632 state that 'for enticing a young maiden unto plaies and into idle yong fellowes company and for enticing her to lend money she is warned and delivered'.

Harvey, Gabriel. In *Foure Letters and certeine Sonnets*, 1592 (3rd letter), he writes of the chance of seeing Tarlton's 'famous play of the seaven Deadly sinnes' in London, and of being invited to it in Oxford by Tarlton himself. His reference to *Hamlet* in his copy of Speght's Chaucer (1598) most likely indicates that he had seen the play, possibly the Cambridge performance mentioned in the Q1 titlepage.

Hattrell, Elizabeth. A serving-woman, aged nineteen or twenty in 1611, she went to the Curtain playhouse for a play by Prince Charles's company.

Hawkins, William. A barber caught at the Curtain in 1600 stealing a purse and £1. 6s. 6d.

Heath, Edward. A student of the Middle Temple. His accounts show that he attended forty-nine plays in eighteen months through 1628–9, and bought ten playbooks. The entries in his diary are transcribed by John R. Elliott, Jr, in *Medieval and Renaissance Drama in England* 6 (1993), pp. 187–91.

Henrietta Maria, Queen. Visited the Blackfriars playhouse four times. The accounts of the Master of the Revels include 13 May 1634: 'the Queene was at Blackfryers, to see Messingers playe . . . Blake Friers, where the Queene saw Lodwick Carlile's second part of *Arviragus and Felicia* acted, which is hugely liked of every one' (a performance in early 1636 when she was accompanied by Prince Charles of the Palatinate). 'The 5th of May at the Blackfryers for the Queene and the prince elector . . . Alfonso . . . At the blackfryers the 23 of Aprill (1638) for the queene . . . the unfortunate lovers.'

Herbert, Philip, fourth Earl of Pembroke. The Lord Chamberlain, quarrelled with the Duke of Lennox over a box at Blackfriars for a new play, January 1636.

Herringe, Robert. A surgeon ('chirugeon') of Shadwell in Stepney, bound over on 16 May 1626 for £50 for his part in an affray at the Fortune with Thomas Alderson and others.

Hewes (Hughes), Joan. A gatherer for the twopenny galleries at the Red Bull in 1607, also on record as a gatherer there in 1618. In 1607 she was involved in a squabble with Luke Bryan, a sixty-year-old member of the king's guard.

Hobart, Sir John. Mentioned in Dering's diary as accompanying him to plays. He was of a Norfolk family which supported the Parliamentary side in the 1640s.

Holdaye, William. A glover accused with Staple and Harrison of picking a purse with 10s. in it from William George 'att the Curten'.

Holles, John, Lord Haughton. On 11 August 1624, urged by Sir Edward Gorge, he went to see *A Game at Chesse*. It was his first visit to a playhouse for ten years.

Howe, John. A barber surgeon, who visited Paul's Boys in 1603 to see himself portrayed as Snipper-Snapper in Chapman's *The Old Joiner of Aldgate*.

Howell, James. In a letter to R. Brown of 20 January 1624, he writes, 'I pray make haste, for *London* streets, which you and I have trod together so often, will prove tedious to me else. Among other things, *Black-Friars* will entertain you with a Play spick and span new, and the *Cockpit* with another; nor, I believe, after so long Absence, will it be an unpleasing object for you to see' (*Epistolae Ho-Elianae*, p. 214).

Hutton, Timothy. Curate of St Giles, Cripplegate, he was denounced along with his vicar in Parliament in 1641 for failing to take funeral services, leaving three parties waiting. 'And at the last, hearing that the said Timothy Hutton his Curate was at the *Fortune* to see a Play, they sent to desire him, to officiate for the three corps: but hee would by no meanes come; then they sent a second, and a third time also, certifying how long they had there waited: yet would the said Timothy Hutton by no means come, untill such time that the play ended' (*The Petition and Articles Exhibited in Parliament against Dr Fuller . . . and Timothy Hutton* (1641), Thomason Tracts E175 (1), Wing Microfilm 256).

Ingram, Sir Arthur. A self-made gentleman, one of the wealthiest in England, he rebuilt Temple Newsam House near Leeds. He stayed in London in 1633–4, when he went to seven plays, at least one of them at the Cockpit, and to another play in October 1638. He paid for links to light his group from the play, and a coachman (Ingram papers, West Yorkshire archive, in Wasson and Palmer, ed. REED, *Derbyshire and the West Riding*, forthcoming).

Jacob, Thomas. Arrested along with William Moolde and John West for brawling at the Red Bull in August 1639.

James, Mrs. She accompanied Humphrey Mildmay to a playhouse in February 1639, and with 'her goodman' to *The Alchemist* in May 1639.

Jenckes, John. A haberdasher with Hugh Oldbury and three feltmakers (Brian, Fryne and Mason), fined for 'a notable outrage' at the Red Bull in 1610.

Johnson, Christopher. A blacksmith of Golding Lane by the Fortune. He testified for Alice Hinckley and Margarett Johnson for being 'taken as common prostitutes at the house of Susan Evans neere the Fortune playehouse, being a noted bawdy house'.

Jones, Captain Ellis. Accompanied other Essex conspirators to the Globe on 7 February 1601.

Jonson, Ben. Playwright. He was satirised in *Satiromastix* for exchanging 'curtezies, and complements with Gallants in the Lordes roomes'. He evidently also saw Shakespeare's *Pericles, The Tempest, Julius Caesar* and *The Winter's Tale*.

Kerbye, John. A victualler of Blackwall in Stepney. He was bound over on 16 May 1626 for his part in an affray at the Fortune with Thomas Alderson and others.

Kiechel, Samuel. A merchant of Ulm, visiting London in 1584, he noted the playhouses in his diary.

Killigrew, Thomas. Playwright. Pepys reports Sir John Mennis as telling him in 1662 that while a boy he used to get free access to the Red Bull's plays by accepting invitations 'to be a devil upon the stage' (*The Diary of Samuel*

Pepys, ed. Robert Latham and William Matthews, 11 vols., London, 1971–83, III.243–4).

Lake, Sir Thomas. He is in the list of people Chamberlain mentioned as attending performances of *A Game at Chesse*, in August 1624.

Lambarde, William. Keeper of the Tower of London. He mentions the Bel Savage and the Theatre as London playhouses in the revised edition, published in 1596, of his 1576 *Perambulation of Kent*.

Lambe, Dr John. In a notorious case, he was killed by a mob after a visit to the Fortune, 18 June 1626.

Le Fevre, Antoine, Sieur de la Boderie, French ambassador. He and his wife took the Venetian ambassador and the Secretary of the Florentine embassy to the Globe in 1607–8 to see *Pericles*.

Lea, Captain Thomas. Went with other Essex conspirators to the Globe on 7 February 1601. He was executed for his part in the plot on 14 February.

Leak or Leke, Father Thomas. A Catholic priest imprisoned in the Clink for his religion in 1618. He regularly went to plays at the nearby Bankside playhouses while in the Clink, and challenged his archpriest's right to forbid his playgoing.

Legh, Sir Peter. An eighteen-year-old MP from Cheshire, killed in a duel after a quarrel at a playhouse in February 1642. 'Being at a play, he hurled a piece of tobacco-pipe at a man, thinking he had known him; but, being mistaken, they fell out in words, and so challenged one another.' His opponent was a Gray's Inn student, twenty-three-year-old Valentine Browne from Lincolnshire (Martin Butler, 'Two Playgoers, and the Closing of the London Theatres, 1642', *Theatre Research International* 9 (1984), pp. 93–9).

Lewis, Prince of Anhalt-Cöthen. A visitor to London in 1596, he mentions four amphitheatres.

Lewis, Prince Frederick of Württemberg. A visitor to London in 1610, he went to the Globe to see *Othello* (William B. Rye, *England as Seen by Foreigners in the Days of Elizabeth and James I*, London, 1865, p. 61).

Ligon, Richard. A gentleman who wrote a book in 1657 about Barbados. Of a dinner in the Cape Verde Islands he mentions a lutenist who entertained them with 'the Passame saves galiear; a tune in great esteeme, in Harry the fourths dayes; for when Sir John Falstaff makes his Amours to Mistress Doll Tear-sheet, sneake and his Companie, the admired fidlers of that age, playes this tune'.

Lionello, Giovanni Battista. Ambassador of Venice. He took Horatio Busino to a play in December 1617, placing, for what Busino saw as a joke, an elegant lady alongside him (*Calendar of State Papers Venetian 1617–19*, p. 67).

Lotto. Secretary to the Florentine embassy. He was in the French ambassador's party at the Globe in 1607–8.

Lynsey, John. A butcher charged with making an affray at the Fortune in 1611 with Ralph Brewyn and others.

Madox, Richard. On 22 February 1583 he 'went to the theater to see a scurvie play set out al by one virgin, which there proved a fyemartin without voice, so that we stayed not the matter' (BL Cotton MS App. xlvii, f. 6).

Manners, Roger, fifth Earl of Rutland. It was reported in 1600 that Rutland and Southampton 'pass away the tyme in London merely in going to plaies every Day' (see under Wriothesley). Imprisoned for his part in the Essex conspiracy, but released by James, he died in 1612. His younger brother, the sixth earl, commissioned an *impresa* from Richard Burbage and Shakespeare in 1613.

Marcy, Charles. A gentleman accused along with Richard Moreton and John Shanke at Middlesex Sessions in December 1614 of selling 'at the Playhouse' stolen bands and cuffs belonging to Henry Udall.

Margrave, Richard. A sailor of Wapping, bound over on 16 May 1626 for 100 marks over his part in a gang mainly of seamen including Thomas Alderson, attacking the Fortune.

Marmion, Shackerley. Playwright at the Salisbury Court and Cockpit in the 1630s, and a 'son of Ben'. He wrote verses to Joseph Taylor for his revival of Fletcher's *Faithful Shepherdess* at court in 1633.

Marston, John. His *Antonio's Revenge* (1601) seems indebted to *Hamlet*, which was not yet in print.

Mason, William. A feltmaker involved with four others (Brian, Fryne, Jenckes and Oldbury) in an affray at the Red Bull in May 1610.

Matthew, Sir Toby. Son of the Archbishop of York, he turned Jesuit. He quoted Falstaff's honour catechism in a letter to Dudley Carleton on 20 September 1598. Chamberlain (II.137) also reported seeing him, when a newly made Catholic priest, on his way to a play at Blackfriars on 6 February 1618. He was then aged about fifty.

Mayne, Jasper. His verses written in the 1630s show him to have been a frequent playgoer.

Melton, John. In *Astrologaster*, 1620, he mentions *Faustus* at the Fortune, and also *Alphonsus of Aragon*, *Friar Bacon and Friar Bungay*, *Byron*, and a player speaking a prologue.

Meres, Francis. In his book *Palladis Tamia*, 1598, culled from his wide reading, he mentions several of Shakespeare's plays which were not yet in print, notably *Two Gentlemen of Verona*, *The Comedy of Errors*, *A Midsummer Night's Dream* and *King John*.

Merrick, Lady Anne. Wrote to her London friend Mrs Lydall on 21 January 1638 saying she wanted to see the London attractions, including *The Alchemist* (*Calendar of State Papers Domestic 1638–9*, 13. p. 342).

Merrick, Sir Gilly. An Essex conspirator, he attended the Globe on 7 February to see *Richard II*.

Middleton, Thomas. Playwright. A lawsuit of 8 February 1601 testified that he 'remaynethe heare in London daylie accompaninge the players'.

Mildmay, Anthony. Recorded as accompanying his brother Humphrey to Blackfriars to see *Volpone* and other plays in 1634, 1638 and other dates.

The brothers were closer to each other than to their third brother Sir Henry. All three became Parliamentarians in 1642. Sir Henry was a judge at the trial of Charles I. Anthony was King Charles's gaoler in 1648. He described himself as 'a great opposer of tyranny and Popery'. His wife Grace wrote in her memoirs that she refused to go to 'the Court, to feastes, marryages, and plays' when asked by court ladies.

Mildmay, Sir Humphrey. The eldest of three brothers and a sister, grandchildren of the puritan founder of Emmanuel College Cambridge. He was born in 1592, knighted in 1616 and married in the same year. His wife, Jane or Joan, was of the famous Crofts family of Saxham, which regularly entertained royalty during its visits to Newmarket. Her sister Ann married Wentworth, the Earl of Cleveland. Mary married Christopher Abdy and Cicely married Thomas Killigrew. She was literate. Mildmay began the diary at the age of forty in 1633. On Saturday 3 February 1638 he failed to get in to a play, 'being full', after supper with Coke. But he saw many other plays at court and in the playhouses. Mostly he went to the Blackfriars, but also the Cockpit and the Globe. In September 1648, when the playhouses were officially closed, he saw a performance at the Red Bull. The plays he saw during the years of regular playgoing included Mabbe's *Spanish Bawd* on 18 May 1632, Fletcher's *Rollo* at the Globe on 23 May 1633, Davenant's *The Wits* at Blackfriars on 22 January 1634, Shirley's *The Gamester* at Whitehall on 6 February 1634, *Cleander* on 21 May 1634, *Catiline* at court on 9 November 1634, Davenant's *Love and Honour* on 12 December 1634, Fletcher's *Elder Brother* at Blackfriars on 25 April 1635, *Othello* at Blackfriars on 6 May 1635, Shirley's *Lady of Pleasure* on 8 December 1635, and Fletcher's *Mad Lover* on 21 May 1639.

Mildmay, Lady Jane. Recorded by her husband as accompanying him to a playhouse six times between 1632 and 1640.

Mildmay, Nan. Accompanied Mildmay and his wife to *Cleander*, a King's Men's play, 21 May 1634.

Milton, John. Went to the Fortune at the age of twelve, in 1621. In 1623 he was again in London attending the amphitheatre playhouses. His first Elegy to Charles Diodati mentions *sinuosi pompa theatri*, the splendour of the curved theatre. (See R. Hosley, *Renaissance Drama Supplement* 10 (1967), p. 14.)

Moolde, William. A lime-man, charged along with John West and Thomas Jacob, 'for committing a great disorder in the Red Bull playhouse and for assaulting and beating divers persons there', on 23 August 1639.

More, James. A secretary to William Darrell of Littlecote, he attended a play at Paul's in 1589 at a cost of sixpence to his master. (See H. Hall, *Society in the Elizabethan Age*, 1888, pp. 101, 211, 206–33, reprinting Darrell's accounts.)

Morton, Sir Albert. Went to *A Game at Chesse* at the Globe in August 1624.

Mulis, Joseph. Servant to Dudley Norton, at the Globe in August 1612.

Murray, Sir James. He 'dilated' the jibes against Scotsmen in *Eastward Ho!* to the king, some time before the text of the play appeared in print.

Murray, Sir William. Fought a duel with Sir Humphrey Tofton after a quarrel at a playhouse in 1625.

Newdigate, John. A student of the Inner Temple, he made eight visits to plays, including two to the Blackfriars, between 22 December 1620 and 11 July 1621 (*Camden Society*, 4th series, 39, pp. 223, 229, 231, 232, 256, 257).

Newdigate, Richard, brother of John. While a student at Oxford he went to a London playhouse in 1619.

Newport, Anne, Countess of. The scandal over her conversion to Catholicism includes mention of her at the Cockpit in November 1637 (*Earl of Strafford's Letters*, ed. Knowles, II.128).

Norton, Dudley. Secretary for Ireland, he went to a play at the Globe in August 1612, as one of a party made up by the recently widowed Elizabeth Wybarn. At a Star Chamber hearing over a fracas he was involved in at the play he claimed that he 'never was above foure or five times in his whole life' at the Globe. He was the executor of her husband's will. (See Wybarn, Elizabeth.)

Norwood, Richard. Scholar and soldier, born at Stony Stratford. His diary reports that in 1612 he 'went often to stage plays wherewith I was as it were bewitched . . . Yea, so far was I affected with these lying vanities that I began to make a play and had written a good part of it. It happened after some time that I fell out with the players at the Fortune (which was the house I frequented) about a seat which they would not admit me to have, whereupon out of anger, and as it were to do them a despite, I came there no more that I remember' (*The Journal of Richard Norwood*, ed. E. C. Craven, London, 1945, p. 42).

Oldbury, Hugh. A haberdasher with John Jenckes and three feltmakers (Brian, Fryne and Mason) fined for 'a notable outrage' at the Red Bull in 1610.

Osborne, Francis. Author of a manuscript pamphlet about the civil war, *The True Tragicomedy formerly played at Court* (transcribed from the manuscript in the British Library by John Pitcher and Lois Potter, ed. with an introduction by Lois Potter, New York, 1983), where he says (p. 4): 'I amongst others hissed *Sejanus* off the stage, yet after sat it out, not only patiently but with content and admiration.' If he was at the first performances at the Globe in 1603 or 1604, when it was derided, he could hardly have been more than eight or nine years old.

Overall, Mrs. Wife of John Overall, Regius Professor of Theology at Cambridge 1596–1607, Dean of St Paul's 1602–18. Aubrey writes, 'She had (they told me) the loveliest Eies that were ever seen, but wondrous wanton. When she came to Court, or to the Play-house, the Gallants would so flock about her' (*Brief Lives*, ed. O. L. Dicks, p. 226).

Palmer, T. A student of Christ Church Oxford, his verses in the preliminaries of the Beaumont and Fletcher Folio (1647) show that he knew the plays in performance.

Parker, William, fourth Baron Monteagle. Attended the Globe on 7 February 1601 as an Essex conspirator. He paid a heavy fine for his part in the plot. In 1605 he received a warning not to attend Parliament, and prompted an investigation which led to the discovery of the Gunpowder Plot.

Peacham, Henry. Saw *Titus Andronicus* in about 1595, and drew a scene together with an extended quotation from the play.

Percy, Sir Charles. In a letter of 27 December 1600 he refers to Justice Silence and Justice Shallow (*Calendar of State Papers Domestic, Elizabeth 1598–1601*, p. 502). He attended the Globe on 7 February 1601 as an Essex conspirator. A short, plump man, he was one of the two horsemen who raced to Edinburgh to tell James of Elizabeth's death.

Perkins, Richard. Principal player at the Red Bull, and later a King's player. In his poem 'To my loving Friend and Fellow, Thomas Heywood', prefixed to *An Apology for Actors* (1612), he writes, 'when I come to playes, I love to sit / That all may see me in a publike place'.

Philip Julius, Duke of Stettin-Pomerania. Visited London in 1602 and went to both the boys' and the adult playhouses, including the Fortune on 14 September (*Transactions of the Royal Historical Society* n.s. 6 (1892), p. 29).

Phillipps, Mary. A gatherer at the Red Bull in 1607.

Pinnocke, Thomas. A silkweaver arrested in January 1638 at the Red Bull 'for menacing and threatening to pull downe the Redbull playhouse and strikinge divers people with a great cudgell as he went alonge the streets'.

Platter, Thomas. Swiss scholar who visited England in 1599. His travels included a visit to the Globe to see *Julius Caesar* on 21 September.

Prince, Mr. Accompanied Mildmay to a play at Blackfriars, 7 February 1634.

Prynne, William. Author of *Histriomastix*, 1633. In his Epistle Dedicatory he writes of 'having upon my first arrival here in London, heard and seene in foure severall Playes (to which the pressing importunity of some ill acquaintance drew me whiles I was yet a novice) such wickednes, such lewdnes as then made my penitent heart to loath, my conscience to *abhorre all Stage-playes ever since*'.

Pudsey, Edward. His commonplace book (Bodleian Library MS Eng. poet. D.3) contains quotations from Jonson's *The Case is Altered*, *Every Man Out of his Humour*, *Cynthia's Revels* and *Poetaster*, Marston's *Antonio* plays and *Jack Drum's Entertainment*, Chapman's *Blind Beggar of Alexandria*, *The Merchant of Venice*, and Dekker's *Satiromastix*. Most of the quotations are inaccurate, and must have been jotted down during or soon after a performance in the years around 1600.

Purfet, Edward. A feltmaker, one of four involved in an affray at the Red Bull, May 1610.

Reignoldes, Elizabeth. A lawsuit reports that she was escorted by John Cotton to plays in 1599.

Reynolds, Henry, esq. A friend of Drayton, who writes of reminiscing with him and hearing him quote from stage plays. He wrote *Torquato Tasso's Aminta Englisht* (1628).

Rich, Henry, Earl of Holland. He attended *Henry VIII* at the Globe in August 1628.

Rich, Mary, née Boyle. The Countess of Warwick, her autobiography records her staying in London in about 1640 with her sister-in-law, who enticed her 'to spend (as she did) her time in seeing and reading plays and romances' (*Autobiography of Lady Warwick*, Percy Society no. 74 (vol. xx), 1848, p. 4).

Rich, Sir Robert. Accompanied the Marchese di Villa, the Savoy ambassador, with Sir Henry Wotton to 'the public plays, where anyone at all can go for a few pence', in May 1613 (John Orrell, 'The London Stage in the Florentine Correspondence, 1604–1618', *Theatre Research International* 3 (1977–8), p. 169).

Richards, Nathanael. Author of *Messallina*. His commendatory verses to *Women Beware Women* say that he had seen the play on stage.

Rowlands, Samuel. Several of his verses refer to plays. His references to Pope and Singer as clowns confirm his familiarity with the public stages.

Rudyerd, Sir Benjamin. According to John Chamberlain he saw *A Game at Chesse* at the Globe in August 1624.

Sackville, Richard, third Earl of Dorset. Husband of Anne Clifford, her diary reports that, on 14 February 1616, he 'sup't at the globe'. This may have been an inn, not the playhouse, but in May she wrote, 'All this time my Lord was at London where he had infinite & great resorte coming to him he went abroade to cocking, to Bowling Alleys, to Plays & Horseraces'.

Savile, William. A country gentleman of Nottinghamshire, he was born in 1612 at Thornhill Hall, Yorkshire. He had a residence in London and went to plays in 1639 and 1641. Charles made him Governor of York in 1643. (See Nottingham Record Office, in Wasson and Palmer, ed. REED, *Derbyshire and the West Riding*, forthcoming.)

Sc., An. (Antony Scoloker?). In *Daiphantus*, 1604, he refers to a man wearing only his shirt, like mad Hamlet, and echoes passages not in the 1603 quarto of the play.

Sewster, Mr. Herbert records him as taking exception to a play performed at Salisbury Court in October 1633. Herbert stopped the play on Sewster's complaint.

Shanke, John. A gentleman accused with Charles Marcy and Richard Moreton of selling stolen bands and cuffs to Henry Udall at a Middlesex playhouse in December 1614. He is unlikely to have been his namesake the player.

Shaw, John. A butcher charged with making an affray at the Fortune in 1611 with Ralph Brewyn and others.

Sidney, Sir Philip. In his *Apology for Poetry* he writes about *Gorboduc* and other plays in ways which indicate he must have been to the amphitheatres.

Skipwith, Sir Henry. Accompanied Mildmay to a play, probably *Cleander*, Massinger's revision of *The Wandering Lovers*, in May 1634.

Smyth, William. Yeoman of St Margaret's, Westminster, bound over on 16 May 1626 for his part with Thomas Alderson and others in an affray at the Fortune.

Speire, Katherine. In a case at Bridewell on 16 April 1629, where she is described as a 'Lewd young Wench will not be ruled by her friends but followeth the company of players and idle company' she was ordered by the court 'to be kept here at her fathers charges to worke'.

Spenser, Edmund. Gabriel Harvey wrote to Spenser in the 1580s, about 'sum maltconceivid comedye fitt for the Theater, or sum other paintid stage whereat thou and thy lively copesmates in London maye laughe ther mouthes and bellyes full for pence or twopence apeece' (*Letter Book*, ed. E. J. L. Scott, Camden Soc. Publications n.s. 33 (1884), pp. 67–8).

Stafferton, Parr. A student of Gray's Inn, he led a 'dysordered companye of gentlemen of the Innes of Court' to attack players of Lord Berkeley's Men in 1581.

Staple, Henry. A cordwainer, accused along with Harrison and Holdaye of picking William George's purse at the Curtain in August 1613.

Strange, William. A glover, aged forty-four in 1611. Testifying in a lawsuit at the London Consistory Court (*Overen* v. *Paine*, 1609–11, f340), he said he 'attendeth the King's players at their plays'.

Stuart, James, second Duke of Lennox. Embroiled in a quarrel with Pembroke, the Lord Chamberlain, over the possession of a box at Blackfriars for a new play in January 1636.

Sweet, Alexander. He was robbed of a purse containing £3 by Alexander Fulsis at the Red Bull in 1614.

Tatham, John. The author of *Fancies Theater*, 1640. It has a poem about meeting a friend at the Globe, and a subsequent meeting being hindered by rain. He also wrote a prologue for the Fortune players on their transfer to the Red Bull in 1639.

Taylor, John. The Water Poet. He describes a visit on 14 October 1618 to a play by Derby's Men about Guy of Warwick. The Globe and Fortune are frequently mentioned in his writings.

Tedcastle, William. A yeoman involved in an affray in May 1610 at the Red Bull, with four feltmakers.

Thorneton, Thomas. A victualler, charged with Thomas Pinnocke and Samuel White with brawling at the Red Bull in January 1638.

Thules. One of the three Catholic priests named as a playgoer in 1618, in correspondence between William Harison and Thomas Leke (Folger MS 4787).

Tofte, Robert. In *The Months Minde of a Melancholy Lover*, 1598, he writes, 'Loves Labour Lost, I once did see a Play / Y-cleped so.' The titlepage calls him 'gentleman'.

Tofton, Sir Humphrey. Fought a duel with Sir William Murray after a quarrel at a playhouse in 1625.

Tomkyns, Nathaniel. He wrote an account of *The Late Lancashire Witches*, which he saw at the Globe on about 14 August 1634. Tomkyns had been an MP, and was then clerk and registrar of the Queen's Council. In 1643 when his plot to raise London for the king was betrayed by his brother-in-law, the poet Edmund Waller, he was executed.

Tufton. A husband and wife who accompanied Dering to a playhouse. One of them was related to Dering's wife.

Udall, Edward. A victualler, witness to the sale of stolen drapery to Henry Udall at a Middlesex playhouse in December 1614.

Udall, Henry. A linen-draper. At one of the Middlesex playhouses in December 1614 he bought 'four network bands and a pair of cuffs at the Playhouse at an under-rate, being part of the goods which were stolen from the said Henry'. The accused were Charles Marcy and John Shanke, gentlemen, and Richard Moreton, ironmonger. Witnesses to the sale were William Fludd, Edward Udall, Richard Caulton, William Boulton and Robert Greene.

Vaux, Sir Ambrose. A younger son of the third Lord Vaux, and an extravagant man-about-town, he was identified in Star Chamber papers of 1612 as trying to abduct Elizabeth Wybarn from her party at the Globe, claiming to have married the recently widowed lady. She was defended by her escort Dudley Norton and a dozen supporters. (See Wybarn, Elizabeth.)

Vennar, Richard. A member of Lincoln's Inn, and author of a notorious trick about an advertised extravaganza 'England's Joy' at the Swan in 1602. In his pamphlet *Apology* of 1614 defending his conduct he wrote that in 1602 'I saw a daily offring to the God of pleasure, resident at the Globe on the Banke side'. The same passage refers to his pursuit as 'the hunting of the fox' (as in *Volpone*), and of another failed play, the 'burning pestle'. Beaumont's play had been published the year before with a note about its failure when first staged (*An Apology*, 1614, B6r).

Verrue, Count di. Ambassador of Savoy. He went in company with the Duke of Buckingham to see *Henry VIII* at the Globe in August 1628. Buckingham, making naval preparations to attack La Rochelle, was seeking an alliance with Savoy and Venice against the French.

Villa, Marchese di. Ambassador Extraordinary from Savoy, in London in early 1613. Sir Robert Rich and Sir Henry Wotton took him to 'the public plays'.

Waldstein, Baron. His London diary for 3 July 1600 reports, 'Went to see an English play. The theatre follows the ancient Roman plan: it is built of wood and is so designed that the spectators can get a comfortable view of everything that happens in any part of the building' (*The Diary of Baron Waldstein, a Traveller in Elizabethan England*, trans. G. W. Gros, London, 1981).

Waller, Edmund. His verses in the preliminaries of the Beaumont and Fletcher Folio (1647) show that he knew the plays in performance. In Parliament in January 1642 he joined with John Pym, one of the 'Five Members', to block a motion proposing to ban all stage playing.

Watton, Mrs. In a London Consistory Court hearing of January 1610 the judge reproved her for going to a play with a man who was not her husband, 'the sayd Mr Curle & mres Watton had byn seene together at playes or at a playe whereupon the Lord chiefe Justice wished Mr Watton to looke better to his wife' (quoted by Loreen L. Giese, 'Theatrical Citings and Bitings: Some References to Playhouses and Players in London Consistory Court Depositions, 1586–1612', *Early Theatre* 1 (1998), 113–28, pp. 115–16).

Webster, John. Playwright, described by Henry Fitzgeoffery in 1617 as in the audience at Blackfriars ('Crabbed (*Websterio.*) / The *Play-wright Cartwright*').

Weever, John. An epigram (1599) indicates that he had attended a performance of *The Spanish Tragedy*. He seems also to have known Shakespeare.

Wenman, Sir Richard. Reported by Chamberlain (II.181) as attending Blackfriars for 'an ordinarie play' in November 1618.

West, John. A hemp-dresser, charged along with Moolde and Jacob for an affray at the Red Bull in August 1639.

Wheaten, Elizabeth. Attended the Globe in the 1630s, possibly as a gatherer. In her will of 1635, Richard Burbage's widow bequeathed her 'the gatheringe Place at the Globe during my Lease'.

White, Thomas. A tailor, charged with Thomas Pinnock and Thomas Thorneton for brawling at the Red Bull in January 1638.

Whitelocke, Bulstrode. Lawyer and politician. Of his life in the 1630s, he wrote, 'I was so conversant with the musicians, and so willing to gain their favour, especially at this time, that I composed an air myself, with the assistance of Mr. Ives, and called it *Whitelock's Coranto*, which being cried up, was first played publicly by the Blackfriars Music, who were then esteemed the best of the common musicians in London. Whenever I came to that house (as I did sometimes in those days), though not often, to see a play, the musicians would presently play *Whitelock's Coranto*, and it was so often called for that they would have played it twice or thrice in an afternoon' (Charles Burney, *A General History of Music from the Earliest Ages to the Present Period*, London, 1782–9, II.299).

Williams, Elizabeth. Married sister of Alice, wife of Sir Dudley Carleton. On 30 June 1614 Chamberlain wrote to Alice Carleton saying that he had tried twice to see her sister, but 'the first time she was at a neighbours house at Cards, and the next she was gon to the new Globe to a play' (*Letters*, I.544).

Williams, Thomas. One of four feltmakers in an affray at the Red Bull, May 1610.

Wilson, Arthur. Author of *The Swisser*. When the King's company staged his play in 1631 Wilson was thirty-six, having served as secretary to the Earl of Essex for fifteen years. It shows a close familiarity with the company's repertory of plays.

22. Bulstrode Whitelocke, from a painting in St John's College, Oxford.

Wilson, George. A note for March 1634 says, 'George Wilson kild at ye play house in salesburie court' (Guildhall MS 6538).

Windsor, Mary. Niece to William Wybarn. Either she or another niece Margaret Franke was in a family group of her aunt's at a play at the Globe in August 1612. (See Wybarn, Elizabeth.)

Wortley, Sir Frank. Recorded as accompanying his cousin Humphrey Mildmay to Blackfriars to see *Volpone* and other plays in January 1632 and October 1638.

Wotton, Sir Henry. Accompanied the ambassador of Savoy to 'the public plays' in 1613, and went to *A Game at Chesse* at the Globe in August 1624. His account of the burning of the Globe in 1613 does not make it clear that he was present for the performance of *Henry VIII* which caused the fire.

Wotton. Possibly Matthew Wotton, a master stationer of Fleet Street. Pepys reported in his Diary for 1660 that while drinking with him in an alehouse 'he told me a great many stories of comedies which he had formerly seen acted and the names of the principal actors' (*Diary*, ed. Latham, I.59).

Wriothesley, Henry, second Earl of Southampton. He was reported by Rowland Whyte in 1600 as in company with the Earl of Rutland passing 'away the tyme in London merely in going to plaies every Day' (Arthur Collins, ed., *Letters and Memorials of State, The Sidney Papers*, 1746, II.132).

Wybarn, Elizabeth. Wife of William Wybarn, who died early in 1612. A Star Chamber lawsuit reveals that she took a party to the Globe in August of that year, when Ambrose Vaux tried to take her away, claiming she was his wife. (See Mary A. Blackstone and Cameron Louis, 'Towards "A Full and Understanding Auditory": New Evidence of Playgoers at the first Globe Theatre', *MLR* 90 (1995), pp. 556–71.)

APPENDIX 2

References to playgoing

References are arranged by date or approximate date.

1. 1563

[An idle noble man] licenciously roames in ryot, coasting the stretes with wavering plumes, hangd to a long side blade, & pounced in silkes . . . haunteth plaies, feastes, bathes and bankettings . . . I allowe him not so much as one ynche of Nobility.

> Laurence Humphrey, *The Nobles, or of Nobilitye*, I1r–2r

2. 1574

. . . the present time requirithe yowe to have good care and use good meanes towchinge the contagion of sickenes, that the sicke be kept from the whole, that the places of persons infected be made plaine to be knowen and the more releeved; that sweetenes and holsomnes of publique places be provided for; that unnecessarie and scarslie honest resorts to plaies, to shewes to thoccasion of thronges and presse, except to the servyce of God; and especiallie the assemblies to the unchaste, shamelesse and unnaturall tomblinge of the Italian Weomen maye be avoided.

> Thomas Norton, 'An Exhortation or Rule wherbie the L. Maior of London is to order him selfe and the Citty' (J. P. Collier, *Illustrations of the Olde English Literature*, III.14)

3. 1577

If you will learne howe to be false and deceyve your husbandes, or husbandes their wyves howe to playe the harlottes, to obtayne one's love, howe to ravishe, howe to beguyle, howe to betraye, to flatter, lye, sweare, forsweare, how to allure to whoredome, howe to murther, howe to poyson, howe to disobey and rebell against princes, to consume treasures prodigally, to moove to lustes, to ransacke and spoyle cities and townes, to bee ydle, to blaspheme, to sing filthie songs of love, to speake filthily, to be prowde, howe to mocke, scoffe, and deryde any nation . . . shall not you learne, then, at such enterludes howe to practise them?

> John Northbrook, *A Treatise wherein Dicing, Dauncing, Vaine playes, or Enterluds, with other idle pastimes, &c., commonly used on the Sabbath day, are reproved by the Authorities of the word of God and the aunteint writers*, p. 92 (mentions 'the Theatre and Curtaine' p. 82)

4. 1578

The Englishman in this quallitie, is most vaine, indiscreet, and out of order: he fyrst groundes his worke, on impossibilities, then in three howers

247

ronnes he throwe the world: marryes, gets Children, makes Children men, men to conquer kingdoms, murder monsters, and bringeth Gods from Heaven, and fetcheth Divels from Hel. And (that which is worst) their ground is not so unperfect, as their working indiscreete: not waying, so the people laugh, though they laugh them (for theyr folleys) to scorne: Manye tymes (To make mirthe) they make a Clowne companion with a Kinge: in theyr grave Counsels, they allow the advise of fooles.

> George Whetstone, *Promos and Cassandra*, prefatory epistle

5. 1578

> Where shall we goe?
> To a playe at the Bull, or else to some other place.
> Doo Comedies like you wel?
> Yea sir, on holy dayes.
> They please me also wel, but the preachers wyll not allowe them.
> Wherefore, knowe you it:
> They say, they are not good.
> And wherefore are they used?
> Because every man delites in them.
> I beleeve there is much knavery used at those comedies:
> So beleeve I also.
>
>> John Florio, *Florio his First Fruites*, 1578, A1r (an English–Italian conversation book)

6. 1580

Some citizens wives, upon whom the Lord for ensample to others hath laide his hands, have even on their deathbeds with teares confessed, that they have received at those spectacles such filthie infections, as have turned their minds from chast cogitations, and made them of honest women light huswives . . .

Whosoever shal visit the chappel of Satan, I meane the Theater, shal finde there no want of yong ruffins, nor lacke of harlots, utterlie past al shame: who presse to the fore-front of the scaffoldes, to the end to showe their impudencie, and to be as an object to al mens eies.

> Anon (Anthony Munday), *A third blast of retrait from plaies and Theaters*, 1580, pp. 125, 139

7. 1581

Parr Stafferton gentleman of Grayes Inne for that he that daye brought a dysordered companye of gentlemen of the Innes of Court & others, to assalte Arthur Kynge, Thomas Goodale, and others, servauntes to the Lord Barkley, & players of Enterludes within the Cyttye.

> City order & Lord Berkeley letter, July 1581 (*ES* IV.282)

8. 1582

The argument of Tragedies is wrath, crueltie, incest, injurie, murther eyther violent by sworde, or voluntary by poyson. The persons, Gods, Goddesses, juries, friendes, kinges, Quenes, and mightie men. The grounde worke of Commedies, is love, cosenedge, flatterie, bawderie, slye conveighance of whoredome; The persons, cookes, knaves, baudes parasites, courtezannes, lecherous olde men, amorous young men . . .

Sometime you shall see nothing but the adventures of an amorous knight, passing from countrie to contrie for the love of his lady, encountering many a terrible monster made of broune paper, and at his retorne, is so wonderfully changed, that he cannot be knowne but by some posie in his tablet, or by a broken ring, or a handkircher or a piece of a cockle shell, what learne you by that? When ye soule of your playes is eyther mere trifles, or Italian bawdery, or cussing of gentlewomen, what are we taught? . . .

The ancient Philosophers . . . called them a monster of many heades . . . The common people which resorte to Theatres being but an assemblie of Tailors, Tinkers, Cordwayners, Saylers, Olde Men, yong Men, Women, Boyes, Girles, and such like . . .

So in Comedies delight being moved with varietie of shewes, of eventes, of musicke, the longer we gaze, the more we crave . . .

As at the first, so nowe, theaters are snares unto faire women. And as I toulde you long ago in my schoole of abuse, our Theaters, and play houses in London, are as full of secrete adulterie as they were in Rome . . . In the playhouses at London, it is the fashion of youthes to go first into the yarde, and to carry theire eye through every gallery, then like ravens where they spye the carion thither they flye, and presse as nere to ye fairest as they can. In stead of pomegranates they give them pippines, they dally with their garments to passe ye time, they minister talke upon od occasions, & eyther bring them home to theire houses on small aquaintance, or slip into taverns when ye plaies are done . . .

The *Poets* send their verses to the Stage upon such feete as continually are rowled up in rime at the fingers endes, which is plaucible to the barbarous, and carrieth a stinge into the eares of common people.

> Stephen Gosson, *Playes Confuted in Five Actions*, C6r, D1r, D4r, F1r, F6r

9. 1584

Uppon Weddensdaye one Browne, a serving man in a blew coat, a shifting fellowe having a perrelous witt of his owne, entending a spoile if he cold have browght it to passe, did at Theatre doore querell with certen poore boyes, handicraft prentises, and strook some of theym, and lastlie he with his sword wonded and maymed one of the boyes upon the left hand; where upon there assembled nere a ml people.

. . . This Browne is a common cossiner, a thieff, & a horse stealer, and colloreth all his doynges here about this towne with a sute that he haithe in the lawe agaynst a brother of his in Staffordshire. He resteth now in Newgate . . .

> Letter of William Fleetwood to Lord Burghley (*ES* IV.297–8)

10. *c.*1584

[Prologue at Blackfriars concludes] . . . wishing that although there bee in your precise judgementes an universall mislike, yet wee maye enjoy by your woonted courtisies a general silence.

> John Lyly, *Campaspe* (*Complete Works*, II.315)

11. *c.*1589

[Prologue at Paul's] . . . Onelie this doeth encourage us, that presenting our studies before Gentlemen, thogh they receive an inward mislike, wee shall not be hist with an open disgrace.

John Lyly, *Midas* (*Complete Works*, III.115)

12. 1589

I am not ignorant how eloquent our gowned age is grown of late; so that every mechanical mate abhorres the English he was borne too, and plucks, with a solemne periphrasis, his *ut vales* from the inkehorne: which I impute, not so much to the perfection of Arts, as to the servile imitations of vainglorious Tragedians, who contend not so seriously to excell in action, as to embowell the cloudes in a speech of comparison, thinking themselves more than initiated in Poets immortality, if they but once get *Boreas* by the beard and the heavenly bull by the deaw-lap. But herein I cannot so fully bequeath them to folly, as their idiot Art-Masters, that intrude themselves to our eares as the Alcumists of eloquence, who (mounted on the stage of arrogance) Think to out-brave better pennes with the swelling bumbast of a bragging blanke verse. Indeede it may bee the ingrafted overflow of some kil-cow conceit, that overcloyeth their imagination with a more then drunken resolution, being not extemporall in the invention of any other meanes to vent their manhoode, commits the digestion of their cholericke incumbrances to the spacious volubilitie of a drumming decasillabon.

Thomas Nashe, epistle 'To the gentlemen Students of Both Universities', prefixed to Greene's *Menaphon* (*Works*, ed. McKerrow, I.311)

13. 1590

At plaies, the Nip standeth there leaning like some manerly gentleman against the doore as men go in, and there finding talke with some of his companions, spieth what everie man hath in his purse, and where, in what place, and in which sleeve or pocket he puts his boung and according to that so he worketh either where the thrust is great within, or else as they come out at the dores.

Robert Greene, *The Second part of Conny Catching*, 1591 (*Life and Works*, ed. Grosart, X.105)

14. 1592

The next, by his sute of russet, his buttond cap, his taber, his standing on the toe, and other tricks, I knew to be either the bodyer resemblaunce of Tarlton, who living for his pleasant conceits was of all men liked, and dying for mirth left not his like.

. . . lette . . . the young people of the Cittie, either abstaine . . . altogether from playes, or at their comming thither to use themselves after a more quiet order . . . The beginners are neither gentlemen, nor citizens, nor any of both their servants, but some lewd mates that long for innovation; & when they see advantage that either Servingmen or Apprentises are most in number, they will be of either side, though indeed they are of no side, but men beside all honestie, willing to make boote of cloakes, hats, purses, or what ever they can lay holde on in a hurley burley. These are the common causers of discord in publike places.

Henry Chettle, *Kind-Harts Dreame*, B2v, D4v

15. 1592

. . . whereas the after-noone beeing the idlest time of the day; wherein men that are their owne masters (as Gentlemen of the Court, the Innes of the Courte, and the number of Captaines and Souldiers about *London*) do wholy bestow themselves upon pleasure, and that pleasure they devide (howe vertuously it skils not) either into gameing, following of harlots, drinking, or seeing a Playe . . .

How would it have joyed brave *Talbot* (the terror of the French) to thinke that after he had lyne two hundred yeares in his Tombe, hee should triumphe againe on the Stage, and have his bones newe embalmed with the teares of ten thousand spectators at least, (at severall times) who, in the Tragedian that represents his person, imagine they behold him fresh bleeding! . . .

Whereas some Petitioners of the Counsaile against them object, they corrupt the youth of the Cittie, and withdrawe Prentises from their worke, they heartily wishe they might bee troubled with none of their youth nor their prentises; for some of them (I meane the ruder handicrafts servants) never come abroade, but they are in danger of undoing . . .

Thomas Nashe, *Pierce Penilesse*, F3r–3v

16. 1592

. . . it is the lucke of some pelting Comedies, to busy the Stage, as well as some graver Tragedies.

Gabriel Harvey, *Foure Letters and certeine Sonnets*, the fourth letter

17. 1592

. . . their gaines lies by all places of resort and assemblies therefore their chief walkes is Paules, Westminster, the exchange, Plaies, Bear-garden, running at Tilt, the L. Maiors day, any festival meetings, fraies, shootings, or great faires.

Robert Greene, *The second and last part of Conny-catching*, 1592, p. 30

18. 1593?

> For as we see at all the play house dores,
> When ended is the play, the daunce, and song:
> A thousand townsemen, gentlemen, and whores,
> Porters and serving-men together throng . . .

Sir John Davies, *Epigrammes* 17, 'In Cosmum' (*Poems*, ed. Krueger)

19. 1593?

> *Rufus*, The Courtier, at the Theater,
> Leaving the best and most conspicuous place,
> Doth either to the stage himselfe transferre,
> Or through a grate, doth shew his double face,
> For that the clamorous fry of Innes of court
> Fills up the private roomes of greater price:

And such a place where all may have resort,
He in his singularity doth despise.

Sir John Davies, *Epigrammes* 3, 'In Rufum'

20. 1593?

Fuscus is free and hath the world at will,
Yet in the course of life that he doth leade,
He's like a horse which turning rounde a mill,
Doth alwaies in the selfe same circle treade:
First he doth rise at 10 and at eleven
He goes to *Gyls*, where he doth eate till one,
Then sees a play til sixe, and sups at seaven,
And after supper, straight to bed is gone,
And there till tenne next day he doth remaine,
And then he dines, then sees a commedy,
And then he suppes, and goes to bed againe:
Thus rounde he runs without variety:
Save that sometimes he comes not to the play,
But falls into a whore-house by the way.

Sir John Davies, *Epigrammes* 39, 'In Fuscum'

21. 1594

. . . toies
Or needlesse antickes imitations,
Or shewes, or new devices sprung a late,
we have exilde them from our Tragicke stage.

Anon., *The Wars of Cyrus*, prologue

22. 1594

. . . the quality of such as frequent the sayed playes, beeing the ordinary places of meeting for all vagrant persons & maisterles men that hang about the Citie, theeves, horsestealers, whoremoongers, coozeners, connycatching persones, practizers of treason, & other such lyke . . .

Lord Mayor to Lord Burghley, 3 November 1594, repeated in petition for abolition of playhouses 28 July 1597 to the Privy Council (*ES* IV.317)

23. 1594

. . . *Item*, Every Knight of this Order shall endeavour to add Conference and Experience by Reading; and therefore shall not only read and peruse *Guizo*, the French Academy, *Galiatto* the Courtier, *Plutarch*, the *Arcadia*, and the Neoterical Writers, from time to time; but also frequent the Theatre, and such like places of Experience.

'Articles of the Orders', *Gesta Grayorum*, 1594 (published 1688)

24. 1594

Faustus not lord, nor knight, nor wise, nor olde,
To every place about the towne doth ride,
He rides into the fieldes, Playes to behold,
He rides to take boate at the water side,
He rides to Powles, he rides to th'ordinarie,

He rides unto the house of bawderie too.
Thither his horse so often will him carry,
That shortlie he will quite forget to go.
    Sir John Davies, *Epigrammes* 7, 'In Faustum'

25. 1595?

A Lady of great Birth, great reputation,
Clothed in seemely, and most sumptuous fashion,
Wearing a border of rich Pearl and stone,
Esteemed at a thousand crowns alone,
To see a certaine Interlude, repaires
To shun the press, by dark and privat staires.
Her page did beare a Torch that burnt but dimly.
Two cozening mates, seeing her deckt so trimly,
Did place themselves upon the stayres to watch her,
And thus they laid their plot to cunny-catch her:
One should as 'twere by chance strike out the light;
While th'other that should stand beneath her, might
Attempt (which modestie to suffer lothes)
Rudely to thrust his hands under her clothes.
That while her hands repeld such grosse disorders,
His mate might quickly slip away the borders . . .
    Sir John Harington, *Letters and Epigrams*, ed. McLure, pp. 245–6

26. 1596

All suddenly they heard a troublous noyes,
That seemd some perilous tumult to desine,
Confusd with womens cries, and shouts of boyes,
Such as the troubled Theaters oftimes annoyes.
    Edmund Spenser, *The Faerie Queene*, IV.iii.37

27. 1596

. . . in publike Theaters, when any notable shew passeth over the stage, the people arise in their seates, & stand upright with delight and eagernesse to view it well.
    Stephen Gosson, *The Trumpet of Warre*, 1598, C7v

28. 1596

. . . the said Burbage is now altering and meaneth very shortly to convert and turne the same into a comon playhouse, which will grow to be a very great annoyance and trouble, not only to all the noblemen and gentlemen thereabout inhabiting but allso a generall inconvenience to all the inhabitants of the same precinct, both by reason of the great resort and gathering togeather of all manner of vagrant and lewde persons that, under cullor of resorting to the playes, will come thither and worke all manner of mischeefe, and allso to the great pestring and filling up of the same precinct, yf it should please God to send any visitation of sicknesse as heretofore hath been, for that the same precinct is allready growne very populous; and besides, that the same playhouse is so neere the Church that the noyse of the drummes and

trumpetts will greatly disturbe and hinder both the ministers and parishioners
in tyme of devine service and sermons.

> Petition to the Privy Council from the inhabitants of Blackfriars (*ES* IV.320)

29. 1597

>One [poet] higher pitch'd doth set his soaring thought
>On crowned kings that Fortune hath low brought:
>Or some upreared, high-aspiring swaine
>As it might be the Turkish *Tamberlaine.*
>Then weeneth he his base drink-drowned spright,
>Rapt to the threefold loft of heavens hight,
>When he conceives upon his fained stage
>The stalking steps of his great personage,
>Graced with hufcap termes, and thundring threats,
>That his poore hearers hayre quite upright sets.
>Such soone, as some brave-minded hungry youth,
>Sees fitly frame to his wide-strained mouth,
>He vaunts his voyce upon an hyred stage,
>With high-set steps, and princely carriage;
>Now soouping in side robes of Royalty,
>That earst did skrub in lowsie brokery.
>There if he can with termes Italianate,
>Big-sounding sentences, and words of state,
>Faire patch me up his pure *Iambicke* verse,
>He ravishes the gazing Scaffolders:
>Then certes was the famous *Corduban*
>Never but halfe so high *Tragedian.*
>Now, least such frightfull showes of Fortune fall,
>And bloudy Tyrants rage, should chance appall
>The dead stroke audience, mids the silent rout,
>Comes leaping in a selfe-misformed lout,
>And laughes, and grins, and frames his Mimick face,
>And justles straight into the princes place.
>Then doth the Theatre eccho all aloud,
>With gladsome noyse of that applauding crowd.
>A goodly *hoch-poch*, when vile *Russettings*,
>Are match'd with monarchs, & with mighty kings.
>A goodly grace to sober *Tragick Muse*,
>When each base clown, his clumbsie fist doth bruise,
>And show his teeth in double rotten-row,
>For laughter at his selfe-resembled show.

> Joseph Hall, *Virgidemiarum II*, Liber I, Satire iii

30. 1597

We have here a new play of humors in very great request, and I was
drawn alonge to yt by the common applause, but my opinion of yt is (as the
fellow sayde of the shearing of hogges) that there was a great crie for so litle
wolle.

> Chamberlain to Carleton, *Letters*, 132 (11 June 1597)

31. 1598

> Luscus what's playd to day? faith now I know
> I set thy lips abroach, from whence doth flow
> Naught but pure *Juliat* and *Romio.*
> Say, who acts best? *Drusus*, or *Roscio?*
> Now I have him, that nere of ought did speake
> But when of playes or Plaiers he did treate.
> H'ath made a common-place booke out of plaies,
> And speakes in print, at least what ere he sayes
> Is warranted by Curtaine *plaudeties.*
> If ere you heard him courting *Lesbias* eyes;
> Say (Curteous Sir) speakes he not movingly
> From out some new pathetique Tragedie?
> He writes, he railes, he jests, he courts, what not,
> And all from out his huge long scraped stock
> Of well penn'd playes . . . O ideot times,
> When gawdy Monkeyes mowe ore sprightly rimes!
> O world of fooles, when all mens judgements set
> And rests upon some mumping Marmoset!
> Yon Athens Ape (that can but simperingly
> Yaule *auditores humanissimi,*
> Bound to some servile imitation,
> Can with much sweat patch an Oration,
> Now up he comes, and with his crooked eye
> Presumes to squint on some faire Poesie;
> . . . O what a tricksie lerned nickering straine
> Is this applauded, sencles, modern vain
> When late I heard it from sage *Mutius* lips,
> How il me thought such wanton Jigging skips
> Beseem'd his graver speech.

John Marston, *The Scourge of Villainy*, G7v, H4r

32. 1598

[at court] There was a French gentleman, a master of requests, and resident of Lyons, brother to Mons. De Vicq, governor of Calais, a man honourably entertained by my Lord of Essex, and greatly commended by the Queen, for his speech and other carriage. There were divers Almains with him, whereof one lost 300 crowns at a new play called Every Man's humour.

Calendar of State Papers Domestic: Elizabeth 1598–1601, ed. Mary Anne Everett Green, HMSO 1869, p. 97

33. 1598

> And she with many a salt *La volto* jest
> Edgeth some blunted teeth, and fires the brest
> Of many an old gray-bearded Citizen,
> *Medea* like making him young againe;
> Who comming from the Curtaine sneaketh in
> To some odde garden noted house of sinne.

Everard Guilpin, *Skialetheia*, Satyre Preludium

34. 1598

> See you him yonder, who sits o're the stage,
> With the Tobacco-pipe now at his mouth?
> It is *Cornelius* that brave gallant youth,
> Who is new printed to this fangled age;
> He weares a Jerkin cudgeld with gold lace,
> A profound slop, a hat scarce pipkin high,
> For boots, a paire of dagge cases; his face,
> Furr'd with Cads-beard: his poynard on his thigh.

Guilpin, *Skialetheia*, Epigram 53, 'Of Cornelius'

35. 1599

> How some damnd tyrant, to obtaine a crowne,
> Stabs, hangs, imprisons, smothers, cutteth throats,
> And then a Chorus too comes howling in,
> And tels us of the worrying of a cat,
> Then of a filthie whining ghost,
> Lapt in some fowle sheete, or a leather pelch,
> comes skreaming like a pigge half stickt,
> And cries *Vindicta*, revenge, revenge:
> With that a little Rosen flasheth forth,
> Like smoke out of a Tabacco pipe, or a boyes squib:
> Then comes in two or three like to drovers,
> With taylers bodkins, stabbing one another,
> Is not this trim? is not here goodly things?
> That you should be so much accounted of . . .
> *Enter Comedie at the other end*
> TRAGEDIE   What yet more Cat guts? O this filthie sound
> Stifles mine eares:
> More cartwheeles craking yet?
> A plague upont, Ile cut your fiddle strings,
> If you stand scraping thus to anger me.

Anon., A *Warning for Fair Women*, Induction

36. 1599

> It chaunced me gazing at the Theater,
> To spie a Lock-Tobacco-Chevalier
> Clowding the loathing ayr with foggie fume
> Of Dock-Tobacco, friendly foe to rume.

Henry Buttes, *Dyets Dry Dinner*, P3v

37. 1599

On September 21st after lunch, about two o'clock, I and my party crossed the water, and there in the house with the thatched roof witnessed an excellent performance of the tragedy of the first Emperor Julius Caesar with a cast of some fifteen people; when the play was over, they danced very marvellously and gracefully together as is their wont, two dressed as men and two as women.

On another occasion not far from our inn, in the suburb of Bishopgate, if I remember, also after lunch, I beheld a play in which they presented diverse nations and an Englishman struggling together for a maiden; he overcame them all except the German who won the girl in a tussle, and then sat down by her side, when he and his servant drank themselves tipsy, so that they were both fuddled and the servant proceeded to hurl his shoe at his master's head, whereupon they both fell asleep; meanwhile the Englishman stole into the tent and absconded with the German's prize, thus in his turn outwitting the German; in conclusion they danced very charmingly in English and Irish fashion. Thus daily at two in the afternoon, London has two, sometimes three plays running in different places, competing with each other, and those which play best obtain most spectators. The playhouses are so constructed that they play on a raised platform, so that everyone has a good view. There are different galleries and places, however, where the seating is better and more comfortable and therefore more expensive. For whoever cares to stand below only pays one English penny, but if he wishes to sit he enters by another door, and pays another penny, while if he desires to sit in the most comfortable seats which are cushioned, where he not only sees everything well, but can also be seen, then he pays yet another English penny at another door. And during the performance food and drink are carried round the audience, so that for what one cares to pay one may also have refreshment. The actors are most expensively and elaborately costumed; for it is the English usage for eminent lords or knights at their decease to bequeath and leave almost the best of their clothes to their serving men, which it is unseemly for the latter to wear, so that they offer them for sale for a small sum to the actors . . .

Good order is also kept in the city in the matter of prostitution, for which special commissions are set up, and when they meet with a case, they punish the man with imprisonment and fine. The woman is taken to Bridewell, the King's palace, situated near the river, where the executioner scourges her naked before the populace. And although close watch is kept on them, great swarms of these women haunt the town in the taverns and playhouses.

Thomas Platter, *Travels in England*, trans. Clare Williams, pp. 166–75

38. 1599

. . . last weeke at a puppet play in St. Johns street the house fell and hurt betwene thirty and forty persons and slew five outright wherof two (they say) were goode handsome whoores.

John Chamberlain, *Letters*, I.85 (23 August 1599)

39. 1599

> . . . in all this front,
> You can espy a gallant of this marke,
> Who (to be thought one of the judicious)
> Sits with his armes thus wreath'd, his hat pull'd here,
> Cryes meaw, and nods, then shakes his empty head.

Jonson, *Every Man Out of his Humour* (*Works*, III.434)

40. 1599

> *Ruffinus* lost his tongue on stage,
> And wot ye how he made it knowne?
> He spittes it out in bloudy rage,
> And told the people he had none:
> The fond spectators said, he acted wrong,
> The dumbest man may say, he hath no tongue.

>   John Weever, *Epigrammes* 6, 'In Ruffinum'

41. 1600

Gentlemen, Gallants, and you my little Swaggerers that fight lowe . . . I recant, beare witness all you Gentle-folkes (that walke i'th Galleries) I recant the opinions which I helde of Courtiers, Ladies, and Citizens, when once (in an assembly of Friars) I railde upon them.

>   Dekker, *Satiromastix*, Epilogus

42. 1600

> Speak gentlemen, what shall we do today? . . .
> Or shall we to the Globe to see a play?
> Or visit Shoreditch for a bawdy house?

>   Samuel Rowlands, *The Letting of Humours Blood in the Head-Vaine*,
>   Epigram 7

43. 1600

I rembred one of them to be a noted Cut-purse, such a one as we tye to a poast on our stage, for all people to wonder at, when at a play they are taken pilfring.

>   Will Kemp, *Kemps nine daies wonder*, B1r

44. 1600

> [If he could paint spotless Chastity truly]
> Then light-taylde huswives which like *Syrens* sing,
> And like to *Circes* with their drugs enchant,
> Would not unto the Banke-sides round house fling,
> In open sight themselves to show and vaunt:
> Then then I say they would not marked goe,
> Though unseene to see those they faine would know.

>   John Lane, *Tom Tell-Troths Message, and His Pens Complaint*, F3r

45. 1600

. . . the gentlewoman that sware by her trouth, *That she was as much edefied at a play as ever she was at any sermon, etc.* will, ere she die, be of another minde, though it may be shee saied true then, in regard of her owne negligence and backwardnes in not giving eare to the word of God with reverence. The like may fall out also to those men too, that have not bene afraid of late dayes to bring upon the Stage the very sober countenances, grave attire, modest and matronlike gestures & speaches of men & women to be laughed at as a scorne and reproch to the world . . . Well to heale, if it may be, or at least, to correct the bad humour of such humorists as these (who in their discovery of humours doe withall fouly discover their own shame and

wretchednes to the world) here is now laied before thee (good Reader) a most
excellent remedie and receipt.

> Richard Schilders, The Printer to the Reader, in Rainolds, *The Overthrow of Stage Playes*, A3v–4r

46. 1600

> [The author's] violence proceeds not from a minde
> That grudgeth pleasure to this generous presence,
> But doth protest all due respect and love
> Unto this choise selected influence . . .
> And vowes not to torment your listning eares
> With mouldy fopperies of stale Poetry . . . (Prologue)
> . . . I saw the Children of *Powles* last night . . .
> Ifaith I like the Audience that frequenteth there
> With much applause: A man shall nor be choakte
> With the stench of Garlicke, nor be pasted
> To the barmy Jacket of a Beer-brewer . . .
> . . . Tis a good gentle Audience . . . (Act 5)

> Marston, *Jack Drum's Entertainment*

47. 1600?

> With those the thronged Theaters that presse,
> I in the Circuit for the Lawrell strove:
> Where, the full Prayse I freely must confesse,
> In heat of Bloud, a modest Mind might move.
> With Showts and Claps at ev'ry little pawse,
> When the proud Round on ev'ry side hath rung,
> Sadly I sit, unmov'd with the Applause,
> As though to me it nothing did belong.

> Drayton, *Idea*, Sonnet 47 (*Works*, ed. Hebel, II.334)

48. 1601

> If thousands flocke to heare a Poets pen,
> To heare a god, how many millions then? . . .
> Wit, spend thy vigour, Poets, wits quintessence,
> *Hermes*, make great the worlds eies with teares:
> *Actors* make sighes a burden for each sentence:
> That he may sob which reades, he swound which
>   heares.

> John Weever, *The Mirror of Martyrs*, A3v, F3v

49. 1601

. . . *sineor Snuffe, Mounsieur Mew*, and *Cavaliero Blirt*, are three of the
most to bee fear'd Auditors . . .

> . . . beleeve it *Doricus* his spirit
> Is higher blouded then to quake and pant
> At the report of *Skoffes* Artillery;
> Shall he be creast-falne, if some looser braine,
> In flux of witte uncively befilth

His slight composures? shall his bosome faint
If drunken *Censure* belch out sower breath,
From *Hatreds* surfet on his labours front?
Nay say some halfe a dozen rancorous breasts
Should plant them-selves on purpose to discharge
Impostum'd malice on his latest Sceane
Shall his resolve be struck through with the blirt,
Of a goose breath? What imperfect borne?
What short-liv'd *Meteor*? what cold-harted Snow
Would melt in dolor? cloud his mudded eyes
Sinck downe his jawes, if that some juicles husk
Some boundlesse ignorance should on sudden shoote
His grosse knob'd burbolt, with *that's not so good,*
Mew, blirt, ha, ha, light Chaffy stuff:

[the Prologue protests that he will be put off by] . . . the female presence; the Genteletza; the women will put me out . . . [to which Doricus replies] . . . and so we leave thee to the kinde Gentlemen, and most respected Auditors.

This is the straine that chokes the theaters:
That makes them crack with full stufft audience,
This is your humor onely in request
Forsooth to raile, this brings your eares to bed,
This people gape for, for this some doe stare
This some would heare, to crack the Authors neck,
This admiration and applause persues.

Marston, *What You Will*, Induction; 3.2

50. 1602

At our feast wee had a play called 'twelve Night, or what you will'; much like the commedy of errores, or Menechmi in Plautus, but most like and neere to that in Italian called *Inganni*. A good practise in it to make the Steward beleeve his Lady widdowe was in Love with him, by counterfayting a letter as from his Lady, in generall termes, telling him what shee liked best in him, and prescribing his gesture in smiling, his apparaile, &c., and then when he came to practise, making him beleeve they tooke him to be mad.

John Manningham, *Diary*, ed. R. Parker Sorlien, p. 48

51. 1602

. . . they did not only presse gentlemen, and sarvingmen, but Lawyers, Clarkes, country men that had lawe causes, aye the Quenes men, knightes, and as it was credibly reported one Earle, quight contrary to that the councell, and especyally my L. Cheif Justice intended.

Philip Gawdy, *Letters*, ed. Jeayes, pp. 120–1

52. 1602

[At Richard Vennar's Swan extravaganza] there was great store of good companie and many noble men.

John Chamberlain, *Letters*, I.172

53. 1602

MISTRESS PURGE. Hither I come from out the harmless fold
        To have my good name eaten up by wolves:
        See, how they grin!
    Middleton (?), *The Family of Love*, 5.3

54. 1603

. . . there was a stage Play plaied by the children of Powles concerning
a barber & others & this defendant thinketh that the same Play was meant
by this defendant & his daughter & Mris Sharles John Flaskett & others, all
which Play he did once sitt together with Flaskett & sawe the same, being
unawares unto him brought to sitt by Flaskett to see the Play. And further he
hath heard manie say that the Play was made of this defendant & his daughter
& also of others.
    John Howe, deposition in Star Chamber, quoted by C. J. Sisson, *Lost Plays
    of Shakespeare's Age*, p. 77

55. 1603

. . . a Play is like a sincke in a Towne, whereunto all the filth doth
runne: or a byle in the body, that draweth all the ill humours unto it . . . is
it fit that the infirmities of holy men should be acted on a Stage . . . there is
no passion wherwith the king, the soveraigne majestie of the Realme was
possest, but is amplified and openly sported with, and made a May-game to
all the beholders.
    Henry Crosse, *Vertues Commonwealth*, P3r

56. 1603

The second moneth of *February* is more fertile of rubricate Martyrs,
then *January*, for that yt hath 8 in number, two Wickliffians, *Syr* John
Oldcastle, a Ruffian-knight as all England knoweth, & commonly brought in
by comediants on their stages: he was put to death for robberyes and rebellion
under the foresaid *K. Henry* the fifth.
    Robert Parsons (Dolman), *The Third Part of a Treatise, Intituled: of three
    Conversions of England*, D2v

57. 1603

. . . my very fine Heliconian gallants, and you my worshipful friends in
the middle region . . .
    Marston, *The Dutch Courtesan*, 5. 3

58. 1603

the whole Neast of Ants . . . made a Ring about her and their restored
friend, serving in stead of a dull Audience of Stinkards sitting in the Penny
Galleries of a Theater, and yawning upon the Players, whilst the Ant began
to stalke like a three Quarter sharer . . . the Campe had bene supplied with
Harlots too, as wel as the Curtaine . . . [a gallant after dinner] must venture
beyond sea, that is, in a choice paire of Noble mens Oares, to the Bank-side,
where he must sit out the breaking up of a Comedie, or the first cut of a
Tragedie; or rather (if his humour so serve him) to call in at the Black-fryers,
where he shall see a neast of Boyes able to ravish a man.
    Middleton (?), *Father Hubburds Tale*, B4r, C1v, D1r

59. 1604

> Faith, that same vein of railing
> Becomes now most applausive; your best poet is
> He that rails grossest.

Chapman, *All Fools*, 2.1

60. 1604

. . . the tragedie of Gowrie with all the action and actors hath ben twise represented by the Kings players, with exceding concourse of all sortes of people, but whether the matter or manner be not well handled, or that yt be thought unfit that princes should be plaide on the stage in theyre life time, I heare that some great counsaillors are much displeased with yt: and so is thought shalbe forbidden.

Chamberlain to Winwood, *Letters*, I.199

61. 1605

> [of a burlesque city pageant]
> O may you find in this our pageant, here,
> The same contentment which you came to seek,
> And as that show but draws you once a year,
> May this attract you hither once a week.

Jonson, *Eastward Ho!* epilogue

62. 1605

> Yet, thus much I can give you, as a token
> Of his PLAYES worth, No egges are broken;
> Nor quaking Custards with feirce teeth affrighted,
> Wherewith your rout are so delighted;
> Nor hales hee in a *Gull*, old ends reciting,
> To stop gappes in his loose writing;
> With such a deale of monstrous, and forc'd *action*
> As might make *Bethlem* a faction . . .
> All gall, and coppresse, from his inke, he drayneth,
> Onelie, a little salt remaineth.

Jonson, *Volpone*, prologue

63. 1605

> . . . like a looker on a Tragedie
> within the Middle Roome, among the meane,
> I see the fall of State and Majesty
> While mongst the Presse t'a Piller sure I leane:
> So see I others sorrowes with delight
> Though others sorrowes do but make me sadd:
> . . .
> In few, there may I see how all Estates
> That lifted are above the myrry Meane,
> Do, falling stand twixt Dangers and Debates,
> Whiles of their Falls I make a swelling Sceane.

John Davies of Hereford, *Wittes Pilgrimage*, 'Fortuna vitrea est', 37–69

64. 1605

> One tould a Drover that beleev'd it not,
> What booties at the playes the Cut-purse got,
> But if twere so my Drovers wit was quicke,
> He vow'd to serve the Cut-purse a new tricke.
> Next day unto the play, pollicy hy'd,
> A bagge of fortie shillings by his side,
> Which houlding fast hee taketh up his stand,
> If stringes be cut his purse is in his hand.
> A fine conceited Cut-purse spying this,
> Lookt for no more, the fortie shillings his,
> Whilst my fine Politique gazed about,
> The Cut-purse feately tooke the bottom out.
> And cuts the strings, good foole goe make a jest,
> This Dismall day they purse was fairely blest.
> Houlde fast good Noddy tis good to dread the worse,
> Your monie's gone, I pray you keepe your purse.
> The Play is done and foorth the foole doth goe,
> Being glad that he cousned the Cut-purse soe.
> He thought to jybe how he the Cut-purse drest.
> And memorize it for a famous jest.
> But putting in his hand it ran quight throw
> Dash't the conceite, heele never speake on't now,
> You that to playes have such delight to goe,
> The Cut-purse cares not, still deceive him so.

Samuel Rowlands, *Humors Antique Faces*, D1r

65. 1606

. . . their houses smoakt every after noone with Stinkards who were so glewed together in crowdes with the Steames of strong breath, that when they came foorth, their faces lookt as if they had beene per boylde . . . tis given out that *Sloth* himselfe will come, and sit in the two pennie galleries amongst the Gentlemen.

Dekker, *Seven Deadly Sinnes* (*Non-Dramatic Works*, II.53)

66. 1606

2 GENT. And where sits [the author's] friends? hath he not a prepard company of gallants, to aplaud his jests, and grace out his play.

PROL. None I protest: Doe Poets use to bespeake their Auditory.

2 GENT. The best in grace doe, and but for that, some that I know, had never had their grace in Poetry till this day . . .

PROL. Alas Gentlemen, how ist possible to content you? you will have rayling, and invectives, which our Author neither dares, nor affects: you baudy and scurrill jests, which neither becomes his modestie to write, nor the eare of a generous Auditory to heare: you must ha swelling comparisons, and bumbast Epithetes, which are as fit for the body of a Comedie, as *Hercules* shooe for the foote of a Pygmey . . .

> Neither quick mirth, invective, nor high state,
> Can content all: such is the boundless hate
> Of a confused audience.

John Day, *The Isle of Gulls*, Induction

67. 1606

At this time there was much speech of a play in the Black Friars, where, in the 'Isle of Gulls', from the highest to the lowest, all men's parts were acted of two divers nations: as I understand sundry were committed to Bridewell.

Sir Thomas Edmondes, February 1606 (*Court and Times of James I*, ed. T. Birch, I.60–1)

68. 1606

> And if yee list to exercise your Vayne,
> Or in the Sock, or in the Buskin'd Strayne . . .
> The thick-brayn'd Audience lively to awake,
> Till with shrill Claps the Theater doe shake.

Michael Drayton, 'The Sacrifice to Apollo', ode (*Works*, ed. Hebel, II.358)

69. 1606

> Spectators know, you may with freest faces
> Behold this Scene, for here no rude disgraces
> Shall taint a publique, or a privat name.

John Marston, *The Fawn*, prologue

70. 1606

Hell being under everie one of their *Stages*, the Players . . . might with a false Trappe doore have slipt [the devil] downe, and there kept him, as a laughing stocke to al their yawning Spectators.

Dekker, *Newes from Hell* (*Non-Dramatic Works*, II.92)

71. 1606

> If sceans exempt from ribaldrie or rage
> Of taxinges indiscreet, may please the stage,
> If such may hope applause, he not commandes
> Yet craves as due, the justice of your hands.

John Marston, *Sophonisba*, epilogue

72. 1606

. . . though *bodies* oft-times have the ill luck to be sensually preferr'd, they find afterwards, the good fortune (when *soules* live) to be utterly forgotten. This it is hath made the most royall *Princes*, and greatest *persons* (who are commonly the *personators* of these *actions*) not onely studious of riches, and magnificence in the outward celebration, or shew: (which rightly becomes them) but curious after the most high, and heartie *inventions*, to furnish the inward parts: (and those grounded upon *antiquitie*, and solid *learnings*) which, though their *voyce* be taught to sound to present occasions, their *sense*, or doth, or should alwayes lay hold on more remov'd *mysteries*.

Jonson, *Hymeniae*, preface

73. *c.*1606

NOBODY . . . *somebody* once pickt a pocket in this Play-house yard, Was hoysted on the stage, and shamd about it.

> Anon., *No-body and Some-body*, I1v

74. 1607

If there be any amongst you, that came to heare lascivious Scenes, let them depart: for I doe pronounce this, to the utter discomfort of all two peny Gallerie men, you shall have no bawdrie in it: or if there bee any lurking amongst you in corners, with Table bookes, who have some hope to find fit matter to feede his – mallice on, let them claspe them up, and slinke away, or stay and be converted. For he that made this Play, meanes to please Auditors so, as hee may bee an Auditor himselfe hereafter, and not purchase them with the deare losse of his eares.

> Francis Beaumont, *The Woman Hater*, Apologetical prologue

75. 1607

A Wench having a good face, a good body, and good clothes on, but of bad conditions, sitting one day in the two-penny roome of a play-house, & a number of yong Gentlemen about her, against all whom she maintaind talke, One that sat over the stage, sayd to his friend: doe you not thinke that yonder flesh will stincke anon, having so many flyes blowing upon it. Oh (quoth his friend) I thinke it stinckes already, for I never saw so many crowes together but there was some carion not far off.

> Dekker, *Jests to Make You Merry* (*Non-Dramatic Works*, II.292)

76. 1607

. . . the basest stinkard in London, whose breth is stronger then Garlicke, and able to poison all the 12. penny roomes.

> Dekker, *The Ravens Almanacke* (*Non-Dramatic Works*, IV.1941)

77. 1608

Pay thy two-pence to a *Player*, in his gallerie maist thou sitte by a harlot.

> Dekker, *Lanthorne and Candlelight* (*Non-Dramatic Works*, III.216–17)

78. 1608

His ma' was well pleased with that which your lo. advertiseth concerning the committing of the players yt have offended in ye matters of France, and commanded me to signifye to your lo. that for ye others who have offended in ye matter of ye Mynes and other lewd words which is ye children of ye blackfriers That though he had signified his mynde to your lo. by my lo. of Montgommery yet I should repeate it again That his G. has vowed they should never play more but should first begg their bred and he wold have his vow performed. And therefore my lo. chamberlain by himselfe or your ll. at the table should take order to dissolve them, and to punish the maker besides.

> Sir Thomas Lake to Lord Salisbury, 11 March 1608 (*Malone Society Collections* II.2, 1923, p. 149)

79. 1608

. . . satiric inveighing at any man's private person (a kind of writing which of late seems to have been very familiar among our poets and players, to their cost).

> H. Parrott, *The More the Merrier*, epistle

80. 1608

[The Profane] . . . comes to Church as to the Theater, saving that not so willinglie, for companie, for custome, for recreation, perhaps for sleepe; or to feed his eyes or his eares.

> Joseph Hall, *Characters* of *Vertues and Vices*, H1r

81. 1608

[referring to *The Puritan*, 1607] . . . now they bring religion and holy things upon the stage . . . Two hypocrites must be brought foorth; and how shall they be described but by these names, *Nicholas S. Antlings, Simon S. Maryoveries* . . . by these miscreants thus dishonoured, and that not on the stage only, but even in print.

> William Crashaw, *The Sermon preached at the Crosse, Feb. xiiij, 1607* (i.e. 1608)

82. 1608

> Is she that Marchants wife? I know that face,
> And sure have seene it, in some other place,
> Lets see, did I not meete her on the way?
> Or se her at a Sermon, or a Play?
> Or where was it? Ifaith t'would pleasse me well,
> If I for certeinty the place could tell:
> Oh now I have't, but tis not worth a louse:
> Twas but her picture, at a baudy house.

> Richard West, *Wits A. B. C., Or a Centurie of Epigrams*, 1608

83. *c.*1608

> [Spongus] Plays at Primero over the stage.

> Farmer-Chetham manuscript (*ES* II.535)

84. 1609

> Ile thinke
> As abjectly of thee, as any Mongrill
> Bred in the Citty; Such a Citizen
> As the Playes flout still.

> Nathaniel Field, A *Woman is a Weathercock*, 2.1

85. 1609

. . . when at a new play you take up the twelve-penny room next the stage; (because the Lords and you may seeme to be haile fellow wel-met) there draw forth this booke, read alowd, laugh alowd, and play the *Antickes*, that all the garlicke mouthd stinkards may cry out, *Away with the fool* . . . The Theater is your Poets Royal Exchange . . . Your Gallant, your Courtier, and your Capten, had wont to be the soundest paymaisters . . . your *Groundling*, and *gallery-Commoner* buyes his sport by the penny . . . Sithence then the place is so free in entertainment, allowing a stoole as well to the Farmers

sonne as to your Templer: that your Stinkard has the selfe-same libertie to
be there in his Tobacco-Fumes, which your sweet Courtier hath: and that
your Car-man and Tinker claime as strong a voice in their suffrage, and sit to
give judgement on the plaies life and death, as well as the prowdest *Momus*
among the tribe of *Critick*: It is fit that hee, whom the most tailors bils do
make roome for, when he comes, should not be basely (like a vyoll) casd up
in a corner . . .

> Dekker, *The Gull's Hornbook*, Proemium and Chapter 6 (*Non-Dramatic
> Works*, II.203, 246–7)

86. 1609

The quick eares [of a Court audience contrast with] those sluggish ones
of Porters, and Mechanicks, that must be bor'd through, at every act, with
Narrations.

> Jonson, *The Masque* of *Queens*, 107–10

87. 1609

> Amazde I stood, to see a Crowd
> Of *Civill Throats* stretcht out so lowd;
> (As at a *New Play*) all the Roomes
> Did swarme with *Gentiles* mix'd with *Groomes*,
> So that I truly thought all These
> Came to see *Shore* or *Pericles*.
>> Anon., *Pimlyco, or Runne Red-Cap*, Clr

88. 1609

Tearme times, when the *Two-peny Clients*, and *Peny Stinkards* swarme
together to heere the *Stagerites*.

> Dekker, *Worke for Armourers* (*Non-Dramatic Works*, IV.96)

89. *c.*1609

It is a pastorall Tragie-comedie, which the people seeing when it was
plaid, having ever had a singuler guift in defining, concluded to be a play
of country hired Shepheards in gray cloakes, with curtaild dogs in strings,
sometimes laughing together, and sometimes killing one another: And
missing whitsun ales, creame, wassel and morris-dances, began to be angry.

> John Fletcher, *The Faithful Shepherdess*, epistle

90. *c.*1609

> The wise, and many headed *Bench*, that sits
> Upon the Life, and Death of *Playes*, and *Wits*,
> (Composed of *Gamster, Captaine, Knight, Knights man,*
> *Lady*, or *Pusill*, that weares maske or fan,
> *Velvet*, or *Taffeta* cap, rank'd in the darke
> With the shops *Foreman* or some such *brave sparke*,
> That may judge for his *sixe-pence*) had, before
> They saw it halfe, damd the whole Play . . .
>> Jonson, *The Faithful Shepherdess*, commendatory verses

91. *c.*1609

> Why should the man, whose wit nere had a straine,
> Upon the publike stage present his vaine,

And make a thousand men in judgement sit,
To call in question his undoubted wit,
Scarce two of which can understand the lawes
Which they should judge by, nor the parties cause . . .
But since it was thy happe to throw away,
Much wit, for which the people did not pay,
Because they saw it not, I not dislike
This second publication, which may strike
Their consciences, to see the thing they scornd,
To be with so much will and art adornd.
Bisides one vantage more in this I see,
Your censurers must have the quallitie
Of reading, which I am afraid is more
Then halfe your shreudest judges had before.

Beaumont, *The Faithful Shepherdess*, commendatory verses

92. *c.*1609

Such art, it should me better satisfie,
Then if the monster clapt his thousand hands,
And drownd the sceane with his confused cry . . .

Nathaniel Field, *The Faithful Shepherdess*, commendatory verses

93. 1610

Momus would act the fooles part in a play,
And 'cause he would be exquisite that way,
Hies me to London, where no day can passe,
But that some play-house still his presence has.
Now at the *Globe* with a judicious eye,
Into the Vice's action doth he prie.
Next to the *Fortune*, where it is a chaunce,
But he marks something worth his cognisance.
Then to the *Curtaine*, where, as at the rest,
He notes that action downe that likes him best.
Being full fraught, at length he gets him home,
And *Momus* now, know's how to play the Mome . . .
Fie on this Mimick still, it marres his part:
Nature would doe farre better without art.

John Heath, *Two Centuries of Epigrammes*, E3r–v

94. 1610

. . . in Playes: wherein, now, the Concupiscence of Daunces, and Antickes
so raigneth, as to runne away from Nature, and be afraid of her, is the onely
point of art that tickles the *Spectators*. (*To* the Reader)
. . . Judging Spectators . . . (Prologue)

Jonson, *The Alchemist*

95. 1611

A GALLANT at a Play, that usde to brall
Abus'd as many as but neere him came;

At last they fell on him, while they could fall,
Till they by Death had made that tiger tame.
For which some were attach'd as murderers:
(Through them on him he with strong hand did draw)
So with the cheife were some cheife furtherers
Arraignd, condemnd and so trust up by law.
    Thus he (like Sampson) on him and his foes
    Puld a whole house, to both their over-throes.
      John Davies of Hereford, *The Scourge of Folly*, [1611], Epigram 159

96. 1611

[Marion Frith] . . . being at a play about three quarters of a yeare since at ye Fortune in man's apparel and in her boots and with a sword at her syde she told the company then present yt she thought many of them were of opinion that she was a man, but if any of them would come to her lodging they should finde she is a woman, and some other immodest and lascivious speaches she also used at yt time. And also sat upon the stage in the public viewe of all the people there present in man's apparel and played upon her lute and sange a song.
      Consistory of London Correction Book, 1611–12 (*JCS* VI.147)

97. 1612

The fashion of play-making, I can properly compare to nothing, so naturally, as the alteration in apparell. For in the time of the Great-crop-doublet, your huge bombasted plaies, quilted with mighty words to leane purpose was onely then in fashion. And as the doublet fell, neater inventions beganne to set up. Now in the time of sprucenes, our plaies followe the nicenes of our Garments, single plots, quaint conceits, letcherous jests, drest up in hanging sleeves, and those are fit for the Times and Tearmers. (Epistle)
    Within one square a thousand heads are laid
    So close, that all of heads, the roome seemes made. (1.2)
      Middleton and Dekker, *The Roaring Girl*

98. 1612

    If then the world a Theater present,
    As by the roundnesse it appeares most fit,
    Built with starre-galleries of hye ascent,
    In which, *Jehove* doth as spectator sit.
    And chiefe determiner to'applaud the best . . .
      Heywood, 'The Author to his Booke', *An Apology for Actors*

99. 1612

Now to speake of some abuse lately crept into the quality, as an inveighing against the State, the Court, the Law, the Citty, and their governements, with the particularising of private mens humours (yet alive) Noble-men, & others. I know it distastes many; neither do I any way approve it, nor dare I by any meanes excuse it. The liberty, which some arrogate to themselves, committing their bitternesse, and liberall invectives against all estates, to the mouthes of Children, supposing their juniority to be a priviledge for any rayling, be it never so violent, I could advise all such, to curbe and limit this presumed liberty within the bands of discretion and government.

Thomas Heywood, An *Apology for Actors*, G3v

100. 1612

. . . it was acted, in so dull a time of Winter, presented in so open and blacke a Theater, that it wanted (that which is the onely grace and setting out of a Tragedy) a full and understanding Auditory: and that since that time I have noted, most of the people that come to that Play-house, resemble those ignorant asses (who visiting Stationers' shoppes, their use is not to inquire for good bookes, but new bookes) I present it to the generall view.

John Webster, *The White Devil*, epistle

101. 1612

> But tis with *Poets* now, as tis with Nations,
> Th'il-favouredst *Vices*, are the bravest *Fashions*.
> A Play whose *Rudenes, Indians* would abhorre,
> Ift fill a house with Fishwives, *Rare, They All Roare*.
> It is not Praise is sought for (Now) but *Pence*,
> Tho dropd, from Greasie-apron *Audience* . . .
> [the verse] Can call the *Banishd* Auditor home, And tye
> His Eare (with golden chaines) to his Melody:
> Can draw with *Adamantine Pen*, (even creatures
> Forg'de out of *th'Hammer*,) on tiptoe, to *Reach*-up,
> And (from *Rare silence*) clap their *Brawny hands*,
> T' *Applaud*, what their *charmd* soule scarce understands.
> That Man give mee; whose Brest fill'd by the *Muses*,
> With Raptures, Into a second, them infuses:
> Can give an Actor, Sorrow, Rage, Joy, Passion,
> Whilst hee againe (by selfe-same Agitation)
> Commands the *Hearers*, sometimes drawing out *Teares*,
> Then smiles, and fills them both with *Hopes* and *Feares* . . .

Dekker, *If This Be Not a Good Play, the Devil is in it*, prologue

102. 1612

I wish a *Faire* and *Fortunate Day*, to your *Next New-Play* (for the *Makers-sake* and your *Owne*), because such *Brave Triumphes of Poesie*, and *Elaborate Industry*, which my *Worthy Friends Muse* hath there set forth, deserve a *Theater* full of very *Muses* themselves to be *Spectators*. To that *Faire Day* I wish a *Full, Free*, and *Knowing Auditor*. And to that *Full Audience, One Honest Doore-Keeper*.

Dekker, *If This Be Not a Good Play*, dedication to the Queen's Men

103. 1612

An Order for suppressinge of Jigges att the ende of Playes – Whereas Complaynte have beene made at this last Generall Sessions, that by reason of certayne lewde Jigges songes and daunces used and accustomed at the playhouse called the Fortune in Goulding lane, divers cutt-purses and other lewde and ill disposed persons in great multitudes doe resorte thither at the end of everye playe, many tymes causinge tumultes and outrages . . .

Middlesex General Session of the Peace, 1 October 1612 (*ES* IV.340–1)

104. 1612.

> . . . silken gulls and ignorant Cittizens.

Robert Daborne, Prefatory epistle to *A Christian Turned Turk*

105. 1613?

> All we have done we aim at your content,
> Striving to illustrate things not known to all,
> In which the learn'd can censure right;
> The rest we crave, whom we unletter'd call,
> Rather to attend than judge; for more than sight
> We seek to please.

Heywood, *The Brazen Age*, prologue

106. 1613

> That's the fat foole of the Curtin,
> and the leane foole of the Bull:
> Since *Shanke* did leave to sing his rimes,
> he is counted but a gull.
> The players of the Banke side,
> the round Globe and the Swan,
> Will teach you idle trickes of love,
> but the Bull will play the man.

William Turner, *A Dish of Lenten Stuffe* (*A Pepysian Garland*, ed. Rollins, p. 35)

107. 1613

> His Poetry is such as he can cul
> From plaies he heard at *Curtaine* or at *Bul*,
> And yet is fine coy Mistres *Marry Muffe*,
> The soonest taken with such broken stuffe.

George Wither, *Abuses Stript and Whipt*, first satire

108. 1613

These are the youths that thunder at a playhouse, and fight for bitten apples: that no audience but the tribulation of Tower Hill, or the limbs of Limehouse, their dear brothers, are able to endure.   (5. 4)

> 'Tis ten to one this play can never please
> All that are here: some come to take their ease
> And sleep an hour or two; but those we fear
> W'have frighted with our trumpets, so 'tis clear
> They'll say 'tis naught: others to hear the City
> Abus'd extremely, and to cry 'That's witty',
> Which we have not done neither. (Epilogue)

Fletcher, *Henry VIII*

109. 1613

The Kings Players had a new Play, called *All is true*, representing some principal pieces of the Reign of *Henry* the *8th*, which was set forth with many extraordinary Circumstances of Pomp and Majesty, even to the matting of the Stage; the Knights of the Order, with their Georges and Garter, the Guards with their embroidered Coats, and the like: sufficient in truth within a while to make Greatness very familiar, if not ridiculous. Now, King *Henry* making a Masque at the Cardinal *Wolsey's* House, and certain Cannons being shot of at his entry, some of the Paper, or other stuff, wherewith one of them was stopped, did light on the Thatch, where being thought at first but an idle smoak, and their Eyes more attentive to the show, it kindled inwardly, and ran round like a train, consuming within less than an hour the whole House to the very ground.

> Henry Wotton, letter to Edmund Bacon, *Reliquiae Wottoniae*, 1685, pp. 425–6

110. 1613

. . . my Pantalone often goes out now all alone, though with a faithful interpreter who walks a little in front to show him the way. He goes about saying that he's travelling incognito, and goodness knows where he ends up. He often goes to the plays in these parts. Among others, he went the other day to a playhouse called the Curtain, which is out beyond his house. It is an infamous place in which no good citizen or gentleman would show his face. And what was worse, in order not to pay a royal, or a scudo, to go in one of the little rooms, not even to sit in the degrees that are there, he insisted on standing in the middle down below among the gang of porters and carters, giving as his excuse that he was hard of hearing – as if he could have understood the language anyway! But it didn't end there because, at the end of the performance, having received permission from one of the actors, he invited the public to the play for the next day, and named one. But the people, who wanted a different one, began to call out 'Friars, Friars' because they wanted the one that they called 'Friars'. Then, turning to his interpreter, my Tambalone asked what they were saying. The interpreter replied that it was the name of a play about friars. Then, he, bursting out of his cloak, began to clap his hands as the people were doing and to yell 'Friars, Friars'. But at this racket the people turned on him, thinking him to be a Spaniard, and began to whistle at him in such a fashion that I don't think he'll ever want to go back there again. But that doesn't stop him frequenting the other theatres, and almost always with just one servant.

> Antimo Galli, in Orrell, 'Letters from the Florentine Correspondence', p. 171

111. 1614

. . . you think you have undone me, think so still, and swallow that belief, till you be company for Court-hand Clarks, and starved Atturnies, till you break in at playes like Prentices for three a groat, and crack Nuts with the Scholars in peny Rooms again, and fight for Apples, till you return to what I found you . . .

> Fletcher, *Wit Without Money*, 4.1

112. 1614

Hee that will sweare, *Jeronimo*, or *Andronicus* are the best playes, yet, shall passe unexcepted at, heere, as man whose Judgement shewes it is constant, and hath stood still, these five and twentie, or thirtie yeeres.

> Jonson, *Bartholomew Fair*, Induction

113. 1614

The Players have all (except the King's Men) left their usuall residency on the Banke-side, and doe play in Middlesex farre remote from the Thames, so that every day in the weeke they doe drawe unto them three or four thousand people, that were used to spend their monies by water, (to the reliefe of so many thousands of poore people, which by Players former playing on the Banke-side are encreased) so that oft-times a poore man that hath five or six children, doth give good attendance to his labour all day, and at night (perhaps) hath not gotten a Groat to relieve himselfe, his wife and family.

John Taylor, *The True Cause of the Water-mens Suit . . .* (*Works*, 1630, p. 172)

114. 1614

. . . a *Water-bearer* on the floore of a *Play-house* [admires] a wide-mouth'de *Player.* (*An Hypocrite*)

. . . he hath heard one mooting, and seen two plaies. (*A Fantasticke Innes of Court man*)

He hath sworn to see *London* once a yeare, though all his businesse be to see a Play, walke a turne in *Paules*, and observe the fashion. (*A meere Fellow of an House* [i.e. a College])

. . . eates Ginger bread at a Play-house. (*A Puny-Clarke*)

He withers his Cloathes on the Stage, as a Sale-man is forc't to doe his Suits in Birchin-Lane; and when the Play is done, if you but mark his rising, 'tis a kind of walking Epilogue between the two Candles, to know if his Suite may passe for currant. (*A Phantastique*)

The Play-houses only keepe him sober; and as it doth many other Gallants, make him an afternoones man. (*A Water-Man*)

Thomas Overbury, *Characters*, ed. Paylor, pp. 41, 45, 46, 52, 60, 68

115. 1615

[at university plays] And who are the spectators? but such like as both Poets and Actors are, even as such as reckon no more of their studies, then spend-all Gentlemen of their cast sutes . . . [against Heywood's *Apology*] In what a doubtfull case would the use of playes then stand, if none but fooles (as commonly they are) or none but blindmen were their auditors? the one kind could not understand, the other could not see, and consequently neither give right judgement of them.

J. G., *A Refutation of the Apology for Actors*, C2r, F1v

116. 1615

And when hee heares his play hissed, hee would rather thinke bottle-Ale is opening. (*A base Mercenary Poet*)

John Stephens, *Satyrical Essayes. Characters and Others*, p. 292 (V4v)

117. 1615

When he doth hold conference upon the stage; and should looke directly in his fellows face; hee turnes about his voice into the assembly for applause-sake, like a Trumpeter in the fields, that shifts places to get an eccho.

J. Cocke, 'A Common Player', in Stephens, *Satyrical Essayes*, p. 292 (V7r)

118. 1615

Sit in a full Theater, and you will thinke you see so many lines drawne from the circumference of so many eares, whiles the *Actor* is the *Center* . . . what we see him personate, we thinke truely done before us: a man of deepe thought might apprehend, the Ghosts of our ancient *Heroes* walk't againe, and take him (at severall times) for many of them . . . He entertaines us in the best leasure of our life, that is betweene meales, the most unfit time, either for study or bodily exercise.

> Anon. (Webster?), 'An Excellent Actor', *New Characters*, M5v–6v

119. 1615

> Ide have a plaie could I but to my mind
> Good actors gett, but thats not now to find
> For (oh) thare dead; this age afordeth none,
> Good actors all longe since are dead and gone
> For beggars parte a Courtyer I would have . . .
> But oh the Divell! I am graveld nowe
> To finde a Divell out I knowe not howe
> And with out one my plaie shall nere come forth
> For with out Divells, plaies are nothing worth
> > *Mas I have thought of one for gold heel come*
> > *An exlent actor is the Pope of Rome* . . .   (Epigram 12)
> Wouldst thou turne Rorer boye? wouldst growe in fashon
> Learne this garbe then, shalt gaine faire reputation
> Tobacco take; run in each mercers score
> Visit plaies, be seene to court thy whore
> Laughe at learning . . .   (Epigram 36)
> Goe to your plaie-howse you shall actors have
> Your baude, your gull, your whore, your pandar knave
> Goe to your bawdie howse, y'ave actors too
> As bawdes, and whores, and gulls: pandars also.
> Besides, in eyther howse (yf you enquire)
> A place there is for men themselves to tire
> > *Since th'are soe like, to choose ther'es not a pinn*
> > *Whether bawdye-howse or plaie-howse you goe in.*   (Epigram 64)
> > William Goddard, *A Neaste of Waspes*

120. 1615

[a rustic clown, Trincalo, woos his mistress] . . . then will I confound her with complements drawn from the Plaies I see at the Fortune and the Red Bull, where I learne all the words I speake and understand not.

> Thomas Tomkis, *Albumazar*, C1r

121. 1615?

> Now talk of this, and then discoursed of that,
> Spoke our owne verses, 'twixt our selves, if not
> Other men's lines, which we by chance had got,

Or some Stage pieces famous long before,
Of which your happy memory had store . . .

Michael Drayton, 'To my most dearely-loved friend, HENRY REYNOLDS Esquire, of Poets & Poesie' (*Minor Poems*, ed. Cyril Brett, p. 108)

122. 1615?

He rather prayes, you will be pleas'd to see
One such, to day, as other playes should be.
Where neither *Chorus* wafts you ore the seas,
Nor creaking throne comes downe, the boyes to please;
Nor nimble squibbe is seene, to make afear'd
The Gentlewomen . . .

Jonson, prologue to *Every Man in his Humour*, 1616 Folio

123. 1616

. . . sweet Poesye
Is oft convict, condem'd, and judg'd to die
Without just triall, by a multitude
Whose judgements are illiterate and rude.
Witnesse *Sceianus*, whose approved worth,
Sounds from the calme South, to the freezing North.
And on the perfum'd wings of *Zephorus*,
In triumph mounts as farre as *Aeolus*,
With more then humane art it was bedewed,
Yet to the multitude it nothing shewed;
They screwed their scurvy jawes and look't awry,
Like hissing snakes adjudging it to die:
When wits of gentry did applaud the same,
With silver shouts of high lowd sounding fame:
Whil'st understanding grounded men contemn'd it,
And wanting wit (like fooles to judge) condemn'd it.
Clapping, or hissing, is the onely meane
That tries and searches out a well writ *Sceane*.
So is it thought by *Ignoramus* crew,
But that good wits acknowledge's untrue;
The stinkards oft will hisse without a cause,
And for a baudy jeast will give applause.
Let one but aske the reason why they roare
They'll answere, cause the rest did so before.

William Fennor, *Fennors Descriptions*, epistle, 'The Description of a Poet', B2r–3r

124. 1616

Player is much out of countenance, if fooles doe not laugh at them, boyes clappe their hands, pesants ope their throates, and the rude rascal rabble cry excellent, excellent: the knaves have acted their parts in print.

T. G[ainsford], *A Rich Cabinet*, Q5r–v

125. 1616

> Or why are *women* rather growne so mad,
> That their *immodest feete* like *planets* gad
> With such *irregular motion* to base *Playes*,
> Where all the *deadly sinnes* keepe *hollidaies*
> There shall they see the *vices* of the *times*,
> *Orestes* incest, *Cleopatres* crimes.

Robert Anton, *The Philosopher's Satyrs*, p. 46

126. 1616

> Today I goe to the *Black-fryers Play-house*,
> Sit i'the view, salute all my acquaintance,
> Rise up between the *Acts*, let fall my cloake,
> Publish a handsome man, and a rich suite
> (As that's a speciall end, why we goe thither,
> All that pretend, to stand for't o' the *Stage*)
> The Ladies aske who's that?

Jonson, *The Devil is an Ass* (*Works*, VI.178)

127. 1617

These theatres are frequented by a number of respectable and handsome ladies, who come freely and seat themselves among the men without the slightest hesitation. On the evening in question [at the Fortune] his Excellency and the Secretary were pleased to play me a trick by placing me amongst a bevy of young women. Scarcely was I seated ere a very elegant dame, but in a mask, came and placed herself besides me . . . she determined to honour me by showing me some fine diamonds on her fingers, repeatedly taking off no fewer than three gloves, which were worn one over the other . . . This lady's bodice was of yellow satin richly embroidered, her petticoat of gold tissue with stripes, her robe of red velvet with a raised pile, lined with yellow muslin with broad stripes of pure gold. She wore an apron of point lace of various patterns: her head-tire was highly perfumed, and the collar of white satin beneath the delicately-wrought ruff struck me as extremely pretty.

Orazio Busino, *Calendar of State Papers Venetian 1617–19*, pp. 67–8

128. 1617

Wee are informed that there are certayne Players or Comedians wee knowe not of what Company, that goe about to play some enterlude concerning the late Marquesse d'Ancre, wch for many respectes wee thincke not fitt to be suffered.

Privy Council Order, 22 June 1617, to the Master of the Revels (*JCS* V.1371)

129. 1617

> See (*Captain Martio*) he ith' *Renounce me* Band,
> That in the middle Region doth stand . . .
> Look next to him to, *One* we both know well,
> (Sir *Iland Hunt*) a Travailer that will tell
> Of stranger Things then *Tatterd Tom* ere li't of,

Then *Pliny*, or *Herodotus* e're writ of . . .
But stay! see heere (but newly Entred,)
A *Cheapside* Dame, by th' Tittle on her head!
Plot (Villain!) plot! Let's lay our heads together!
We may devise perchance to get her hither.
(If wee to-gether cunningly compact)
Shee'l holde us dooing till the Latter *Act*
And (on my life) Invite us Supper home,
Wee'l thrust hard for it, but wee'lc finde her rome,
Heer *Mrs* – (pox ont! she's past, she'l not come ore,
Sure shee's bespoken for a box before . . .
Knowest thou yon world of fashions now comes in
In *Turkie* colours carved to the skin.
Mounted *Pelonianly* untill hee reeles,
That scornes (so much) plaine dealing at his heeles.
His Boote speakes *Spanish* to his *Scottish* Spurres,
His Sute cut *Frenchly*, round bestucke with Burres . . .
Now *Mars* defend us! seest thou who comes yonder?
Monstrous! *A Woman* of the *masculine Gender*.
Looke! thou mayst well descry her by her groath,
Out, point not man! Least wee be beaten both.
Eye her a little, marke but where shee'l goe,
Now (by this hand) into the Gallants Roe.
Let her alone! What ere she gives to stand,
Shee'l make her selfe a gayner, *By the Hand* . . .
What think'st thou of yon plumed *Dandebrat*,
Yon Ladycs *Shittle-cocke, Egyptian Rat*:
Yon *Musk-ball, Milke-sop:* yon *French Sincopace*:
That Ushers in, with a *Coranto* grace.
Yon Gilded *March-pane:* yon *All Verdingall*,
This is the *Puppet*, which the Ladyes all
Send for of purpose and solicite so
To *daunce* with them . . .
A Stoole and Cushion! Enter *Tissue slop!*
Vengeance! I know him well, did he not drop
Out of the *Tyring-house?* Then how (the duse)
Comes the mishapen *Prodigall so* spruce,
His year's *Revenewes* (I dare stand unto't,)
Is not of worth to purchase such a *Sute* . . .
Who woo'd not all his Land spend had hee more,
Then in a day a *Kite* could hoover ore . . .
T'injoy the pleasant *Harmony* that wee
Finde in this *Microcosme*, Man's societie . . .
. . . yon Spruse *Coxcombe*, yon Affecting *Asse*,
That never walkes without his *Looking-glasse*,

In a *Tobacco box*, or *Diall* set,
That he may privately conferre with it . . .
But h'st! with him Crabbed (*Websterio*).
The *Play-wright Cart-wright:* whether? either! ho –
No further. Looke as yee'd bee look't into:
Sit as ye woo'd be *Read:* Lord! who woo'd know him?
Was ever man so mangled with a *Poem*?
See how he drawes his mouth awry of late,
How he scrubs: wrings his wrests: scratches his Pate.
A *Midwife!* helpe!

H[enry] F[itzgeoffery], *Satyres: and Satyricall Epigrams: with Certaine Observations at Blackfryers*, E8v–F2v, F4v, F6v–7r

130. 1617

Fourth dutie is, to love her owne house best,
And be no gadding gossippe up and downe,
To heare and carry tales amongst the rest.
That are the newes reporters of the towne:
A modest womans home is her delight,
Of businesse there, to have the oversight.
At publike plays she never will be knowne,
And to be taverne guest she ever hates,
Shee scornes to be a streete-wife (Idle one,)
Or field wife ranging with her walking mates.
She knows how wise men censure of such dames . . .

Samuel Rowlands, *The Bride*, E1r–1v

131. 1617

Why doe our *lustfull Theaters* entice,
And personate in lively action *vice*:
Draw to the *Cities* shame, with guilded clothes,
Such *swarmes* of *wives* to breake their *nuptiall othes*?

Robert Anton, *The Philosophers Satyrs*, I3v

132. 1618

[Of Robert Shute, the King's candidate for Recorder] I am sory that Shute was brought upon the stage . . .

Chamberlain to Carleton, *Letters*, II.181

133. 1618

Mine host was full of ale and history . . .
Besides what of his knowledge he could say,
He had authenticke notice from the Play;
Which I might guesse, by's mustring up the ghosts,
And policyes, not incident to hosts;
But cheifly by that one perspicuous thing,
Where he mistooke a player for a King.
For when he would have sayd, King Richard dyed,
And call'd – A horse! a horse! – he, Burbidge cry'de.

Richard Corbet, 'Iter Boreale', *Poems*, 1807, pp. 193–4

134. 1619

> oft have I seene him, leap into the Grave
> suiting the person, wch he seem'd to have
> of A sadd Lover, with soe true an Eye
> that theer I would have sworne, he meant to dye,
> oft have I seene him, play this part in jeast,
> soe livly, that Spectators, and the rest
> of his sad Crew, whilst he but seem'd to bleed,
> amazed, thought even then hee dyed in deed.

> Funeral elegy for Richard Burbage (C. M. Ingleby, *Shakespeare, the Man and the Book*, II.180)

135. 1619

He had ane intention to have made a play like Platus Amphitrio but left it of, for that he could never find two so like others that he could persuade the Spectators they were one.

> Jonson, *Conversations with Drummond of Hawthornden*, p. 18

136. 1619

> We hope, for your owne good, you in the Yard
> Will lend your Eares, attentively to heare
> Things that shall flow so smoothly to your ear;
> That you returning home, t'your Friends shall say,
> How ere you understand't, 'Tis a fine Play:
> For we have in't a Conjurer, a Devill,
> And a Clowne too; but I feare the evill,
> In which perhaps unwisely we may faile,
> Of wanting Squibs and Crackers at their taile . . .

> J. C., *The Two Merry Milkmaids*, prologue

137. 1620

Another will fore-tell of Lightning and Thunder that shall happen such a day, when there are no such Inflamations seene, except men goe to the *Fortune* in *Golding-Lane*, to see the Tragedie of Doctor *Faustus*. There indeede a man may behold shagge-hayr'd Devills runne roaring over the Stage with Squibs in their mouthes, while Drummers make Thunder in the Tyring-house, and the twelvepenny Hirelings make artificial Lightning in their Heavens.

> John Melton, *Astrologaster*, E4r

138. 1620

[Every poet] must govern his Penne according to the Capacitie of the Stage he writes too, both in the Actor and the Auditor.

> The printer, *The Two Merry Milkmaids*

139. 1620

> Nor Lord, nor Lady we have tax'd; nor State,
> Nor any private person.

> Fletcher, *The Custom of the Country*, prologue

140. 1620

. . .(in the midst of his pride or riches) at a Play house . . . (before he dare enter) with the *Jacobs*-Staffe of his owne eyes and his Pages, hee takes a full survay of himselfe, from the highest sprig in his feather, to the lowest spangle that shines in his Shoo-string.

Anon., *Haec-Vir: or the Womanish-Man*, C2r

141. 1620

Our pulpits ring continually of the insolence and impudence of women: and to helpe the matter forward the players have likewise taken them to taske, and so to the ballades and ballad-singers.

Chamberlain to Carleton, *Letters*, II.289

142. 1621

> fly to ye Globe or Curtaine with your trul,
> Or gather musty phrases from ye Bul.
> This was not for your dyet he doth bring
> what he prepar'd for our Platonique King.

Peter Heylyn, verse on the performance of *Technogamia*, for the king at Woodstock (*JCS* VI.135)

143. 1621

> Yet have I seene a beggar with his Many
> Come in at a Play-house, all in for one penny.

John Taylor, *The praise, antiquity, and commodity of beggery, beggers and begging*, C3v

144. 1623

. . . no true Puritanes will endure to bee present at playes . . . few of either sex come thither, but in theyr holy-dayes appareil, and so set forth, so trimmed, so adorned, so decked, so perfumed, as if they made the place the market of wantonnesse, and by consequence to unfit for a Priest to frequent.

William Harison (quoted in Harbage, *Shakespeare's Audience*, pp. 71, 113)

145. 1623

> So have I seene, when Cesar would appeare,
> And on the Stage at halfe-sword parley were,
> Brutus and Cassius: oh how the Audience,
> Were ravish'd, with what wonder they went thence,
> When some new day they would not brooke a line,
> Of tedious (though well laboured) Catilines;
> Sejanus too was irksome, they priz'de more
> Honest Iago, or the jealous Moore.
> And though the Fox and subtill Alchimist,
> Long intermitted could not quite be mist . . .
> Yet these sometimes, even at a friend's desire
> Acted, have scarce defraied the Seacoale fire
> And doore-keepers: when let but Falstaffe come
> All is so pester'd: let but Beatrice
> And Benedicke be seene, loe in a trice
> The Cockpit Galleries, Boxes, are all full
> To heare Malvolio that crosse garter'd Gull . . .
> But if you needs must write, if poverty
> So pinch, that otherwise you starve and die,

On Gods name may the Bull or Cockpit have
Your lame blancke Verse, to keepe you from the grave:
Or let new Fortunes younger brethren see,
What they can picke from your leane industry.
I do not wonder when you offer at
Blacke-Friers, that you suffer.

Leonard Digges, commendatory verses for the First Folio, published with
Shakespeare's *Poems*, 1640 (*WS* II.233)

146. 1624

Here are no Gipsie Jigges, *no* Drumming stuffe,
Dances, *or other* Trumpery *to delight,*
Or take, by common way, the common sight.

W. B., commendatory verses to Massinger's *The Bondman*

147. 1624

[to the ladies in the audience]
Nor blame the Poet if he slip aside,
Sometimes lasciviously if not too wide.
But hold your Fannes close, and then smile at ease,
A cruell Sceane did never Lady please.

Fletcher, *Rule a Wife and Have a Wife*, prologue

148. 1624

I doubt not but you have heard of our famous play of Gondomar, which hath
ben followed with extraordinarie concourse, and frequented by all sorts of
people old and younge, rich and poore, masters and servants, papists and
puritans, wise men *et.ct.*, churchmen and statesmen as Sir Henry Wotton, Sir
Albert Morton, Sir Benjamin Ruddier, Sir Thomas Lake, and a world besides;
the Lady Smith would have gon yf she could have persuaded me to go with
her. I am not so sowre nor severe but that I wold willingly have attended her,
but I could not sit so long, for we must have ben there before one a clocke at
farthest to find any roome. They counterfeited his person to the life, with all
his graces and faces, and had gotten (they say) a cast sute of his apparell for
the purpose, and his Lytter, wherin the world sayes lackt nothing but a couple
of asses to carry yt, and Sir G. Peter or Sir T. Mathew to beare him company.

John Chamberlain to Carleton, 21 August 1624, *Letters*, II.577–8

149. 1625

A worthy story, howsoever writ
For Language, modest Mirth, Conceit or Wit,
Meets oftentimes with the sweet commendation
Of hang't, 'tis scurvy, when for approbation
A Jigg shall be clapt at, and every rhime
Prais'd and applauded by a clamorous chime.
Let ignorance and laughter dwell together,
They are beneath the Muses pity. Hither
Come nobler Judgements, and to those the strain
Of our inventions is not bent in vain.

Fletcher, *The Fair Maid of the Inn*, prologue

150. 1625

. . . the hearers and beholders, who being baptised into the name of Christ are brought into danger of Gods wrath, and theire owne condemnation, in as much as they are partakers of the sinnes of the Players and of the Playes in approving them.

> Anon., *A Shorte Treatise of Stage-Playes*, ch. 4

151. 1625

The action of the theatre, though modern states esteem it but ludicrous, unless it be satirical and biting, was carefully watched by the ancients, that it might improve mankind in virtue; and indeed many wise men and great philosophers have thought it to the mind as the bow to the fiddle; and certain it is, though a great secret in nature, that the minds of men in company are more open to affections and impressions than when alone.

> Francis Bacon, *The Advancement of Learning*, Bk II, ch. 13

152. 1625?

> [A youth from Cornwall]
> Most of my money being spent,
>   To *S. Johns* street to the *Bull* I went,
> Where I the roaring Rimer saw,
>   And to my face was made a daw:
> And pressing forth among the folke,
>   I lost my purse, my hat and cloke.

> Anon., '[Dice, Wine, and Women] or the Unfortunate Gallant Gulled at London' (in *The Pepysian Ballads*, ed. Rollins, I.239)

153. 1626

> For your owne sakes, not his, he bad me say
> Would you were come to heare, not see a Play.
> Though we his *Actors* must provide for those,
> Who are our guests, here, in the way of showes,
> The maker hath not so; he'ld have you wise,
> Much rather by your eares, then by your eyes.

> Jonson, *The Staple of News*, prologue

154. 1626

Whereas wee are informed that on thursday next, divers loose and Idle persons, some Saylors, and others, have appointed to meete at the Playhouse called the Globe, to see a Play (as it is pretended) but their ende is thereby to disguise some Routous and Riotous action . . .

> Privy Council to Surrey Justices of the Peace, 17 May 1626 (*JCS* I.21)

155. 1628

[a gallant] . . . his business is the street: the Stage, the Court, and those places where a proper man is best showne . . .

[Paul's Walk is] the other expence of the day, after Playes, Taverne, and a Baudy house . . . [a player] The waiting-women Spectators are over-eares in love with him, and Ladies send for him to act in their Chambers. Your Innes of Court men were undone but for him, hee is their chiefe guest and imployment, and the sole business that makes them Afternoones men.

> John Earle, *Microcosmographie*, D4r, H3v

156. 1629?

. . . you may now at last falsifie that ignominious Censure which some *English Writers* in their printed Workes have passed upon Innes of Court Students; of whom they record: . . . (p) That Innes of Court men were undone but for Players, that they are their chiefest guests and imployment, & the sole busines that makes them afternoons men; (q) & take smoke at a Play-house, which they commonly make their Studie . . .

William Prynne, *Histriomastix*, Epistle Dedicatory

157. 1629

[A young gallant loves Jonson's] booke of Playes . . .
The Cockpit heretofore would serve his wit,
But now upon the Fryers stage hee'll sit . . .
His silken garments, and his sattin robe,
That hath so often visited the Globe,
And all his spangled rare perfum'd attires
Which once so glistred in the Torchy Fryers,
Must to the Broakers . . .

F[rancis] L[enton], *The Young Gallants Whirligig*, C3r–4v

158. 1629

. . . that last daye certaine vagrant French players, who had beene expelled from their owne contrey, *and those women*, did attempt, thereby giving just offence to all vertuous and well-disposed persons in this town, to act a certain lacivious and unchaste comedye, in the French tonge at the Blackfryers. Glad am I to saye they were hissed, hooted, and pippin-pelted from the stage . . .

Letter by Thomas Brande, 8 November 1629 (*JCS* I.25)

159. 1629

[Joseph Taylor complains against]
some sowre censurer who's apt to say
No one in these times can produce a Play
Worthy his reading since of late, 'tis true
The old accepted are more than the new.

Massinger, *The Roman Actor*, 1.1

160. 1629?

. . . first prepare to admire my Capacity, for thy knowledge never owned such a parlous Plot before. Which was, that I should go to see a Play in *Black-Fryars*: and there (by all necessary consequences, or rather inspired assurance) some rich Lady would cast her Eie on me, and the same night me on her. Be not thou astonish'd Reader, neither suppose it impossible that Nature can be so opulent, or he that is mortall, possesse such a strong Brain. For (alas Man!) heretofore I was as full of these learned-Stratagems, as an Egge is full of meat.

Fifty pounds accroutred me from Top to Toe: having been very thrifty in laying out my Money, and carefull to refuse *Bunges* [his servant] advice, for he brought me a *Taylor*, whom Custome had made to steale from himself. A Slave that the Devill durst not trust with his old Clothers; no, though he might gaine his Soul in lue of the Theft.

Thus like a true *English-man* (who wears his Mother too much in his Aparell) I entered the *Theater*, and sat upon the Stage: making low Congies to divers Gentlemen; not that I knew them, but I was confident, they would requite me in the same kinde: which made the Spectators suppose us of very olde, and familiar acquaintance. Besides (that I might appear no *Novice*) I observ'd all fashionable Customes; As delivering my Sute to a more apparent view, by hanging the Cloak upon one shoulder: or letting it fall (as it were) by chance. I stood up also at the end of every *Act*, to salute those, whom I never saw before. Two *Acts* were finished before I could discover any thing, either for my Comfort then, or worth my relation now. Unlesse it were *punycall* absurdity in a Country-Gentleman: who was so caught with the naturall action of a Youth (that represented a ravish'd Lady), as he swore alowd, he would not sleep untill he had killed her ravisher: and how 'twas not fit such Rogues should live in a Common-wealth. This made me laugh, but not merry.

Anon after, I spied a Gentlewomans Eie, fix'd full upon me. Hope and Despaire threw me into such Distractions, that I was about to bid a Boy (who personated *Cupid* in the play) to shoot at her with his counterfeit Arrow. But she presently disclaimed me her Object: and with the like inconstancy gaz'd upon another. About the beginning of the Fourth *Act*, my Face withstood a fresh encounter, given me by a Ladies Eie, whose Seate opposed mine. She look'd stedfast on me, till the Play ended; seeming to survey my Limbs with amorous curiosity: whilst I advanced them all, to encounter her approbation. A great desire I had to see her Face: which she discovered, by unmasquing it to take her leave of a Gentleman. But if I ever beheld one so ill-favour'd? do thou abhorre my Book. She look'd like *December*, in the midst of *April*, old and crabbed in her Youth. Her Nose stood towards the *South-East* point: and *Snot* had fretted a preposterous *Channell* in the most remote corner of her Lip. Sure she was chast, *chast* because *deformed*: and her *deformitie* (repugnant to the common course of *Nature*) might beget that *Chastitie*: but in whom? in others, not in her selfe; unlesse *Necessitie* did force it. For no doubt she would be as leacherous as the Mountaine-*Goate*, had not Natures qualmishnesse proved a strong contradiction to her desire: who heaved the Gorge, at her *imperfect* perfecting: therefore had no Stomach to make a Man fitting her embracements. Yet she wore *Jewells*, for the which I could willingly have kiss'd her in the *dark*. And perhaps too (by guilded provocation) supplied the Office of a Husband.

Her uglinesse made me suppose that nothing could be too base for her acceptance: therefore I (following her down the Staires) resolved to discover a goodwill to her, either by a wanton gesture of my Body, or whispering in her Ear just as she came forth into the Street, (her Usher being step'd aside to complement with parting Company) I proffer'd my service to attend her home, if she missed any of her Friends. She suspecting that I thought her to be a Whore, told me aloud I was much mistaken. Her Brother (unknown to me) stood behind us, and asked her; what the matter was? *Marry* (quoth she) this Gentleman takes me for some common Creature. He with all violent dexterity strucke me in the Face; and afterwards went about to draw his Sword. But I slunk through the presse of people, and very *tamely* conveied my selfe home. My man *Bunge* (who attended there all the Play-time, to save charges) saw this: and heard the *Young-Gallant* swear (after I was gone) if ever he met me, he would make my Heart the *Scabbard* of his Sword. These woful tydings hee brought to my Chamber, so that my costly *Experiment* was now concluded, and my glorious Garments altogether uselesse. For I durst not visit *Theaters* any more, lest I should meete with him, or Women elsewhere, as fearfull of the like entertainment.

> T. M., *The Life of a Satyrical Puppy called Nim*, 1657, pp. 102–7 (sig. H3v–H6)

161. 1630

Your Majesty will give me leave to tell you another general calamity; we have had no plays this six months, and that makes our statesmen see the good use of them, by the want: for if our heads had been filled with the loves of Pyramus and Thisbe, or the various fortunes of Don Quixote, we should never have cared who had made peace or war, but on the stage. But now every fool is enquiring what the French do in Italy, and what they treat in Germany.

> Sir Thomas Roe, letter to the Queen of Bohemia, 29 October 1630, about the plague. *Calendar of State Papers Domestic Chas I*, 174. Doc. 102

162. 1630?

> The world's a Theatre. The earth, a Stage
> Placed in the midst: where both Prince and Page,
> Both rich and poor, fool, wise man, base and high,
> All act their Parts in Life's short Tragedy.
>   Our Life's a Tragedy. Those secret Rooms,
> Wherein we tire us, are our mothers' wombs.
> The Music ush'ring in the Play is mirth
> To see a man-child brought upon the earth.
> That fainting gasp of breath which first we vent,
> Is a Dumb Show; presents the Argument.
> Our new-born cries, that new-born griefs bewray,
> Are the sad Prologue of th'ensuing Play.
> False hopes, true fears, vain joys, and fierce distracts,
> Are like the Music that divides the Acts.
> Time holds the Glass; and when the Hour's outrun,
> Death strikes the Epilogue, and the Play is done.

> Francis Quarles, 'On the Life and Death of a Man'

163. 1630

>   . . . they'l still slight
> All that exceeds Red Bull, and Cockpit flight.
> These are the men in crowded heapes that throng
> To that adulterate stage, where not a tong
> Of th'untun'd Kennell, can a line repeat
> Of serious sence: but like lips, meet like meat;
> Whilst the true brood of Actors, that alone
> Keepe naturall unstrayn'd Action in her throne

Behold their Benches bare, though they rehearse
The tearser *Beaumonts* or great *Johnsons* verse.
> Thomas Carew, verses for Davenant's *The Just Italian*, A3v–4r

164. 1630

You've seen the Muses Looking Glass, ladies fair,
And gentle youths: and others too whoeer
Have fill'd this orb: it is the end we meant:
Yourselves unto your selves still to present.
A soldier shall himself in Hector see;
Grave councillors, Nestor, view them selves in thee;
When Lucrece' part shall on our stage appear,
Every chaste lady sees her shadow there.
Nay, come who will, for our indifferent glasses
Will show both fools and knaves, and all their faces,
To vex and cure them: but we need not feare
We do not doubt but each one now thats here
That has a fair soul and a beauteous face,
Will visit of the Muses Looking Glass.
> Thomas Randolph, *The Muses' Looking Glass*, epilogue

165. 1631

[A yong Innes a Court Gentleman]: His Recreations and loose expence of time, are his only studies (as Plaies, Dancing, Fencing, Taverns, Tobacco,) and Dalliance . . .
> Francis Lenton, *Characterismi*, F5r

166. 1631

[A Ruffian] . . . To a play they will hazard to go, though with never a rag of money: where after the *second Act*, when the *Doore* is weakly guarded, they will make *forcible entrie*, a knock with a Cudgell is the worst; whereat though they grumble, they rest pacified upon their admittance. Forthwith by violent assault and assent, they aspire to the two-pennie roome; where being furnished with Tinder, Match, and a portion of decayed *Barmoodas*, they smoake it most terribly, applaude a prophane jest unmeasurably, and in the end grow distastefully rude to all the Companie. At the Conclusion of all, they single out their *dainty Doxes*, to cloze up a fruitlesse day with a sinnefull evening.
> Clitus-Alexandrinus (i.e. Richard Brathwait), *Whimzies: or a New Cast of Characters*, pp. 134–5

167. 1631

In this following *Act*, the *Office is* open'd, and shewn to the *Prodigall*, and his *Princesse Pecunia*, wherein the *allegory*, and purpose of the *Author* hath hitherto beene wholly mistaken, and so sinister an interpretation beene made, as if the soules of most of the *Spectators* had liv'd in the eyes and eares of those ridiculous Gossips that tattle betweene the *Acts*.
> Jonson, Address to the reader, before Act 3, *The Staple of News*

168. 1631

Many gentlemen
Are not, as in the days of understanding,
Now satisfied without a Jig, which since
They cannot, with their honour, call for after
The play, they look to be serv'd up in the middle.

James Shirley, *The Changes*, 4.2

169. 1631

. . . though on each hand
To over-top us, two great Lawrels stand;
The one, when she shall please to spread her traine,
The vastness of the Globe cannot containe;
Th'other so high, the Phoenix does aspire
To build in, and takes new life from the fire
Bright Poesie creates.

Shackerley Marmion, *Holland's Leaguer*, prologue for Salisbury Court

170. 1632

Especially, and above all the rest, she was most taken with the report of three famous *Amphytheators*, whicstood so neere scituated, that her eye might take view of them from the lowest *Turret*, one was the *Continent of the World*, because halfe the yeere a World of *Beauties*, and brave *Spirits* resorted unto it; the other was a building of excellent *Hope*, and though *wild beastes* and *Gladiators* did most possesse it, yet the Gallants that came to behold those combats, though they were of a mixt Society, yet there were many Noble worthies amongst them.

Nicholas Goodman, *Holland's Leaguer*, F2v

171. 1632

[Players] love not the company of Geese or Serpants, because of their hissing.

Donald Lupton, *London and the Countrey Carbonadoed*, G1v

172. 1632

. . . the faeces or grounds of your people, that sit in the oblique caves and wedges of your house, your sinful sixpenny mechanicks.

Jonson, *The Magnetic Lady*, Induction

173. 1632

Is this the childe of your bed-ridden witt,
An none but the Black-friers foster ytt?
If to the Fortune you had sent your ladye,
Mongst prentizes and apell-wyfes, ytt may bee
Your rosie foole might some sport have gott.
But when as silkes and plush, and all the witts
Are calde to see, and censure as befitts,
And yff your follye take not, they, perchance,
Must here them selfes stilde, gentle ignorance.

Alexander Gill, verses against *The Magnetic Lady*

174. 1632

>[Ann Frugal, a city magnate's wife, wants to imitate a court lady]
>. . . A friend at court to place me at a masque;
>The private box took up at a new play
>For me, and my retinue; a fresh habit,
>(Of a fashion never seen before) to draw
>The gallants' eyes that sit on the stage upon me . . .
>>Massinger, *The City Madam*, 2.2

175. 1632

This Captaine attending and accompanying my Lady of Essex in a boxe in the playhouse at the blackfryers, the said lord coming upon the stage, stood before them and hindred their sight. Captain Essex told his lordship they had payd for their places as well as hee, and therefore intreated him not to deprive them of the benefitt of it. Whereupon the lord stood up yet higher and hindred more their sight. Then Capt. Essex with his hand putt him a little by. The lord then drewe his sword and ran full butt at him, though he missed him, and might have slaine the Countesse as well as him.

>PRO C115/8391 (quoted by Herbert Berry, 'The Stage and Boxes at Blackfriars', p. 165)

176. 1632

Item: That no tobacco be taken in the Hall nor anywhere else publicly, and that neither at their standing in the streets, nor before the comedy begin, nor all the time there, any rude or immodest exclamations be made; nor any humming, hawking, whistling, hissing, or laughing be used, or any stamping or knocking, nor any such other uncivil or unscholarlike or boyish demeanour, upon any occasion; nor that any clapping of hands be had until the *Plaudite* at the end of the Comedy, except his Majesty, the Queen, or others of the best quality here, do apparently begin the same.

>Order to Cambridge students over play for royal visit, March 1632 (quoted in Masson, *Life of Milton*, I.218)

177. 1632?

>. . . yet had hee longer sin'd I doubt
>he had but foold this long life out,
>as other Courtiers spend their dayes
>wearing good clothes, seeing bad Playes,
>In Courting Ladyes, begging favours,
>in perfuming 'gainst ill savours,
>powdring his hayre, ruffing his boote,
>matching points unto his suite,
>all the morning spent in dressing,
>all the afternoone in kissing,
>or to Hide parke his mistresse squiring,
>or with his tayler is Conspiring . . .

John Earle, mock epitaph on Viscount Falkland, Malone MS 13, 29 (quoted in Kurt Weber, *Lucius Cary*, pp. 43–4)

178. 1633

The comedy called *The Yonge Admirall*, being free from oaths, prophaness, or obsceanes, hath given mee much delight and satisfaction in the
readinge, and may serve for a patterne to other poetts, not only for the bettring
of maners and language, but for the improvement of the quality, which hath
received some brushings of late.

When Mr. Sherley hath read this approbation, I know it will encourage him
to pursue this beneficial and cleanly way of poetry, and when other poetts
heare and see his good success, I am confident they will imitate the original
for their own credit, and make such copies in this harmless way, as shall speak
them masters in their art, at the first sight, to all judicious spectators . . .

[3 July] Exception was taken by Mr. Sewster to the second part of The Citty
Shuffler, which gave me occasion to stay the play till the company had given
him satisfaction; which was done the next day, and under his hande he did
certifye mee that he was satisfyed . . .

On friday the nineteenth of October, 1633, I sent a warrant by a messenger
of the chamber to suppress The Tamer Tamd, to the Kings players, for that
afternoone, and it was obeyd; upon complaints of foule and offensive matters
conteyned therein.

They acted The Scornful Lady instead of it . . .

On saterday morninge followinge the booke was brought mee, and at my lord
of Hollands request I returned it to the players ye monday morninge after,
purgd of oaths, prophaness, and ribaldrye . . .

All ould plays ought to bee brought to the Master of the Revells, and have his
allowance to them for which he should have his fee, since they may be full
of offensive things against church and state; ye rather that in former time the
poetts tooke greater liberty than is allowcd by me.

Henry Herbert, *Diary*, pp. 19–21

179. 1633

Blesse mee you kinder Stars! How are wee throng'd?
Alas! whom, hath our long-sick-Poet wrong'd,
That hee should meet together in one day
A Session, and a Faction at his Play?
. . . But 'bove the mischiefe of these feares, a sort
Of cruell Spies (we heare) intend a sport
Among themselves; our mirth must not at all
Tickle, or stir their Lungs, but shake their Gall.

Davenant, *The Wits*, prologue

180. 1633

. . . If I winne
Your kinde commends, 'twill bring more *custome* in.
When others fill'd *Roomes* with neglect disdaine ye
And if such *Guests* would dayly make it shine,
Our POET should no more drinke *Ale*, but *Wine*.

Nabbes, *Tottenham Court*, 1638, epilogue

181. 1633

> When this smooth Pastorall was first brought forth,
> The Age twas borne in, did not know it's worth.
> Since by thy cost, and industry reviv'd,
> It hath a new fame, and new birth atchiv'd.

> Shackerley Marmion, 'Unto his worthy friend Mr. *Joseph Taylor* upon his
> presentment of the *Faithfull Shepherdesse before the King and Queene, at
> the Whitehall, on Twelfth night last* 1633.'

182. *c*.1634

. . . it is the *Ingeniousness* of the Speech, when it is fitted to the Person; and the *Gracefulness* of the *Action*, when it is fitted to the Speech; and
therefore a Play *read*, hath not half the pleasure of a Play *Acted*: for though it
have the pleasure of *ingenious Speeches*, yet it wants the pleasure of *Gracefull
action*: and we may well acknowledg, that *Gracefulness* of *action*, is the
greatest pleasure of a Play, seeing it is the greatest pleasure of (the Art of
pleasure) *Rhetorick* in which we may be bold to say; there never had been so
good Oratours, if there had not first been Players.

> Richard Baker, *Theatrum Redivivum*

183. 1634

Here hath been an Order of the Lords of the Council hung up in a
Table near *Paul's* and the *Black-Fryars*, to command all that Resort to the
Play-House there to send away their Coaches, and to disperse Abroad in *Paul's
Church-Yard*, *Carter-Lane*, the Conduit in *Fleet-Street*, and other Places, and
not to return to fetch their Company, but they must trot afoot to find their
Coaches, 'twas kept very strictly for two or three Weeks, but now I think it is
disorder'd again.

> 9 January, *Strafforde's Letters*, I.175–6

184. 1634

> [The players reject]
> All bitter straines, that suit a Satyr Muse:
> And that which so much takes the Vulgar Eare,
> Loosenes of speech, which they for jests do heare.

> William Rutter, *The Shepherd's Holiday*, Prologue to the Stage

185. 1634

> . . . where before great Patriots, Dukes and Kings
> Presented for some hie facinorious things,
> Were the Stage-Subject; now we strive to flie
> In their low pitch, who never could soare hie:
> For now the common argument intreats,
> Of puling Lovers, craftie Bawdes or cheates.

> Heywood, *A Challenge for Beauty*, prologue

186. 1634

> If any meete here, as some men i'th age
> Who understand no sense, but from one stage,
> And over partiall will entaile like land
> Upon heires male all action, and command

Of voice and gesture, upon whom they love,
These, though cal'd Judges, may delinquent's prove.

Shirley, *The Example*, prologue

187. 1634

[female Prologue at the Cockpit]
. . . is there not
A blush upon my cheekes that I forgot
The Ladies, and a Female Prologue too?
Your pardon noble Gentlewomen, you
Were first within my thoughts, I know you sit
As free, and high Commissioners of wit . . .
You are the bright intelligences move,
And make a harmony this sphere of Love.

Shirley, *The Coronation*, prologue

188. 1635

For all your pretious Morning-hours are given
For you to paint and decke you till eleven;
And then an houre or two must be the least
To jeere your foolish Lover, or to feast,
Or court your amorous cringing Favorite
With a bare-bathed breast to feed delight,
And purchase more Spectators: – but time's lost
Till a Play-bill be sever'd from the Post
T'informe you what's to play; then comes your Coach,
Where numerous light-ones, like your selfe approach,
But where's Devotion all this while? asleepe,
And for her selfe sole Centinall may keepe.
But now you'r seated, and the Music sound
For th'Actors entry; pleasures doe abound
In ev'ry Boxe; sometimes your eye's on th' Stage,
Streight on a lighter Object, your loose *Page*,
Or some phantastike *Gallant*, or your *Groome*,
But when this Embleme of your life is done,
This piece of witty art, what doe you then?
To your sinne-shrouding Coaches streight againe,
You make repaire, where you relaters bee
Of what your Eare did heare, or Eye could see.
Then to a luscious Supper, after this
To a reere banket, or to some quaint dish
To move a sensuall slumber, and delight
But never sate your boundless appatite.
Thus you in painted joyes mis-spend your dayes
More to your *Suiters* than your *Makers* praise.

Richard Brathwait, *Anniversaries upon his Panarete; Continued*, A6r–v

189. 1635

These things now we that live in *London* canot help, and they are as great news to men that sit in Boxes at *Black-Fryars*, as the affairs of Love to Flannel-Weavers.

> John Suckling, letter to Mary and Anne Bulkeley (*Works*, I.134)

190. 1635

> The places thou dost usually frequent,
> Is to some Play-house in an afternoone.
> And for no other meaning, and intent,
> But to get company to sup with soone,
> More changeable, and wavering then the moone.
> And with they wanton lookes, attracting to thee,
> The amorous spectators for to wooe thee.
> Thether thou com'st, in severall formes, and shapes,
> To make thee still a stranger to the place:
> And traine new lovers, like young Birds to scrapes . . .
> Now in the richest colours maybe had,
> The next day, all in mourning blacke, and sad.
> In a Stuffe Wastcote, and a Peticote
> Like to a chamber-mayd, thou com'st to day:
> The next day after thou dost change thy note,
> Then like a countrey wench, thou com'st in gray,
> And sittest like a stranger at the Play.
> The morrow after that, thou comest then
> In the neate habit of a Citizen.
> The next time, rushing in thy Silken weeds,
> Embroyder'd, lac't, perfum'd, in glittering shew,
> Rich like a Lady, and attended so,
> As brave as any Countesse dost thou goe.

> Thomas Cranley, *Amanda, or The Reformed Whore*, F2r

191. 1635

Here hath bin lately a newe comedie at the globe called *The Witches of Lancasheir*, acted by reason of ye great concourse of people 3 dayes togither: the 3rd day I went with a friend to see it, and found a greater apparence of fine folke gentmen and gentweomen then I thought had bin in town in the vacation.

> Nathaniel Tomkyns, letter to Robert Phelips, quoted in Berry, 'The Globe Bewitched and *El Hombre Fiel*', in *Medieval and Renaissance Drama in England* 1 (1984), p. 215

192. 1635

The Gallants of the Court are more impatient to hear the News of a Battle, than they are to have a Play begin at *Black-Fryars*.

> Viscount Conway, 14 November, *Strafforde's Letters*, I.478

193. 1635

> *The speaker enter'd with a Sword drawne*
> For your owne sakes (Poore Soules!) you had not best

Beleeve my fury was so much supprest
I'th'heat of the last Scene, as now you may
Boldly, and safely too, cry downe our Play!
For you if you dare but Murmure one false Note,
Here in the House, or going to take Bote,
By Heav'n I'le mowe you off with my long Sword;
Yeo'man, and Squire, Knight, Lady, and her Lord!

William Davenant, epilogue to *News from Plymouth*, at the Globe

194. 1636

A little Pique happened betwixt the Duke of Lenox and the Lord Chamberlain about a Box at a new Play in the *Black Fryars*, of which the Duke had got the Key; Which if it had come to be debated betwixt them as it was intended, some Heat or perhaps other Inconvenience might have happen'd. His Majesty hearing of it, sent the Earl of *Holland* to commend them both not to dispute it, but before him, so he heard it and made them Friends.

25 January, *Strafforde's Letters*, I.511

195. 1636?

[Applauds the audience, despite]
        ... this long neglect
Of Court and Citie Gentry, that transfer
In Terme their visits to our Theater ...
And now we hope you've leisure in the Citie
To give the World cause to suspect you witty.
We would intreat you then put off a while
That formall brow you wear when you beguile
Young Chapmen with bad wares; pray do not look
On us, as on the Debtors in your Book.
        ... tis your care
To keepe your Shops, 'lesse when to take the Ayr
You walke abroad, as you have done to day,
To bring your Wives and Daughters to a play.

Henry Glapthorne, 'To a Reviv'd Vacation Play' (*Plays and Poems*, II.194–5)

196. 1638

Thine were *land-Tragedies*, no Prince was found
To swim a whole *Scoene* out, then oth'*Stage* drown'd;
Pitch'd fields, as *Red-Bull* wars, still felt thy doome,
Thou laidst no sieges to the *Musique-Roome* ...

Jasper Mayne, *Jonsonus Virbius*, E4r

197. 1638

[Twenty years ago] ... they ... to th'Theatre would come
Ere they had din'd to take up the best room;
Then sit on benches, not adorn'd with mats,
And graciously did vail their high-crowned hats
To every half dress'd Player, as he still
Through th'hangings peep'd to see how th'house did fill.

> Good easy judging souls, with what delight
> They would expect a jig, or target fight.
>
> Davenant, *The Unfortunate Lovers*, prologue

198. 1638?

> How is't possible to suffice
> So many Ears, so many Eyes?
> Some in wit, some in shows
> Take delight, and some in Clothes;
> Some for mirth they cheifly come,
> Some for passion, for both some,
> Some for lascivious meetings, that's their arrant;
> Some to detract and ignorance their warrant . . .
> How is't possible to please
> Opinion toss'd in such wild seas?
> Yet I doubt not, if attention
> Seize you above, and apprehension
> You below, to take things quickly,
> We shall both make you sad, and tickle ye.
>
> Anon., *No Wit, No Help Like a Woman's*, prologue

199. 1638

> The sneaking Tribe, that drinke and write by fits,
> As they can steale or borrow coine or wits,
> That Pandars fee for Plots, and then belie
> The paper with – *An excellent Comedie,
> Acted* (more was the pitty) *by th' Red Bull
> With great applause,* of some vaine City Gull;
> That damne Philosophy, and prove the curse
> Of emptinesse, both in the Braine and Purse;
> These that scrape legs and trenchers to my lord,
> Had starv'd but for some scraps pick'd from thy board . . .
>
> R. Bride-oake, *Upon Mr. Randolph's Poeme, collected and published after his death*, **1r

200. 1638

. . .to drive away griefe, I would sometimes see a Play, and heare a Beare-baiting; whereas a handsome formall Bearded man made me roome, to sit downe by him, and he tooke such good notice of my Civility, in laughing at the sport, that indeed Love strucke him to the heart with the glaunces of mine eyes, in such sort as within short space we met at a Taverne, where with a Contract we made our selves as sure as sacke and sugar.

> John Taylor, *A Juniper Lecture*, p. 213

201. 1638

> [to the Clown]
> LETOY. But you Sir are incorrigible, and
> Take licence to your selfe, to adde unto
> Your parts, your owne free fancy; and sometimes

To alter, or diminish what the writer
With care and skill compos'd: and when you are
To speake to your coactors in the Scene,
You hold interloquutions with the Audients.
BIPLAY. That is a way my Lord has bin allow'd
On elder stages to move mirth and laughter.
LETOY. Yes in the dayes of *Tarlton* and *Kempe*,
Before the stage was purg'd from barbarisme,
And brought to the perfection it now shines with.

> Richard Brome, *The Antipodes*, D3v

202. *c.*1638

LANDL. Why I would have the Fool in every Act,
Be't Comedy or Tragedy, I'ave laugh'd
Untill I cry'd again, to see what Faces
The Rogue will make: O it does me good
To see him hold out's Chin hang down his hands,
And twirle his Bawble. There is nere a part
About him but breaks jests.
THRI . . . his part has all the wit,
For none speaks Craps and Quibbles besides him:
I'd rather see him leap, laugh, or cry,
Then hear the gravest speech in all the *Play*.
I never saw Rheade peeping through the Curtain,
But ravishing joy enter'd into my heart . . .
[The Courtier and gallant leave, and the country gentleman follows]
I'le follow them, though't be into a Box.
Though they did sit thus open on the Stage
To shew their Cloak and Sute, yet I did think
At last they would take sanctuary 'mongst
The Ladies, lest some Creditor should spy them.
'Tis better looking o're a Ladies head
Or through a Lettice-window, then a grate.

> Thomas Goffe, *The Careless Shepherdess*, Praeludium

203. 1638?

. . . The Company's my Merchant, nor dare they
Expose my weak frame on so rough a Sea,
'Lesse you (their skilful Pilots) please to stear
By mild direction of your Eye and Ear
Their new rigg'd Bark . . .

> Henry Glapthorne, 'For *Ezekiel Fen* at his first Acting a Mans Part', *Poems*,
> 1639 (prologue spoken by Fenn)

204. 1639

Troth Gentlemen, we know that now adayes
Some come to take up Wenches at our Playes;
It is not in our power to please their sence,

We wish they may go discontented hence.
And many Gallants do come hither, we think
To sleep and to digest there too much drink:
We may please them; for we will not molest
With Drums and Trumpets any of their rest.
If perfum'd Wantons do for eighteen pence,
Expect an Angel, and alone go hence;
We shall be glad with all our hearts: for we
Had rather have their Room then companie;
For many an honest Gentleman is gon
Away for want of place, as looke you yon!
We guess some of you Ladies, hither come
To meet your Servants, wh'are at dice at home:
You'l be deceive'd . . .

Aston Cockayne, *The Obstinate Lady*, prologue

205. 1639

Thursday last the players of the Fortune were fined £1,000 for setting up an altar, a bason, and two candlesticks, and bowing down before it upon the stage, and although they allege it was an old play revived, and an altar to the heathen gods, yet it was apparent that this play was revived on purpose in contempt of the ceremonies of the church.

Edmond Rossingham to Viscount Conway, 8 May 1639 (*JCS* V.1300)

206. 1639

Order of the King in Council. Complaint was this day made that the stage-players of the Red Bull have for many days together acted a scandalous and libellous play in which they have audaciously reproached and in a libel represented and personated not only some of the aldermen of the city of London and some other persons of quality, but also scandalised and libelled the whole profession of doctors belonging to the Court of Probate, and reflected upon the present Government.

Malone Society Collections, I.4 & 5, pp. 394–5

207. 1639

Here are no bumbast raptures swelling high
To pluck *Jove* and the rest downe from the sky.
Here is no sence that must be thee be scann'd,
Before thou canst the meaning understand.
Here is not any glorious Scene of state;
Nor Christning set out with the Lottery plate.
There's no disguise in't; no false beard, that can
Discover severall persons in one man.
No politician tells his plots unto
Those in the Pit, and what he meanes to doe.
But now me thinkes I heare some Criticke say,
All these left out there's nothing in the play.
Yes: Thou shalt find plaine words, and language cleane;

That *Cockram* needs not tell thee what they meane.
Shalt find strict method in't, and every part
Severely order'd by the rules of Art.
A constant Scene: the business it intends
The two houres time of action comprehends.

Thomas Nabbes, *The Unfortunate Mother*, Proeme to the Reader

208. 1640

You shall not here be feasted with the sight
Of anticke showes, but Actions, such as might
And have beene reall, and in such a phrase,
As men should speake in . . .

Henry Glapthorne, *The Ladies Privilege*, prologue

209. 1640

Wee've cause to fear yours, or the Poets frowne
For of late day's (he know's not how) y'are grown,
Deeply in love with a new strayne of wit
Which he condemns, at least disliketh it,
And solemnely protests you doe expect the same;
Hee'l tread his usuall way, no gaudy Sceane
Shall give instructions, what his plot doth meane;
No handsome Love toy shall your time beguile
Forcing your pitty to a sigh or smile,
But a slight piece of mirth . . . (Prologue)
Ladyes . . . Cavaliers and Gentry . . . the City friends . . .
    my Countrey
folkes too if here be any o'em. (Epilogue)

Richard Brome, *The Court Beggar*

210. 1640

            . . . others that have seen,
And fashionably observ'd the English scene,
Say (but with lesse hope to be understood)
Such titles unto Playes are now the mood,
Aglaura, *Claracilla*, names that may
(Being Ladies) grace, and bring guests to the Play.

James Shirley, prologue to the Dublin performance of *Rosania*, performed at the Globe in 1640 as *The Doubtful Heir*

211. 1640

Gentlemen, I am onely sent to say,
Our Author did not calculate his Play,
For this Meridian; the Bank-side he knowes
Is far more skilful at the ebbes and flowes
Of water then of Wit: He did not mean
For the elevation of your Poles this Scene.
No shews, no frisk, and what you most delight in,
(Grave understanders) here's no Target fighting

Upon the Stage, all work for cutlers barrd,
No Bawd'ry, nor no Ballads; this goes hard.
The wit is clean, and (what affects you not)
Without impossibilities the plot;
No Clown, no squibs, no Divell's in't; oh now
You Squirrels that want nuts, what will ye do?
Pray do not crack the benches, and we may
Hereafter fit your palats with a Play.
But you that can contract your selves, and fit
As you were now in the *Blackfriers* pit,
And will not deaf us with lewd noise, or tongues,
Because we have no heart to break our lungs,
Will pardon our vast Scene, and not disgrace
This Play, meant for your persons, not the place.

Shirley, *The Doubtful Heir*, prologue; *Poems*, 1646, D4v–5

212. 1640

Who would rely on Fortune, when *shee's* knowne
An *enemie* to Merit, and hath shewne
Such an example here? Wee that have pay'd
Her tribute to our losse, each night defray'd
The charge of her attendance, now growne poore,
(Through her expences) thrusts us out of doore.
For some peculiar profit; shee has t'ane
A course to banish Modesty, and retaine
More dinn, and *incivility* than hath been
Knowne in the *Bearward Court*, the *Beargarden*.
Those that now sojourne with *her*, bring a noyse
Of *Rables*, *Apple-wives* and Chimney-boyes,
Whose shrill confused Ecchoes loud doe cry,
Enlarge your *Commons*, We hate *Privacie*.
Those that have plots to *undermine*, and strive
To blow their Neighbours up, so *they* may thrive,
What censure they deserve, *wee* leave to you,
To whom the judgement on't belongs as due.
Here Gentlemen, our Anchor's fixt; And wee
(Disdaining Fortune's mutability)
Expect your kinde acceptance; then wee'l sing
(Protected by your smiles our ever-spring;)
As pleasant as if wee had still possest
Our lawfull Portion out of Fortunes brest:
Onely wee would request you to forbeare
Your wonted custome, banding *Tyle*, or Peare,
Against our *curtaines*, to allure us forth.
I pray take notice *these* are of more Worth,
Pure Naples silk, not *Worsted*, we have ne're
An Actour here has mouth enough to teare

Language by th'eares; this forlorne Hope shall be
By Us refin'd from such grosse injury.
And then let your judicious Loves advance
Us to our Merits, them to their Ignorance.

John Tatham, 'A Prologue spoken upon removing of the late Fortune Players to the Bull', *The Fancies Theater*, H2v–H3

213. 1640

When last we did encounter with the G LOBE ,
The Heav'ns was pleas'd to grace us with his robe
Of settled motions; but *Aquarius*, hee,
Like an ambitious Churle, disdaines that wee
Should have another meeting . . .

John Tatham, 'Upon the hinderance of meeting by raine, sent to his friend Mr. W. B.', *The Fancies Theater*, C1v

214. 1641

[Plays are] First for strangers, who can desire no better recreation, then to come and see a Play: then for Citizens, to feast their wits: then for Gallants, who otherwise perhaps would spend their money in drunkennesse, and lasciviousnesse, doe find a great delight and delectation to see a Play: then for the learned, it does increase and adde . . . to their knowledge.

Anon., *The Stage-Players Complaint*, p. 24

215. 1641?

His *Schollars* school'd, sayd if he had been wise
He should have wove in one two comedies.
The first for th'gallery, in which the throne
To their amazement should descend alone,
The rosin-lightning flash and monster spire
Squibs, and words hotter than his fire.
Th'other for the gentlemen o'th'pit
Like to themselves all spirit, fancy, wit.

Richard Lovelace, *The Scholars*, epilogue, in *Poems*, 1649

216. 1643

. . . we shall for the future promise, never to admit into our sixpenny-roomes those unwholesome inticing Harlots, that sit there meerely to be taken up by Prentizes or Lawyers Clerks; nor any female of what degree soever, except they come lawfully with their husbands, or neere allies: the abuses in Tobacco shall be reformed, none vended, not so much as in three-penny galleries, unless of the pure *Spanish* leafe. For ribaldry, or any such paltry stuffe, as may scandall the pious, and provoke the wicked to loosenesse, we will utterly expell it, with the bawdy and ungracious Poets, the authors to the *Antipodes*.

Anon., *The Actors Remonstrance, or Complaint*, conclusion

217. 1653

The Gentry of our Nation were as much civiliz'd by the *Stage*, as either by *Travail*, or the *University*, in beholding the abridgment there of the best Fashions, Language, and Behaviour of the Time. And here if any one object, that on the *Stage* much *Ribaldry* and *Scurrility* was *Introduc'd* and *Represented*: I answer, as little here as in any place of the *Christian world* besides. Our *English* eare (what time the *Stage* was most frequented, and in request) having been the least *corrupted* part of the Nation, and that sense still so *neate* and *nice* in us, as no *obscenity*, but well *washt* was ever suffered or admitted on the *Stage*.

> Richard Flecknoe, *Miscellanea*, p. 104

218. 1653

. . . passing on to Black-fryers, and seeing never a *Play-bil* on the Gate, no *Coaches* on the place, nor *Doorkeeper* at the *Play-house* door, with his Boxe like a *Church-warden*, desiring you to remember the poor *Players*, I cannot but say for *Epilogue* to all the *Playes* were ever Acted there:

> *Poor House, that in dayes of our Grand-sires,*
> *Belongst unto the* Mendiant Fryers:
> *And where so oft in our Fathers dayes*
> *We have seen so many of* Shakspears *Playes,*
> *So many of* Johnsons, Beaumonts, *&*Fletchers,
> *Untill I know not what* Puritan *Teachers:*
> *(Who for their* Tone, *their* Language, *&* Action,
> > *Might 'gainst the Stage make* Bedlam *a faction)*
> > *Have made with their Raylings the Players as poore*
> > *As were the* Fryers *and* Poets *before.*

> Richard Flecknoe, *Miscellanea*, pp. 141–2

219. 1654

The players have been appointed, notwithstanding their bills to the contrary, to act what the major part of the company had a mind to. Sometimes *Tamerlane*, sometimes *Jugurtha*, sometimes *The Jew of Malta*, and sometimes parts of all these; and at last, none of the three taking, they were forced to undress and put off their tragick habits, and conclude the day with *The Merry Milkmaides* And unless this were done, and the popular humour satisfied (as sometimes it so fortun'd that the players were refractory), the benches, the tiles, the laths, the stones, oranges, apples, nuts, flew about most liberally; and as there were mechanicks of all professions, who fell every one to his trade, and dissolved a house in an instant, and made a ruin of a stately fabric.

> Edmund Gayton, *Pleasant Notes upon Don Quixot*, p. 272

220. 1654

. . . men come not to study at a Play-house, but love such expressions and passages, which with care insinuate themselves into their capacities.

> Gayton, *Pleasant Notes*, p. 46

221. 1659

The chief of the Spectators sit in the *Gallery* . . . the common sort stand on *the ground* . . . and clap the hands if anything please them.

> Comenius, *Orbis Sensualium Pictus*, English Edition, 1659, p. 264

222. 1671

We may remember that the Red Bull writers, with their Drums, Trumpets, Battels, and Hero's, have had this success formerly.

> Edward Howard, *The Six Days' Adventure*, A4v

223. 1673

[An Appendix] without which a Pamphlet now a dayes, finds as small acceptance as a Comedy did formerly, at the *Fortune* Play-House, without a Jig of *Andrew Kein's* into the bargain.

> Henry Chapman, *The City of Bath Described*, epistle

224. 1699

Before the Wars, there were in being all these Play-houses at the same time. The *Black-friers*, and *Globe* on the Bankside, a Winter and Summer House, belonging to the same Company called the King's Servants; the *Cockpit* or *Phoenix*, in *Drury-lane*, called the Queen's Servants; the private House in *Salisbury-court*, called the Prince's Servants; the Fortune near *White-cross-street*, and the *Red Bull* at the upper end of St. *John's-street*: the two last were mostly frequented by Citizens, and the meaner sort of People. All these Companies got Money, and Liv'd in Reputation, especially those of the *Blackfriars*, who were Men of grave and sober Behaviour.

> James Wright, *Historia Histrionica*, B3

Notes

1. INTRODUCTION

1. See David Bevington, *Action is Eloquence: Shakespeare's Language of Gesture*, Cambridge, Mass., 1984; Alan C. Dessen, *Elizabethan Stage Conventions and Modern Interpreters*, Cambridge, 1984; Jean E. Howard, *Shakespeare's Art of Orchestration*, Urbana, 1984; and for a more detailed account of properties, Jonathan Gill Harris and Natasha Korda, eds., *Staged Properties in Early Modern Drama*, Cambridge, 2002.

2. Previous studies of Shakespearean audiences had different leanings. Alfred Harbage, *Shakespeare's Audience*, New York, 1941, and its development in *Shakespeare and the Rival Traditions*, New York, 1952, created two categories, the citizen and artisan audience at the amphitheatres, opposed by a 'coterie' audience at the hall playhouses. Ann Jennalie Cook, *The Privileged Playgoers of Shakespeare's London, 1576–1642*, Princeton, 1981, found a much higher proportion of the richer sort in all playhouses. Neither book takes much note of the historical changes.

3. See Martin Butler, 'Two Playgoers and the Closing of the London Theatres, 1642', *Theatre Research International* 9 (1984), 93–9.

4. See Janet S. Loengard, 'An Elizabethan Lawsuit: John Brayne, his Carpenter, and the Building of the Red Lion Theatre', *Shakespeare Quarterly* 35 (1984), 298–310.

2. PHYSICAL CONDITIONS

1. See map, illustration 2, and Glynne Wickham, *Early English Stages 1300–1660*, 3 vols., London, 1959–81, II.2.60–78, 101–16 (*EES*). Evidence about the Red Lion is supplied by Janet S. Loengard, 'An Elizabethan Lawsuit'.

2. See Glynne Wickham's discussion of the relationship between the baiting houses and the playhouses, *EES* II.1.161–3, 204–5.

3. Samuel Kiechel, quoted in E. K. Chambers, *The Elizabethan Stage*, 4 vols., Oxford, 1923, II.358 (*ES*).

4. The evidence about the entrance-ways is examined thoroughly by Richard Hosley, *The Revels History of Drama in English III, 1576–1613*, pp. 157–64 (*Revels History*). The phrase 'twopenny galleries' came into use at the end of the century, suggesting that a single payment of twopence for a place in the galleries replaced the penny-by-penny system at about the time the Globe was built. Questions about the use of external stair turrets for

access directly into the galleries are bedevilled by contradictory evidence. See Gurr, 'The Bare Island', *ShS* 47 (1994), 29–43, pp. 40–3, and 'Entrances and Hierarchy in the Globe Auditorium', *Shakespeare Bulletin* 14 (1996), 11–13.

5. John Orrell, *The Quest for Shakespeare's Globe*, Cambridge, 1982, p. 136, allows 1,848 square feet for the Globe yard, almost exactly the Fortune's yard space, but for this calculation he ignores the area on each flank of the stage platform.

6. John Marston, *Jack Drum's Entertainment*, 1600, 5.1; Thomas Dekker, *Seven Deadly Sins* (1606), *The Ravens Almanacke* (1609), *Worke for Armourers* (1609) and *The Gull's Hornbook* (1609), where the Proemium refers to 'all garlic-mouthed stinkards'.

7. Orrell, *The Quest for Shakespeare's Globe*, p. 135.

8. G. E. Bentley, *The Jacobean and Caroline Stage*, 7 vols., Oxford, 1940–68, IV.871 (*JCS*).

9. Richard Hosley suggested that the balcony rooms over the stage, where De Witt shows audience, were the 'lord's room'. He put the word in the singular, on the grounds that they were set aside for the company's patron. But only the Globe was owned by the company that played in it, and all the playhouses had spare space for seating on either side of their central stage balcony. The argument that the lords' rooms were positioned where Henslowe had his 'gentlemen's rooms', in the middle gallery next to the stage, do not satisfy either the point about spare space or access through the tiring house. For a contrary view, see Gabriel Egan, 'The Situation of the "Lords' Rooms": A Revaluation', *Review of English Studies* 48 (1997), 297–309.

10. John Harington, *Letters and Epigrams*, ed. N. E. McClure, Philadelphia, 1930, pp. 245–6. The autograph (BL Add. MS 12049) is addressed to his friend Sir John Lee. Most of Harington's epigrams can be dated between 1585 and 1603.

11. *Henslowe's Diary*, ed. R. A. Foakes and R. T. Rickert, Cambridge, 1961, pp. 22–30 (*Diary*); J. Leeds Barroll, *Revels History* III.48. Extrapolating from the *Diary* figures, it seems that in 1594–5, with two amphitheatres offering plays, about 15,000 people went to plays each week. With three or more amphitheatres and two indoor playhouses open in 1605, the attendances would have been nearer 21,000 a week.

12. Orrell, *The Quest for Shakespeare's Globe*, p. 137.

13. *ES* II.535. Harington's Epigram 195 (*Letters and Epigrams*, pp. 227–8) describes the game succinctly.

14. Ann Jennalie Cook, *The Privileged Playgoers*, p. 187, notes a comment by Middleton about the Fortune, that 'Within one square a thousand heads are laid' (*The Roaring Girl*, 1.2) and concludes that it indicates the capacity of the yard. I would suspect that the galleries, also in the square, would be included in Middleton's figure, and that it shows the expected total attendance in a playhouse of at least twice that capacity.

15. See Orrell, *The Quest for Shakespeare's Globe*, p. 129.
16. See Reavley Gair, *The Children of Paul's*, Cambridge, 1982, chapter 2. Herbert Berry, 'Where was the Playhouse in which the Boy Choristers of St Paul's Cathedral Performed Plays?' *Medieval and Renaissance Drama in England* 13 (2001), 101–16, reckons it was not where Gair locates it, and had a capacity of perhaps as few as eighty people.
17. The full story of the Chamberlain's Men's plan to use an amphitheatre for summer and a hall playhouse for winter, not fully realised until 1608, has been told elsewhere, for instance in Gurr, *The Shakespeare Company 1594–1642*, Cambridge, 2004.
18. For a more detailed account of this exceptional deal, see Gurr, *The Shakespeare Company*, pp. 65–77.
19. The most careful survey of the evidence for the design of the second Blackfriars hall playhouse is by Richard Hosley, *Revels History* III. 197–226. Irwin Smith, *Shakespeare's Blackfriars Theater: Its History and Its Design*, New York, 1964, provides the fullest body of information, including many quotations about the playhouse.
20. The evidence for pricing is summarised in Gurr, *The Shakespearean Stage*, p. 214. William Cavendish's accounts for his visits to the Blackfriars and Paul's in 1600–2 list sums varying from one shilling to 4s 6d (fifty-four pennies), plus threepence for his servant (see Appendix 1, Sir William Cavendish). Oddly, the smallest price he paid was just under a shilling, of which ninepence was for a stool on the stage. Charges probably varied according to the customer and how much the gatherer could winkle out of him or her.
21. In the prologue to *Jack Drum's Entertainment* (1600) they are addressed as 'this choise selected influence'.
22. Hosley, *Revels History* III.212. See also John Orrell, 'The Private Theatre Auditorium', *Theatre Research International* 9 (1984), 79–94.
23. The letter describing the incident was by the professional letter-writer John Pory. Herbert Berry used it to prove where the boxes were located at Blackfriars, in 'The Stage and Boxes at Blackfriars', *Studies in Philology* 63 (1966), 163–86.
24. *The Gull's Hornbook*, 1610, chapter 6.
25. John Marston, *The Malcontent*, 1604, Induction. The Induction was written for the Shakespeare company by John Webster.
26. Beeston probably called his hall playhouse the Cockpit because it was adapted from an old game house (he called its replacement, after apprentices attacked and burned it, the Phoenix). Inigo Jones's drawings seem to be an enlargement of the originally circular building. See John Orrell, *The Theatres of Inigo Jones and John Webb*, Cambridge, 1985, chapter 3.
27. *ES* IV.316.
28. See George Whetstone, prefatory epistle to *Promos and Cassandra*, 1578; Thomas Dekker, *The Ravens Almanacke*, 1609, and other instances, including the prologue to *Romeo and Juliet*, quoted in *ES* II.243.

29. *JCS* I.5.
30. See 2.58. John Taylor the Water Poet, in his 1614 pamphlet *The True Cause of the Water-mens Suit concerning Players*, probably exaggerated the numbers ferried to the Bankside playhouses: 'the Players have all (except the King's men) left their usuall residency on the Bankeside, and doe play in Middlesex farre remote from the Thames, so that every day in the weeke they doe draw unto them three or four thousand people, that were used to spend their monies by water' (*Works*, 1630, p. 172). Thomas Overbury's Character 'A Water-Man', also published in 1614, suggests that his favourite element was stronger than water. 'The Play-houses only keepe him sober, and as it doth many other Gallants, make him an afternoons man' (*Characters*, ed. W. J. Paylor, 1936, p. 68). The term 'afternoon's man' was a euphemism for a chronic drunkard.
31. *JCS* I.4–5. According to Edmund Howes's additions to Stow's *Annales*, the 'ordinary use of coaches' did not begin until 1605 (*Annales*, 1631, p. 867).
32. John Tatham, in a poem 'Upon the hindrance of meeting by raine, sent to his friend Mr. W. B.', exonerates the Globe in verses punning heavily on the signs of the zodiac which decorated the stage cover at the playhouse. The hindrance seems to have been over getting to the playhouse in the rain rather than getting wet in its yard.
33. *The City Match*, 1639, prologue.
34. *Thomas Platter's Travels in England*, trans. Clare Williams, London, 1937, p. 176.
35. Epigram 36, 'Of Tobacco', in *The Poems*, ed. Robert Krueger, Oxford, 1975, p. 144.
36. *Travels in England*, pp. 170–1.
37. 'To the Gentleman Reader', *The Letting of Humours Blood in the Head-Vaine*, 1600. Rowlands also wrote in 1619 about a gallant demanding that the feather-seller 'plume my head with his best Estridge tayle' (*A pair of Spy-knaves*, 1619).
38. That was Dekker's term in the prologue to *If This Be Not a Good Play*, 1612. Donald Lupton in *London and the Countrey Carbonadoed*, 1631, acknowledged hissing as a mark of an audience's disapproval when he wrote '[players] love not the company of Geese or Serpants, because of their hissing' (G1v).
39. Fletcher wrote bitterly of the hostile reception his *Faithful Shepherdess* received when played by the boys at a hall playhouse in about 1608 (2.89). Edmund Gayton, amongst other notes on playing written in Oxford in the 1650s, wrote sarcastically of an amphitheatre audience demanding a change of play and later wrecking the playhouse (2.219).
40. The original order was given in Latin. This is David Masson's translation, from his *Life of Milton*, I.218.
41. *Jests to make you Merie*, 1607, F3.
42. *ES* IV.297–8; *JCS* I.21, 222.

3. SOCIAL COMPOSITION

1. Lawrence Stone, *Family and Fortune: Studies in Aristocratic Finance in the Sixteenth and Seventeenth Centuries*, Oxford, 1973, pp. 59–61. Other London wage rates are in *Proclamations*, ed. P. L. Hughes and J. F. Larkin, 2 vols., New Haven, 1964, II.22–3. Carol Chillington Rutter, *Documents of the Rose Playhouse*, 2nd edn, Manchester, 2002, has an appendix listing the relevant statutes.

2. Louis B. Wright, *Middle-Class Culture in Elizabethan England*, Chapel Hill, 1935. The notion of an identifiable social rank coming into existence in the sixteenth century is too gross an oversimplification to be of much use. Ann Jennalie Cook's second chapter in *The Privileged Playgoers*, about the more privileged class, offers a useful correction to Wright.

3. Sir Thomas Smith, *De Republica Anglorum*, 1583. Mary Dewar's edition (1982) discusses in detail the date of original composition and the relationship between Smith's description and Harrison's. She dates both in the early 1560s, and reckons Smith to be the borrower from Harrison.

4. Thomas Wilson, 'The State of England (1600)', ed. F. J. Fisher, *Camden Miscellany*, 3rd series, 52 (1936), pp. i–vii, 1–47.

5. Keith Wrightson, *English Society 1580–1680*, London, 1981, p. 13, emphasises two major social developments in this period. The first was an enhanced sense of national identity, the second an intensified polarisation between the poor and the wealthy.

6. The young Earl of Southampton spent over £40,000 in the six years up to the time he was arrested for supporting Essex in the attempted coup of 1601, more than half of it financed by the sale of land. See Stone, *Family and Fortune*, pp. 217–19.

7. Roger Finlay, *Population and Metropolis: the Demography of London 1580–1650*, Cambridge, 1981, p. 6.

8. Holinshed, *Chronicles*, 1577, vol. I, Bk ii, chapter 5. All the quotations from Harrison come from this chapter.

9. Wilfred R. Prest, *The Inns of Court under Elizabeth I and the Early Stuarts*, London, 1972, pp. 6–8.

10. Wrightson, *English Society 1580–1680*, p. 28.

11. A. L. Beier, 'Social Problems in Elizabethan London', *Journal of Interdisciplinary History* 9 (1978), 209, 214. (See also the author's *Masterless Men. The Vagrancy Problem in England 1560–1640*, London, 1985.)

12. Ibid., p. 204.

13. David Cressy, *Literacy and the Social Order: Reading and Writing in Tudor and Stuart England*, Cambridge, 1980, p. 129. Cressy makes the basis for his calculations the ability to sign one's name instead of using a cross. This is not a very dependable basis for determining true literacy, since illness or other difficulties might hinder the use of a complete signature, particularly in wills, which are Cressy's chief evidence. The printer Lionel Snowden, working in a trade demanding thorough literacy, signed his will with a cross in 1616. A cross might be used as a religious token

instead of a name. Moreover Shakespeare's father, wholly literate, sometimes signed official papers with his craft mark. Women were often taught to read but not to write, and might have valued plays precisely because they did not have to read them. Comments from the time are unhelpful because of their prejudice. The prologue to Davenant's *Platonic Lovers*, written to please Henrietta Maria and staged at the Blackfriars in 1635, claimed that half the city-dwellers were illiterate: "'Bove half our City audience would be lost, / That knew not how to spell [the play's name] on the post.'

14. Cressy, *Literacy and the Social Order*, p. 134.
15. Ibid., p. 128. The publishing of escapist prose fiction, characterised by the preference the citizen's wife expresses in *The Knight of the Burning Pestle*, increased threefold in the forty years up to 1600.
16. J. H. Wiffen, *Historical Memoirs of the House of Russell*, 2 vols., 1833, I.499.
17. The play was probably *2 Tamburlaine*. Gawdy's letter says that 'My L. Admyrall his men and players having a devyse in ther playe to tye one of their fellows to a poste and so to shoote him to deathe, having borrowed their callyvers one of the players handes swerved his peece being charged with bullet missed the fellowe he aymed at and killed a child, and a woman great with child forthwith, and hurt an other man in the head very soore' (*The Letters of Philip Gawdy*, ed. I. H. Jeayes, London, 1906, p. 23).
18. John Taylor, *The praise, antiquity, and commodity of beggery, beggers and begging*, London, 1628, C3.
19. *The Autobiography of Anne Lady Halkett*, Camden Society, 1875, p. 3. See also Richard Levin, 'Women in the Renaissance Theatre Audience', *Shakespeare Quarterly* 40 (1989), 165–74.
20. Graham Parry gives a succinct account of her life in *The Seventeenth Century. The Intellectual and Cultural Context of English Literature, 1603–1700*, London, 1989.
21. 'T. M.' is sometimes said to have been Tom May, a playwright, poet and translator of Lucian in the 1620s. He wrote a play, *The Heir*, published in 1622, translations of Virgil's *Georgics*, Lucan and other classics, and after 1642, when he was Secretary to the Long Parliament, he wrote *The History of the Parliament of England which began Nov 3, 1640*, taking it up to the Battle of Newbury in 1643, the period through which he was Secretary. The chapter from *The Life of a Satyricall Puppy Called Nim* is reprinted in full in Appendix 2.160.
22. Quoted by Cyrus Hoy, *Introductions, Notes and Commentaries to Texts in 'The Dramatic Works of Thomas Dekker'*, 4 vols., Cambridge, 1980, III.2.
23. *JCS* VI.146.
24. *ES* I.264, II.447.
25. *ES* III.387.
26. *ES* IV.280.

27. Frederic Gerschow, printed and translated in *Transactions of the Royal Historical Society* n.s. 6 (1892), p. 29.
28. Sir Hugh Cholmley, *Memoirs*, 1787, p. 18.
29. E. K. Chambers, *William Shakespeare*, 2 vols., Oxford, 1930, II.335 (*WS*).
30. William B. Rye, *England as Seen by Foreigners in the Days of Elizabeth and James I*, London, 1865, p. 61.
31. Alfred Harbage, who first developed this thought, in his book on audiences, elaborated in *Shakespeare and the Rival Traditions*, overstates the case in its polarising into two distinct audience types, but he assembles too much supporting evidence to be ignored. G. E. Bentley asserted in 1948 that Shakespeare's last plays were affected by the acquisition of the Blackfriars in 1608 ('Shakespeare and the Blackfriars Theatre', *Shakespeare Survey* 1 (1948), 38–50), but his view has worn even less well.
32. Induction, 1–3. The first quarto of 1613 mispunctuates these lines, putting the comma which should end the first line at the end of the second. See J. C. Maxwell, 'Conservative Principles', *Essays in Criticism* 21 (1971), 389.
33. *An Apology for Actors*, 1611, G3v; Anon., *Mucedorus* 1611, epilogue. See also *ES* IV.35–6.
34. *Middlesex County Records*, II.71, cited by Cook, *The Privileged Playgoers*, p. 137.
35. *JCS* IV.225.
36. E. M. Symonds, 'The Diary of John Greene (1635–1657)', *English Historical Review* 43 (1928), 385–94.
37. BL MS Egerton 2983.
38. BL Harleian 454, summarised in *JCS* II.673–81.

4. MENTAL COMPOSITION

1. *Discoveries, Works*, VIII.578.
2. *The Diary of John Manningham of the Middle Temple, 1602–1603*, ed. R. Parker Sorlien, Hanover, N.H., 1976, p. 202.
3. Kurt Weber, *Lucius Cary*, New York, 1940, p. 63.
4. *The Complete Works of John Webster*, ed. F. L. Lucas, 4 vols., London, 1927, III.327. I am indebted to Michael Neill for drawing this reference to my attention.
5. T. W. Baldwin, *William Shakespeare's Small Latine and Lesse Greeke*, 2 vols., Urbana, 1944, I.344.
6. George Puttenham, *The Arte of English Poesie*, ed. Gladys Willcock and Alice Walker, Cambridge, 1936, p. 145. Puttenham condemned the rhetorical figure of '*Barbarismus* or Forrein speech' (p. 250). His view represents the hostility of his time, prompted by anti-Catholic prejudice, against the use of Latinisms and neologisms based on Latin called 'ink-horn terms'. He wrote (p. 36) of the 'beholders' of ancient tragedies, and translated *theatrum* as 'a beholding place'. He also referred (p. 291) to 'the hearer

or beholder'. But by the time his book was published some years after its composition Sidney had already introduced the word 'spectator', and the Latin term easily prevailed. A reference in an anti-playing pamphlet of 1625 to 'hearers and beholders' is a sign of its derivation from the diatribes of the 1580s (*A Shorte Treatise of Stage Playes*, 1625, chapter 4).

7. 'An Expostulation with Inigo Jones', *Works*, VIII.402.

8. Ibid., IV.43. In *The Masque of Queens* (1609), lines 107–10, Jonson contrasted the 'quick eares' of a court audience with 'those sluggish ones of Porters, and Mechanicks, that must be bor'd through, at every act, with Narrations'.

9. See 2.153. The point about poets preferring the ear to the eye has been made by Alan C. Dessen, *Elizabethan Drama and the Viewer's Eye*, Chapel Hill, 1977, p. 11. Some playgoers of course also preferred the poetry. Lord Falkland, writing in the 1630s about a playbook in manuscript, asked for a copy on the grounds that 'if I valued it so at the single hearing, when myne eares could not catch half the wordes, what must I do now, in the reading when I may pause upon it'. It might be argued that Falkland viewed the stage presentation of poetry as inadequate compared with reading. Sir Richard Baker in the same decade took the opposite view, affirming his preference for the stage over reading. He also affirmed that sight is more influential than hearing. Both writers are cited by Martin Butler, *Theatre and Crisis 1632–1642*, Cambridge, 1984, pp. 106–7.

10. *The Anatomy of Melancholy*, Part I, Section I, Memb. 2, Subsection 6. The author of *A third blast of retrait from plaies*, 1580, attacked playgoing for its effect on the eyes: 'There commeth much evil in at the eares, but more at the eies, by these two open windowes death breaketh into the soule.' Gosson even includes music as a seduction of the eyes: 'In Comedies delight being moved with varietie of shewes, of events, of musicke, the longer we gaze, the more we crave.' *Playes Confuted in Five Actions*, 1582, 4th Action.

11. Puttenham, *The Arte of English Poesie*, p. 55.

12. T. G., *The Rich Cabinet*, 1616, Q4.

13. *The Works of Geoffrey Chaucer*, ed. F. N. Robinson, London, 1933, *Canterbury Tales* Fragment III, lines 1935–7.

14. Quoted by David Bevington, *From 'Mankind' to Marlowe*, Cambridge, Mass., 1962, p. 41. Despite the emphatically English lexis, 'audiens' is the classical Latin for a single hearer. In this context where the term is clearly plural it presumably is a variant spelling for 'audience', from Latin *audientia*, an audience or attentive hearing.

15. See 2.40. Other writers who used 'spectator' include Daniel, *The Civil Wars*, 1595, II.58; *A Warning for Fair Women*, 1599, Induction; *The Fair Maid of the Exchange*, c.1602, G2, and most pointedly William Percy, who began *Cuckqueans and Cuckolds Errant*, 1600, with a prologue spoken by Tarlton's ghost, who addresses the audience as 'Spectators', and goes on to claim that who he is must be visible to all, so that he need not 'recapitulate

into your eares now, either my name or my Person'. The only writer who does not seem to have been sensitive to the distinction between hearing and seeing was William Cornwallis, who wrote in his *Essayes*, 1600, 'Let ape-keepers and players catch the eares of their Auditory and Spectators with faire bumbaste words & set speeches' (H3).

16. See Andrew Gurr, 'The Bear, the Statue, and Hysteria in *The Winter's Tale*', *Shakespeare Quarterly* 34 (1983), 420–5.

17. 3.2.35–7. The contrast between a told tale which is incredible and a visual presentation which convinces is affirmed by Paulina when the statue comes to life, 5.3.115–17.

18. N. W. Bawcutt, *The Control and Censorship of Caroline Drama. The Records of Sir Henry Herbert, Master of the Revels 1623–73*, Oxford, 1996, p. 180.

19. J. H., *This World's Folly*, 1615. The same writer has an 'Oyster-crying Audience' and a 'Monster-headed Multitude' (B2v).

20. Epistle to Henry Fitzgeoffery, *Satyres and Satyricall Epigrams*, 1617.

21. The anti-democratic image of the 'many-headed monster' was integral to the term 'multitude'. As early as 1582 Gosson was writing of a playhouse audience that 'the auncient Philosophers . . . called them a monster of many heades' (*Plaies Confuted in Five Actions*, 2nd Action). Nathaniel Field in his verses sympathising over the hostile reception for Fletcher's *The Faithful Shepherdess* wrote of the audience as a 'monster' clapping its 'thousand hands' (2.92).

22. *A Treatise at Playe*, 1598, reprinted in *Nugae Antiquae*, 1804, I.186–232, pp. 190–1.

23. *Letters and Epigrams*, p. 31.

24. Richard Levin, *New Readings vs. Old Plays*, Chicago, 1979, Appendix, 'The Figures of Fluellen'; and 'The Relation of External Evidence to the Allegorical and Thematic Interpretation of Shakespeare', *Shakespeare Studies* 13 (1980), 1–29.

25. See R. H. MacDonald, *The Library of Drummond of Hawthornden*, Edinburgh, 1971. Drummond's reading between 1606 and 1619 is strikingly similar in its range if not in its detail to Gabriel Harvey's, judging from Harvey's marginalia made in the years 1582–99.

26. Carleton is quoted in Ralph Winwood, *Memorials of Affairs of State*, 2 vols., London, 1725, II.44; Busino in *Calendar of State Papers Venetian 1617–1619*, pp. 67–8.

27. The boys unofficially 'apprenticed' to those players who as members of London's twelve trading guilds could claim the authority to give them bed and board for seven years had to be younger than the official apprentices. In London apprentices were not officially taken on until they were seventeen, usually too old for the unbroken voices needed for the women's roles.

28. See F. W. Brownlow, *Shakespeare, Harsnett, and the Devils of Denham*, Newark, 1993, and Gurr, 'Metatheatre and the Fear of Playing', in *Neo-Historicism*, ed. Robin Headlam Wells, Glenn Burgess and Rowland Wymer, Cambridge, 2000, pp. 91–110.

29. 21 September 1604, *Dudley Carleton to John Chamberlain 1603–1624*, ed. Maurice Lee, Jr, New Brunswick, 1972, p. 65.
30. Forman's text is accurately transcribed in *WS* II.337–41. Barbara Traister, *The Notorious Astrological Physician of London. Works and Days of Simon Forman*, Chicago, 2001, is a detailed study. For an analysis of Forman's account of *Macbeth*, see Leah Scragg, 'Macbeth on Horseback', *Shakespeare Survey* 26 (1973), 81–8.
31. Holles Letter Book, Nottingham University Library, Ne C 15,405, quoted in *A Game at Chesse*, ed. T. H. Howard-Hill, Manchester, 1993, pp. 198–200.
32. Quoted by Herbert Berry, *Shakespeare's Playhouses*, New York, 1987, pp. 123–4.
33. Levin, 'The Relation of External Evidence', pp. 10, 21.
34. *The Diary of Samuel Pepys*, ed. Robert Latham and William Matthews, 9 vols., 1973, II.156.
35. *Calendar of State Papers Domestic Chas* Doc. 102. The Duke of Buckingham's visit to the Globe in 1628 to see *Henry VIII*, and his departure after watching the execution of his predecessor in Act 2 marks another use of playgoing for politics.
36. David Lindley, *The Trials of Frances Howard: Fact and Fiction at the Court of King James*, Basingstoke, 1993.

5. THE EVOLUTION OF TASTES

1. Scott McMillin and Sally-Beth MacLean make a strong case for the political role of the company founded in 1583 to show the queen's livery to the nation. See *The Queen's Men and their Plays*, Cambridge, 1998.
2. Ann Righter (Barton), *Shakespeare and the Idea of the Play*, London, 1962, p. 53. A good account of the 'romantic narrative' plays of 1570–90 is Patricia Russell's essay in *Elizabethan Theatre*, ed. J. R. Brown and Bernard Harris, London, 1966, pp. 106–29.
3. J. Leeds Barroll, in *Revels History* III.4–14.
4. *ES* IV.280.
5. Pistol's fortuitously searching question to the disguised king, *Henry V*, 4.1.38.
6. The phrase is by An. Sc. of *Hamlet*, in *Daiphantus*, written in 1600 but published in 1604.
7. Gabriel Harvey, *Foure Letters and certeine sonnets*, 1592, p. 19. Harvey writes in the third letter of being invited by Tarlton to see his *Seven Deadly Sins* at Oxford. Alexandra Halasz, in ' "So beloved that men use his picture for their signs": Richard Tarlton and the Uses of Sixteenth-Century Celebrity', *Shakespeare Studies* 23 (1995), 19–38, rehearses the evidence for Tarlton's 'star' quality and his place in the development of a 'national' or class identity. Richard Helgerson, *Forms of Nationhood*, Chicago, 1993, discusses Tarlton in chapter 5. Peter Womack's essay ('Imagining Communities: Theatres and the English Nation in the Sixteenth Century', in

Culture and History 1350–1600, ed. David Aers, London, 1992, pp. 91–146) makes a more general point about the role of playgoing in shaping a sense of the nation in these years.

8. *Tarltons Jestbook*, titlepage. The only extant edition was printed in 1613, but previous ones had appeared before 1600.

9. The only surviving fragment is in the Folger Shakespeare Library. It is described and quoted by M. C. Bradbrook, *The Rise of the Common Player*, London, 1964, pp. 173–6.

10. Both passages are quoted in Gurr, *The Shakespearean Stage*, 3rd edn, pp. 87–8.

11. *Poems*, ed. Krueger, p. 181.

12. For instance Samuel Rowlands, *The Letting of Humours Blood in the Head-Vaine*, Sat. 4, D8.

13. Richard Jones, the publisher of the 1590 edition, wrote of the omissions as 'far unmet for the matter . . . though haply they have been of some vain conceited fondlings greatly gaped at'.

14. *ES* II.75.

15. Reavley Gair, *The Children of Paul's*, p. 98.

16. Ibid., p. 109.

17. See O. L. Brownstein, 'A Record of London Inn Playhouses from *c.* 1565–1590', *Shakespeare Quarterly* 22 (1971), p. 22. Richard Flecknoe, however, writing in the 1660s, declared that the Bull and Cross Keys both had inn-yards still in existence (*A Discourse of the English Stage*, p. 2). Glynne Wickham discounts Flecknoe's comment (*EES* II.1.190–1).

18. *JCS* II.361.

19. See 2.8. Sidney was equally derisive.

20. *Revels History* III.256.

21. For imitations of *Tamburlaine* in plays see Peter Berek, '*Tamburlaine's* Weak Sons, Imitation as Interpretation before 1593', *Renaissance Drama* n.s. 13 (1982), 55–82.

22. 'La "Tragédie espagnole" face à la critique élisabethaine et jacobéenne', in *Dramaturgie et société*, ed. Jean Jacquot, 2 vols., Paris 1968, II.607–31.

23. Bradbrook, *The Rise of the Common Player*, pp. 130–1.

24. T. M. (Middleton?), *The Blacke Booke*, B4r.

25. Quoted in *ES* III.425.

26. *The Knave of Clubs*, 1609, p. 29. Aubrey cites a legend that Alleyn was frightened by a devil when playing Faustus and vowed to found Dulwich College as a result.

27. Starting with Greene, *Perimedes the Blacksmith*, 1588, preface.

28. *Thomas Platter's Travels in England*, p. 170.

29. Lyly, *A Whip for an Ape* (*Complete Works*, III.421); Nashe, *Martins Months Minde* (*Works*, ed. R. B. McKerrow, 10 vols., London, 1904, I.166).

30. The fourth Martinist tract, *Hay any worke for Cooper*, issued early in 1589, cheekily proposed candidates for Martin's identity, including both Penry and Wiggington (p. 31).

31. *Chronicles of England, Scotlande and Irelande*, 2nd edn, 1587, III.1062–6.

32. *ES* I.267 note 4.
33. Quoted by C. J. Sisson, *Lost Plays of Shakespeare's Age*, London, 1936, p. 58.
34. One ballad was entered in the Stationers' Register in July 1624, as *The repentance of* NATHANAEL TINDALL *that killed his mother*, and the other in September as *A Most bloudy unnaturall and unmatchable murther Committed in Whitechappel by* NATHANAELL TINDALL *upon his owne mother.* See *JCS* III.186 [i.e. 286].
35. *JCS* III.75–6.
36. Sisson, *Lost Plays of Shakespeare's Age*, p. 78.
37. Quoted in *ES* I.322 note 2.
38. On 10 May 1601 the Privy Council instructed the Middlesex magistrates to suppress a play at the Curtain because it portrayed 'the persons of some gentlemen of good desert and quality that are yet alive, under obscure manner, but yet in such sort as all the hearers may take notice both of the matter and of the persons that are meant thereby' (*ES* I.324). The 'obscure manner' of their representation probably meant that the persons portrayed were notable enough for the players to anticipate censure. The offence over Chapman's *Byron* was committed by the boys of Blackfriars. Sir Thomas Lake wrote to Lord Salisbury on 11 March 1608 that 'His ma' was well pleased with that which your lo. advertiseth concerning the committing of the players that have offended in the matters of France, and commanded me to signifye to your lo. that for the others who have offended in the matter of the Mynes and other lewd words which is the children of the blackfriers That though he had signified his mynde to your lo. by my lo. of Montgommery yet I should repeate it again That his G. had vowed they should never play more but should first begg their bred and he would have his vow performed.' *Malone Society Collections*, II.2, 1923, p. 149.
39. *Calendar of State Papers Domestic, Eliz*, CCLXXIV.138.
40. Guilpin, *Skialetheia*, Sat. 1, 'In Foelix', C3v; the attack on Raleigh, 1603, is in *Poetical Miscellanies*, ed. J. O. Halliwell, London, 1845, p. 17.
41. See L. G. Salingar, Gerald Harrison and Bruce Cochran, 'Les Comédiens et leur public en Angleterre de 1520 à 1640', *Dramaturgie et société* II.553 (table 10).
42. See John C. Meagher, 'Hackwriting and the Huntingdon Plays', in *Elizabethan Theatre*, ed. Brown and Harris, pp. 197–219.
43. Roslyn Lander Knutson, *The Repertory of Shakespeare's Company 1594–1613*, Fayetteville, 1991, gives a careful analysis of both repertories for this period.
44. See Judith Doolin Spikes, 'The Jacobean History Play and the Myth of the Elect Nation', *Renaissance Drama*, n.s. 8 (1977), 117–49.
45. *Singing Simkin* is reprinted in C. R. Baskerville, *The Elizabethan Jig*, Chicago, 1929, pp. 444–9.
46. Neil Carson, 'John Webster: the Apprentice Years', *Elizabethan Theatre* 6 (1978), 76–87.

47. See Frank Kerins, 'The Crafty Enchaunter: Ironic Satires and Jonson's *Every Man Out of his Humour*', *Renaissance Drama* n.s. 14 (1983), 132–3.
48. See 2.99. Heywood's pamphlet was probably originally written in 1607–8. Marston in *Jack Drum's Entertainment* aims Heywood's kind of animus directly at Jonson, who, he claims, takes pleasure 'to Gull / Good honest soules, and in thy arrogance / And glorious ostentation of thy wit, / Thinke God infused all perfection / Into thy soule alone . . .' (5, conclusion).
49. See Raman Selden, *English Verse Satire, 1590–1765*, London, 1978, p. 72.
50. See Brian Gibbons, *Jacobean City Comedy*, 2nd edn, London, 1980, p. 285.
51. I am inclined to think that *Twelfth Night* was written after *Every Man Out* and partly as a reply to the idea of dramaturgy expressed in that play. See Henk Gras, '*Twelfth Night, Every Man Out of his Humour*, and the Middle Temple Revels of 1597–98', *MLR* 84 (1989), 545–64.
52. Two books appeared in 2001 that deal in different ways with the Jonson/Shakespeare rivalry and the questions about the Chamberlain's Men's staging of *Satiromastix*. James P. Bednarz, *Shakespeare and the Poets' War*, New York, 2001, and Roslyn Lander Knutson, *Playing Companies and Commerce in Shakespeare's Time*, Cambridge, 2001.
53. *The Court and Times of James I*, ed. Thomas Birch, 2 vols., London, 1848, I.60–1.
54. Chapman, *All Fools*, 2.1; Jonson, *Volpone*, prologue: Day, *Isle of Gulls*, prologue; Marston, *The Fawn*, prologue; *Sophonisba*, epilogue; Beaumont, *The Woman Hater*, Apologetical prologue; Barry, *Ram Alley*, prologue; *Mucedorus* (1610), epilogue.
55. According to Alfred Harbage, *Shakespeare and the Rival Traditions*, p. 71.
56. Alexander Leggatt, *Citizen Comedy in the Age of Shakespeare*, Toronto, 1973, p. 4.
57. Ibid., p. 130.
58. Anne Barton, *Ben Jonson, Dramatist*, Cambridge, 1984, p. 68.
59. L. C. Knights, *Drama and Society in the Age of Jonson*, London, 1937, especially chapter 7.
60. Gibbons, *Jacobean City Comedy*, pp. 76–7.
61. The Fortune company tried to set up a similar arrangement with their landlord Alleyn in 1618. Unfortunately for them, their playhouse burned down in 1622 at midnight, when nobody was there to save the costumes and playbooks, unlike Shakespeare's company when the Globe burned in 1613. After that impoverishment the new arrangement could not survive. See Gurr, *The Shakespearian Playing Companies*, Oxford, 1996, pp. 249–50.
62. *The Diary of Lady Margaret Hoby 1599–1605*, ed. Dorothy M. Meads, London, 1930, p. 49.
63. A more detailed account of how the King's Men gained their Blackfriars dominance, in repertory and social catchment, is in Gurr, *The Shakespeare Company 1594–1642*, Cambridge, 2004.

64. G. E. Bentley, 'Shakespeare and the Blackfriars Theatre', *Shakespeare Survey* 1 (1948), 38–50. See also Andrew Gurr, ed., *Philaster*, pp. xliii–l, and J. A. Lavin, 'Shakespeare and the Second Blackfriars', *Elizabethan Theatre* 3 (1973), pp. 66–81.

65. See Gurr, '*The Tempest's* Tempest at Blackfriars', *Shakespeare Survey* 41 (1988), 91–102.

66. See Gurr, 'Playing in Amphitheatres and Playing in Hall Theatres', *Elizabethan Theatre* 13 (1994), 27–62.

67. *JCS*, II.365.

68. John Orrell, *The Theatres of Inigo Jones and John Webb*, Cambridge, 1985, chapter 3. For the argument that the Blackfriars' galleries were curved although the hall was rectangular, see Orrell, 'The Private Theatre Auditorium'.

69. Beeston's tangled finances and the litigation they involved him in are explained by C. J. Sisson, 'Notes on Early Stuart Stage History', *Modern Language Review* 37 (1942), 25–36.

70. *Letters*, II.59–60.

71. See *JCS* I.214–17 and *The Shakespearian Playing Companies*, ch. 22. The only title to have survived from the first period is the lost play *The Younger Brother*. *A Fair Quarrel* and *All's Lost by Lust* can reasonably be identified as Red Bull plays of this period.

72. Leonard Digges, in verses prefixed to the 1640 edition of Shakespeare but probably written in 1622 for the first Folio, wrote of poetasters: 'On Gods name may the Bull or Cockpit have / Your lame blancke Verse, to keepe you from the grave: / Or let new Fortunes younger brethren see, / What they can picke from your leane industry.' The reference to the 'new' Fortune places this close to its rebuilding at the end of 1622. Evidently Digges also regarded the Cockpit and Red Bull as equivalent venues in their judgement of poetry.

73. The phrase is Jonson's, from *Bartholomew Fair*, Induction. Brome addresses the three main categories, plus 'my Countrey folkes too if here be any o' em' in the epilogue to *The Court Beggar*, written for the Cockpit in 1639–40. Shirley's *The Coronation*, written for the Cockpit in 1634–5, has a prologue addressing the 'noble Gentlewomen'.

74. Ford, *The Broken Heart*, 1633, epilogue. Ford's play was written for the Blackfriars. Michael Neill, '"Wit's most accomplished Senate": the Audience of the Caroline Private Theatres', *Studies in English Literature* 18 (1978), pp. 353–8, analyses the new critical sense in detail.

75. Jonson, 'Ode to Joseph Rutter', *Works*, VIII.414–15.

76. Abraham Wright's reading of plays in the 1630s is examined by James McManaway, 'Excerpta Quaedam per A. W. Adolescentem', in *Studies in Honor of DeWitt T. Starnes*, ed. Thomas P. Harrison *et al.*, Houston, 1967, pp. 117–29. Humphrey Mildmay occasionally commented on the plays he went to. He saw 'a base play att the Cockpitt' in March 1634, but also at the Cockpit 'a pretty & Merry Comedy' in June 1633, and Shirley's

Lady of Pleasure, 'that rare play', in 1635. Three plays he marked down as 'foolish'. *JCS* II.673–81.

77. Peter Beal, 'Massinger at Bay: Unpublished Verses in a War of the Theatres', *Yearbook of English Studies* 10 (1980), 190–203, especially p. 194.

78. *Herbert*, p. 19. See Marvin Morillo, 'Shirley's "Preferment" and the Court of Charles I', *Studies in English Literature* 1 (1961), 101–17.

79. Goffe was a clergyman who died in 1629, the year Salisbury Court first opened. The Praeludium refers to Brome's *Antipodes*, produced at Salisbury Court in 1638. Either Shirley or Brome (as G. E. Bentley suggests, *JCS* IV.504) may have revised the play and inserted the Praeludium.

80. *JCS* VI.238–47.

81. *Timber*, in *Works*, VIII.587; Gayton, *Pleasant Notes*, p. 24; Anon., 'The Unfortunate Gallant Gulled at London', *The Pepys Ballads*, ed. Rollins, I.239; Abraham Cowley, *The Guardian*, 1650, C3v.

82. Richard Flecknoe, *Ænigmaticall Characters*, 1658, I8r.

83. Anon., *The Two Merry Milkmaids*, 1620, prologue; Davenant, *The Unfortunate Lovers*, 1673, prologue. See also 2.196, 222.

84. *JCS* I.274–5.

85. *The Rebellion*, 1639, 5.2.

86. *Knavery in All Trades*, 1664, III, E1r.

87. See Butler, *Theatre and Crisis*, pp. 198–203, 206–10.

88. Margot Heinemann in her analysis of censorship in the political aspects of Jacobean and Caroline drama runs the risk of assuming the absence of comment is a token of censorship. See *Puritanism and Theatre*, Cambridge, 1980, especially chapters 9–12. Annabel Patterson, *Censorship and Interpretation*, Wisconsin, 1984, provides some striking examples of tacit censorship in Sidney and in seventeenth-century writers. Much of this is likely to remain unknown territory.

89. See Butler, *Theatre and Crisis*, p. 194.

90. *Herbert*, p. 66.

91. *JCS* V.1106.

92. *Revels History* IV.167.

Select bibliography

(A) PRIMARY TEXTS

In this section, all texts were first printed in London, unless otherwise noted.

Adams, John Quincey, ed. *The Dramatic Records of Sir Henry Herbert, Master of the Revels, 1623–1673*, New Haven, Conn., 1917.

Anon. *The Actors Remonstrance, or Complaint*, 1643.

Gesta Grayorum, 1688.

Haec-Vir: or the Womanish-Man, 1620.

Mucedorus, 1611.

No-body and Some-body, c.1606.

No Wit, No Help Like a Woman's, 1657.

Pimlyco, or Runne Red-Cap, 1609.

A Shorte Treatise of Stage-Plays, 1625.

The Stage-Players Complaint, 1641.

A Warning for Fair Women, 1599.

The Wars of Cyrus, 1594.

Anton, Robert. *The Philosophers Satyrs*, 1617.

Bacon, Francis. *The proficiencie and advancement of Learning, divine and humane*, 1605, revised 1625.

Baker, Richard. *Theatrum Redivivum*, 1662.

Barry, Lording. *Ram Alley*, 1611.

Beaumont, Francis. *The Woman Hater*, 1607; *The Knight of the Burning Pestle*, 1613.

Beaumont, Francis and Fletcher, John. *Dramatic Works*, gen. ed. Fredson Bowers, 10 vols., Cambridge, 1966–96.

Brathwait, Richard [Clitus-Alexandrinus]. *Whimzies: or a New Cast of Characters*, 1631; *Anniversaries upon his Panarete; Continued*, 1635.

Brome, Richard. *The Antipodes*, 1640; *The Court Beggar*, 1653.

Burton, Robert. *The Anatomy of Melancholy*, 1621.

Buttes, Henry. *Dyets Dry Dinner*, 1599.

C., J. *The Two Merry Milkmaids*, 1620.

Carleton, Sir Dudley. *Dudley Carleton to John Chamberlain 1603–1624. Jacobean Letters*, ed. Maurice Lee Jr, New Brunswick, 1972.

Chamberlain, Sir John. *The Letters of John Chamberlain*, ed. N. E. McClure, 2 vols., Philadelphia, 1939.

Chapman, George. *All Fools*, 1605.

Chapman, Henry. *The City of Bath Described*, 1673.

Chettle, Henry. *Kind-Harts Dreame*, 1592.

Cholmley, Sir Hugh. *Memoirs*, 1787.

Cockayne, Aston. *The Obstinate Lady*, 1657.

Comenius [Jan A. Komensky]. *Orbis Sensualium Pictus*, 1659.

Corbet, Richard. *Poems*, 1807.

Cowley, Abraham. *The Guardian*, 1650.

Cranley, Thomas. *Amanda, or The Reformed Whore*, 1635.

Crashaw, William. *The Sermon Preached at the Crosse, Feb. xiiij, 1607*, 1608.

Crosse, Henry. *Vertues Commonwealth*, 1603.

Daborne, Robert. *A Christian Turned Turk*, 1612.

Davenant, William. *The Just Italian*, 1630; *The Wits*, 1636; *The Platonick Lovers*, 1636; *The Unfortunate Lovers*, 1643; *News from Plymouth*, 1673.

Davies, John, of Hereford. *Wittes Pilgrimage*, 1605; *The Scourge of Folly*, 1611.

Davies, Sir John. *Poems*, ed. Robert Krueger, Oxford, 1975.

Day, John. *The Isle of Gulls*, 1606.

Dekker, Thomas. *Dramatic Works*, ed. Fredson Bowers, 4 vols., Cambridge, 1955–61; *The Non-Dramatic Works*, ed. A. B. Grosart, 5 vols., 1884–6.

Dekker, Thomas and Middleton, Thomas. *The Roaring Girl*, 1612.

Drayton, Samuel. *Works*, ed. J. William Hebel, 3 vols., Oxford, 1931–41.

Earle, John. *Microcosmographie*, 1629.

Fennor, William. *Fennors Descriptions*, 1616.

Field, Nathaniel. *A Woman is a Weathercock*, 1612.

F[itzgeoffery], H[enry]. *Satyres: and Satyricall Epigrams: with Certaine Observations at Blackfryers*, 1617.

Flecknoe, Richard. *Miscellanea*, 1653; *Ænigmaticall Characters*, 1658; *A Discourse of the English Stage*, [1664].

Fletcher, John. *The Faithful Shepherdess*, c.1610.

Florio, John. *Florio his first Fruites*, 1578.

G., J. *A Refutation of the Apology for Actors*, 1615.

G[ainsford], T[homas]. *The Rich Cabinet furnished with variety of excellent discriptions*, 1616.

Gawdy, Philip. *Letters*, ed. I. H. Jeayes, 1906.

Gayton, Edmund. *Pleasant Notes upon Don Quixot*, 1654.

Glapthorne, Henry. *Plays and Poems*, ed. R. H. Shepherd, 2 vols., 1874.

Goddard, William. *A Neaste of Waspes*, 1615.

Goffe, Thomas. *The Careless Shepherdess*, 1656.

Gosson, Stephen. *Playes Confuted in Five Actions*, 1582; *The Trumpet of Warre*, 1598.

Greene, Robert. *Life and Complete Works*, ed. A. B. Grosart, 1881; *The Second part of Conny Catching*, 1591; *The second and last part of Conny-catching*, 1592.

Guilpin, Everard. *Skialetheia*, 1598.

H., J. *This World's Folly*, 1615.

Halkett, Anne. *The Autobiography of Anne Lady Halkett*, Camden Society, 1875.

Hall, Joseph. *Virgidemiarum*, 1597; *Characters of Vertues and Vices*, 1608.

Harington, Sir John. *A Treatise at Playe*, 1598; *Letters and Epigrams*, ed. N. E. McClure, Philadelphia, 1930.

Harvey, Gabriel. *Works*, ed. A. B. Grosart, 3 vols., 1884; *Gabriel Harvey's Marginalia*, ed. G. C. Moore Smith, Stratford, 1913.

Hawthornden, Sir John Drummond of. R. H. MacDonald, *The Library of Drummond of Hawthornden*, Edinburgh, 1971.

Heath, John. *Two Centuries of Epigrammes*, 1610.

Henslowe, Philip. *Henslowe's Diary*, ed. R. A. Foakes and R. T. Rickert, Cambridge, 1961.

Heywood, Thomas. *An Apology for Actors*, 1612; *The Brazen Age*, 1613; *A Challenge for Beauty*, 1636.

Hoby, Dame Margaret. *The Diary of Lady Margaret Hoby 1599–1605*, ed. Dorothy M. Meads, 1930.

Howard, Edward. *The Six Days' Adventure*, 1671.

Hughes, P. L. and Larkin, J. F., eds. *Tudor Royal Proclamations*, 3 vols., New Haven, Conn., 1964–9.

Humphrey, Laurence. *The nobles, or of Nobilitye*, 1563.

Jonson, Ben. *Works*, ed. C. H. Herford, P. and E. Simpson, 11 vols., Oxford, 1925–52.

Kemp, William. *Kemps nine daies wonder*, 1600.

Lane, John. *Tom Tell-Troths Message, and His Pens Complaint*, 1600.

L[enton], F[rancis]. *The Young Gallants Whirligig*, 1629; *Characterismi*, 1631.

Lovelace, Sir Richard. *Poems*, 1649.

Lupton, Donald. *London and the Countrey Carbonadoed*, 1632.

Lyly, John. *Complete Works*, ed. R. W. Bond, 3 vols., Oxford, 1892.

M., T. *The Life of a Satyrical Puppy called Nim*, 1657.

Manningham, John. *The Diary of John Manningham*, ed. Robert Parker Sorlien, Hanover, N.H., 1976.

Marmion, Shackerly. *Holland's Leaguer*, 1632.

Marston, John. *The Scourge of Villainy*, 1598; *Jack Drum's Entertainment*, 1601; *The Dutch Courtesan*, 1605; *The Fawn*, 1606; *Sophonisba*, 1606; *What You Will*, 1607.

Massinger, Philip. *The Bondman*, 1624; *The Roman Actor*, 1629; *The City Madam*, 1658.

Mayne, Jasper. *Jonsonus Virbius*, 1638.

Melton, John. *Astrologaster*, 1620.

Middleton, Thomas (?). *Father Hubburds Tale*, 1603; *The Family of Love*, 1608.

Munday, Anthony. *The third blast of retrait from plaies and Theaters*, 1580.

Nabbes, Thomas. *Tottenham Court*, 1638; *The Unfortunate Mother*, 1640.

Nashe, Thomas. *Works*, ed. R. B. McKerrow, 5 vols., 1904–10.

Northbrook, John. *A Treatise wherein Dicing, Vaine playes, or Enterluds, with other idle pastimes, &c., commonly used on the Sabbath day, are reproved by the Authorities of the word of God and the auntient writers*, 1577.

Osborne, Francis. *The True Tragicomedy Formerly Acted at Court*, ed. John Pitcher and Lois Potter, New York and London, 1983.

Overbury, Sir Thomas. *Characters*, ed. W. J. Paylor, Oxford, 1936.

Parrot, Henry. *The More the Merrier*, 1608.

Parsons, Robert. *The Third Part of a Treatise, Intituled: of three Conversions of England*, Paris?, 1603.

Peacham, Henry. *The Compleat Gentleman*, 1622; *The Art of Living in London*, 1642.

Percy, Sir William. *Cuckqueans and Cuckolds Errant*, 1600.

Platter, Thomas. *Thomas Platter's Travels in England 1599*, trans. Clare Williams, 1937.

Prynne, William. *Histriomastix*, 1633.

Puttenham, George. *The Arte of English Poesie*, ed. Gladys Willcock and Alice Walker, Cambridge, 1936.

Rainolds, John. *The Overthrow of Stage Playes*, 1600.

Randolph, Thomas. *The Muses' Looking Glass*, 1638; *Poems*, 1652.

Rowlands, Samuel. *The Letting of Humours Blood in the Head-Vaine*, 1600; *Humors Antique Faces*, 1605; *The Bride*, 1617; *A pair of Spy-knaves*, 1619.

Rutter, William. *The Shepherd's Holiday*, 1635.

Sc., An. *Daiphantus*, 1604.

Shirley, James. *The Changes*, 1632; *The Example*, 1637; *The Coronation*, 1640; *Poems*, 1646.

Smith, Sir Thomas. *De Republica Anglorum*, ed. Mary Dewar, Cambridge, 1982.

Spenser, Edmund. *The Faerie Queene*, ed. A. C. Hamilton, London and New York, 1977.

Stephens, John. *Satyrical Essayes. Characters and Others*, 1615.

Stowe, John. *Annales of England*, 1592; revised by Edmund Howes, 1631.

Suckling, Sir John. *Works*, ed. A. Hamilton Thompson, 1910.

Tatham, John. *The Fancies Theater*, 1640.

Taylor, John. *Workes*, 1630.

Tomkis, Thomas. *Albumazar*, 1615.

Turner, William. *A Dish of Lenten Stuffe*, 1613.

Webster, John. *The Complete Works*, ed. F. L. Lucas, 4 vols., 1927.

Weever, John. *Epigrammes*, in E. A. J. Honigmann, *John Weever*, Appendix, Manchester, 1987; *The Mirror of Martyrs*, 1601.

Wentworth, Thomas. *The Earl of Strafforde's Letters and Dispatches*, ed. William Knowler, 2 vols., 1739.

West, Richard. *Wittes ABC. A Centurie of Epigrammes*, 1608.

Whetstone, George. *Promos and Cassandra*, 1578.

Wilson, Thomas. 'The State of England [1600]', ed. F. J. Fisher, *Camden Miscellany*, 3rd ser., 52 (1936), pp. 1–47.

Wither, George. *Abuses Stript and Whipt*, 1613.

Wotton, Henry. *Reliquiae Wottoniae*, 1685.
Wright, James. *Historia Histrionica*, 1699.

(B) SECONDARY TEXTS

Periodicals are cited by these abbreviations: *ELH: English Literary History*;
HLQ: Huntington Library Quarterly; *JEGP: Journal of English and Germanic Philology*; *JIH: Journal of International History*; *MLR: Modern Language Review*; *MRDE: Medieval and Renaissance Drama in England*; *NQ: Notes and Queries*; *SEL: Studies in English Literature*; *ShS: Shakespeare Survey*; *SQ: Shakespeare Quarterly*; *SP: Studies in Philology*; *TN: Theatre Notebook*; *TRI: Theatre Research International*; *YES: Yearbook of English Studies*

Ashton, Robert. *The City and the Court 1603–1643*, Cambridge, 1979.
Astington, John H. 'The Origins of the *Roxana* and *Messallina* Illustrations',
    ShS 43 (1991), 149–69.
    'Rereading Illustrations of the English Stage', *ShS* 50 (1997), 151–70.
Baldwin, T. W. *William Shakespeare's Small Latine and Lesse Greeke*, 2 vols.,
    Urbana, 1944.
Barish, Jonas. *The Anti-Theatrical Prejudice*, Berkeley, 1981.
Barroll, J. Leeds. *Politics, Plague and Shakespeare's Theater: the Stuart Years*,
    New York, 1991.
Barton, Anne. 'Harking back to Elizabeth: Ben Jonson and Caroline Nostalgia',
    ELH 48 (1981), 706–31.
Baskervill, C. R. *The Elizabethan Jig*, Chicago, 1929.
Bawcutt, N. W. *The Control and Censorship of Caroline Drama. The Records of Sir Henry Herbert, Master of the Revels 1623–73*, Oxford, 1996.
Beal, Peter. 'Massinger at Bay: Unpublished Verses in a War of the Theatres',
    YES 10 (1980), 190–203.
Beckermann, Bernard. *Shakespeare at the Globe 1599–1609*, New York, 1962.
Bednarz, James P. *Shakespeare and the Poets' War*, New York, 2001.
Beier, A. L. 'Social Problems in Elizabethan London', *JIH* 9 (1978), 205–18.
    Masterless Men. The Vagrancy Problem in England 1560–1640, London,
    1985.
Bennett, H. S. *English Books and Readers 1558–1603*, Cambridge, 1965.
Bennett, Susan. *Theatre Audiences, a Theory of Audience and Reception*, 2nd
    edn, London, 1997.
Bentley, J. C. *The Jacobean and Caroline Stage*, 7 vols., Oxford, 1940–68.
    'Shakespeare and the Blackfriars Theatre', *ShS* 1 (1948), 38–50.
    The Profession of Dramatist in Shakespeare's Time, 1590–1642, Princeton,
    N.J., 1971.
    The Profession of Player in Shakespeare's Time 1590–1642, Princeton, N.J.,
    1984.
Berek, Peter. '*Tamburlaine*'s Weak Sons: Imitation as Interpretation before
    1593', *Renaissance Drama* 13 (1982), 55–82.

Berry, Herbert. 'The Stage and Boxes at Blackfriars', *SP* 63 (1966), 163–86. [Repr. in *Shakespeare's Playhouses*, New York, 1987.]

'The Globe Bewitched and El Hombre Fiel', *Medieval and Renaissance Drama in England* 1 (1984), 211–30. [Repr. in *Shakespeare's Playhouses*, New York, 1987.]

'Where was the Playhouse in which the Boy Choristers of St Paul's Cathedral Performed Plays?' *Medieval and Renaissance Drama in England* 13 (2001), 101–16.

Berry, Ralph. *Shakespeare and the Awareness of the Audience*, London, 1984.

Bevington, David. *From 'Mankind' to Marlowe: Growth and Structure in the Popular Drama of Tudor England*, Cambridge, Mass., 1962.

Tudor Drama and Politics, Cambridge, Mass., 1968.

Action is Eloquence: Shakespeare's Language of Gesture, Cambridge, Mass., 1984.

Birch, Thomas. *The Court and Times of James I*, London, 1849.

The Court and Times of Charles I, 2 vols., London, 1849.

Blackstone, Mary A. and Cameron, Louis. 'Towards "A Full and Understanding Auditory": New Evidence of Playgoers at the First Globe Theatre', *MLR* 90 (1995), 556–71.

Blayney, Peter. *The Texts of 'King Lear' and their Origins*, Cambridge, 1982.

Bradbrook, M. C. *The Rise of the Common Player*, London, 1962.

Bristol, Michael D. *Carnival and Theater: Plebeian Culture and the Structure of Authority in Renaissance England*, New York, 1985.

Bromham, A. A. and Bruzzi, Zara. *'The Changeling' and the Years of Crisis, 1619–24: a Hieroglyph of Britain*, New York, 1990.

Bruster, Douglas. *Drama and the Market in the Age of Shakespeare*, Cambridge, 1992.

Bulman, James C., ed. *Shakespeare, Theory, and Performance*, London, 1996.

Burnett, Mark Thornton. *Masters and Servants in English Renaissance Drama and Culture: Authority and Obedience*, New York, 1997.

Butler, Martin. 'Massinger's *The City Madam* and the Caroline Audience', *Renaissance Drama* 13 (1982), pp. 157–88.

Theatre and Crisis 1632–1642, Cambridge, 1984.

'Two Playgoers and the Closing of the London Theatres, 1642', *TRI* 9 (1984), 93–9.

Calendar of State Papers Domestic: Elizabeth 1598–1601, ed. Mary Anne Everett Green, London, 1869.

Carson, Neil. 'John Webster: the Apprentice Years', *Elizabethan Theatre* 6 (1978), 76–87.

A Companion to Henslowe's Diary, Cambridge, 1988.

Carte, Thomas. *An History of the Life of James Duke of Ormonde*, 2 vols., London, 1736.

Cartelli, Thomas. *Marlowe, Shakespeare and the Economy of Theatrical Experience*, Philadelphia, 1991.

Cartwright, Kent. *Shakespearean Tragedy and its Double: the Rhythms of Audience Response*, University Park, Pa., 1991.

Ceresano, S. P. 'Competition for the King's Men? Alleyn's Blackfriars Venture', *MRDE* 4 (1989), 173–86.

'Philip Henslowe, Simon Forman, and the Theatrical Community of the 1590s', *SQ* 44 (1993), 145–58.

Chambers, E. K. *The Elizabethan Stage*, 4 vols., Oxford, 1923.

William Shakespeare, 2 vols., Oxford, 1930.

Clare, Janet. *'Art made tongue-tied by authority': Elizabethan and Jacobean Censorship*, Manchester, 1990.

Cogswell, Thomas. 'Thomas Middleton and the Court, 1624: *A Game at Chesse* in Context', *HLQ* 47 (1984), 273–88.

'England and the Spanish Match', in *Conflict in Early Stuart England*, ed. Richard Cust and Ann Hughes, London, 1989.

Collier, J. P., ed. *Illustrations of Old English Literature*, 3 vols., London, 1886.

Cook, Ann Jennalie. *The Privileged Playgoers of Shakespeare's London, 1576–1642*, Princeton, 1981.

'Audiences: Investigation, Interpretation, Invention', in *A New History of Early English Drama*, New York, 1997, pp. 305–20.

Cox, John D. *The Devil and the Sacred in English Drama 1350–1642*, Cambridge, 2000.

Cressy, David. *Literacy and the Social Order: Reading and Writing in Tudor and Stuart England*, Cambridge, 1980.

Davies, H. Neville. 'Beaumont and Fletcher's *Hamlet*', in *Shakespeare, Man of the Theater*, ed. Kenneth Muir, Jay L. Halio and D. J. Palmer, Newark, N.J., 1983.

Dawson, Anthony B. and Yachnin, Paul. *The Culture of Playgoing in Shakespeare's England. A Collaborative Debate*, Cambridge, 2001.

Dessen, Alan C. *Elizabethan Drama and the Viewer's Eye*, Chapel Hill, N.C., 1977.

Elizabethan Stage Conventions and Modern Interpreters, Cambridge, 1984.

Recovering Shakespeare's Theatrical Vocabulary, Cambridge, 1995.

Dessen, Alan C. and Thomson, Leslie. *A Dictionary of Stage Directions in English Drama, 1558–1642*, Cambridge, 1999.

Diehl, Huston. *Staging Reform, Reforming the Stage*, Ithaca, 1997.

Dutton, Richard. *Mastering the Revels. The Regulation and Censorship of English Renaissance Drama*, Basingstoke, 1991.

Edmund, Mary. *Rare Sir William Davenant*, Manchester, 1987.

Elliott, J. R., Jr. 'Four Caroline Playgoers', *Medieval and Renaissance Drama in England* 6 (1993), 179–93.

Essays on Audience Perception in Elizabethan and Jacobean Literature, Salzburg Studies in English Literature: Elizabethan and Renaissance Studies 124, Salzburg, 1997.

Finlay, Roger. *Population and Metropolis: the Demography of London 1580–1650*, Cambridge, 1981.

Gair, W. Reavley. *The Children of Paul's: the Story of a Theatre Company, 1553–1608*, Cambridge, 1982.

Gibbons, Brian. *Jacobean City Comedy*, 2nd edn, London, 1980.

Giese, Loreen L. 'Theatrical Citings and Bitings: Some References to Playhouses and Players in London Consistory Court Depositions, 1586–1611', *Early Theatre* 1 (1998), 113–28.

Gordon, Donald. 'Poet and Architect: the Intellectual Setting of the Quarrel between Ben Jonson and Inigo Jones', in *The Renaissance Imagination*, ed. Stephen Orgel, Berkeley, Calif., 1975.

Gowing, Laura. *Domestic Dangers. Women, Words, and Sex in Early Modern London*, Oxford, 1996.

Grantley, Darryll. *Wit's Pilgrimage. Drama and the Social Impact of Education in Early Modern England*, Aldershot, 2000.

Gras, Henk. '*Twelfth Night, Every Man Out of his Humour*, and the Middle Temple Revels of 1597–98', *MLR* 84 (1989), 545–64.

Gurr, Andrew. 'The Bear, the Statue, and Hysteria in *The Winter's Tale*', *SQ* 34 (1983), 420–5.

'Money or Audiences: the Impact of Shakespeare's Globe', *TN* 42 (1988), 3–14.

The Shakespearean Stage, 1574–1642, 3rd edn, Cambridge, 1992.

'Playing in Amphitheatres and Playing in Hall Theatres', *Elizabethan Theatre* 13 (1994), 27–62.

'The Bare Island', *ShS* 47 (1994), 29–43.

The Shakespearian Playing Companies, Oxford, 1996.

The Shakespeare Company 1594–1642, Cambridge, 2004.

Halasz, Alexandra. '"So beloved that men use his picture for their signs": Richard Tarlton and the Uses of Sixteenth-Century Celebrity', *Shakespeare Studies* 23 (1995), pp. 19–38.

Harbage, Alfred. *Shakespeare's Audience*, New York, 1941.

Shakespeare and the Rival Traditions, New York, 1952.

Haynes, Jonathan. 'The Elizabethan Audience on Stage', in *The Theatrical Space*, ed. James Redmond (Themes in Drama 9), Cambridge, 1987.

Heinemann, Margot. *Puritanism and Theatre*, Cambridge, 1980.

Helgerson, Richard. *Forms of Nationhood: the Elizabethan Writing of England*, Chicago, 1993.

Howard, Jean E. *Shakespeare's Art of Orchestration*, Urbana, 1984.

Howard-Hill, T. H. 'Political Interpretations of Middleton's *A Game at Chesse* (1624)', *YES* 21 (1991), 274–85.

Hoy, Cyrus. *Introductions, Notes and Commentaries to Texts in 'The Dramatic Works of Thomas Dekker'*, 4 vols., Cambridge, 1980.

Ingram, William. *The Business of Playing: the Beginnings of the Adult Professional Theater in Elizabethan London*, Ithaca, 1992.

Jones, Ann and Stallybrass, Peter. *Renaissance Clothing and the Materials of Memory*, Cambridge, 2001.

King, T. J. *Casting Shakespeare's Plays: London Actors and their Roles, 1590–1642*, Cambridge, 1992.

Knutson, Roslyn Lander. *The Repertory of Shakespeare's Company, 1594–1613*, Fayetteville, 1991.
Playing Companies and Commerce in Shakespeare's Time, Cambridge, 2001.
Laroque, François. *Shakespeare's Festive World: Elizabethan Seasonal Entertainment and the Professional Stage*, trans. Janet Lloyd, Cambridge, 1991.
Leggatt, Alexander. *Citizen Comedy in the Age of Shakespeare*, Toronto, 1973.
Jacobean Public Theatre, London, 1992.
Leinwand, Theodore. *The City Staged: Jacobean Comedy, 1603–1613*, Madison, Wis., 1986.
Theatre, Finance and Society in Early Modern England, Cambridge, 1999.
Lesser, Zachary, 'Mixed Government and Mixed Marriage in *A King and No King*: Sir Henry Neville Reads Beaumont and Fletcher', *ELH* 69 (2002), 947–77.
Levin, Harry. 'Two Magian Comedies: *The Tempest* and *The Alchemist*', *ShS* 22 (1971), 47–58.
Levin, Richard. 'The Relation of External Evidence to the Allegorical and Thematic Interpretation of Shakespeare', *Shakespeare Studies* 13 (1980), 1–29.
'The Contemporary Perception of Marlowe's *Tamburlaine*', *Medieval and Renaissance Drama in England* 1 (1984), 51–70.
'Women in the Renaissance Theatre Audience', *SQ* 40 (1989), 165–74.
Lindley, David. *The Trials of Frances Howard: Fact and Fiction at the Court of King James*, Basingstoke, 1993.
Loengard, Janet. 'An Elizabethan Lawsuit: John Brayne, his Carpenter, and the Building of the Red Lion Theatre', *SQ* 35 (1984), 298–310.
Lopez, Jeremy. *Theatrical Convention and Audience Response in Early Modern Drama*, Cambridge, 2003.
Lunney, Ruth. *Marlowe and the Popular Tradition: Innovation in the English Drama before 1595*, Manchester, 2002.
McJannet, Linda. *The Voice of Elizabethan Stage Directions. The Evolution of a Theatrical Code*, Newark, 1999.
McLuskie, Kathleen E. *Renaissance Dramatists. Feminist Readings*, London, 1989.
Dekker and Heywood, Professional Dramatists, Basingstoke, 1994.
McManaway, James G. 'Excerpta Quaedam per A. W. Adolescentem', in *Studies in Honor of DeWitt T. Starnes*, ed. Thomas P. Harrison, Houston, Tex., 1967.
McMillin, Scott. *The Elizabethan Theatre and the Book of Sir Thomas More*, Ithaca, 1987.
'The Queen's Men and the London Theatre of 1583', *Elizabethan Theatre* 10 (1988), 1–17.
McMillin, Scott and MacLean, Sally-Beth. *The Queen's Men and their Plays*, Cambridge, 1998.

Mann, David. *The Elizabethan Player. Contemporary Stage Representation*, London, 1991.

Masson, David. *The Life of John Milton*, Cambridge, 1859–94.

Maus, Katherine Ensaman. *Inwardness and the Theater in the English Renaissance*, Chicago, 1995.

Montrose, Louis. *The Purpose of Playing. Shakespeare and the Cultural Politics of the Elizabethan Theatre*, Chicago, 1996.

Morillo, Marvin. 'Shirley's "Preferment" and the Court of Charles I', *SEL* 1 (1961), 101–17.

Morse, David. *England's Time of Crisis: from Shakespeare to Milton, a Cultural History*, New York, 1989.

Mowat, Barbara A. '"The Getting up of the Spectacle": the Role of the Visual on the Elizabethan Stage, 1576–1600', *Elizabethan Theatre* 9 (1983), 60–76.

Mullaney, Steven. *The Place of the Stage: License, Play and Power in Renaissance England*, Chicago, 1988.

Mulryne, J. R. and Shewring, Margaret, eds. *Theatre and Government under the Early Stuarts*, Cambridge, 1993.

Neill, Michael. '"Wit's most accomplished Senate": the Audience of the Caroline Private Theaters', *SEL* 18 (1978), 341–60.

Nethercot, Arthur. *Sir William Davenant*, New York, 1938; revised edn, 1967.

Orgel, Stephen. *The Authentic Shakespeare, and Other Problems of the Early Modern Stage*, London, 2002.

Orrell, John. 'The London Stage in the Florentine Correspondence, 1604–1618', *TRI* 3 (1977–8), 155–81.

  The Quest for Shakespeare's Globe, Cambridge, 1982.

  'The Private Theatre Auditorium', *TRI* 9 (1984), 79–94.

  'Sunlight at the Globe', *TN* 38 (1984), 69–76.

  The Theatres of Inigo Jones and John Webb, Cambridge, 1985.

  The Human Stage: English Theatre Design, 1567–1640, Cambridge, 1988.

Parry, Graham. *The Seventeenth Century. The Intellectual and Cultural Context of English Literature, 1603–1700*, London, 1989.

Patterson, Annabel. *Censorship and Interpretation: the Conditions of Writing and Reading in Early Modern England*, Madison, Wis., 1984.

Pearson, Jacqueline. *Tragedy and Tragicomedy in the Plays of John Webster*, Manchester, 1980.

Peck, Linda Levy. *Court Patronage and Corruption in Early Stuart England*, London, 1989.

  ed. *The Mental World of the Jacobean Court*, Cambridge, 1991.

Pettit, Thomas. 'The Seasons of the Globe: Two New Studies of Elizabethan Drama and Festival', *Connotations* 2 (1992), 234–56.

Prest, Wilfred R. *The Inns of Court under Elizabeth I and the Early Stuarts*, Totowa, N.J., 1972.

Pugliatti, Paola. *Beggary and Theatre in Early Modern England*, Aldershot, 2003.

Rackin, Phyllis. *Stages of History: Shakespeare's English Chronicles*, Ithaca, 1990.

Rappaport, Steve. *Worlds within Worlds: Structures of Life in Sixteenth-Century London*, Cambridge, 1989.

The Revels History of Drama in English, vol. III: *1576–1613*, J. Leeds Barroll, Alexander Leggatt, Richard Hosley and Alvin Kernan, London, 1975; vol. IV: *1613–1660*, Philip Edwards, Gerald Eades Bentley, Kathleen McLuskie and Lois Potter, London, 1981.

Reynolds, George F. *The Staging of Elizabethan Plays at the Red Bull Theater, 1605–1625*, New York, 1940.

Schoenbaum, Samuel. *William Shakespeare: a Compact Documentary Life*, Oxford, 1977.

Scragg, Leah. 'Macbeth on Horseback', *ShS* 26 (1973), 81–8.

Selden, Raman. *English Verse Satire, 1590–1765*, London, 1978.

Sisson, C. J. *Lost Plays of Shakespeare's Age*, London, 1936.

Smith, Bruce R. *The Acoustic World of Early Modern England*, Chicago, 1999.

Smuts, R. Malcolm. *Court Culture and the Origins of a Royalist Tradition in Early Stuart England*, Philadelphia, 1987.

'Cultural Diversity and Cultural Change at the Court of James I', in *The Mental World of the Jacobean Court*, ed. Linda Levy Peck, Cambridge, 1991.

Spikes, Judith Doolin. 'The Jacobean History Play and the Myth of the Elect Nation', *Renaissance Drama* 8 (1977), 117–49.

States, Bert O. *Great Reckonings in Little Rooms. On the Phenomenology of Theater*, Berkeley, 1985.

Steggle, Matthew. *Wars of the Theatres: the Poetics of Personation in the Age of Jonson*, Victoria, BC, 1998.

Stone, Lawrence. *Family and Fortune: Studies in Aristocratic Finance in the Sixteenth and Seventeenth Centuries*, Oxford, 1973.

Symonds, E. M. 'The Diary of John Greene (1635–1657)', *English Historical Review* 43 (1928), 385–94.

Thompson, Marvin and Thompson, Ruth, eds. *Shakespeare and the Sense of Performance*, Newark, N.J., 1989.

Traister, Barbara. *The Notorious Astrological Physician of London. Works and Days of Simon Forman*, Chicago, 2001.

Tricomi, Albert H. 'Philip, Earl of Pembroke, and the Analogical Way of Reading Political Tragedy', *JEGP* 85 (1986), 332–45.

Anticourt Drama in England 1603–1642, Charlottesville, Va., 1989.

Trousdale, Marion. 'Coriolanus and the Playgoer in 1609', in *The Arts of Performance in Elizabethan and Early Stuart Drama. Essays for G. K. Hunter*, ed. Murray Biggs, Philip Edwards, Inga-Stina Ewbank and Eugene M. Waith, Edinburgh, 1991, pp. 124–34.

Underdown, David. *Revel, Riot, and Rebellion: Popular Politics and Culture in England 1603–1660*, Oxford, 1985.

Ungerer, Gustav. 'Prostitution in Late Elizabethan London: the Case of Mary Newborough', *Medieval and Renaissance Drama in England* 15 (2003), 138–223.

Wagenheim, Sylvia Stoler. Alfred Harbage, *Annals of English Drama 975–1700*, 3rd edn revised, London, 1989.

Weber, Kurt. *Lucius Cary*, New York, 1940.

Weimann, Robert. *Shakespeare and the Popular Tradition in the Theater*, ed. and trans. Robert Schwartz, Baltimore, 1978.
   Author's Pen and Actor's Voice. Playing and Writing in Shakespeare's Theatre, Cambridge, 2000.

White, Paul Whitfield. *Theatre and Reformation: Protestantism, Patronage and Playing in Tudor England*, Cambridge, 1993.

White, R. S., Edelman, Charles and Wortham, Christopher, eds. *Shakespeare. Readers, Audiences, Players*, Nedlands, 1998.

Whitney, Charles. 'Out of Service and in the Playhouse: Richard Norwood, Youth in Transition, and Early Response to *Dr. Faustus*', *Medieval and Renaissance Drama in England* 12 (1999), 166–89.
   '"Usually in the Werking Daies": Playgoing Journeymen, Apprentices, and Servants in Guild Records, 1582–92', *SQ* 50 (1999), 433–58.
   'The Devil his Due: Mayor John Spencer, Elizabethan Civic Antitheatricalism, and *The Shoemaker's Holiday*', *Medieval and Renaissance Drama in England* 14 (2001), 168–85.

Wickham, Glynne. *Early English Stages, 1300–1660*, 3 vols., London, 1959–81.

Wiffen, J. H. *Historical Memoirs of the House of Russell*, 2 vols., London, 1833.

Wiles, David. *Shakespeare's Clown: Actor and Text in the Elizabethan Playhouse*, Cambridge, 1987.

Wilson, Richard. *Will Power: Essays on Shakespearean Authority*, Detroit, 1993.

Womack, Peter. 'Imagining Communities: Theatres and the English Nation in the Sixteenth Century', in *Culture and History 1350–1600*, ed. David Aers, London, 1992.

Woodbridge, Linda. *Vagrancy, Homelessness, and the English Renaissance*, Urbana, 2001.

Wright, Louis B. *Middle-Class Culture in Elizabethan England*, Chapel Hill, N.C., 1935.

Wrightson, Keith. *English Society 1580–1680*, London, 1981.

Zitner, Sheldon P. 'Gosson, Ovid, and the Elizabethan Audience', *SQ* 9 (1958), 206–8.

Index